This Band of Heroes

James M. McCaffrey

This
Band
of
Heroes

Granbury's Texas Brigade, C.S.A.

TEXAS A&M UNIVERSITY PRESS
College Station

Originally published in 1985 by Eakin Press, Austin, Texas

The paper used in this book meets the minimum requirements
of the American National Standard for Permanence
of Paper for Printed Library Materials, Z39.48-1984.
Binding materials have been chosen for durability.

Library of Congress Cataloging-in-Publication Data

McCaffrey, James M., 1946–
    This band of heroes : Granbury's Texas Brigade, C.S.A. / by James
M. McCaffrey. — 1st Texas A&M University Press ed.
        p.   cm.
    Includes bibliographical references (p.   ) and index.
    ISBN 0-89096-727-X (alk. paper)
    1. Confederate States of America.   Army.   Granbury's Infantry
Brigade—History.   2. United States—History—Civil War, 1861–1865—
Regimental histories.   3. Texas—History—Civil War, 1861–1865—
Campaigns.   4. United States—History—Civil War, 1861–1865—
Campaigns.   I. Title.
E580.5.G73M33   1996
973.7'464—dc20   96-3005
                                                              CIP

For my wife Ellen

Camp Butler as it appeared during the Civil War.
— Courtesy Illinois State Historical Library.

Contents

Illustrations

Preface

Few works of this type are ever accomplished entirely alone and this book is no exception. I deeply appreciate the use of many fine books from the libraries of Rice University and the University of Houston. A great deal of unpublished material was also made available to me by the U.S. Army Military History Institute at Carlisle Barracks, Pennsylvania, the Confederate Research Center at Hill Junior College in Hillsboro, Texas, and the Texas State Archives in Austin. I wish to thank the staffs of those institutions for their help.

The photographs used in this book came from several sources — as indicated in the accompanying captions — and I thank all of those who made them available.

I also wish to thank Confederate flag expert H. Michael Madaus who shared his research with me on flags associated with Granbury's Brigade.

Last and most important, I wish to thank my wife Ellen. It was she who originally suggested that I write this book. And it was she who put up with the fact that her sewing room has become my writing room, and not a very orderly one at that. I thank her for all of this and dedicate this book to her and to her ancestors who served in the Texas regiments comprising Granbury's Texas Brigade: Claborn J. Hodges of Company A, Eighteenth Texas Cavalry (killed in action in 1864); Nathaniel Green Hodges of Company A, Eighteenth Texas Cavalry; Thomas M. Hodges of Company A, Eighteenth Texas Cavalry (died in 1862); and Lieutenant Eugenio Navarro of Company K, Sixth Texas Infantry.

JAMES M. McCAFFREY
Houston, Texas, 1984

Hiram Bronson Granbury.
— Courtesy of Library of Congress.

Introduction

Brigades in the Confederate army were known by the names of their commanders, unlike the Union army where the brigades were numbered within the divisions to which they belonged. Sometimes — due to death, transfer, or promotion — a brigade had more than one commander during the war. In these cases the brigade was quite often known by its most popular commander. Thus it was that a brigade of predominantly Texas soldiers in the Army of Tennessee came to be known as Granbury's Texas Brigade even though Brigadier General Hiram B. Granbury only led them for less than nine months.

The men in this brigade had other commanders both before and after Granbury's brief stint — Thomas Churchill, James Deshler, Roger Q. Mills, James Smith, and Edward T. Broughton. The men who preceded Granbury in command lent their names to the brigade but Granbury was so highly regarded by the men that after his death they continued to refer to themselves as members of "Granbury's Brigade." Even long after the war, when they got together at reunions, they retained the name of their slain leader.

What follows is the story of this brigade. It traces its history from the formation of each individual Texas regiment until the end of the war and beyond. These regiments fought together for the first time as elements of three separate brigades at Arkansas Post in January 1863. It wasn't until four and a half months later that they were consolidated into one brigade. This unit retained its identity until the waning days of the Civil War when, due to the heavy losses it had suffered, it was reduced to a single consolidated regiment.

1

Sadly, but not fearfully, this band of heroes left the hill they had held so well . . .

— Patrick R. Cleburne
Major General, C.S.A.
Referring to performance
of the Texas Brigade, during
the Battle of Missionary Ridge

CHAPTER ONE

Texans Go To War

Early in 1861, patriotic fervor swept across America as young men by the thousands rushed to the colors. After the fall of Fort Sumter in April, President Lincoln issued a call for 75,000 volunteer soldiers to put down the rebellion. President Davis likewise called on the states of the fledgling Confederacy to furnish troops to protect Southern soil. Quotas were set for each state and these goals were quickly reached. Many prospective soldiers even had to be turned away. There was just not enough war materiel to equip all of them!

The war was viewed as a glorious adventure and there was quite a rush to enlist. Many observers felt that the entire matter would be decided by one — or at most two — great battles, and young men all over the country wanted a crack at the enemy before the war ended.

In Texas, the methods of raising troops were fairly typical of the rest of the Confederacy. Militia companies already in existence sometimes enlisted *en masse,* thus forming the nuclei of new units. In most cases, however, prominent local citizens raised troops expressly for the emergency at hand. These individuals were often rewarded for their zeal by being appointed commanders of these units. This method did not always produce qualified officers and was later abandoned in favor of letting the soldiers elect their own officers and noncommissioned officers. These popularity contests — for that is what they were — still did not always provide adequate leadership. The soldiers often voted for whichever candidate they were more acquainted with, or for whichever one treated them to the most drinks. In spite of these methods there were good officers.

The best officers were those with prior military training. Most Southern-born officers of the United States Army resigned their commissions and cast their lots with the Confederacy. One such officer was Captain Robert R. Garland, late of the Seventh United States Infantry Regiment. Garland had over thirteen years of experience as an officer. He was a Southerner, though not a Texan, and when war came he sided with his homeland. He left his last assigned post at Fort Fillmore, in what is now New Mexico, and headed east with his family. Men with his military credentials were sorely needed in the South. In the fall of 1861, he served as the mustering officer for the Texas cavalry regiments of Colonels B. Warren Stone and Middleton T. Johnson. After completing this assignment Garland was promoted to the rank of colonel and took command of the newly formed Sixth Texas Infantry Regiment.

The Sixth Texas would later become part of a brigade commanded by Brigadier General Hiram B. Granbury. Granbury's Texas Brigade also included the Tenth Texas Infantry Regiment, the Fifteenth, the Seventeenth, the Eighteenth, the Twenty-fourth, and the Twenty-fifth Texas Cavalry Regiments (Dismounted). Also attached to the brigade were the independent Texas cavalry companies of Captains Sam Richardson and Alf Johnson, and the Louisiana cavalry companies of Captains L. M. Nutt and William Denson. Other units that served with the brigade for varying periods of time were the Nineteenth and the Twenty-fourth Arkansas Infantry Regiments, the Thirty-fifth Tennessee Infantry Regiment, the Third Confederate Infantry Regiment, and Granbury's own Seventh Texas Infantry Regiment.

The Sixth Texas formed at a camp of instruction known as Camp McCulloch. Camp McCulloch was located on the prairie about four miles from Victoria, Texas, at a place called Nuner's Mott. Several hundred recruits assembled there during the summer and fall of 1861. By the beginning of 1862, seven infantry companies had arrived and begun their training. The soldiers at Camp McCulloch underwent several months of training — a luxury not afforded to many other Confederate regiments. Much of what the troops learned probably came from a book entitled *Rifle and Light Infantry Tactics* written by Lieutenant William J. Hardee, United States Army. This manual did not teach the finer points of warfare as might be inferred from the title. Rather it instructed the recruit in the basics of military life — the manual of arms, the articles of war, and various marching movements. The men at Camp McCulloch who had to spend hours mastering these skills probably did not think very highly of Lieutenant Hardee.

Another point of irritation for the soldiers was the vast gulf that existed between the professional soldiers from the "old Army" and the volunteers. The old soldiers, for example, were used to hearing officers addressed as "Sir" or "Captain." It was not at all unusual to hear the new troops addressing their company commanders by their first names. The volunteers, in like manner, looked upon the regulars as stuffed shirts. In light of these feelings it is not surprising that Colonel Garland was not universally loved by his men. He was a hard taskmaster on the drill field. One soldier, in a letter to his wife, accused the colonel of being insensitive to the needs and hardships of his men, "because he hopes to procure a higher position for himself." [1] Another called him a martinet, though, in fairness to the colonel, this same soldier admitted that Garland "converted the regiment into a machine which would move with a clock-like precision." [2]

The fact that this motley array of citizen-soldiers could be molded into anything resembling a military machine was a credit to the officers entrusted with this assignment. Difficulties abounded. First of all, the men had to be uniformly equipped with clothing and weapons. Each company had arrived in camp with its members either garbed in some distinctive type of militia uniform or simply wearing whatever clothes they had happened to put on when they went to enlist. Company G from Travis County, for instance, looked very military in their uniforms of salt-and-pepper gray, trimmed in green. The good ladies of Austin had formed a Needle Battalion to make uniforms and they saw to it that their boys were properly clothed. The men of Company A, sported blue flannel frock coats and jeans trousers, all trimmed in red. Sometime during the regiment's stay at Camp McCulloch the entire unit received uniforms made of cloth manufactured at the State Penitentiary at Huntsville. They were not gray, as Hollywood would have us believe was the *only* color for Confederate uniforms, but were a light brown color often referred to as "butternut."

Another logistical problem that faced the regiment was that of weaponry. Again, each company was armed differently than the others. There were all sorts of firearms in evidence — old military muskets, hunting rifles, and shotguns. Company G arrived at Victoria armed with obsolete flintlock muskets that an Austin gunsmith had converted to percussion. Many of these weapons were older than the men who carried them! This was a problem that stayed with the Sixth Texas until at least mid-1863.

Amid all the drudgery of life in an army camp at least one soldier was able to see the lighter side of life. Robert R. Gilbert of Company B wrote a series of letters, tongue in cheek, to the Victoria *Advocate* and the Houston *Telegraph* detailing army life. One such letter purported to give the oath of enlistment required of each soldier. "You solemnly swear that you will stay in the army as long as this war lasts and fight to the best of your ability; that you will not growl at your rations, and be content with eleven dollars a month, whether you get them or not, so help you God." [3]

By the spring of 1862, the men of the Sixth Texas were ready to go to war. Indeed, some of them had been at the camp of instruction for seven or eight months and were as well instructed as they would ever be. Companies H, I, and K joined the regiment at this time bringing it up to full ten-company strength.

On May 22, 1862, the ten companies left Camp McCulloch. Marching at a leisurely pace of ten miles per day, the regiment reached Camp Number Eight at Eagle Lake a week later. There the men rested for a week before resuming their journey. They rode the train from Eagle Lake through Richmond and Houston, and on to Navasota, where they again rested for a few days.

While at Navasota, a little military justice was dispensed. One of the soldiers stole a revolver belonging to Captain C. P. Naunheim of Company I. The culprit was quickly apprehended when he foolishly offered the gun for sale later the same day. Justice was swift. He was immediately sentenced to be drummed out of the service. Half of his head was shaved and he was put astraddle a fence rail. Then, while his comrades lined the street and the drums rolled, some Negroes carried the rail through the streets of Navasota and the unfortunate soldier was discharged from the army.

A couple of days later the Sixth Texas left Navasota and took up the line of march for Tyler. Another week was spent there, at Camp Number Twenty-five, before the regiment left for Arkansas. After three weeks on the road the men arrived at Rockport, Arkansas, for a stay of some ten days. They left Rockport about August 3d, en route to Camp Holmes, near Pine Bluff, where they were later joined by the Twenty-fourth and the Twenty-fifth Texas Cavalry Regiments.

By this time enlistments into the Confederate Army had fallen off drastically. The early flood of enlistees slowed to a trickle after the first year of the war. People on both sides then realized that the war was not a circus where well-fed, smartly uniformed troops were able to scare the enemy into retreat by their mere presence on the battlefield. It was hungry, dirty, painful work, and as word filtered back to the homefolk of another local boy buried far away, it became more difficult to lure the remaining young men into the army. In order to maintain the strength of the forces in the field the Confederate government resorted to conscription. A Conscription Act was passed by Congress and went into effect on April 16, 1862. By the terms of this law all able-bodied men between the ages of eighteen and thirty-five were subject to the draft. There were loopholes in the law and one of them granted exemptions to those who owned twenty or more slaves. This unfair provision was very unpopular among the average men in the South since most of them did not own slaves and they soon dubbed it the "20 nigger law." The existence of this clause in the law only served to emphasize the feeling already current that it was to be a "rich man's war and a poor man's fight."

The Conscript Act had a definite impact, both directly and indirectly, on the number of men entering the army in the spring of 1862. Recruiting notices published in newspapers all across the South urged young men to volunteer for service in order to avoid the social stigma of being drafted. Southern women also applied pressure to the men to enlist. Many of them would have absolutely nothing to do with a man romantically unless he was in uniform. Another method the women used to encourage enlistments involved questioning the masculinity of any man who was slow to respond to his country's call. This took the form of mailing the unfortunate fellow items of feminine underclothing with the obvious implication that if he wasn't man enough to fight for his country perhaps he wasn't a man at all.

Some men went to great lengths to avoid military service, even to the point of purposely maiming themselves so as to be unfit for the army. A Dallas newspaper commented dryly on two such cases:

> A conscript in Austin cut three of his fingers off last week to free himself from military duty. The next day he was sent to a camp of instruction. A German, in Brenham, blew his brains out on Saturday for the same reason. He was not sent to a camp of instruction. [4]

For one reason or another the spring of 1862 saw a great number of new recruits being raised in Texas. All five of the cavalry regiments that would become part of Granbury's Brigade formed at this time. Cavalry service just naturally appealed to Texans. Living, as they did, on the very edge of the frontier, Texans were usually accomplished horsemen at an early age. It seemed quite natural to continue with this mode of transportation when war came. After all, why would a man want to walk to war when he could ride? Consequently, there were more cavalry regiments organized in Texas than infantry or artillery units.

Two of these cavalry regiments were brigaded with the Sixth Texas Infantry in 1862. The Twenty-fourth and the Twenty-fifth Texas Cavalry Regiments both sprang from the same parent organization. In the spring of 1861, the Reverend George W. Carter resigned his position as president of Soule University at Chappell Hill, Texas, to follow another calling. He set about recruiting a regiment of Texas Lancers! These men were to be armed with long lances in addition to their standard armament of double-barreled shotguns, revolvers, and bowie knives. The reason for the lances, according to a recruiting poster, was the impossibility of obtaining cavalry sabers. An added advantage of the lances was that they were "much the most formidable weapon in a Cavalry charge." [5]

Young men were urged to enlist in companies, in squads, or as individuals and report to Chappell Hill. The assembly point was later changed to Hempstead, and by April 1, 1862, enough men had joined up to form thirty companies. Colonel Carter received permission from the Secretary of War to divide his oversize command into three regiments. This reorganization took place on April 24th and Colonel Carter designated the three newly formed regiments as the First, Second, and Third Texas Lancers. Officially they were known as the Twenty-first, the Twenty-fourth, and the Twenty-fifth Texas Cavalry Regiments, respectively. (There is no record of lances ever being issued to the men in these units.) Colonel Carter retained control of the Twenty-first Regiment and of the brigade formed by the union of the three regiments. Colonel Franklin C. Wilkes, who had served as the lieutenant colonel of Carter's original unit, led the Twenty-fourth Regiment. Colonel Clayton C. Gillespie, Carter's former major, commanded the Twenty-fifth Regiment. Like Carter, both Wilkes and Gillespie were Methodist clergymen.

Colonel Carter's brigade camped just outside of Hempstead, on Clear Creek. The camp was named Camp Hebert in honor of Brigadier General Paul O. Hebert, Confederate commander of the Texas District. A Confederate infantryman who was camped across the railroad tracks from Camp Hebert, at Camp Groce, has painted a rather idyllic word picture of the trials and tribulations of his cavalry counterparts. He described the dinner of an officer and his staff (probably Colonel Carter) as follows:

> . . . It consists of stewed beef, boiled ham, mashed potatoes, and a couple of chickens, which some of the Austin County housekeepers were kind enough to raise for them — *at least the officers' servants thought so*; for dessert, a couple of bottles of old rye, which some of the planters sent them — for their especial benefit; all these flanked by a respectable force of negro waiters.

The enlisted men were similarly described:

> . . . Some are playing cards, pitch and toss, or a thousand other games known only in the army; others are dining, and grumbling at their rations, while dining, perhaps, on turkey. The cooks are busy around a huge camp-kettle, placed on the fire, in which a joint of bacon and some peas are bubbling and bubbling around, as if they were patriotic enough to enjoy being eaten for the good of the soldier. A smaller vessel simmers near it; but, as the lid is on it, I cannot see its contents — most likely a brace of chickens under the wing of a fat turkey. This is the way the cavalry lived at "Camp Hebert." [6]

These conditions soon changed.

Carter received orders to take his brigade to Arkansas. He retained a skeleton crew at Camp Hebert and furloughed the rest of the men with orders to meet at Crockett, Texas, in early May. From Crockett the brigade travelled in a generally northeastern direction toward Shreveport, Louisiana. The good life enjoyed at Hempstead had apparently become a habit for some of the men — much to the annoyance of civilians along the line of march. The protests of outraged citizens marked the route travelled by Carter's brigade. Mr. W. W. Frizzell of Alto, Texas, complained in a letter to his friend, Postmaster General John H. Reagan, that the soldiers were "marching eastward slowly . . . remaining in each neighborhood just long enough to ravage the corn-cribs and smoke-houses of the defenseless country." [7] Frizzell's was not an isolated complaint. Similar events were brought to the attention of the authorities by other private citizens and, a short time later, by the governor of Louisiana. It was not a bright page in the history of these Texas troops. One of them even wrote: "I think that we will rove around over the country until we eat up all we can get." [8] The shock waves over the Texans' conduct reverberated all the way to Richmond and back to Texas. Orders were issued to Colonel Carter to investigate the matter and bring charges against the guilty parties but there the official correspondence ceased. It seems unlikely that any formal punishment was meted out but the lack of further reports of such shameful behavior indicates that stern warnings were given to the men of the three regiments.

Part of the pillaging engaged in by Carter's men was due to the need to obtain adequate forage for their horses. As the troops rode northward from Shreveport, it became increasingly difficult to maintain the health of the animals. By the time the column reached Pine Bluff, Arkansas, Major General Theophilus H. Holmes decided these troopers should be dismounted and used as infantry. The protests were long and loud. If these men had wanted to serve as infantry they would have joined the infantry regiments! Instead, they had joined the cavalry, furnishing their own horses in order to do so. All of the complaining was, of course, to no avail. After July 29, 1862, Wilkes's and Gillespie's regiments became known as the Twenty-fourth and the Twenty-fifth Texas Cavalry Regiments (Dismounted). The Twenty-first Regiment retained its mounts and joined Colonel William H. Parsons's cavalry brigade. The Twenty-fourth and Twenty-fifth Regiments were assigned, on August 27th, to Colonel Garland's new Brigade, which also included the Sixth Texas Infantry.

Paralleling the early experiences of the Sixth Texas, were those of another infantry regiment destined to become part of Granbury's Brigade. This was the Tenth Texas Infantry Regiment. Thirty-nine-year-old Colonel Allison Nelson of Bosque County, was the prime mover behind the organization of this command. A Georgian by birth, Nelson had served in that state's legislature before moving to Texas in the 1850s. He quickly gained political stature in his adopted state, serving in the Texas legislature and in the Secession Convention. While Nelson no doubt enjoyed the political life his main interest seems always to have been in the military. He led a company of Georgia volunteers in the Mexican War and later participated in the bloody border warfare in Kansas prior to the Civil War. Becoming colonel of the regiment he raised, however, was not Nelson's first taste of high rank. He had served under General Narcisco Lopez in the cause of Cuban independence from Spain, and was rewarded with a generalship in the Cuban army.

Virginia Point, on the Texas coast across from Galveston Island, was the assembly point for the various companies of Nelson's regiment. The installation there was also named Camp Hebert, or Fort Hebert. The latter title was probably due to wishful thinking, at least early in the war, for the fort only mounted a handful of medium size cannons and was protected by nothing stouter than earthen walls. Companies of men arrived intermittently during the fall of 1861. Between October 13th and 31st, Companies A through H were mustered into the service of the Confederacy and the regiment was accepted even though it lacked two companies of being up to full strength.

Life at Virginia Point soon became a bore for the men stationed there. Early in November they drilled vigorously for three or four hours every day. As soldiers everywhere know, this martial routine soon degenerates into nothing more than sweat and toil. So it was at

Camp Hebert. By the end of the month drill time had been drastically reduced and the men were "learning next to nothing." [9] They had plenty to eat though. In fact, they had all the beef and bread they wanted. This unimaginative diet could be supplemented by bacon and molasses, but only if an individual could afford to purchase them from outside sources. The health of the regiment remained good until mid-February of 1862. By that time foul weather set in and there was a marked increase in the length of the sick list.

The addition of Companies I and K in January 1862, brought the number of companies in the regiment up to the required number of ten. The regiment finally left Camp Hebert in two columns on March 29th and 30th and headed for Millican, Texas. After a few days there the men moved off in a northerly direction, passing through the towns of Wheelock and Fairfield, before turning east. On May 14, 1862, the regiment passed through Shreveport and swung north again, entering Arkansas three days later. The tired Texans arrived at Camp Texas, near Little Rock, on June 4th and settled down for a short stay.

A couple of months earlier a Federal army under Major General Samuel R. Curtis had left Missouri, and was now in northeastern Arkansas. Curtis's forward progress was stalled in the vicinity of Batesville, and Secretary of War Edwin M. Stanton called on the navy for help. He requested that navy gunboats drop down from Memphis on the Mississippi River and enter the White River. They were then to steam upriver as far as Jacksonport, Arkansas, destroying all Confederate shipping as they went. By gaining control of this much of the river, Curtis's army could easily be kept supplied and his offensive could resume. This naval expedition led to the baptism of fire of the Tenth Texas almost.

On June 16th the naval convoy started up the White River in single file. Colonel Graham Fitch's Forty-sixth Indiana Infantry Regiment, acting as marines, accompanied the ships to protect against Confederate snipers along the banks. When the Federals arrived within about eight miles of St. Charles, they halted. A tugboat probed cautiously ahead while a scouting party landed with orders to reconnoiter toward St. Charles. Both detachments returned with the word that gun emplacements, supported by an unknown force of infantry, commanded the river at St. Charles.

Confederates had hastily fortified a bluff overlooking the river. Two 32-pounder rifled guns removed from the Confederate gunboat *Pontchartrain* were emplaced there. Two three-inch rifled guns were also set up about a quarter of a mile downstream. On the night of the 16th, two small artillery pieces from another Confederate gunboat, the *Maurepas*, were added to the river's defenses. The defenders then scuttled the *Maurepas* along with two merchant steamers to further obstruct the river. Confederate sailors manned the artillery while a small force of thirty-five infantrymen provided support.

Early on the morning of June 17th the Union ships raised anchors and steamed slowly up the river. The blue clad sailors closely scanned the banks for evidence of enemy sharpshooters. When the fleet was about two and a half miles below St. Charles, Confederate scouts were sighted and the ironclads *Mound City* and *St. Louis* began blasting the underbrush with grape and cannister. Under cover of this fire the Indiana infantrymen went ashore. Then, with naval gunfire preceding them, the Federals worked their way forward.

Soon the ironclads came within sight of the upper portions of the three sunken ships. Commander Augustus H. Kilty, the leader of the expedition, knew that enemy artillery was close at hand but he didn't know exactly where. The ships moved boldly forward. When the lead ship, the *Mound City*, came abreast of the lower Confederate battery the Southern artillerists opened up. As their shots rattled harmlessly off the armored sides of the ships the battle began.

The ironclads passed slightly above the lower battery and, when they were within point-blank range of the 32-pounders, these big guns joined in. The gunboats and the shore batteries duelled ineffectually for a time before one of the big Confederate shells pierced the *Mound City*. The shot hit the steam drum and sent scalding steam throughout the ship. Over a hundred men died as a result of this hit and the *Mound City* was out of the battle. The amount of fire poured onto the *St. Louis* then doubled.

What seemed like a Confederate victory in the making soon turned the other way. The Federal infantrymen, after observing all the fireworks, were then ready to go to work. The *St. Louis* ceased firing and the foot soldiers swept forward. Before long it was over. The small force of Confederate infantry was no match for an entire enemy regiment. The cannoneers spiked their guns and scattered.

Meanwhile, the new commander of the Confederate Trans-Mississippi District, Major General Thomas C. Hindman, ordered the Tenth Texas to the defense of St. Charles. The Texans left their camp at about 10:00 A.M. on June 16th and covered almost thirty miles by midnight. They arrived at DeVall's Bluff, on the White River, the next morning about nine o'clock. They could have boarded transports immediately and gone to the rescue of St. Charles except for a logistical problem — they had no ammunition. By the time a sufficient amount of ammunition could be procured to allow each man forty rounds, it was late afternoon. Finally, near four o'clock, Colonel Nelson and two companies left for St. Charles. Six hours later three more companies followed. Action at last.

The next morning the reinforcements continued down the river. The captain of the second ship transporting the Texans was hailed from shore and told that the enemy was only a short distance below. Proceeding carefully he caught sight of smoke from an approaching vessel. Not wanting to confront a Yankee gunboat, the captain quickly turned his ship and headed back upstream. As soon as he was able, he landed his craft and sent scouts out to learn the identity of the other ship. Meanwhile, Colonel Nelson, in the lead ship, found out that it was too late to save St. Charles and ordered his ship turned around. The brave Texans in the second craft, eager for a chance at the Yankees, were chagrined to find that they had been chased away by their commanding officer returning up the river. After that dismal beginning, Colonel Nelson led his men back to DeVall's Bluff to await the inevitable approach of the victorious enemy.

The regiment spent the next couple of weeks nervously expecting an attack that never came. Reinforcements rushed to DeVall's Bluff and Colonel Nelson took command of all these hastily assembled troops. Reports of enemy activity in the area were constant. The men were issued ammunition and were more than once ordered into battle lines only to be dismissed when the immediate threat subsided. One threat that did not subside, however, was that of death by disease. Sickness killed as many men as bullets during the Civil War, and it was sickness rather than bullets which took the first lives from the Tenth Texas. Measles and mumps, for which we now have easily administered vaccines, raged through the camp. Fully two-thirds of the regiment was incapacitated at once and there were many deaths.

By the middle of July, Nelson's regiment left DeVall's Bluff and moved back to Camp Texas. The health of the men was still poor and when orders were issued requiring two hours of drill in the morning and two more in the afternoon there were not enough able-bodied men to make the drill meaningful. The combination of poor health, rigid discipline, too much drill, and no pay led to a rebellion in the ranks.

On July 16, 1862, the regiment was ordered to fall in for roll call at noon. The men were not in the habit of doing this. Companies G and K formed up as ordered but the rest of the regiment refused to obey. It is not clear just what the leaders of the revolt intended to do but the men still had the ammunition that had been issued to them at DeVall's Bluff and they felt that they could enforce whatever course they chose to pursue. Colonel Nelson appeared and once again ordered the men to fall in on the parade ground. Most of the soldiers relented this time and followed orders. There were fifty or sixty diehards, though, who steadfastly refused. They were promptly arrested and taken to Little Rock to see General Hindman. After a fiery lecture the general ordered the men back to camp with the stern admonition to behave themselves or he would have every tenth one of them shot. This apparently did the trick. All of the underlying causes of the mutiny were still present but the men of the Tenth Texas never again gave in to these pressures. They were lucky. Their transgressions required nothing more serious than a reprimand. Some other Confederates at Camp Texas were not so lucky.

On August 1, 1862, the Texans saw four fellow soldiers die. These men did not die facing the enemy. They were shot by other Confederates. They were deserters from an Arkansas regiment who had had the misfortune of falling back into Confederate hands. They were tried and sentenced to be shot. Everyone in the camp marched out to the field where the executions were to take place. Nineteenth century military leaders felt that if their soldiers witnessed these events they would be less likely to do anything to incur the same penalty. Many of the onlookers that day must have felt a twinge of anxiety as they thought back to their abortive uprising two weeks earlier. It could just as easily have been Texans being shot that day. One man philosophically wrote in his diary: "It is hard fer a man to be marched out in an old field and shot tho according to the Army reg[u]lations it has to be done." [10]

While the Tenth Texas was at Camp Texas it was brigaded with several dismounted Texas cavalry regiments. Three of these regiments — the Fifteenth, the Seventeenth, and the Eighteenth — would fight shoulder to shoulder with the Tenth until the end of the war. These three cavalry regiments were originally intended to be placed under the command of Colonel Middleton T. Johnson along with two other regiments. Late in 1861, Johnson was authorized to raise a cavalry brigade to serve for twelve months. As a result of this recruiting effort, the Fourteenth, the Fifteenth, the Sixteenth, the Seventeenth, and the Eighteenth Texas Cavalry Regiments were formed. The Fifteenth, the Seventeenth, and the Eighteenth Regiments gained lasting fame as elements of Granbury's Texas Brigade.

The Fifteenth Texas Cavalry Regiment was organized on March 10, 1862, at Dallas, Texas. As was the case with most Texas mounted units, the men of the Fifteenth Texas were equipped with a hodgepodge of arms. Most of the men carried single or double-barreled shotguns, squirrel rifles, or obsolete military muskets. There was no uniformity with respect to size, age, caliber, or condition. A few men, mostly officers, had pistols but these were just as varied as the long arms. Whereas most of their Northern counterparts carried bright, shiny sabers, the Texans preferred the use of large knives. These knives — called side knives — were often made by local blacksmiths out of old files. They were large — almost the size of swords in some cases — and fierce looking. The men proudly displayed them when they had their pictures made for the folks back home.

The tactical value of the big knives was doubtful. The men liked to ride through the woods swinging their knives like swords at the tops of young trees, imagining with every sweep of their arms that they were beheading hapless Yanks. One Texas trooper, albeit not from the Fifteenth,[11]

> . . . had whetted his till it bore the edge of a razor, and then went out in the woods to practice, and in an attempt to make a grand right and left cut against an imaginary foe, the first whack he made he cut off his horse's right ear, and the next stroke he chipped a chunk out of his left knee, when he immediately dismounted and poked the dangerous thing up a hollow log . . .

These weapons generally went out of favor after a short while because of their dubious value balanced against their weight. Most men didn't want to carry the extra pound or two. For many men of the Fifteenth Texas, the deciding factor in whether to keep the knives or not was a spring rain shower. After the sun came back out and dried the rawhide scabbards they shrunk until "they fit as tight as the bark on a black jack, and [the knives] were as hard to draw as a nigger's eye teeth." [12] At this point many of the big knives were unceremoniously dumped into the Arkansas River.

The regiment was reorganized on March 20, 1862, and shortly thereafter moved to Clarksville in Red River County, Texas. The men spent a month there drilling and learning how to be soldiers. The young ladies of Clarksville presented a beautiful silk flag to the men of Company G. Miss Ida DeMorse gave the presentation speech and urged the men to follow the flag "into the very jaws of destruction . . . and if counted amid the unreturning braves, make it your martial cloak without regret, and proudly fill a warrior's grave . . ." [13] Captain Alsdorf Faulkner accepted the Bonnie Blue Flag on behalf of his men, pledging their lives in its defense: "And rather than permit it, for a moment, to hang trailing in the dust, or see its beautiful folds stained with dishonor, it shall be dyed with the best blood that chambers in our hearts." [14] Such impassioned oratory at flag presentations prevailed throughout the South.

Events outside of Texas soon caused the regiments assembled at Clarksville to head east. The bloody Battle of Shiloh was fought in southwestern Tennessee on April 6th and 7th, 1862, and the Confederate troops were forced to withdraw into Mississippi. Confederate General Pierre G. T. Beauregard rested his men at Corinth, Mississippi, while Union Major General Ulysses S. Grant slowly considered his next move. Observers on both sides felt that another great battle was imminent. Consequently, the Confederate high command began to hurriedly send reinforcements to Beauregard. Among the many units west of the Mississippi that were summoned was the Fifteenth Texas Cavalry. As the regiment moved into Arkansas in response to this call, the men felt confident that they would be able to teach the Yankee invaders a sobering lesson. Few, if any, could possibly have realized that the regiment would not return to Texas for three long years. Nor could the effects of upcoming campaigns have been fathomed at that time. Many of these happy-go-lucky troopers would never see home again.

By the time the Fifteenth reached Pine Bluff, Arkansas, it received revised orders. It was to remain in Arkansas. After spending a few days at Pine Bluff, the men headed toward Little Rock. Because of the Conscript Act it became necessary once again to reorganize the regiment and all soldiers under the age of eighteen or over the age of thirty-five were discharged. This left many vacancies in the officer ranks, so new elections were held on May 20, 1862, to fill them. Captain George H. Sweet of Company A had been elected colonel back in March and he was reelected to the command of the regiment. The men chose Captain George B. Pickett of Company B to be lieutenant colonel and Captain William H. Cathey of Company K to be major. Within a week of the reorganization, Brigadier General Albert Rust took command of the Twelfth, the Fourteenth, the Fifteenth, the Sixteenth, the Seventeenth, and the Eighteenth Texas Cavalry Regiments.

The Seventeenth Texas Cavalry was mustered into Confederate service at Dallas on March 15, 1862. Colonel George F. Moore, Lieutenant Colonel Sterling B. Hendricks, and Major John McClarty were the regimental officers. The composition of the unit did not remain stable for long. On April 22nd Captain Patrick Henry's Company I transferred to the Twenty-eighth Texas Cavalry Regiment where it became Company B. Then, in November 1862, Captain James G. McKnight's Company K of the Eighteenth Texas Infantry Regiment transferred into the Seventeenth Texas Cavalry.

The regiment left Texas early in May and marched across the northwest corner of Louisiana and into Arkansas on its way to Corinth. Measles hit the regiment hard and a soldier in Company A wrote his wife that about "half of our company has the measles. We leave from four to six every day. Our company is strewed from Shreveport [to] here . . ." [15] Sympathetic civilians along the way took in the men thus left behind and nursed them back to health. Periods of rainy weather contributed to the men's health problems and morale suffered. Every day or so one company or another circulated petitions asking that its officers resign. On May 11th six of the nine companies petitioned Colonel Moore to order a regimental reorganization.

The reorganization which followed took place in Little Rock on May 22, 1862. It was a result of the Conscript Act (as had been the reorganization of the Fifteenth Texas) and was not due to the wishes of the men in the ranks. It is not clear whether Colonel Moore stood for reelection but most of the balloting was between Captain Sebron M. Noble of Company A and Captain James R. Taylor of Company B. Captain Taylor won the election and Captain Noble retained command of his company. The men of Company B elected Oliver C. Taylor to take over their company. Likewise, the men of Companies C, D, H, and K, elected new captains.

Fifty-five-year-old Nicholas H. Darnell raised and commanded the Eighteenth Texas Cavalry Regiment. Darnell had been born in Tennessee, and had come to Texas in 1838. He served in the Sixth and Seventh Congresses of the Republic of Texas and lost a bid for the governor's office in 1847. In the fall if 1861, he journeyed to the Confederate capital at Richmond seeking a military appointment. He returned to Dallas in early November with the authority to raise a regiment of either infantry or cavalry for twelve months' service. The branch of service was to be left up to the recruits.

Darnell was beyond the age of wanting to walk to war so his recruiting notices sought only young men interested in joining the cavalry. No mention was made of infantry. Darnell played upon the emotions of the prospective soldiers by stating that "an appeal to the valor and patriotism of my fellow-citizens is wholly unnecessary, when our border and our sister states are threatened with invasion. The fate of Missouri is enough to call together our brave boys and save our homes from the torch of the enemy." [16] Darnell authorized John N. Bryan, one of the founding settlers of Dallas, to raise a company for his regiment and Bryan's recruiting tactics were a little different. He told of a recruit in his company who had fought the British at the Battle of New Orleans in 1815, and invited any young man who wanted "to see how an old soldier can fight, let him take a place by him and learn a lick or two." [17] What self-respecting young man could allow himself to be outshone by a man old enough to be his grandfather?

Companies destined for Darnell's regiment arrived in Dallas throughout January and February of 1862. The recommended equipment for each man included a double-barreled shotgun, a revolver, and a large knife. Most of the men rode into town in civilian garb and carrying all sorts of firearms. One noteworthy exception to this generally unmilitary appearance was provided by Captain Hiram S. Morgan's company from Bastrop, Texas. Morgan spent a good deal of his own money equipping his men, "The Morgan Rangers." They were outfitted in gray double-breasted coats and gray trousers with yellow cavalry stripes on the legs. The fabric used for these uniforms was also a product of the state penitentiary at Huntsville.

The companies rendezvoused at the fairgrounds in Dallas and began learning the cavalry drill. While at this campsite Darnell's regiment suffered one of its first casualties. On the morning of February 10th the aforementioned Captain Morgan prepared for his day's activities. He finished dressing and reached for his cap, which was hanging against a tent pole. As he did so he knocked down a loaded revolver which discharged when it hit the ground. The bullet passed through the calf of the captain's leg and, while the wound was not serious, caused Captain Morgan a considerable amount of discomfort and embarrassment.

Ten companies were finally assembled and the Eighteenth Texas Cavalry Regiment was mustered into Confederate service on March 15, 1862. The men elected Darnell to be their colonel; Jonathon T. Coit, formerly captain.of Company E, was elected lieutenant colonel; and Charles C. Morgan was elected major.

The regiment remained in Dallas for another few weeks before heading into Indian Territory. The twelve hundred men of the Eighteenth Texas occupied quite a long stretch of road as they headed north. The next several weeks passed uneventfully and the regiment finally started for Arkansas about the first of June.

Darnell's men were not in Arkansas long before becoming embroiled in an incident with Brigadier General Albert S. Pike. Pike was a Confederate emissary to the various tribes in the Indian Territory early in the war and had led a mixed command of Indians and whites at the Battle of Elk Horn Tavern (Pea Ridge), in early March of 1862. Apparently some of Darnell's men found his performance at that battle less than exemplary. On July 3d General Pike wrote to General Thomas C. Hindman complaining that his reputation was being damaged. "There has been a regular deluge of lies poured out about me in Arkansas and Texas, and the men of the regiments of Darnell and Dawson [Colonel Charles L. Dawson of the Nineteenth Arkansas Infantry Regiment], who owe me nothing but favors and kindness, have sown them broadcast over these two states . . ." [18] The exact nature of the stories being spread about General Pike has not been discovered. In fact, any stories spread by the men of the Eighteenth Texas would have to have been secondhand since they were not in the Battle of Pea Ridge. At any rate, the matter was allowed to die without any apparent further repercussions.

The Fifteenth, the Seventeenth, and the Eighteenth Texas Cavalry Regiments were brigaded with the Twelfth, the Fourteenth, and the Sixteenth Texas Cavalry Regiments under General Rust whose first act was to lead a raid into northern Arkansas. Union foraging parties were active in the neighborhood of Batesville, and Rust intended to break up those operations. When the Confederates reached Izard County, just northwest of Batesville, they received word that a party of Federals was threshing wheat about twenty miles away. That sounded like just what the general was looking for. He instructed Colonel Sweet to hold the Fifteenth Texas on the bank of the White River and wait for further orders while he took the other five regiments in the direction of Batesville, hoping to bar the Yanks from returning to their camp.

It was dusk when the soldiers of the Fifteenth Texas reached their assigned place on the river. People living in the area reported to Colonel Sweet that a group of Federals was just across the river. The colonel found himself between the proverbial rock and hard place. Here was a chance to have a go at the Yanks but to do so meant that he would have to disobey the orders of a superior officer. He polled his subordinates and the decision was unanimous — disregard the general's orders and cross the river.

The night sky was pitch-black by the time the horsemen forded the river. The men nervously fingered their weapons as they rode slowly through the darkness. Suddenly the column halted. The nerves of some of the men, stretched taut by waiting for action, seemed to snap now that action had arrived. They put spurs to horseflesh and splashed noisily back across the river. It proved to be another cruel joke of fate, as it was found that what had startled the troopers was General Rust and his men returning from a fruitless ride. General Rust left about a hundred and fifty men of the Fifteenth Texas to keep an eye on Union troop activity in the neighbor-hood while he led the rest of the brigade into camp at Searcy.

Late on the afternoon of June 6th, the Seventeenth Texas started out to break up a small enemy foraging operation on the Lit-tle Red River. During the night march that followed, the rear guard separated from the main body and time was lost as the two groups sought each other in the darkness. The regiment was finally re-united and reached the Little Red about midnight. As the men began fording the river, shots rang out from the opposite side and they scurried for safety. After retreating for half a mile, Colonel Tay-lor sent ten men back to keep watch at the ford. At daylight a few more shots were fired but there was no further activity and the guard detachment rejoined the regiment.

Taylor's cavalrymen crossed the river a short distance away and soon sighted the enemy. The Yankee pickets fired on the Con-federate vanguard and fell back. The Texans needed no further in-vitation to fight. They galloped forward in a column of fours, the piercing rebel yell in their throats and blazing shotguns in their hands. The effect was overpowering. Most of the Federals took flight, leaving a small guard to stem the tide. "The little rear guard melted before us like straw before the wild fire on the prairie," wrote one of the Texans.[19] A handful of prisoners and several wagons and teams were taken and the Confederates were quite proud of them-selves. The Seventeenth Texas's baptism of fire had proved success-ful, and the men were ready for more.

And they got more. Later the same day, after returning to Searcy, Confederate pickets received fire from across the Little Red River. The alarm spread quickly through the town and the Texas cavalrymen sprang into their saddles. This time the Twelfth and the Sixteenth Regiments accompanied the Seventeenth, all under the command of Colonel William H. Parsons of the Twelfth. As the Confederates prepared to move out, an advance guard of one hundred men from the Seventeenth Texas went ahead to locate the enemy. Riding about eight miles ahead of the main force, the de-tachment found the enemy some fifteen miles east of Searcy. The Federals opened fire. The Confederates were ordered to respond with only one barrel of their shotguns, saving the other for a charge. The Texans fired a volley and urged their horses into a gallop. Once again the blue-coated soldiers were unable to stand up to the on-rushing horsemen. After most of the surviving Yankees had made good their escapes, the Confederates stopped to rest their mounts and wait for the rest of the command to catch up with them.

Night came and the Confederates bedded down. They were

within a few miles of a large Federal camp which they intended to attack in the morning. The men had barely fallen asleep when shots were heard. Pulses raced as the men quickly formed another battle line. It was a false alarm. One of the pickets, nervous perhaps, or sleepy, fired at what he thought was a Yankee. The dead Yankee turned out to be a dead cow.

Meanwhile Colonel Parsons waited anxiously for the arrival of the Sixteenth Texas. He had detached that regiment earlier with orders to rejoin the main body in the evening. By midnight the reunion still had not taken place so Parsons called off his plans for an early morning attack on the enemy camp. The sleeping soldiers were again awakened and ordered into their saddles. At sunup on the morning of June 8th, the tired troopers rode back into Searcy. They had once again faced the foe and emerged victorious.

The ride back to camp was without incident. The men shared a laugh over the dead cow and the resulting disorder. The cow was not the only casualty. In the darkness there had been much confusion. During the cow's attack, other Confederate pickets had mistaken some of their comrades for the enemy and had opened fire on them. Before the mistake could be rectified, Solomon V. Mace, of Company C, was wounded in the thigh and his horse was killed. Such mishaps were bound to occur in such a large gathering of relatively untrained troops. Less than a week earlier a more tragic accident had occurred. Several men from Company G had stacked their rifles in pyramid fashion, and were relaxing on the grass while their horses grazed nearby. One of the horses somehow knocked the guns down, and one of them discharged and hit two men, killing one and wounding the other.

By the end of the third week in June, Union General Curtis's situation at Batesville was becoming desperate. He informed his superiors that he could not advance without reinforcements and he could not stay where he was without being resupplied. So, in addition to the naval relief expedition led by Commander Kilty up the White River, a cavalry brigade started out from Missouri to bolster the garrison at Batesville. Kilty's infantry contingent was increased after the Battle of St. Charles to a total strength of about four thousand. To counter the threat posed by Kilty, Confederate troops hurried to DeVall's Bluff. General Rust's cavalry were among those sent there.

As the Union gunboats proceeded slowly up the river, the infantry fought its way through the undergrowth along the banks. Near Clarendon, Arkansas, the Yanks met with stiff resistance and that was the final straw for Commander Kilty. He sent a message to

Curtis informing him that the gunboats could not ascend any higher up the river. Curtis would have to come to him. Fortunately for the Confederates, a copy of this message was taken from a captured courier. As Curtis made his plans to evacuate Batesville, General Hindman also made plans. He would leave a small force at DeVall's Bluff and send some of his cavalry to intercept Curtis.

As the Union troops vacated Batesville, and moved down the river to Jacksonport, the way was clear for Colonel Sweet to lead his men into town. Not all of the residents were avid secessionists but those who were made the Texans feel welcome. The Unionists of the area soon became victims of a prank played by Lieutenant Gilbert B. Hathaway and some of his troopers from Company A. Upon the departure of the Federal soldiers from the town, the publishers of the pro Union Batesville *Eagle* also left rather than face the Confederates. With the newspaper offices empty, Lieutenant Hathaway and his men promptly moved in and set up shop. They ran off an issue full of anti Union invective and secessionist editorials and sent it out to all of the regular subscribers. The readers, unaware of the hoax, rushed to the *Eagle* office, paid their bills, and cancelled their subscriptions. Lieutenant Hathaway and his men, eighty dollars richer, then ended their literary endeavors.

The men of the Fifteenth Texas were not at Batesville long before they finally met the enemy. On Tuesday, July 8th, scouts galloped breathlessly into camp with word that a Federal supply train was a few miles away with an escort of only about two hundred men. These Federals were part of the relief force from Missouri. Colonel Sweet quickly assembled his men and set out in pursuit. Just before sunset they caught up with the Yankees at a place on the Black River known as Orient Ferry. The bluecoats, members of Colonel Powell Clayton's Fifth Kansas Cavalry, had already begun crossing the river when the Rebel horsemen came thundering down the road. The Yanks were surprised by the sudden onslaught but recovered quickly. The men on the near side of the river took refuge in some buildings and behind their wagons and returned the Confederates' fire. Meanwhile, their comrades across the river formed a battle line and poured a destructive rifle fire into the gray ranks. The fight was short. The Confederates found themselves in an area too small in which to deploy effectively. In addition, their shotguns could not compete with the enemy's rifled carbines. After ten or fifteen minutes of confusion the Texans hastily retreated back up the road, leaving their dead and wounded behind them.

The Fifteenth Texas lost seven men killed and seven men wounded. While this first engagement was certainly not a Southern victory it was not without value. The men learned a valuable lesson. The Yankees could fight! Gone were the notions that the war would be one vast picnic.

The Fifteenth Texas licked its wounds, while the rest of the brigade underwent a similar experience farther south. General Rust had been ordered to cross White River near Jacksonport and block Curtis's force near there. When Rust found a crossing at Jacksonport to be impracticable, General Hindman ordered him to cross farther downstream, near Des Arc, to prevent Curtis from crossing the Cache River. Hindman instructed Rust to hold out until the last man. He was to leave nothing in Curtis's path that would be of any use to him. He was to destroy crops, burn bridges and poison the water by dumping dead and gutted cattle into the streams. He had the Twelfth, the Sixteenth, and the Seventeenth Texas Cavalry Regiments at his disposal and to these were added five regiments of Arkansas infantry — some of which were composed of poorly-armed conscripts. General Pike, still smarting from the libelous tales spread about him, was ordered to send Colonel Dawson's Nineteenth Arkansas Infantry Regiment to General Rust. Pike complied with the request to the letter. He sent the men. He did not send them with any weapons, however. After much scrounging around for men and arms, General Rust's force numbered about five thousand.

Curtis marched his ten thousand man Army of the Southwest down the east side of the White as he endeavored to reach safety at Helena. The clash between the two forces occurred close to the Cache River near Round Hill on July 7, 1862. When the Federal First Division reached the river, Brigadier General Frederick Steele sent Colonel Charles E. Hovey with one small cannon and four hundred men from the Thirty-third Illinois Infantry and the Eleventh Wisconsin Infantry as skirmishers. Confederate pickets fired on these men near Hill's plantation and fell back. The Federals moved down the road toward Des Arc, and fell into a Confederate ambush. They quickly unlimbered their little field gun and put it into action.

Colonel Parsons led the Confederate cavalry in this engagement. He ordered the Seventeenth Texas to ride around the enemy's left flank to hit him with a rear assault. He then led the Sixteenth Texas and his own Twelfth Texas in a frontal assault. The Union infantry fired a volley at the attacking cavalry and staggered them momentarily. The second volley emptied more saddles. Terrified, riderless horses galloped in all directions. The third time the Yanks fired completed the demoralization of the remaining horsemen and they began a precipitous retreat that turned into a rout. The fighting ended before the Seventeenth Texas could become engaged. The Texas and Arkansas troops fled for their lives. Five thousand Confederate soldiers were put to flight by four hundred enemy troops. This brief action, known as the Battle of Cotton Plant, did little to enhance the image of the dashing Texas cavalry soldier.

A short time after the battle the disposition of the Texas cavalry was modified. The Fifteenth, the Sixteenth, the Seventeenth, and the Eighteenth Regiments were removed from the command of General Rust and ordered to report to Camp Texas. In mid-July these regiments suffered the same fate meted out to the Twenty-fourth and the Twenty-fifth — they were dismounted. The men in these regiments would henceforth serve as infantry, but still retained their cavalry designations. These four regiments were brigaded with the Tenth Texas Infantry under the command of Colonel Sweet of the Fifteenth Texas. The new brigade spent the last few days of July and the first few days of August moving to a new campsite. The new location was called Camp Chrystal Hill and was twelve to fifteen miles northwest of Little Rock. After only about three weeks, the brigade moved again, this time to Camp Hope, near the town of Austin, Arkansas. The water was better there and it was hoped that the health of the men would improve.

While at Camp Hope the brigade drilled hard in infantry tactics — four hours a day for the men and an extra two hours for the officers. This all seemed quite natural to the men of the Tenth Texas but it galled the ex-cavalrymen. They were still fuming over the loss of their horses and it seemed logical to them to blame whoever was in charge. In this case it was Colonel Sweet.

The colonel was a proud man and very vain about his military appearance. One night some men from the Eighteenth Texas crept over to Sweet's quarters and cut off the mane and tail of his horse, Bay Bob, a practice generally reserved for untrained and skittish army horses and mules. After that, whenever the colonel appeared on his horse the men would hoot derisively, "Whoa, Bob," as loud as they could.[20] These antics were common in all camps in both armies and the victims were almost always officers. The charm and good breeding of Sweet's men were also evident at a party given by him for the brigade on September 9, 1862. There were only thirty or forty women in attendance amid several thousand men. To say that the behavior of the men was rowdy would be to grossly understate the case. In fact, "the men behaved so bad that the ladys left in dysgust and went home — this is no place fer women." [21] So much for Southern chivalry.

The men heard many rumors while at Camp Hope. The most

persistent of these was that they would be ordered into Missouri for the winter. They were told to obtain warm clothing from home because the government could not provide it for them. Letters home at this time read like shopping lists: "If it is convenient, send me a Double brested Jeans vest and one or two Pr. pants and a shirt or two." [22] "I want one good thick pair of breeches[,] an over shirt, both of wool or part wool and a couple of pairs of drawers, soft wool if you can get it, a vest, a couple of homespun cotton shirts . . . three or four pair of socks, a pair of homemade suspenders and a soldiers cloak or overcoat." [23] "I want you to make us som overshirts; make mine geens [jeans] and dy[e] them purple and brown . . ." [24] "I would like to have a heavy jeans, well lined overcoat, also a linsey or cotton overshirt, one pair of pants, and pair of slips and socks." [25]

Early on the morning of October 1, 1862 the men at Camp Hope received marching orders. General Curtis was believed to be headed that way with a strong Federal force. Clarendon, on the White River, was designated as the point to which Confederate troops were to be sent to parry the Union thrust. About midnight, after the first day's march, rain began to fall. It poured all the next day as the men floundered along through knee-deep mud. There were no campfires that night, but it didn't really matter. All of the food supplies were drenched anyway. After a miserable night in the mud, the march continued the next day. Finally, on October 4th, the troops reached Clarendon. The sun eventually made an appearance and the soldiers were able to dry out. Fortifications were erected but no enemy appeared. On October 9th the Texans started back to Camp Hope.

The weather during the march back to camp was, if anything, worse than it had been during the trip to Clarendon. On the second day's march the heavens parted again and icy, cold, wind-driven rain stung the faces of men and animals. The rain occasionally alternated with sleet. Mules, exhausted by straining to pull wagons along in hub-deep mud, dropped in their tracks and were left. Men, also, too weary to go on, dropped out of line to lie on any spot of ground they could find that was above water. When the troops at last reached Camp Hope, on October 11th, they found that Allison Nelson, who had been promoted to brigadier general a few weeks before, had died of typhoid fever on October 7, 1862. As a mark of respect for the man, the name of Camp Hope was changed to Camp Nelson.

After the death of General Nelson a new brigade commander was named. He was a former artillery colonel named James Deshler. Deshler was an 1854 graduate of West Point and had gained military experience against the Sioux before joining the Confederate Army as a captain. He fought in western Virginia in 1861 in the Cheat Mountain Campaign where he was severely wounded. After recovering, he was made a colonel and served as General Holmes's chief of artillery in the battles around Richmond in May of 1862. Colonel Deshler rapidly earned the respect of the men in his new command and a strong bond of friendship was forged between commander and commanded.

CHAPTER TWO

The Battle of
Arkansas Post

Hundreds of miles from Arkansas, the bloodiest one-day battle of the war took place at Sharpsburg, Maryland, on September 17, 1862. The three Texas infantry regiments that took part in that battle were badly cut up. In fact, the Fourth Texas Infantry suffered over fifty percent casualties and the First Texas was almost annihilated as it lost over eighty percent of its men. These Texas troops had already earned reputations as intrepid fighters and the authorities in Richmond wanted more Texans in the Army of Northern Virginia. To that end General Thomas C. Hindman was ordered, on October 17, 1862, to dispatch seven more regiments of Texans to Richmond. He decided to send, as part of this requirement, Colonel Robert R. Garland's brigade. The departure of these troops for Virginia was delayed — as it turned out no more Texas regiments were ever sent to General Lee — and Garland's men stayed in Arkansas for a few more months.

On September 28, 1862, Major General Theophilus H. Holmes issued Special Order Number 39. By this order Colonel John Dunnington was placed in command of the river defenses of Arkansas, with instructions to fortify suitable points on the White and Arkansas Rivers. Lieutenant Colonel William A. Crawford's Arkansas Infantry Battalion and Colonel Charles L. Dawson's Nineteenth Arkansas Infantry Regiment were ordered to report to Colonel Dunnington and Colonel Garland was ordered to assemble his brigade near the Post of Arkansas. Garland's men were already there when the order was issued.

Garland's Texans had departed Camp Holmes and slowly made their way toward Arkansas Post when messengers arrived on September 19th with word that a large enemy force was on its way to destroy the fort then under construction at the Post. The men had already stopped for the night by this time so volunteers were called for to make a forced march to the Post. Four hundred men, mostly from the Sixth and Twenty-fourth Texas, left just after dark. At dawn the next morning the exhausted Texans reached their objective. They had crossed the Arkansas River on a ferryboat and marched all night on roads, through fields, and over rough trails. When they arrived they found everything peaceful. Captain L. M. Nutt's independent company of Louisiana cavalry were the only troops present and they were immediately sent out to lure the enemy to the Post where the Texans waited. Instead of snapping at the bait that Captain Nutt dangled before them, the Federals retreated back to their base. The Texans felt a keen sense of disappointment at not getting into action. They had hoped to have heroic stories to tell by the time the rest of the brigade arrived the next day. Instead, however, they had to content themselves with the boredom of routine camp life.

Arkansas Post, or the Post of Arkansas, stood on the Arkansas River about a hundred miles southeast of Little Rock and about forty miles above the river's confluence with the Mississippi. The Post existed as a French trading post as early as 1686 but it is believed that the expedition of Hernando de Soto may have visited the site as early as 1541. During the American Revolution, the small Fort San Carlos III was located there and its Spanish garrison fought with British partisans in one of the westernmost engagements of that war. The United States acquired Arkansas Post from Napoleon in 1803, along with the rest of the Louisiana Territory. The first territorial capital of Arkansas was located there in 1819, but was removed to Little Rock in 1821, due in part to the unhealthiness of the area. The Post then served as county seat of Arkansas County until 1855 when the seat of government shifted to DeWitt. Few persons remained after that and the town fell into ruin.

The Confederates decided to fortify Arkansas Post in September 1862, to keep the enemy from using his superior naval strength to steam up the river into the very heart of the state. Slaves, under the close supervision of Confederate engineers, built the fort. It was named Fort Hindman in honor of Major General Thomas C. Hindman, Confederate commander of the Trans-Mississippi Department. The fort was roughly square in shape, each side measuring about three hundred feet. The eight foot high earthen walls were

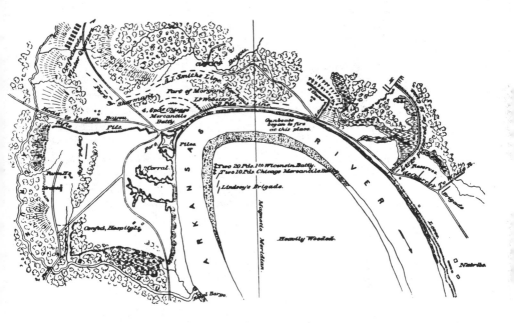

Diagram of Arkansas Post and outworks, from surveys by Captain Sidney S. Lyon, acting topographical engineer 19th Army Corps.

— From the *Official Records*

eighteen feet thick at the top and wider at the base. A deep ditch, or moat, lay just outside the walls. It was eight feet deep, twenty feet across, and usually filled with water. Entrance to the fort was gained by a drawbridge on the northwest side. On the eastern face, the side nearest the river, were two casemates for heavy guns. These structures measured about eighteen feet square on the inside and resembled small houses. Any similarity to dwellings ceased, however, upon closer inspection. Three layers of fourteen-inch oak timbers formed the walls and roofs. The casemates were then buried up to their eaves on the sides toward the river and the three and a half foot thick roofs were covered with almost an inch of railroad iron. These emplacements housed an eight-inch gun and a nine-inch gun, respectively. A third heavy gun — another nine-inch — was mounted on the parapet on the same side of the fort. The Confederates had several nicknames for this big gun. It was affectionately known as "Big Susan", "Long Tom", and "Lady Davis." [1] All three of the big guns came from the Confederate Navy ram *Pontchartrain,* and were manned by Confederate sailors. Four three-inch rifled guns and four six-pounders completed the fort's armament.

In conjunction with the fort was a series of outlying works. Stretching out to the west was a partially finished trench extending seven hundred yards, almost to Post Bayou. Piles were driven into the riverbed east of the fort and connected with heavy chains. These obstructions were located near the opposite shore and were designed to force any ships passing up or down the river to come directly under the muzzles of the fort's guns. Downriver were two sets of earthworks extending inland from the river's edge. The uppermost of these defenses was about a mile and a quarter from the fort and had embrasures for six cannons. The lower works were another three-quarters of a mile downstream and were designed to accommodate ten fieldpieces as well as provide for a large number of infantry.

As the days grew shorter the Confederates settled into the daily routine of garrison life. Log huts, resembling slave cabins, were built for winter quarters. They were typically about sixteen feet square with the chinks between the logs filled with mud. Chimneys were built, wooden roofs were added and every effort was made to make the huts as comfortable as possible.

The monotony of daily drill was eased somewhat by occasional scouting expeditions, but the enemy was seldom seen. The soldiers' boredom was further alleviated by the endless stream of rumors which always seem to surround an idle army. Most of the rumors were of an optimistic nature. It was said, for instance, that President

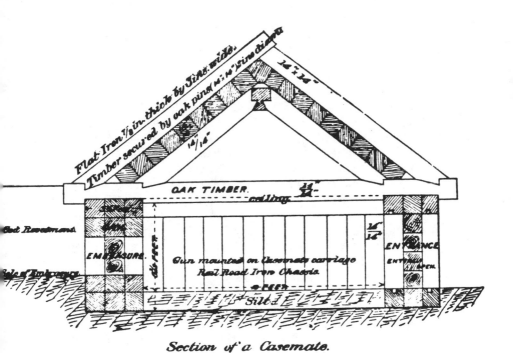

Section of a Casemate.

SCALE OF FEET.

— From the *Official Records*

Lincoln was trying to arrange a compromise with the Confederacy because of his fear of the ten Rebel ironclads reported to be at Mobile! *(There were no ironclads at Mobile.)* General Braxton Bragg had soundly defeated General Don Carlos Buell. *(This was true. It was a reference to the Battle of Munfordsville, Kentucky, in which Union casualties numbered thirty-six hundred as opposed to seven hundred for the Confederates.)* General Sterling Price had won an important battle at Iuka, Mississippi, and had captured ten thousand prisoners and five million dollars worth of supplies! *(Union losses were actually about seven hundred and fifty while the Rebels lost over fifteen hundred.)* Another great Confederate victory was won at Perryville, Kentucky! With only a slight loss to themselves, the rumor went, the Confederates had killed two thousand Yanks and wounded another thirteen thousand! *(The Battle of Perryville was fought on October 8, 1862. The two thousand Yanks that were killed, actually numbered about eight hundred and fifty, and the thirteen thousand wounded were less than three thousand. The Confederates lost over three thousand men in this battle.)* It was reported in camp in early December that General Ambrose Burnside had been defeated in Virginia. This was a reference to the Battle of Fredericksburg. Another wild rumor had to do with a big battle fought at Vicksburg, with Yankee losses of twelve thousand killed, six gunboats sunk and twenty-two hundred prisoners taken! *(The battle referred to here was the Battle of Chickasaw Bluff, in which Union losses were two hundred killed and about a thousand wounded. No gunboats were lost.)*

There were also occasional negative rumors. Stonewall Jackson had been killed! *(Not true.)* General Hindman had lost six transports at Fort Smith and fallen back to within fifty miles of Little Rock! *(This apparently referred to Hindman's loss at Prairie Grove, although the rumor made its appearance in camp a couple of days before the battle took place.)*

No matter how absurd some of the rumors sound now, the soldiers were more than willing to believe them. Captain Samuel F. Foster of the Twenty-fourth Texas wrote:[2]

> Since our arrival at this Post these rumors still come. I suppose they are told partly to keep our soldiers in good sperits and partly because we all like to hear just such reports, and wether true or not makes no difference, we believe it when we hear it, and that is an end to it, for soon another rumor [appears,] greater than the last one before it, and so on.

On November 21, 1862, Colonel Deshler's brigade broke camp and headed for Little Rock. The brigade reached the Arkansas capital the next day. While there the troops were reviewed by General

Holmes and on the 25th they boarded steamers bound for Arkansas Post. The river was low and the ships frequently ran aground. At the end of each day's journey the men camped on the banks of the river and they finally reached the Post on the 28th after a cold, miserable trip. The new arrivals wasted little time in erecting comfortable quarters, spurred on by winter weather which was already upon them.

During the fall and winter of 1862, the health problems that had plagued the civilian inhabitants of Arkansas Post throughout its existence were visited in full force upon the soldiers. Diaries and letters home record over and over again the alarming amount of sickness and death. Pneumonia was one of the principal killers. Men died so fast for a while that funerals were held from sunup until sundown, and sometimes far into the night. One of the few remaining buildings in the village of Arkansas Post, the bank, was pressed into service as a hospital and was quickly filled with the sick. Morale was severely undermined and Captain Gil McKay of the Seventeenth Texas likened Fort Hindman to Fort Donelson which had been captured the year before. His morbid prediction was soon fulfilled.

During the last week of December, a party of Captain Nutt's Louisiana cavalrymen fired into and captured the Union transport *Blue Wing* at Cypress Bend on the White River. In addition to a large quantity of ammunition and commissary stores, the steamer carried sixteen mailbags full of letters and newspapers. Soldiers who were starved for news, pored over the latest Northern newspapers and letters. A young man in the Eighteenth Texas wrote home to his mother that "we have plenty of Northern papers of the latest dates to reade and some of the most interesting letters that I ever saw. They was written by the young ladies to thare sweet hearts in the army. From what I can learn from these papers I think they are as tired of the war as we are." [3]

While the Southern soldiers thus passed the time in relative inactivity, forces were in motion which would cause great changes for them. Before the new year of 1863 would scarcely have begun, some of these men would lie in shallow graves, some would be suffering from wounds, and most of them would be on their way to cold prison camps in the North. Northern military leaders were anxious to capture Vicksburg and Port Hudson. They were the last two bastions of defense on the Mississippi River and their capture would open up the river for navigation all the way to the Gulf of Mexico. It would also mean that the Confederacy would be cut in two.

The most recent attempt by the Yankees to capture Vicksburg, had resulted in a bloody repulse of Major General William T. Sherman's four divisions at Chickasaw Bluff on December 29, 1862. While the Federals recovered from that debacle, Major General John A. McClernand arrived on January 1st with orders placing himself in command. Both generals felt that the war effort could be materially aided by the elimination of the Confederate threat posed by the garrison of Fort Hindman. The recent capture of the *Blue Wing* proved to them that the Union supply line along the Mississippi was vulnerable as long as such a large enemy force remained in the area.

The success of any attempt to capture Fort Hindman would require the close cooperation of the navy. McClernand asked Admiral David D. Porter to provide the necessary support. Porter hesitated because of his personal dislike of McClernand but he relented and placed his ships at the general's disposal. The army troops making the expedition were the Thirteenth Army Corps, commanded by Brigadier General George W. Morgan, and the Fifteenth Army Corps, led by General Sherman. General McClernand officially dubbed his command the "Army of the Mississippi," and cast off from Milliken's Bend on January 5, 1863.

The Federals reached the Notrib farm, about three miles below the Post, on the evening of January 9th. The ships anchored and preparations were begun to land the troops on the following morning. A heavy rain fell during the night but by dawn it had stopped and the disembarkation commenced. By noon most of the men were ashore.

Meanwhile, the commander of Fort Hindman, Brigadier General Thomas Churchill, became aware on the morning of January 9th of the enemy's approach. He issued orders for the men to be given ammunition and told them to prepare three days' cooked rations. When this was done he ordered them into the lower defenses. By the time the Confederates reached the upper works, however, they learned that the Federals had already landed near the lower trenches so they stopped and began to strengthen the upper line instead.

The Confederate troop disposition at this point stood as follows: Colonel James Deshler's brigade was on the right with its right resting on the river; the six fieldpieces of Captain William E. Hart's Arkansas Battery were also posted near the river so they could return the expected fire of the gunboats; extending from Deshler's left was the Nineteenth Arkansas Infantry Regiment; five companies from Colonel Garland's brigade were detached as skirmishers with the rest of his brigade held in reserve; and the Louisiana cavalry companies of Captains William B. Denson and Nutt, and Captain Sam

Richardson's Texas cavalry company were sent out in front of the skirmishers as advance pickets.

About dusk, one of Admiral Porter's ironclad gunboats steamed up to within about a half mile of the Confederate trenches. Most of the soldiers had never seen such a craft before, so many of them left their positions and strolled down toward the river to get a closer look. The sailors on board soon opened fire and the first shot sent the curious onlookers scurrying for their protective earthworks. The ship fired several more shells during the evening but they did very little damage.

The Confederates spent most of the night strengthening their position. Trees were felled in front of their line and dragged around so that their sharpened branches pointed toward the enemy. The trenches were deepened and the breastworks improved as much as possible with the makeshift tools available. It rained most of the night and that only added to the misery and discomfort of soldiers on both sides.

The morning of Saturday, January 10th, found the Union fleet busy unloading troops at Notrib's farm. General Sherman's Fifteenth Corps was the first to debark and Major General Frederick Steele led the First Division inland in a circuitous march so he could come upon the fort from the north and west. Brigadier General David Stuart led the Second Division up the river road so as to approach the fort from the northeast. The Thirteenth Corps was to follow Stuart's division up the river and take a position on its left.

Steele's division started off as directed but soon became bogged down in a swamp. By the time the head of the column came to solid ground it was discovered that to reach their objective — the back side of the fort — these men would have several more miles of hard marching through difficult terrain. General McClernand felt that the delay involved in such a march would endanger his overall strategy and so, after a hurried consultation with General Sherman, he ordered Steele's division to retrace its steps and advance upon the fort via the river road.

While these Federal troop movements took place the Confederates waited. They had spent most of the night improving their position and now awaited further developments. These developments were not long in coming as the gunboats commenced shelling the Rebel works about 8:00 A.M. Reply by Hart's battery was futile against the heavily-armored vessels and the heavy guns in the fort were unable to reach the fleet with their shells due to the inferior grade of gunpowder with which they were supplied. Shortly after noon, word reached the Confederates of the attempted flank move-

ment of General Steele's division. Fearing envelopment, General
Churchill ordered his men to retire to the main line of trenches at the
fort. Colonel Deshler detached five companies of the Tenth Texas to
help Colonel Garland's five companies of skirmishers cover the
withdrawal. These men succeeded in protecting their retiring comrades even though they were constantly harassed by the Sixth and
the Eighth Missouri Infantry Regiments of Colonel Giles A. Smith's
brigade. General Churchill recognized the gravity of the situation
and began requesting reinforcements. At least two relief columns
started out, one from St. Charles and one from Pine Bluff. Captain
Alf Johnson's Spy Company, a small independent company of Texas
cavalry, arrived on the scene on the evening of January 10th. In the
meantime, General Hindman told Churchill that he was "to hold
out till help arrived or until all dead." [4]

The Southerners began digging in again as soon as they
reached the fort. In front of part of their line were some of the log
huts in which they had been living. They tore these down to provide
a clear field of fire and used the logs to improve their breastworks.
Again the lack of proper tools hampered their efforts and pieces of
planks were used as shovels. As the Confederates worked, the enemy
came even closer. Colonel Roger Q. Mills led a patrol out in front of
the lines to discourage some Yankee skirmishers who had ventured
too close. He brought several prisoners in but similar forays by the
Federals during the evening netted them some Confederate prisoners too. As the Rebels continued to work, the gunboats made another appearance.

The *Louisville, Baron de Kalb, Cincinnati,* and *Lexington* steamed
upriver to test the mettle of the fort. The first three were of the heavily-armored Eads class of river gunboats while the *Lexington* was just
slightly less menacing. At one point in the action which followed, the
tinclad *Rattler* tried to move past the fort and take it in reverse. Unfortunately for the lightly armored ship, she became entangled in the
piles that obstructed the river beneath the Confederate guns. Before
she could extricate herself she was riddled with shot and shell. She
withdrew down the river while the rest of the fleet continued to trade
salvoes with the fort until about 9:00 P.M. Several of the naval shells
sailed past the fort and landed near the Confederate trenches causing some casualties among the artillery horses but doing little damage beyond that.

The night was very cold with snow expected. The Confederates,
by their labors, were able to ward off some of the chill even though
they had left their warm clothes in their quarters when the first
alarm sounded. The Union troops, however, suffered greatly from

the cold. In order to keep their positions from being known by the Confederates they were forbidden to make campfires. They, too, had left warm clothes behind when they got off the ships since they were anticipating an immediate battle.

By mid-morning on January 11th, all was in readiness for a fierce battle. General McClernand had placed Brigadier General Charles E. Hovey's brigade on the extreme right of the Federal line. (Hovey had been promoted since the Battle of Cotton Plant.) Next to Hovey stood the brigades of Brigadier General John M. Thayer, Colonel Giles A. Smith and Colonel Thomas Kilby Smith. Next were the Thirteenth Corps brigades of Brigadier General Stephen G. Burbridge and Colonel Lionel A. Sheldon. Meanwhile, Colonel Daniel W. Lindsey had taken a position across the river and above the fort. With a company of cavalry and four pieces of rifled artillery he had the responsibility of preventing any reinforcements from reaching Fort Hindman from upriver.

The Confederate force was stretched very thin. Colonel Dunnington's brigade held the fort and serviced the heavy guns. Extending from the fort toward the bayou was Garland's brigade — Sixth Texas Infantry, Twenty-fourth Texas Dismounted Cavalry, and Twenty-fifth Texas Dismounted Cavalry, right to left. The left of the Confederate line was held by Deshler's brigade — Eighteenth Texas Dismounted Cavalry, Seventeenth Texas Dismounted Cavalry, Tenth Texas Infantry, Fifteenth Texas Dismounted Cavalry, and the Nineteenth Arkansas Infantry (borrowed from Colonel Dunnington), right to left. Deshler also sent two companies from each of his regiments to the far left to act as skirmishers and protect the flank from a surprise attack from across the bayou. Hart's Battery was in place near the right of Deshler's brigade and the cavalry companies were distributed within the fort and along the bayou as pickets. Help was on the way. Colonel E. E. Portlock, leading one hundred and ninety men of the Twenty-fourth Arkansas Infantry Regiment in a forced march from St. Charles, was only a short distance from the fort by midday. Major General John G. Walker, near Pine Bluff, had just received word of Churchill's predicament and soon had his infantry division on the road for the Post. A race against the clock then ensued.

The Battle of Arkansas Post started in earnest about one o'clock on the afternoon of January 11, 1863. The *Louisville, Baron de Kalb,* and *Cincinnati* led the attack while the less heavily armored gunboats opened fire from long-range. Admiral Porter, in his battle orders, warned his captains not to overshoot the fort since General Sherman's troops would be on the far side of the fort and "it is desirable

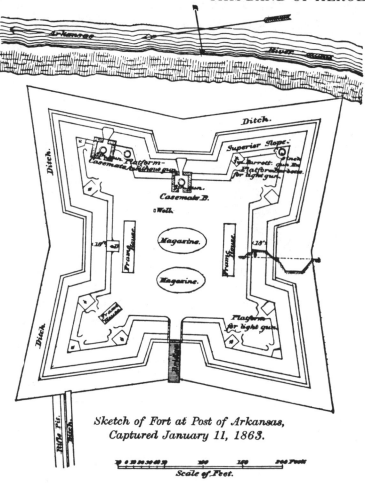

Sketch of Fort at Post of Arkansas,
Captured January 11, 1863.

Scale of Feet.

MEMOIR.

Casemate A—8-inch shell gun. One-half of the chase of the gun knocked away by a shot
through embrasure. Gun totally disabled. Carriage shattered. Embrasure side of
casemate forced inwards by numerous shots, several of which penetrated the entire
thickness of timber. Roofing badly shattered, but the ceiling of casemate uninjured.
Casemate B—8-inch shell gun. Similarly damaged, but to a less extent. Gun struck on
face of muzzle, but not seriously damaged.
Nine-inch barbette shell gun at *C*, mounted on full traverse circle. Gun cut in two in
front of reinforce by a 30-pound Parrott shot. Carriage badly broken; completely disabled.
D—3-inch Parrott gun, mounted on field carriage. Large piece of muzzle knocked off.
Carriage shattered.
Three other 3-inch Parrott guns and four 6-pounder iron smooth-bore guns on platforms in
the angles. Two of the 6-pounders injured; one of them much broken.
Houses injured. Magazines well secured.

                                        WM. L. B. JENNEY,
                                Captain and Aide-de-Camp, on Engineer duty.

                                            — From the *Official Records*

to drop our shells in or near the fort, that we may not trouble him as he advances." [5] As soon as the ships began hammering away at the fort, the Confederate artillery responded. Soon the Federal field artillery was also ablaze all along the line. After about a half hour of artillery preparation, the Union infantry began its advance. The movement began on the Federal right with the other units joining *en echelon* to the left.

General Hovey started the action in his sector by sending forth the Seventeenth Missouri Infantry as skirmishers. As the Missourians moved forward they came under heavy fire from the front and from their right flank. The flank fire came from the Confederate cavalry posted along the bayou and it became so hot that the Seventeenth wheeled to the right while the rest of the brigade swept past behind it and on toward the Rebel breastworks. The Missourians stayed on the flank until their ammunition was exhausted and they were forced to retire.

The long lines of blue infantry, with their bayonets glinting in the sunlight, must have been a fearful sight to the entrenched Confederates. Fear knows no flag, however, and sixty-five men from the Twenty-fifth Iowa Infantry (including a major) decided they had seen enough for one day and hastily absented themselves from further action. As the Yankees continued their forward progress they came under Captain Hart's artillery fire at a distance of two hundred and fifty yards. It took a couple of shots for the Southern gunners to establish the correct range but by the third round much damage was done in the blue ranks. As the attackers advanced to within a hundred yards of the Rebel works the rifles and shotguns of Deshler's brigade opened up on them. Unable to advance further, the Yankees dug in.

Because of the wooded character of the terrain in its front, General Thayer's division occupied a rather narrow space. The general placed the First Iowa Battery on his right with the Twenty-sixth Iowa and the Thirtieth Iowa making up the rest of the front. He put the Thirty-fourth Iowa in close support and kept his other regiments in reserve. The Iowans were able to get no closer to the Confederate lines than their comrades to the right and spent the next several hours trying to pick off the Rebel cannoneers with rifle fire.

Colonel Giles Smith deployed his brigade on the left of General Thayer. He placed the Sixth Missouri on the right with the 116th Illinois in the center and the 113th Illinois on the left. By late afternoon, this brigade appeared to be isolated from the rest of the attacking troops and Colonel Smith sent the Eighth Missouri in to bolster his right, and borrowed the Fifty-seventh Ohio from Colonel Thomas Smith's brigade to support the Missourians.

Meanwhile, the Confederates kept busy pouring artillery and small arms fire into the Northerners. The fire into which the Federals advanced was as varied as the weapons which fired it. In Deshler's brigade there were three hundred and fifteen Enfield rifles, a few sporting rifles, and a multitude of double-barreled shotguns. In Garland's brigade, the Sixth Texas was armed with Enfields, the Twenty-fourth Texas had the Model 1841 (or Mississippi) Rifles, and the Twenty-fifth Texas carried obsolete flintlock muskets that had been converted to the percussion system of ignition. The muskets and shotguns were loaded with "buck and ball."

As the Federal advance began, Confederate officers moved up and down the line encouraging the men. General Churchill told his junior officers to "instruct your men having short range guns to hold their fire until the Yankees come in thirty or forty yards. The buck and ball guns will commence firing at seventy-five to one hundred yards. Minie rifles will fire on them from the time they come in sight." [6] Colonel Wilkes of the Twenty-fourth Texas told his men to "shoot at their knees." [7] In spite of this sound advice the men tended to shoot too high. In fact, the commander of the Seventy-sixth Ohio later stated in his report of the battle that "this fire would probably have annihilated the Seventy-sixth Regiment had it not been . . . too high." [8]

General Burbridge's brigade was on the right of the Thirteenth Corps. When he finally heard the clamor of battle on his right he ordered his men to advance. After driving in the Confederate skirmishers the blue lines hesitated in the awful shower of shot and shell being sent their way. The men of the Sixtieth Indiana found themselves in a particularly perilous situation. Not only were they under murderous fire from the Confederates but they also received heavy fire from their right rear. (This misdirected fire appears to have come from either the Eighty-third Indiana or the 127th Illinois.) General Burbridge soon noticed gaps on both ends of his line and hurriedly sent in the Twenty-third Wisconsin on the right and the Sixty-seventh Indiana on the left.

As on other parts of the battle line the attackers and defenders settled down to a long afternoon of hot work. As the heat of battle increased, General Burbridge found it necessary to again strengthen his right. He borrowed the Nineteenth Kentucky and the Ninety-seventh Illinois from Colonel William J. Landrum, commanding a portion of one of the reserve brigades. The Kentuckians were sent in to support some Wisconsin troops while Burbridge held the Illinoisans in close support. As fresh troops went into battle they often passed over, or through, a regiment that was pinned down and either unable or unwilling to advance. In this manner the Seventy-seventh Illinois shifted to its right and passed over the Eighty-third Ohio. An officer of the Seventy-seventh wrote many years later that the "83d refused to advance, and we were compelled to charge over them in the face of a terrible fire from the fort. As we passed over them we made it a matter of necessity to tramp on as many as possible, at which they threw a few old fashioned anathemas after us. This we considered very ungentlemanly, and especially so as it was Sunday." [9]

Colonel Sheldon's brigade, near the river, was not as heavily engaged as the rest of the army. He sent two companies from the Sixty-ninth Indiana forward as skirmishers but held the rest of that regiment in reserve. Most of the action in this sector was between the opposing artillerists. Lieutenant Webster of the First Wisconsin Battery played the fire of his two twenty-pounder Parrott Rifles against the larger guns of the fort while Captain Charles G. Cooley of the Chicago Mercantile Battery used his four six-pounder brass smoothbores against the Confederate fieldpieces and infantry.

On the other side of the breastworks the Confederates held their own against the enemy infantry. Since the initial attack occurred on the Confederate left, Colonel Garland's brigade was subject at first to only artillery and skirmish fire. As the din of battle increased in front of Colonel Deshler he sent to Garland for reinforcements. Five companies each from the Twenty-fourth and the Twenty-fifth Texas and two companies from the Sixth Texas were immediately dispatched to the left. By this time the action on the left was so intense that these men had to crawl on their hands and knees in single file through the trenches to avoid being shot. A short time later, Colonel Garland further weakened his position by sending a hundred men to Colonel Dunnington inside the fort. Colonel Portlock finally arrived with his men and Confederate spirits were temporarily buoyed as these reinforcements were thrown into the fray.

The fort was slowly battered to pieces. Great gaps began to appear in the earthen walls and the parade ground was plowed up by the constant barrage of heavy projectiles. The wooden barracks buildings inside the fort caught fire and the smoke from these fires, mingled with the heavy pall of gunsmoke hanging over the entire area, was stifling. Even when the fires approached the powder magazine, the brave defenders still fought on. One soldier described the scene as "more like one of the pits of the infernal regions than a part of this fair earth." [10]

The gunboats continued to duel with the fort and the seemingly impregnable casemates were repeatedly penetrated by the shells from the ironclads. The freshwater sailors had coated the sloping sides of their ships with an inch of tallow so the Rebel shells would have a tendency to skid off when they hit, but this measure provided only a token protection. The *Baron de Kalb*, the *Louisville,* and the *Rattler* suffered serious damage from Colonel Dunnington's well served guns. The *Baron de Kalb* was repeatedly hit. One shot hit the muzzle of one of her ten-inch guns, rendering it useless, and another round destroyed the carriage of a thirty-two pounder. The *Louisville* had a couple of shells enter her gunports and explode on her gundeck, sending shards of steel and splinters of oak flying in all directions. After a couple of hours of pounding, though, the last of the three big Confederate guns fell silent and the ships began to move past the fort so they could enfilade the rifle pits to the west.

The plight of the Rebels was indeed grim. There was some talk of surrender in the fort until one of Dunnington's sailors grabbed a rifle and threatened to shoot anyone who would attempt to lower the flag. By this time one section of the First Wisconsin Battery and a section of the Chicago Mercantile Battery had opened fire from across the river. One of the shells struck the flagpole near the top and the flag, defended so courageously, floated to the ground.

The Confederates in the trenches now faced the fire of infantry and field artillery in their front and field and naval artillery from their right rear. Two brothers in Company A of the Twenty-fourth Texas, J. C. and O. Greer, were among the casualties by this time. They were loading and firing as fast as they could when a shell hit them. One of the brothers was killed instantly and the other had both of his legs blown off. The crippled soldier turned to his brother for aid. Seeing that his brother could not help him, and unable to endure the pain, he drew his pistol and killed himself.

After enduring almost an hour of this terrible cross fire, white flags began appearing in the area occupied by the Twenty-fourth Texas. These symbols of capitulation seem to have been raised spontaneously as no officer ever admitted giving a surrender order. Colonel Deshler at first refused to accept defeat.

> I looked and saw the flags, but I could not believe them to be white flags . . . moreover . . . everything had gone on so well on the left wing, and as far as I knew in Garland's brigade also, and knowing that it was General Churchill's determination to fight to desperation, I did not think it possible that a surrender could be intended . . .[11]

Although Deshler expressed surprise at the surrender, most of the private soldiers recognized it as the only way to prevent a useless effusion of blood. One Texas soldier, writing in 1906, said that it "has always seemed providential to surrender just at that time, as the next charge would have annihilated us." [12]

Casualties on both sides were relatively light. Best estimates place the number of Confederate killed at sixty to seventy with about two hundred wounded. Four thousand seven hundred and ninety-one were captured. Federal losses totaled one hundred and thirty-four killed and almost nine hundred wounded in the army, with the navy suffering losses of seven killed and twenty-six wounded. Colonel Garland's reputation was also a casualty. It would never recover. He was blamed, along with Colonel Wilkes, for the surrender. Secretary of War James A. Seddon recommended a court of inquiry be established to look into the affair but nothing immediate came of this and Garland spent the rest of his life unsuccessfully seeking exoneration.

The Battle of Arkansas Post was over. Not a Shiloh or a Gettysburg, its effect on the outcome of the war proved negligible. Any threat to the Federal supply line from Memphis to Vicksburg posed by the garrison of Fort Hindman, could have been easily nullified at any time by merely employing a sufficiently large force — as was done — to overwhelm the Confederates. General Ulysses S. Grant, in fact, in a telegram to General-in-Chief Henry W. Halleck, reported that General McClernand had "gone on a wild-goose chase to the Post of Arkansas." [13] Still, to the soldiers and sailors involved in this battle it was important. It taught them the value of breastworks, even rudimentary ones. It demonstrated the superiority of the large rifled guns of the navy. It lowered Confederate morale and raised that of the Union. Soldiers on both sides fought valiantly and the reports are full of commendations. General Churchill, writing of the surrender, said: "No stigma should rest upon the troops. It was no fault of theirs; they fought with a desperation and courage yet unsurpassed in this war . . ." [14]

CHAPTER THREE

Prison

Fort Hindman was badly battered during the battle and the Federals spent the next few days completing its destruction. They dumped the Confederate cannons, which were already damaged beyond the point of reasonable reclamation, down a well. They leveled the frame barracks buildings and destroyed all the log huts. In later years nature and the Corps of Engineers completed the obliteration of the fort. The course of the river has been altered slightly and the site of Fort Hindman is now completely under water.

After the surrender the Confederates were ordered to stack their arms and assemble on the riverbank. Many of the dejected prisoners simply dropped their weapons at their feet while others threw all of their guns, knives, and swords into a small pond. Union soldiers of the Ninety-seventh Illinois Infantry added their obsolete Belgian muskets to the pile of Confederate weapons and replaced them with brand new Enfield rifles with which some of the Rebels had been fighting. Not all of the defeated Southerners gave up their weapons. Some merely slipped away over the bayou amidst all the confusion. Others, such as Colonel Darnell of the Eighteenth Texas Cavalry, escaped capture by virtue of the fact that they were away from the Post at the time of the battle. Those who were so unfortunate as to be made prisoners, however, were a cold and hungry lot as they huddled together on the riverbank under the watchful eyes of their captors. They were not allowed to return to their cabins for coats or blankets, and the cold weather of January added to their feelings of despair. The Union soldiers passed out food to the hungry Rebels,

many of whom had not eaten since early the previous morning. Captors and captives engaged in some good-natured ribbing and soon
there was an impromptu singing contest going on. While the Yanks
sang such patriotic airs as the *Star Spangled Banner* and *Hail Columbia,
Happy Land,* the Confederates answered with *Dixie* and *Bonnie Blue
Flag* as well as such universal favorites as *The Girl I Left Behind Me.*

On Monday, January 12th, the Confederate prisoners began
boarding the transports *Tigress, Nebraska, John J. Roe,* and *Sam Gatey*
for trips to Northern prisons. After the *Nebraska* was loaded, her captain arranged for the Confederate officers to occupy staterooms and
eat their meals in the cabin just as if they were civilian passengers
out for a weekend cruise. The enlisted men and noncommissioned
officers would have to be content to make themselves as comfortable
as they could on deck and in the hold. Since the prisoners wore little,
if any, indication of rank it was very difficult to distinguish between
the officers and the enlisted men. Because of this it was an easy matter for the hungry Confederates to take advantage of the well inten-
tioned skipper. It didn't take the captain long to see that he had
been taken in and "he cussed like a good sailor, and said he didn't
know that every man in the outlay was an officer, or he certainly
would not have undertaken the job of feeding and bedding them in
the cabin." [1] During the night several men slipped over the sides of
the ships into the icy waters of the Arkansas River and made their
escapes.

On the morning of the 13th, the ships lifted anchor and started
down the river toward the Mississippi. The prisoners all thought
that they would be taken to Vicksburg where they would sign paroles and be released. After all, the Federals taken on the *Blue Wing*
had been quickly paroled. When the ships bearing the prisoners
reached the Father of Waters, however, they did not turn south, in
the direction of Vicksburg, but north. The weather continued cold
and a heavy snow soon blanketed everything in sight except the river
itself.

The vessels steamed past Helena, Arkansas, and by late on the
afternoon of January 16th they reached Memphis. Some fraterniza-
tion was allowed between the prisoners and civilians and the unfortunate Confederates were thus able to obtain some food and blankets. The ships lay anchored at Memphis for a day or two and on the
morning of the eighteenth, Federal sentries discovered that the
yawls of the *Sam Gatey* were gone — as were sixteen enterprising
Rebels. Captain Denson also slipped ashore at Memphis. He had
some civilian clothes smuggled aboard and, after donning the new
apparel, calmly walked ashore. These escapes provided heartwarm-

ing, though false, hope to the folks at home. By the time the news of the sixteen escaped Confederates reached the readers of the Dallas *Herald,* their number had been inflated to twenty-five hundred. The inaccurate report went on to say that these men, after "becoming exasperated by cruel treatment and the absence of absolute necessities . . . overcame their guards, burned the boats and escaped." [2] Individual escapes took place whenever there was the slightest chance for success. On the afternoon of January 20th the *Nebraska,* while manuevering close to shore, ran aground. In an instant, several Confederates jumped from the hurricane deck to the ground and were gone.

The journey up the river was one of continued misery. Some prisoners suffered from wounds. Many were sick. All were victims of the intense cold. Some went to sleep sharing a blanket with another man only to wake up the next morning to find that their companion had frozen to death in the night. As they huddled together for warmth they occasionally saw the blackened remains of burned-out houses along the river. Such was the stark reality of war!

On January 21st, the steamers passed Cairo headed for St. Louis. The paddle wheel of the *Sam Gatey* broke on the 22d — for the second time — and the *Nebraska* went hard aground again on the morning of the 23d. The *Sam Gatey* and the *John J. Roe* unloaded their prisoners and guards and then ferried off the *Nebraska*'s load. The Nebraska was finally free by eleven o'clock that night and the journey continued.

The prisoners reached St. Louis on Saturday, January 24th, and the ships stopped at Arsenal Island below the city. For the next few days the prisoners were guarded by a regiment of soldiers that was unique in either army. It was the Thirty-seventh Iowa Infantry and it was composed almost entirely of men over the age of forty-five. These men — over the maximum age being drafted — had volunteered to perform these rear echelon duties so that younger men would be free for active combat assignments. These patriotic older soldiers were dubbed the "Graybeards" and performed yeoman service until the end of the war. Over the next few days the ships left the island one at a time to deposit their human cargoes on the Illinois side of the river just above St. Louis at Alton. There the prisoners boarded trains for their final destinations. The enlisted men went to Camp Butler, near Springfield, Illinois, and Camp Douglas, just outside of Chicago. Officers went to Camp Chase, near Columbus, Ohio.

Camp Butler, named for Illinois State Treasurer William Butler, was established in August 1861, about six miles east of Springfield. It was built as a recruit depot for Illinois soldiers but on February 23, 1862, two thousand Confederate prisoners arrived from Fort Donelson, and Camp Butler served as a prison camp for most of the rest of the war. The camp was located on the Great Western Railroad about a half mile from the Sangamon River. A wooden fence enclosed the fifteen-acre camp and twenty-one poorly ventilated wood frame barracks with tar paper roofs housed the prisoners. The inhabitants of these buildings shivered in the winter and sweltered in the summer. Some of the barracks were used as hospitals where the sick Confederates supposedly received the same medical treatment as their captors.

The prisoners of war were supposed to receive the same rations as the Union soldiers. In the latter half of 1862, this ration consisted of the following portions calculated to feed one hundred men:

> 75 pounds of bacon
> Or 125 pounds of fresh beef
> 137$^1/_2$ pounds of fresh baker's bread
> Or 125 pounds of corn-meal
> Or 100 pounds of pilot bread
> Or 137$^1/_2$ pounds of flour
> 10 pounds of green coffee
> Or 8 pounds of fine-grained coffee
> 10 pounds of rice
> Or 10 pounds of hominy
> 15 pounds of sugar
> 1 gallon of vinegar
> 1$^1/_4$ pounds of Star candles
> 2 quarts of salt
> 8 quarts of beans
> 42 84/100 pounds of potatoes
> Molasses
> 4 pounds of soap[3]

Throughout the war, however, the amount of rations prescribed and the amount received rarely matched. The prison fare at Camp Butler was no exception and many men were hungry.

As at other prisons, many of the Confederates confined at Camp Butler spent the major part of their time plotting escape. They dug tunnels under the fence. They bribed guards to look the other way. Some prisoners even made their escapes in coffins. When a prisoner died a wooden coffin was sent into the camp and the body was removed to the dead house which was outside the walls and unguarded. Within a day or so a detail of prisoners would be formed to lay to rest their late comrade. Knowing the system of things some men, who were very much alive, were put into these pine boxes about dusk and taken to the dead house. Then "when it was dark these men kicked the tops off the boxes, got out and pulled their freight for a more congenial clime." [4]

Details from the Fifty-eighth Illinois Infantry Regiment and the Sixteenth Illinois Cavalry Regiment formed the guard detachment at Camp Butler. Some of the guards took their duties quite seriously while others were not quite so patriotic. For instance, late in March, a prisoner and a sentinel exchanged insults until the guard ended the conversation with a rifle shot that narrowly missed its mark. A couple of mornings later guards discovered a hole in the fence and a quick roll call confirmed the fact that fourteen Confederates had escaped. Six guards had also gone!

The weather at Camp Butler was a constant source of hardship for the prisoners. What little clothing they had was pitifully inadequate in the cold. When the winter wind whistled across the prairies of central Illinois it penetrated the barracks so that most of the men either stayed in their bunks wrapped in blankets or paced up and down the floor trying to combat the cold with constant movement. There was also much snow and rain in February and March and this dampness contributed to the steady stream of prisoners to the hospital and the equally unbroken routine of the burial parties. During these two months inmates died at the rate of almost thirty per week.

By the end of the prisoners' first week in camp the hardships began to tell on them in another way. Of course, they all wanted out of prison and some quickly decided to use any means possible to gain their freedom. Many of them petitioned the commandant, Colonel W. F. Lynch of the Fifty-eighth Illinois, to be allowed to take the oath of allegiance to the United States so that they might be released. This oath was not freely given and before it could be administered Federal officials had to be convinced that the applicants were sincere. The most frequent story used by the Camp Butler prisoners was that they were unwillingly conscripted into the Rebel Army and were really Unionists at heart. They wanted to be released from prison and remain in the North because if they waited to be formally exchanged they would have to remain in the army and risk being killed, wounded, or recaptured. Some of these men may have been pressured into enlisting but they had all volunteered before the Conscription Act was enacted and none of them were conscripts. A few may have had Unionist leanings but it seems certain that most of them looked upon the oath as a convenient way to get out of prison and out of the war.

During the early part of February 1863, the corpses of the men who had died were allowed to remain unburied in the dead house for several days. When a burial party was finally sent they found that most of the bodies had been horribly disfigured by the gnawing of rats and cats. By February 21st, the first cases of smallpox appeared among the prisoners and this dreaded disease added regularly to the population of the prison cemetery.

Prisoners assisted the Federal doctors in easing the suffering of their fellows, although one young Rebel nurse was anything but a volunteer. William J. Oliphant of the Sixth Texas was lounging near the door of his barracks one day when a Federal surgeon walked by and then stopped. He demanded to know why Oliphant had not saluted him. At this, the teenaged Confederate suggested that the officer "emigrate to a country where the climate was much warmer than any to be found in America." [5] The outraged doctor returned shortly with some guards to escort Oliphant to the smallpox ward. He was thrust in among the patients and ordered to nurse them. Men died around him every day but he did the best he could for them. Apparently disappointed when Oliphant showed no signs of coming down with the disease after ten days, the doctor finally ordered him back to his barracks. Unknown to the doctor Oliphant had already had smallpox and had thus acquired a certain amount of immunity to any recurrence.

On March 11th a supply of clothing was distributed to the inmates. Many of them had been reduced to rags by that time and the clothes were of great benefit. Within a few days the weather began to warm up and when the ground was dry the men were able to play town ball (similar to baseball). When Mother Nature occasionally made this form of recreation impossible, they retreated inside and talked of the ever-present rumors of exchange.

The spirits of the prisoners were buoyed up by the arrival from Louisiana of Captain Nutt's wife on April 4th. After visiting her husband at Camp Chase she obtained a supply of clothing in Louisville for dispersal among the men at Camp Butler. Upon her arrival at the camp the men greeted her as if she had descended straight from heaven. The clothes were to follow her by a few days, but it is not clear whether they got there in time to be issued because on April 7, 1863 the first contingent of prisoners started for Virginia and exchange.

The first troops to leave were the members of the Sixth Texas Infantry and the cavalry companies of Captains Nutt, Denson, Johnson, and Richardson. Some men were too sick to leave but the others crowded aboard the boxcars of the Great Western Railroad and by one o'clock in the afternoon they were on their way east.

Their route carried them through the towns of Decatur, Bement, Danville, and, shortly after midnight, the train crossed into Indiana bearing northeast.

By daylight on April 8th the trainload of hopeful prisoners reached Lafayette, Indiana, and some of the men began to wonder just where they were going. This certainly did not seem to be the way to Virginia! At least they were moving, however, and that was better than languishing in prison. As their journey continued they passed through Logansport, Huntington, and Fort Wayne. By late afternoon they were in Ohio. They reached Toledo by dark and transferred to regular passenger cars. At midnight they stopped at Cleveland.

The next morning the train followed the tracks of the Cleveland and Erie Railroad over a freshly fallen mantle of snow. The Confederates continued their journey along the southern shore of Lake Erie through the northwest tip of Pennsylvania, and into the state of New York. By the middle of the afternoon they reached Dunkirk, where they changed trains again. Now aboard the New York and Erie Railroad they ceased their northeasterly travel and began bearing a little south of east to Elmira. Elmira was the site of a Union recruit camp which was later to become, like Camp Butler, a prison camp.

By the morning of April 10th the prisoners were finally moving almost due south. They had changed trains again and were now the guests of the Elmira and Williamsport Railroad as they steamed through the Pennsylvania villages of Ralston and Trout Run. At Williamsport, they transferred to the cars of the Sudbury and Erie Railroad and from there to York, their line of travel paralleled the Susquehana River. By nightfall the Confederates were once again below the Mason– Dixon line and by midnight they rolled into Baltimore.

Upon reaching Baltimore, the prisoners were taken off the train and marched through the streets to Fort McHenry. After a couple of hours they countermarched back through the city where they found temporary lodging in the St. Charles Hotel. Their quarters were cramped and dirty and their rations were scant. The next morning some local ladies sent two wagons full of provisions to the Rebels but the guards turned them back. Late that evening, aboard the *State of Maine,* the prisoners began moving down the Chesapeake.

The next day was Sunday and it dawned clear and bright. The prisoners signed their paroles and were fed a good meal. By the middle of the afternoon the *State of Maine* dropped anchor off Fortress Monroe. The ship remained there for a couple of days in company with the *John Brooks* and the *W. H. Wilder,* which were also laden with Confederate prisoners of war. Tuesday the prison ships steamed up the James River to City Point, Virginia, and their passengers once more set foot on Confederate soil.

From City Point the prisoners, or former prisoners, rode the train to Petersburg. There they debarked and marched to the Model Farm barracks nearby. Most of the new arrivals were sick and went to the hospitals while the healthy ones were divided into companies of one hundred men each. They were put up in tents and fed regular, though somewhat scanty, rations. Life there was rather easy, although there was still a lot of sickness. They stayed in this camp for a couple of weeks with little to do.

The prisoners at Camp Douglas had similar experiences. Camp Douglas was located on the estate of the late Senator Stephen A. Douglas near Chicago. The site of the camp is now bounded by Cottage Grove Avenue, South Parkway, Thirty-first Street, and Thirty-sixth Street. It was established in 1861 as a rendezvous point and training facility for Illinois volunteers. Later the camp was used to house paroled Union prisoners of war awaiting exchange and, by early 1862, it was utilized as a prisoner of war camp.

Camp Douglas was laid out with wood-framed, single story barracks and wide fifty-foot streets. The camp sat on a low, marshy area and during wet weather these streets became quagmires. Because of this the barracks were built up on piers. A fourteen-foot high fence surrounded the prisoners and there were the customary guard towers, sentinels, and dead line. The "dead line" was a line, usually marked by a low railing, which paralleled the prison walls and was several feet inside them. Any prisoners going past the dead line toward the walls would automatically draw the fire of the sentries. Hence the name, dead line. The camp had a prisoners' hospital within the compound and another smaller infirmary outside the walls for the treatment of smallpox patients.

The Arkansas Post prisoners who were bound for Camp Douglas boarded the cars of the Chicago, Alton and St. Louis Railroad in Alton. They passed through Carlinville, Springfield, Bloomington, Pontiac, and Joliet, before reaching their destination. (Pontiac and Joliet are the sites of present-day Illinois prisons.) Exposure to the elements had already taken its toll on the men. About 800 of the almost 3900 Confederate captives were ill.

The sick Confederates were put into the care of Doctor George H. Park, regimental surgeon of the Sixty-fifth Illinois Infantry Regiment. Doctor Park was assisted by four contract surgeons and four medical men from among the captives. The latter group included D. F. Stewart and Thomas C. Foster who were the surgeon and assistant surgeon of the Tenth Texas; John A. Schomblin, assistant surgeon of the Fifteenth Texas; and James W. Motley, assistant surgeon of the Seventeenth Texas. Despite this abundance of aid, there were 387 fresh graves at Camp Douglas within a month. During the month of February 1863, the mortality rate among the Camp Douglas prisoners was the highest of any prison camp during the entire war — worse even than the more widely publicized Confederate prison at Andersonville, Georgia. Fully ten percent of the inmates died. In a month which saw the temperature plummet to a reported low of forty degrees below zero, a dozen men froze to death in one night. By the middle of March the situation was still so bad that the medical director requested Major General Ambrose Burnside, who commanded the department, to move the prison to Des Plaines, Illinois. When Burnside passed the request along to Major General Henry W. Halleck, the general-in-chief, he was told that the camp could not be relocated without a "full report and the order of the Secretary of War." [6] The machinery of bureaucracy moves slowly, however, and the camp remained where it was throughout the war.

The quality of the food provided the prisoners was marginal and the quantity seemed always to be less than satisfactory. Cats and rats soon disappeared from the prison compound and at least once during the history of Camp Douglas a dog was eaten by the inmates. The owner of the dog, who some say was the prison commandant, posted a notice and offered a reward for its safe return when he realized the mutt was missing. One of the prisoners added the following postscript to the notice: "For want of meat, That dog was eat" [7]

Since the prisoners had a lot of time on their hands they often thought of their loved ones and talked about the general progress of the war. They sometimes sang a song called "Camp Douglas by the Lake" [8] to the tune of *Cottage by the Sea.*

> Childhood's days have long since faded,
> Youth's bright dreams like lights gone out;
> Distant homes and hearths are shaded
> With the future's dread and doubt.

> Here old Michigan before us,
> Moaning waves that ever break,
> Chanting still the one sad chorus,
> At Camp Douglas by the Lake.   (Repeat)

> Exiles from our homes, we sorrow
> O'er the present's darkening gloom;
> Well we know that with the morrow
> We'll wake to feel the same hard doom.

Oh, for one short hour of gladness,
One hour of hope, this pain to break,
And chase away the heavy sadness,
At Camp Douglas by the Lake.

I would some Southern bird were singing,
Warbling richest, softest lays,
Back to eager memory bringing
Sweetest thoughts of happy days.

I dread the night's uneasy slumber,
Hate the day that bids me wake,
Another of that dreary number
At Camp Douglas by the Lake.

Never Sabbath bells are tolling —
Never words of cheer and love;
Wintry waves are round us rolling
Clouds are hiding heaven above.

Dixie Land! still turn toward you.
Hearts that now in bondage ache,
Hearts that once were strong to guard you,
Wasting here beside the lake.

Another constant topic of thought and conversation was escape. While many Confederates escaped from Camp Douglas, the percentage of those who avoided recapture was very low. Some of the escapees went over the walls, some went under the walls, and others enlisted the aid of sympathetic Chicagoans to help them escape. Private Miles Beeler of the Eighteenth Texas went over the wall and made his way back to Texas. Once out of the prison he had very little difficulty in passing himself off as a civilian as he headed south through Illinois and Missouri. He even claimed to have used Confederate money to buy supplies in those states.

As at other prisons, many of the Confederates despaired of ever being exchanged so they took the oath of allegiance to the United States. During the month of February, fifty-one prisoners took the oath and many more applied to take it.

Early in April, orders were issued for all of the Rebel prisoners who were well enough to travel to prepare to go to City Point for exchange. This news was met with great enthusiasm and many men who really should have stayed behind in the hospital summoned up enough strength to make the trip. Their journey across the country was similar to the one experienced by the men from Camp Butler and they arrived at the Model Farm at about the same time as the other enlisted prisoners.

The officers captured at Arkansas Post, about three hundred in number, were sent to Camp Chase. They were carefully escorted to the waiting cars of the Ohio and Mississippi Railroad at Alton. Some of the prisoners enjoyed the relative luxury of riding in passenger cars but others were forced to ride in cattle cars. The train left in the middle of the night and headed for Ohio.

The weather was cold and the officers in the cattle cars suffered considerably. One froze to death before morning. The train passed through Vincennes, and on across Indiana to Cincinnati, where all of the captives transferred to coaches. During this leg of their trip to prison the Rebel officers were treated well. The only mistreatment they suffered was having to listen to a guard sing *We Will Hang Jeff Davis to a Sour Apple Tree,* over and over again.

The train reached Columbus at about midnight on January 30th, and the prisoners were unloaded and prepared for marching. While standing in the cold, with their teeth chattering and their fingers and ears freezing, the prisoners were treated to gifts of food from some of the ladies of the town. The men had not had a lot to eat on the train and greedily accepted the proferred kindness.

Finally the prisoners began the four-mile march to the prison. They arrived at about 3:30 in the morning amidst a heavy snowstorm. They were marched one at a time into a small building where they were thoroughly searched and relieved of their money and any kind of weapons, such as pocketknives. This search seemed a little redundant to at least one Rebel who wrote that the purpose of the search was to "be sure that we had no gunboats, torpedoes, shotguns, or mountain howitzers about our old clothes." [9] After being searched the men were ushered abruptly outside into the cold confines of the prison yard.

The men sought out their friends in the dark and together began to enter the barracks to find places to sleep. The barracks were not quite the same as at Camps Butler and Douglas. At the two Illinois prisons the barracks each contained one large room which housed as many as one hundred men. At Camp Chase the barracks were divided up into several small rooms, each of which included a stove and some crude bunks. The bunks in some rooms were bare of any kind of mattresses or bed clothing while others were well supplied with heavy government issue blankets.

The next morning the Rebel officers walked outside to survey their new surroundings. They found that they were in the middle of an enclosure made up of fifteen-foot walls with warmly clad Yankee sentries pacing to and fro on platforms on the outside of the walls. In the street between the barracks was a water pump and a large washtub. Braving the cold, many of the prisoners bathed themselves in the icy waters of the tub. Thus, with tolerably clean bodies and reasonably well filled stomachs, the men began to feel a little more like human beings again.

In the afternoon of their first full day in prison the inmates were given back their money, if it was less than one hundred dollars, and their pocketknives, if they were small enough. They learned that they could patronize the sutler's store which was located against the outside of one of the walls with a small window cut through to the prison yard. Those who had been carrying more than one hundred dollars had it placed to their accounts with the sutler. This arrangement was very favorable to the Confederate officers as they usually either had money or had friends or relatives who would send them money. Their spending habits were so lavish as to prompt the prison commandant, Captain Edwin L. Webber, to write to Washington for instructions. "There are many of them who wish to purchase uniforms . . . and large supplies of extra clothing that they cannot obtain in the South; also the best quality of boots. I am at a loss to know where to draw the line in this respect." [10] Within a week a reply came which stated that the prisoners should only be allowed enough clothing and shoes for their immediate needs and that these items "must be of a quality such as to insure its not lasting for any length of time on their return to the South." [11]

The days dragged slowly by and the men searched for ways to occupy their time. When the weather permitted, they played ball or ran foot races with one another. At other times they played cards, carved rings out of overcoat buttons, played chess with chessmen occasionally whittled out of carrots, or engaged in spirited debates on topics ranging from escape to theology. There was no shortage of fuel for the religious discussions that went on. The Reverends Gillespie and Wilkes of the Twenty-fourth and Twenty-fifth Texas, respectively, were joined by Lieutenant Colonel Coit of the Eighteenth Texas who was a devout Presbyterian, Captain Sebron G. Sneed of the Sixth Texas who had once studied for the Roman Catholic priesthood, and many others of different faiths.

One morning in March, several distinguished visitors came to Camp Chase, as if to a zoo, to see the Rebel prisoners. Among the party were Andrew Johnson, governor of Tennessee (and future U.S. president), and David Todd, governor of Ohio. At first they walked around the prison on the platforms looking down on the prisoners, both literally and figuratively. The entourage then entered the compound and sought an interview with General Churchill. The other Confederate officers crowded around the general's quarters and waited with the governors while Captain Webber went inside to talk to Churchill. When he emerged and reported that Churchill had absolutely no desire to see the visitors the rest of the Rebels cheered enthusiastically. At this reaction Governor Johnson turned and gave them "a look of contempt and withering scorn that would have made ordinary mortals quake in their boots." [12]

Finally, early in April, the long-awaited orders came for the officers held at Camp Chase to get themselves ready for exchange. Many of the men had accumulated considerable quantities of clothing and blankets, notwithstanding orders to the contrary, and they attempted to devise ways of getting home with all of them. When departure time came the men marched through the prison gate one at a time. When they were outside, guards carefully searched them and confiscated all excess clothing and other contraband. A crowd of soldiers and civilians gathered to watch the humiliation of the Southerners as they were systematically relieved of their possessions. Each man was allowed to keep one suit of clothes, the one he was wearing, and one blanket. Any excess was added to the growing pile on the ground. Lieutenant Bill Brown and Lieutenant Jonathan Chitwood of the Eighteenth Texas were each caught wearing ten shirts. When Lieutenant William Cook of the Fifteenth Texas tried the same trick he was caught by a big Federal sergeant who said: "Aren't you rather too broad across the shoulders, and too large across the corset for that pair of legs you are marchin' on?" [13]

After this final inspection the Confederates marched back to Columbus and boarded eastbound passenger cars. They were not to be exchanged right away, but were being sent to the prison at Fort Delaware. The train twisted its way through the mountains of Pennsylvania, through Pittsburg, and Harrisburg, and finally pulled into the outskirts of Philadelphia on Sunday, April 12th. As the train moved slowly through the city an unruly mob began pelting the cars with rocks and insults. One woman singled out Nicholas Darnell, Jr., of the Eighteenth Texas as the one man in the entire Confederate Army she imagined was responsible for the recent death of her soldier son and she tried, unsuccessfully, to climb onto the train to avenge her son. The engineer pulled his locomotive into the depot and a big iron gate closed quickly behind the last car to keep the rabble from the Confederates. The men were relieved to see the gate closed and they were soon on a ship taking them from the City of Brotherly Love to Fort Delaware.

Fort Delaware was built on Pea Patch Island, thirty miles below Philadelphia in the middle of the Delaware River. The island formed, according to an eighteenth century legend, when a boat loaded with peas sark near there. The peas sprouted and trapped sediment as it floated downstream until, over a period of many years, the island was formed. Regardless of the geological history of the island the government decided it was a good location for a fort. Army engineers drove seven thousand piles into the marshy ground to support the weight of the masonry fort that was completed in 1859. A fifty-five-foot moat surrounded the five-sided fort and also served as a primitive sanitary system. When the river was low, the moat could be flushed of its sewage through a system of locks.

The Texas officers' stay at Fort Delaware only lasted about two and a half weeks but it seemed much longer. The captives were housed in wooden barracks built upon ground that was several feet below sea level. A dike kept the water out and for the first few days the men were allowed to stroll along the top of this dike. The privilege was revoked, though, when several escape attempts originated there. The usual method of escape was to bribe a Yankee soldier to bring a small boat around just after dark. Sometimes these endeavors failed when the guards pocketed the bribes and then reported the prisoners to the commandant. Another procedure, more ingenious than the first, was to strap several empty canteens together and use them for floats while paddling to the mainland.

While at Camp Chase many of the Confederates had actually gained weight on prison fare supplemented by what they bought from the sutler. Things were different at Fort Delaware! The prisoners were served only two meals per day and they were far from delicious. They consisted of either bread, bacon, and coffee or bread and soup. "The bread was regular gun-wadding, the coffee was about one grain to every forty gallons of water, and, as to the bacon, it is safe to say it was a lot of sow-belly General Jackson had left over after the War of 1812. It was green all the way through and was rank, ranky, rankishly rancid." [14] Most of the prisoners felt that if Brigadier General Albin Schoepf, the commandant of the fort, would only give them enough to eat in one meal again, they would not find a single objection to the fort.

The day after the Confederates arrived at Fort Delaware, General Churchill wrote a letter to Colonel William Hoffman, Commissary-General of Prisoners, complaining of the treatment received upon leaving Camp Chase.[15]

> Upon leaving there I was subjected to the grossest and most inhuman treatment, my baggage robbed of all it contained, my overcoat and gloves taken and some of the officers of my staff even had their shirts stripped from their persons. Certain little articles of no

pecuniary value or use to your Government but of peculiar value
to me (articles which I had purchased in and brought from the
South and which had been reserved to me by General Mc-
Clernand at the time of my capture) were taken from me apparently from no other motive than the meanest malice.

The destitute condition of the prisoners was verified by an endorse-
ment from Lieutenant Colonel Robert C. Buchanan who commanded the prison at Fort Delaware. "I have been compelled to
issue 422 blankets . . . to the prisoners who arrived last night and
want some 30 more to supply them all." [16] Colonel Hoffman was
sympathetic but he had been a prisoner himself early in the war, and
he was still under the influence of the war psychosis. He told Colonel Buchanan to assure General Churchill that the acts of robbery
had been committed wholly without authorization. He noted that
Churchill had "been made to suffer by an unauthorized retaliation
for innumerable outrages which have been committed on our people
if not by authority of his Government at least in its immediate presence and which have given rise to the bitter feelings he so much de-
precates." [17]

Toward the end of April the Arkansas Post prisoners were
again told to get ready for exchange. They boarded the *State of Maine*
on April 29th, and after a two day journey fraught with seasickness
they arrived off Fortress Monroe in Hampton Roads. The wrecks of
the *Cumberland* and the *Congress* were still visible a year after the fa-
mous duel between the ironclads USS *Monitor* and CSS *Virginia* —
formerly the USS *Merrimac*. After lying at anchor overnight, the *State
of Maine* steamed up the James River to City Point, where the prisoners spent their third night on board.

The next day they were free! Some of the officers were admitted
to hospitals in Petersburg. Others went to Richmond, where they
drew a year's back pay in brand new Confederate currency. The
printing presses had just started rolling out the fifty million dollars
per month authorized under an act dated March 23, 1863. The first
important purchases made with this money were for new uniforms
and boots. The newly clad Texans drew scant notice in the busy
Richmond streets, for the city was alive with richly caparisoned officers, many of whom did their best to avoid combat.

The enlisted men, meanwhile, spent a couple of weeks at Petersburg recuperating from their ordeal in prison. On April 30, 1863,
on the eve of the Battle of Chancellorsville, those men who were not
in hospitals were hastily armed and sent to Richmond. Union Major
General George Stoneman, at the head of thirty-five hundred battle-

hardened cavalrymen, had interposed his force between Lee's army and the Confederate capital. His objective was to destroy communications and, in the event of a Union victory at Chancellorsville, he was to obstruct Lee's retreat. Confederate officials knew only that a large enemy cavalry force was moving in the general direction of Richmond. All available manpower in the city was sent to picket the roads leading north. Clerks from War Department offices, militia, and the paroled Arkansas Post prisoners were all pressed into service. By this time Stoneman had divided his force and, while occasional small parties of Federal horsemen neared the outskirts of Richmond and there was some light skirmishing, the hastily assembled defense force discouraged any concerted effort to enter the city. When news reached General Stoneman of the Confederate victory at Chancellorsville, he recalled his men to the main army lest they be cut off by Lee.

CHAPTER FOUR

Assigned to the Army
of Tennessee

After Lee defeated Major General Joseph Hooker at the Battle of Chancellorsville, the Texans were no longer needed in the Richmond defenses. Orders were issued that sent them west. They were to be sent to Jackson, Mississippi, to bolster General Joseph E. Johnston's force there. The men received this news with great enthusiasm since it meant that they would be much closer to home. As their train wound its way through the mountains of North Carolina, and eastern Tennessee, they congratulated themselves on their good fortune. Their luck did not last very long. Upon reaching Chattanooga, new orders were received assigning them to Major General Braxton Bragg's Army of Tennessee.

Braxton Bragg was not the Confederacy's most highly esteemed military leader. His army fought well at Perryville, Kentucky, in October and at Murfreesboro, Tennessee in January, but after each of these seemingly victorious battles the army had retreated. After the Battle of Murfreesboro Bragg decided to fall back only after most of his corps and division commanders advised him that retreat was the best course to follow. The soldiers in the ranks, however, and the general public placed the blame entirely on Bragg. It was, therefore, a dispirited army that settled into winter quarters around Tullahoma, and Shelbyville, Tennessee.

Because of the depleted ranks so common in the Confederate armies by this time, the regiments captured at Arkansas Post were consolidated into a single brigade under General Churchill about May 25, 1863. The Sixth and the Tenth Texas Infantries and the

60

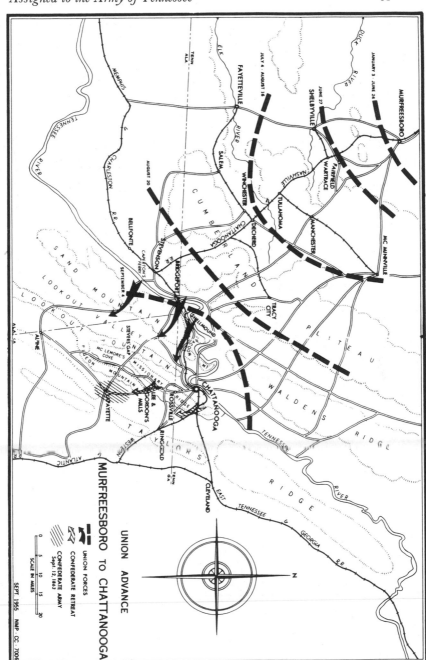

MURFREESBORO TO CHATTANOOGA

UNION ADVANCE

UNION FORCES
CONFEDERATE RETREAT
CONFEDERATE ARMY
Sept. 12, 1863

SCALE IN MILES

SEPT. 1955   NMP · CC · 7006

Fifteenth Texas Cavalry formed one consolidated regiment under Colonel Roger Q. Mills. The Seventeenth, the Eighteenth, the Twenty-fourth, and the Twenty-fifth Texas Cavalries were put together under the command of Colonel Wilkes and the Nineteenth and the Twenty-fourth Arkansas Infantries were combined under Colonel Portlock to form a third regiment. The independent cavalry companies of Captains Nutt, Richardson, Johnson, and Denson were combined and became Company L of the Sixth, Tenth and Fifteenth Regiment. In most cases the newly-formed regiments were commanded by the senior colonels present. Based on seniority, therefore, Colonel Garland should have led the first of these regiments but because of the stain of Arkansas Post on his honor it was felt that the men would not be happy under him and Colonel Mills was appointed to lead the regiment. Colonel Moore of the Seventeenth Texas had returned to Texas before the battle at the Post to become an associate justice of the Texas Supreme Court and Colonel Darnell of the Eighteenth Texas was also in Texas, not having been captured in Arkansas. This left Colonel Wilkes of the Twenty-fourth Texas as the ranking officer of this second consolidated regiment. Colonel Dawson of the Nineteenth Arkansas was still in the Trans-Mississippi so command of the third regiment devolved upon Colonel E. E. Portlock of the Twenty-fourth Arkansas. Company commanders were chosen in a similar manner. For instance, the senior captain from among the captains of Company A of the Sixth Texas, Company A of the Tenth Texas, and Company A of the Fifteenth Texas became the captain of Company A of the Sixth, Tenth and Fifteenth Texas. Those officers who were left without commands were transferred to the Trans-Mississippi Department.

The recently incarcerated Texas and Arkansas soldiers arrived at Tullahoma to anything but open arms. They were assigned to Major General Patrick R. Cleburne's division — it was rumored that Cleburne was the only one who would have them. The veteran Alabama and Mississippi troops in this division viewed them with scorn and ridiculed them for having surrendered to the Yankees a few months before. "Who raised the white flag in Ark?" "We don't want you here if you can't see a Yank without holding up your shirt to him"—"Lie down I am going to pop a cap—don't pull off your shirt it won't hurt you." [1] This verbal abuse continued until the newcomers proved themselves in battle.

The men of Churchill's brigade were issued new gray uniforms and captured tents and camp equippage and the men began to feel like soldiers again. If the new clothes and equipment *didn't* make them feel like soldiers the amount of drill which they were required to perform soon erased any doubt. General Cleburne had learned the value of military discipline and training as an enlisted man in the British army. Consequently, Churchill's men spent a considerable amount of time during the next few weeks practicing company, battalion, and regimental drill.

Meanwhile, the Union Army of the Cumberland, under Major General William Starke Rosencrans, had been encamped near Murfreesboro, Tennessee, ever since the battle near there. On June 24, 1863, the campaign for Chattanooga got under way when Rosencrans sent a large cavalry force under Major General David S. Stanley against the Confederate left at Shelbyville. At the same time he sent Union infantry pouring through the gaps in the foothills that separated Murfreesboro from Tullahoma. The main push came at Hoover's Gap where Colonel John T. Wilder's brigade of mounted infantry, armed with Spencer repeating rifles, cleared the way for Major General George H. Thomas's Fourteenth Corps.

Simultaneously, Major General Alexander McD. McCook's Twentieth Corps was instructed to seize Liberty Gap and hold it. This action was intended to occupy a large part of the Confederate army and keep it from aiding in the defense of Hoover's Gap. It would also keep any large Rebel force from going through Liberty Gap and falling upon Thomas's rear. Five companies of the Thirty-ninth Indiana Mounted Infantry led McCook's advance. Confederate cavalry pickets fired on them as they neared the northern end of the gap, but a Federal brigade soon came up and dispersed the bothersome Rebels. The Yankees spent the rest of that rainy afternoon slowly pushing back the Fifth, the Thirteenth, and the Fifteenth Arkansas Infantry Regiments to the lower end of the gap.

During the night, reinforcements arrived on both sides but the Union soldiers were ordered to merely hold the gap and not to pass beyond it. June 25th saw heavy skirmishing at Liberty Gap, and on the morning of the 26th, Churchill's brigade was sent up as a ready reserve force. Most of the heavy fighting was over and the men amused themselves at the expense of some of the other troops in their division who were near. These other troops were the very ones who had been taunting them ever since they had joined the Army of Tennessee. At Liberty Gap part of the Arkansas Post brigade was posted on the side of a hill slightly above its friendly antagonists from Mississippi. There was still scattered firing going on in their front when the Texans began throwing small rocks low over the heads of their comrades. The Mississippians, thinking that the pebbles were minié balls, "stuck their heads so close to the ground that their mustaches took root and commenced to grow." [2]

During the night of June 26th word was received that the Confederates had been forced back from Hoover's Gap, and unless those at Liberty Gap retreated very soon they would be cut off from the main army concentrating at Tullahoma. Early on the morning of the 27th, therefore, Churchill's brigade withdrew to Wartrace. The wet and muddy men ate a hasty meal of corn bread baked on the sides of fence rails and bacon that was broiled on sticks held over the fire. Then the men, many of them shoeless, pushed on to the fortifications at Tullahoma. There was no pursuit through Liberty Gap, because the Union forces there also left that morning for Hoover's Gap.

The Confederates spent the next few days waiting for the Federals to attack. The incessant rain made marching difficult, and it wasn't until June 30th that the Yankees were ready to advance on Tullahoma from Manchester, where they had assembled. In the interim, Bragg had asked counsel of Lieutenant Generals William Hardee and Leonidas Polk and both advised against making a stand for fear that their supply and communication lines would be cut, forcing them to retire into northern Alabama. If this happened, Rosecrans would have a clear field to Chattanooga, and then on to Atlanta. Heeding the advice of his subordinates, Bragg evacuated Tullahoma during the night of June 30th. Churchill's brigade formed part of the rear guard of the army and was supported by another well-known Texas unit, the Eighth Texas Cavalry — Terry's Texas Rangers. The army crossed the Elk River near Allisona, and began a rain soaked march across the Cumberland Mountains to Chattanooga. In their haste to escape, the Confederates discarded everything that might slow them down. The route over the mountain was strewn with extra clothing, cooking gear, etc. as the men strove to lighten their loads. Amid the refuse were the fine new tents that had been issued to Churchill's men. Some of the tents were still emblazoned with the unit marking of their original owners — "33d Indiana." There was some skirmishing with the Union advance guard near Elk River, but Rosecrans seemed content not to push very hard and the Army of Tennessee reached Chattanooga on July 5th.

At the end of the first week in July things looked bleak for the Southern Confederacy. In the east, Lee's army was hurrying to cross the Potomac back into Virginia after the disastrous three day battle at Gettysburg. In the west, Vicksburg had surrendered and Port Hudson was about to follow suit, thus opening the Mississippi River to Union navigation all the way to the Gulf of Mexico. And in Tennessee, the Southern army had fallen back to Chattanooga with scarcely a fight.

On July 14th Colonel Garland officially requested that a board of inquiry be convened to look into the matter of who had ordered the white flags to be displayed at Arkansas Post. The request was denied with the terse statement that the "exigencies of the service will not admit of assembling a court of inquiry at this time." [3] But there *was* an official hearing! Hoping to clear his own name by pinning the blame on someone else, Garland preferred charges against Colonel Wilkes of the Twenty-fourth Texas. In the ensuing court-martial, Colonel Wilkes was charged with allowing white flags to be displayed in his regiment at the Battle of Arkansas Post thereby causing the surrender of the entire force at that place. He was also charged with inciting a mutiny when he allegedly urged officers in Colonel Garland's command to refuse to serve under him. This latter event was said to have taken place on May 8, 1863, in Richmond. Wilkes was found not guilty on both counts and was returned to his regiment. An officer in Wilkes's regiment wrote that the "investigation could not ascertain who gave the order to raise the white Flag on the Fort, at Ark Post. They came very near finding <u>where</u> it started; but not <u>who</u> started it. <u>Nor will it ever be known in this world</u>." [4]

In July, Churchill's brigade lost its corps commander when General Hardee was transferred to Mississippi. His replacement came from Lee's army in the person of Lieutenant General Daniel H. Hill who arrived on July 19th. The Texans also received a new brigade commander when General Churchill was replaced by Brigadier General James Deshler, who had been recently promoted.

July passed into August and still the two opposing armies seemed content to remain inactive. The Texans, who had been camped at Tyner's Station on the East Tennessee and Georgia Railroad east of Chattanooga, were sent a little farther east, to the town of Harrison, where occasional skirmish activity broke the monotony of camp life. President Davis set August 21st aside as a day of fasting and prayer for the Confederate cause. While the citizens of Chattanooga were thus engaged in church services a Federal artillery battery opened up from a point on Stringer's Ridge, overlooking the city. When the shots began landing in and near the city the civilians were thrown into a near panic and the soldiers all hurried back to their camps.

The Army of the Cumberland was on the move. Rosecrans sent Major General Thomas L. Crittenden's Twenty-first Corps east across the Cumberland Plateau to threaten Chattanooga from the north. It was artillery from this corps that disrupted church services. Meanwhile, General Thomas's corps was proceeding from Jasper up over the mountains and across the Tennessee River at Shell Mound near the Tennessee–Georgia–Alabama border. McCook's corps passed into northern Alabama and prepared to cross the Tennessee at Caperton's Ferry. Rosecrans took a calculated risk by dividing his force but he meant to cross the various mountain ranges and get behind Bragg and isolate him from his base of supply at Atlanta. Rosecrans wanted Bragg to think that Crittenden's corps was spearheading the main Federal effort. Bragg, befuddled by the enemy movements, remained in Chattanooga, apparently waiting for Crittenden to attack. Rosecrans had things just the way he wanted them. While one of his corps occupied Bragg near Chattanooga, the other two corps travelled around the left side of the Confederate army, angling toward the supply line.

Even though Bragg was not sure of the details of Rosecrans's plan, he knew that he must have more men to counter whatever it was that his opponent intended. Reinforcements were started toward Chattanooga from all directions. General Joseph E. Johnston sent two divisions from Mississippi, totalling nine thousand men. Major General Simon B. Buckner was ordered to abandon Knoxville, and fall back toward Bragg with his corps. In Virginia, preparations were being made to send Major General James Longstreet west with two divisions from Lee's army.

By early September Bragg had a fairly good idea about where all the enemy troops were. The Union troops had been on the move since August 16th, so it was about time that he learned their whereabouts! He knew that Thomas and McCook were in the valleys on his left, but he did not know their precise locations. He did not know through which of the mountain passes the Federals would come. He complained to General Hill that the mountain range separating the two armies was "like the wall of a house full of rat-holes. The rat lies hidden at his hole, ready to pop out when no one is watching. Who can tell what lies hidden behind that wall!" [5] A military commander of Bragg's training and experience should never have let himself be put into a position like that. He should have known within a day that Rosecrans's army was moving and he should have had scouts in constant contact with it so he would know exactly where to find his foe.

Bragg finally realized that Crittenden's force was not the main threat and that if he wanted to save his army he would have to evacuate Chattanooga. Deshler's brigade marched in from its camp east of town, and on September 7, 1863, the army started south. Bragg hoped to deceive Rosecrans into thinking that the Confederates were in headlong flight. Rosecrans was taken in by this deception almost as badly as Bragg had been fooled earlier. In fact, he wrote General Halleck in Washington that: "The [Confederate] army has retreated to Rome. If we pursue vigorously they will not stop short of Atlanta." [6] Bragg, meanwhile, intended to meet and defeat each of the widely separated Union corps in detail. This strategy almost worked. Almost.

The Confederate army soon reached the vicinity of La Fayette, Georgia. At about the same time, Major General James S. Negley led his division of Thomas's corps through one of the passes in the Lookout Mountain Range and into a small valley known as McLemore's Cove. When Bragg saw the exposed position of this Union force he ordered General Hill — at about midnight on September 9th — to lead or send Pat Cleburne's division across Pigeon Mountain and into McLemore's Cove. There Cleburne was to link up with General Thomas Hindman's division, which was coming down from near Lee and Gordon's Mill, and together they would crush the invader. Had Hill and Hindman acted with alacrity the plan might have been successful.

Hill did not actually receive the order to advance, however, until almost dawn on the 10th. He informed Bragg that Cleburne was sick and that Dug Gap and Catlett's Gap, through which Cleburne would have had to have moved, were impassable due to felled trees and other obstructions. Bragg then ordered Buckner down from Lee and Gordon's Mill to cooperate with Hindman. By late afternoon the junction was effected but then the movement stalled.

At 4:20 A.M. on September 11th Hindman received a message from army headquarters at La Fayette, which said in part, that

> Crittenden's corps is advancing on us from Chattanooga. A large force from the south has advanced within 7 miles . . . General Bragg orders you to attack and force your way through the enemy to this point at the earliest hour that you can see him in the morning. Cleburne will attack in front the moment your guns are heard.[7]

This was not the type of order that would instill confidence in a subordinate. Hindman vacillated, trying to decide whether to seek the destruction of Negley's force or the salvation of his own. He cautiously moved his troops forward and ran into Federal cavalry skirmishers about 8:00 A.M. Driving the Yankees as they went, the Confederates continued their deliberate advance until they encountered enemy infantry about noon. By this time Deshler's brigade had come through the reopened Dug Gap along with the rest of Cleburne's division and joined up with the main Confederate battle line in the cove.

Both armies spent the afternoon probing, reconnoitering, and skirmishing, but a full-scale battle did not develop. In the latter part of the afternoon, Hindman received more disturbing news from headquarters, now at Dug Gap.[8]

> The enemy, estimated 12,000 or 15,000, is forming line in front of this place. . . . The general is most anxious and wishes to hear from you by couriers once an hour. . . . The enemy are advancing from Graysville to LaFayette.

After consultation with Generals Buckner and Patton Anderson, Hindman decided to fall back through Catlett's Gap. At this time, shortly after sundown, Hindman noted that the Union army was retreating too! Seeing this, he delayed the implementation of his withdrawal order and ordered his men forward, hoping to annihilate the Federals before they could escape back through Stevens Gap. The attack was finally broken off, without ever really developing, at about dark. The men of Deshler's brigade saw only limited action during this sparring match in the valley. Before many more days were gone, though, they would witness scenes of carnage more awful than they could have imagined.

CHAPTER FIVE

The Battle of
Chickamauga

General Bragg had squandered another chance to destroy one of the isolated segments of the Union army but opportunity continued to knock. Bragg next intended to attack Crittenden's Twenty-first Corps and instructed Lieutenant General Leonidas Polk: "You must not delay attack . . . or another golden opportunity may be lost. . . . Action, prompt and decided, is all that can save us." [1] But when Polk's men moved out on the morning of September 13th, the enemy was gone. Crittenden had realized how vulnerable he was, and had consolidated his force on the west side of Chickamauga Creek near Lee and Gordon's Mill, and the Confederate attack in that quarter never came to fruition.

By this time Rosecrans recognized that his entire army was in grave danger and he hurried to concentrate it. He ordered Mc-Cook's corps, which was the farthest away from Crittenden's imperiled position, to link up with Thomas's corps as soon as possible and, together, march for Lee and Gordon's Mill. The time left for Bragg to deliver a series of knockout punches was rapidly dwindling. By late on September 17th, both armies were in position — on opposite sides of Chickamauga Creek. The lines were roughly parallel to one another but the right side of the Confederate line overlapped the Union left. This alignment fit Bragg's battle plan perfectly. He intended that the upcoming battle should start on his right with the men in that sector crossing the creek, turning to the left and pushing the Federals back into McLemore's Cove. As the enemy was rolled up, other Rebel forces would cross the creek and join battle. Rosecrans, meanwhile, saw that his left could be turned and that if he allowed that to happen he would be cut off from his base at Chattanooga. He shuffled troops toward his threatened flank throughout the night of the 17th and all the next day.

On the morning of the 18th, Brigadier General Bushrod Johnson set his division in motion toward Reed's Bridge over the Chickamauga. A little before noon his men encountered Union skirmishers near Pea Vine Creek. There followed three hours of very heavy skirmishing between Johnson's five brigades of Confederate infantry and Colonel Robert H. G. Minty's three and a half regiments of Federal cavalry. As the bluecoats finally retired across the bridge they took up some of the planking in a further effort to impede the Confederate advance.

While this was going on, Brigadier General St. John R. Liddell's Confederate division was ordered to cross the stream at Alexander's Bridge, a little farther south. Liddell's men also faced spirited resistance but were able to make the crossing in much less time than had been required by Johnson's division. The Federals posted here belonged to Colonel John T. Wilder's "Lightning Brigade" of mounted infantry, and they were able to fire fifteen rounds per minute from their Spencer rifles. Liddell lost one hundred and five men to Wilder's repeaters while killing only a handful of Yanks.

By the time the battle opened on the 19th, the Union left was no longer in danger of being turned. In fact, it now extended beyond the Confederate right. The fighting started in this area, as Bragg had planned, but a victory was not to be easily won. The battle seesawed back and forth with charge followed by countercharge. During most of the action that first day, Cleburne's division was posted on the Confederate left and remained inactive until mid-afternoon, when it was ordered to the right.

By 4:30 in the afternoon, the men of Deshler's brigade were splashing across the waist-deep Chickamauga at Thedford's Ford, and hurrying toward the sounds of battle. General Polk was in command of the right wing and he ordered Cleburne to place his men on the right of the second Confederate line. The front line troops had been roughly handled and were about used up for the day. Cleburne advanced his men through the ranks of their comrades and on toward the entrenched enemy.

The enemy, as far as Deshler's brigade was concerned, was the Union brigade of Colonel Joseph B. Dodge, part of the Twentieth Corps. These men had been under fire most of the afternoon and had lately taken part in a counterattack that had pushed the Rebels back some distance. After making this move Colonel Dodge discov-

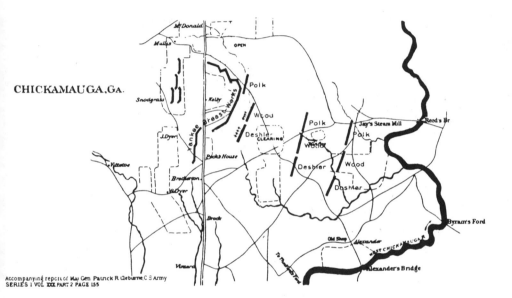

CHICKAMAUGA, GA.

Accompanying report of Maj Gen Patrick R Cleburne C S Army
SERIES 1 VOL XXX PART 2 PAGE 155

ered that he had advanced farther than most of the other Federal troops. Not wanting to remain in this exposed position and risk being subjected to an annihilating cross fire he ordered his men to retire slightly. After Dodge re-formed his brigade, he found that he was only loosely connected on his left with General August Willich's brigade while on his right there was a gap of almost three-quarters of a mile to General John B. Turchin's brigade. Scouts brought reports of a strong Confederate picket force nearby so Dodge strengthened his own pickets. As darkness approached he might have felt reasonably secure until the next day. If so, he was soon to be disappointed.

The Confederate force that had been spotted by Dodge's scouts was a company of skirmishers thrown out by Colonel Wilkes. As they groped about in the darkness they stumbled into the Union lines and were immediately captured. Very shortly thereafter the main Confederate battle line approached. The men of Deshler's brigade occupied the left of the line with the Sixth, Tenth and Fifteenth Texas on the extreme left, the Nineteenth and Twenty-fourth Arkansas in the center and the Seventeenth, Eighteenth, Twenty-fourth and Twenty-fifth Texas on the right, next to the brigade of General Sterling A. M. Wood.

A large open field which had been the scene of recent heavy fighting had to be traversed by part of the brigade, and dead and wounded men lay everywhere. The dry grass had been ignited by shells and muzzle blasts and the flames licked their way up the dead trees nearby. In the deepening darkness the burning trees cast weird shadows over the field. Facing a continuous Federal fire from the far side of the field the oncoming Confederates had no time to stop and minister to the wounded or to pull them from the path of the fire. They had all they could handle just looking out for themselves. They charged on through the field yelling like demons and drove off the enemy in that sector.

The firing along this part of the line soon became general. Under cover of darkness some of the daring Confederate artillerymen ran their pieces up to within pistol shot of the Federals and began filling the air with iron. The ground shook and the gunners were briefly silhouetted each time the cannons fired. Individual targets could not be distinguished and the riflemen on both sides fired at each other's muzzle flashes. Confusion reigned and many men were hit by the cross fires of their own troops.

The bulk of Deshler's brigade passed into the gap on Colonel Dodge's right. Dodge's men thus came under fire from two sides and quickly fell back. In the confusion, the recently captured Confederate skirmishers were freed. In addition, hundreds of men were captured from the Seventy-ninth Illinois Infantry and the Seventy-seventh Pennsylvania Infantry along with their regimental battle flags. Credit for capturing the flags went to Sergeant Calvin L. Martin of the Twenty-fourth Texas, and Privates Louis Montgomery and Benjamin G. Pippen of the Eighteenth Texas. Capturing the enemy's flags was always cause for exultation but it must have been especially gratifying for the men from Arkansas Post, as it helped to restore their damaged pride. The fighting soon stopped, and many of the captured Federals slipped away into the darkness. Both sides then began preparing for a resumption of hostilities on the morrow.

By the end of the first day's battle the relative positions of the two armies remained the same. The Confederates still faced in a northwesterly direction but they had fought their way across Chickamauga Creek all along the line. Rosecrans still worried that Bragg would interpose between him and Chattanooga, and Bragg still clung to his earlier battle plan of turning the Union left and pushing Rosecrans back into McLemore's Cove. General Polk, before retiring that night, sent written battle orders to his subordinate commanders directing that the Confederate attack should begin on the extreme right at dawn with Major General John C. Breckinridge's division initiating the action followed by Cleburne's division and the other Confederate forces from right to left.

The night of September 19, 1863, was unusually cool. The first frost of the season had set in and many men suffered, especially the wounded of both sides who lay helpless in the dark. One wounded Union officer, Captain W. P. Herron of the Seventy-second Indiana, spent the night lying in a pool of his own blood on the cold ground. The next morning he had to be chopped free of the earth because his bloody clothes had frozen to the ground. Another Federal officer lay in front of the Sixth, Tenth and Fifteenth Texas. His cries of pain so touched the Texans that they begged Colonel Mills for permission to bring him in. Mills consented and the injured man was stealthily retrieved. Upon examination it was found that in addition to his wound the man was suffering greatly from the cold. He was carried back behind a small house where, contrary to orders, a small campfire was built to warm him. His rescuers kept a vigil over him throughout the night. It is not known what ultimately became of this man but this event illustrates well the irony of this fratricidal war. Men on both sides often risked their lives to help a wounded enemy soldier. Then, when they had done what they could for him, they resumed the business of killing one another. Another such example occurred the next morning. Confederate skirmishers slowly pushed forward. Here and there lay a dead or wounded Federal. One of the wounded Yanks gave the Masonic sign of distress to a soldier from the Fifteenth Texas and begged the Confederate for water. The Texan used the man's knapsack to fashion him a pillow, left his own canteen full of water with him, and then hurried to rejoin the skirmish line. This wounded man recovered and after the war he prospered greatly. Years later he located the kindhearted Reb and returned his canteen to him — along with a gift of $10,000.

Shortly before the appointed hour for the attack the courier carrying D. H. Hill's orders returned to General Polk to say that he had been unable to find Hill and deliver the orders. As the eastern sky began to show the first hint of daylight Polk hastily scribbled out orders to Breckinridge and Cleburne.[2]

> The Lieutenant-General commanding, having sought in vain for Lieutenant-General Hill, gives you directly the following orders: Move upon and attack the enemy so soon as you are in position. Major-General Cheatham, on our left, has been ordered to make a simultaneous attack.

When Polk's staff officer arrived at Cleburne's headquarters with the above order he found Generals Hill and Breckinridge there also. By this time the sun was up and still Bragg could hear no gunfire on his right. Irritated by the apparent disregard of his orders, he mounted his horse and rode off to investigate. He found that Breckinridge's troops were not yet in a position from which to launch an attack, and Cleburne's men were just then being issued their breakfast rations. Finally, at 9:30, the offensive began.

The Yankees had spent the chilly night felling trees and beefing up their defenses. Earlier in the war such protection was scoffed at by both sides as being unmanly. After all, these men were soldiers, not ditch diggers. Let slaves (or ex-slaves) be employed to do any fortifying that might be necessary. By September 1863, this line of thinking had become obsolete. Soldiers would often throw up some sort of protection even if they were going to stay in an area for only a few hours. Fieldworks went through an evolution of trial and error. At first, dirt was simply dug up and piled in front of the resulting trench. Then logs or fence rails were used to further strengthen the piled up earth. This type of defense protected the soldiers from the shoulders down, but left their heads and arms exposed whenever they rose to fire. The next step was something called a "head log." It was propped up on top of the parapet in such a way that it left a large enough gap beneath it to allow the soldier to stick his rifle through and fire while the head log protected him. This system worked well unless the log was the victim of a direct hit from a cannon. When this happened the log tumbled into the trench where it could severely injure many men at once. The last step in the development of these breastworks was the use of poles to brace the head log against the back side of the trench. A properly entrenched force could usually hold out against a vastly superior attacking force for a considerable length of time.

The Federal works bristled with muskets and cannons as Deshler's brigade began its advance about 10:00 A.M. As the Confederates moved into the open they were met by a tremendous artillery and small arms fire. They halfheartedly cracked jokes to relieve the tension and they pulled the brims of their hats down low as they leaned forward into the fury of lead as if it were a rainstorm. An artillery shell hit a large pine tree and snapped it off about forty feet above the ground. When it fell it landed lengthwise on the men of Company G of the Sixth, Tenth and Fifteenth Texas. Almost miraculously, no one was seriously hurt.

As the Confederates continued toward the Federal lines, the left wing advanced obliquely and soon overlapped the other wing. This put Deshler's brigade temporarily out of action behind the troops of General William B. Bate's brigade. By this time the brigades to the right of Deshler — those of General Wood and Brigadier General Lucius Polk — had come within two hundred yards of the enemy and were unable to go further because of the ferocity of the Federal defense. Casualties were heavy in these two brigades and Cleburne finally ordered them back about four hundred yards to regroup. He then shifted Deshler's brigade to its right to take the position just vacated.

Upon arriving at their new position — the crest of a small hill — the Texas and Arkansas troops were ordered to lie down and commence firing. Private George Cagle, of Nutt's company, tried to increase the odds in his favor. While approaching the hill he collected several rifles from slain and wounded soldiers. He then began firing each of the weapons and giving mock commands to himself. "Attention, CAGLE'S BATTERY, make ready, load, take aim, fire." [3] While his overall rate of fire remained unaltered by the additional armament, Cagle was able to provide a note of humor in a grim situation. The Federal troops, General William B. Hazen's brigade of the Twenty-first Corps, were well protected behind their breastworks. They greeted Deshler's men with sheets of flame and lead as they fired by volley throughout the afternoon. There was almost no protection from the enemy fire on the hill and losses began to mount. By noon, ammunition was dangerously low in Confederate cartridge boxes. Colonel Mills sent Lieutenant Robert Collins to report this fact to General Deshler and await instructions. Collins found Deshler carefully observing the battle but before the message from Colonel Mills could be delivered the general was struck full in the chest by an artillery projectile and instantly killed. Upon hearing this distressing news Colonel Mills, as the senior colonel present, took command of the brigade.

His ammunition was now almost entirely gone so Mills ordered the cartridge boxes of the dead and wounded to be gathered up. The men were issued one round apiece and told to fix bayonets. The Yankees would surely counterattack when it became obvious that the Confederates were not firing any longer. At about this time, Lieutenant Colonel Thomas Anderson sent word to Mills that he had four companies on the far left that had not been engaged. Mills ordered Anderson to lead these men to the center of the brigade where the fire was hottest. Shortly thereafter the rest of the brigade fell back about twenty yards to the reverse slope of the hill where their supply of ammunition was replenished. By this time the fire had slackened to a contest between Confederate sharpshooters and the well protected Federal riflemen. Some of the Rebel snipers climbed trees so they could deliver a plunging fire over the logs which shielded Hazen's Ohio and Indiana troops. The sniper fire was answered by fusillades fired blindly into the treetops. Some of the Confederates were seen to drop from their lofty perches and the idea was given up.

Federal skirmishers soon moved out against the right of Deshler's brigade. Major William A. Taylor, who had assumed command of Wilkes's regiment after that officer was wounded, sent out a company to meet them. The Confederates were slowly driven back until Colonel Mills ordered them reinforced by a company from the Arkansas regiment and, still later, by a company of his own regiment. By late afternoon the action in this area had diminished to desultory skirmish fire.

While the Union left was kept busy by Cleburne's and Breckinridge's divisions, the right and center were crumbling under the fierce onslaught directed by General Longstreet. The center of the Union line was occupied by Brigadier General Thomas J. Wood's division. Immediately to his left were the divisions of Brigadier General John M. Brannan and Major General Joseph J. Reynolds. At about 11:00 A.M., just when Deshler's men were becoming hotly engaged, Federal Captain Sanford C. Kellogg observed what he thought to be a misalignment of troops near the center of the Federal line. He reported to General Rosecrans that Brannan's division was out of line and that Reynolds's right flank was in the air. Rosecrans then committed a blunder that probably cost him the battle. Without verifying the reported deviation in his battle line he ordered Wood to immediately close up on Reynolds. This order must have struck General Wood as being somewhat unusual. Nevertheless it was a direct order from the army commander and was not something to be questioned by a professional soldier like General Wood. He pulled his troops out of line and started them around behind Brannan's men toward Reynolds. And then disaster struck!

General Longstreet began his attack just after the last of Wood's men had left his position. Longstreet's timing was purely accidental but the results were terrific. The five Confederate divisions — twenty-three thousand men — advanced in a compact column of brigades. They burst out of the woods with wild Rebel yells. Immediately, they received an intense fire. However, as they pressed forward they noticed that the fire they were under was coming obliquely from the right and left but not from the positions directly in front of them. When they reached the works formerly occupied by Wood's division some of the attackers turned left, some turned right, and others poured straight through. Two Federal divisions led by Brigadier General Jefferson C. Davis and Major General Phillip H. Sheridan were struck in the flank and scattered as they moved from the Federal right to plug the hole in the line. Generals Rosecrans, McCook, and Crittenden narrowly escaped capture as the Confederates swept away all before them. The right wing of the Army of the Cumberland dissolved and began a hasty retreat through McFarland's Gap and on toward Chattanooga.

In the early afternoon some of the fiercest fighting of the campaign took place on the Federal left. The defenders there, and remnants of other brigades which had withdrawn from the right, formed a defensive perimeter on some small hills near the home of George W. Snodgrass. Colonel Wilder's brigade was among the units gathered there. As the charging Confederates came into their gunsights, these Yanks worked the levers of their Spencers so fast that the Rebels thought they faced an entire division. Longstreet kept up the pressure as Confederate infantry again and again strove to dislodge the enemy from the southern slopes of Snodgrass Hill. He asked for reinforcements from the, by now, inactive right wing. Bragg was reluctant to order Polk's men into action again feeling that the morning's fighting had worn these troops out. Instead, Thomas's tired men were reinforced.

Major General Gordon Granger commanded the Union Reserve Corps of two divisions. He had been stationed at Rossville to

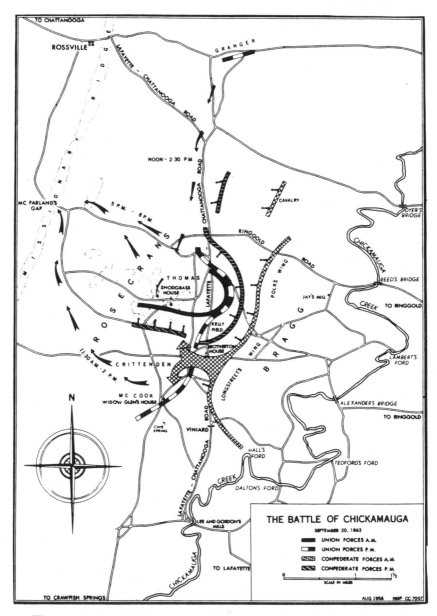

This map is from Chickamauga and Chattanooga Battlefields *by James R.
Sullivan. The map's key appears to have the positions of the "Union
Forces* A.M." *and the "Union Forces* P.M." *reversed.*

cover the retreat of the Union army, should that become necessary. By 11:00 A.M. Granger heard the sounds of battle intensify as Longstreet began his breakthrough. He immediately dispatched Brigadier General James B. Steedman's division toward the sound of the firing. By the time Steedman arrived at Snodgrass Hill the Confederates were about to envelop the right flank there. The fresh blue troops arrived just in time to repulse this attempt. Thomas's men enthusiastically welcomed Steedman's forty-five hundred troops and the ninety-five thousand rounds of extra ammunition that they brought with them.

Longstreet continued to hammer away at Thomas and finally, about four o'clock that afternoon, Deshler's brigade and the rest of Polk's wing were ordered forward. The Confederates on the far right swung around until they gained brief control of the Layfayette-Chattanooga Road. By this time the Union line was bent back upon itself so that it looked like the letter U. By five o'clock, Thomas started pulling his men out of the lines and heading them in the direction of Rossville. Darkness came and the bloody battle was over.

Daylight of September 21st revealed scenes of destruction that were awful to behold. Large trees on the battlefield were literally cut in half by small arms fire. Some of the log breastworks resembled porcupines, with all of the ramrods stuck into them. Many a Southern soldier, in his haste to fire, forgot to withdraw the ramrod before pulling the trigger. The ramrod, when thus fired, became a steel arrow. The unfortunate man who fired away his only means of loading his rifle, however, was left defenseless until he could pick up another gun.

Deshler's brigade had handled itself well in its first full-scale battle since Arkansas Post. It entered the battle with an aggregate strength of seventeen hundred and eighty-three men. By the end of the fighting the brigade had lost fifty-two men killed and three hundred and sixty-six wounded for a casualty rate of just over twenty-three percent. The Arkansas regiment suffered a higher rate of loss than the brigade as a whole. It lost over forty-two percent of its men.

The Battle of Chickamauga, like all battles, was full of instances that could have been termed the turning points of the battle. If General Wood had not pulled his division out of line when he did, Longstreet's attack might have been stopped and the outcome of the battle might have been different. Likewise, if Colonel Wilder's brigade had been armed with the more conventional single shot muskets instead of the seven shot Spencer repeaters, General Thomas might have been overwhelmed at Snodgrass Hill and his entire command destroyed.

CHAPTER SIX

Missionary Ridge

On the morning of September 21, 1863, General Longstreet sought out General Bragg for pursuit orders. Lee's "War Horse" wanted to chase the Union army into Chattanooga, and then bypass the city and march on either Knoxville or Nashville. Such a move could not go unchallenged by Rosecrans. He would have to leave the relative security of the defenses of Chattanooga and fight another battle in which his army might well be destroyed. Bragg seemed to agree with this plan, albeit reluctantly.

Meanwhile, Brigadier General Nathan Bedford Forrest was leading a party of four hundred Confederate cavalry on a scout toward Rossville when he ran into a Federal cavalry patrol. The blue-coated horsemen fired a volley and turned tail with the Confederates in hot pursuit. One of the Yankee bullets severed an artery in the neck of Forrest's mount. The general, not wanting to give up the chase, stuck his finger into the wound to slow the bleeding. When the brief skirmish ended a few minutes later he removed his finger from the bullet hole and dismounted as the horse, one of twenty-nine that were shot from under him during the war, sank to the ground and died. Forrest had gotten close enough to Chattanooga to observe through a captured telescope what he thought was Rosecrans's entire army hurrying to cross the Tennessee River on its way north. He scribbled a quick message to Bragg in which he said, in part, "I think they are evacuating as hard as they can go . . . I think We ought to push forward as rapidly as possible . . ." [1]

General Bragg ultimately acted upon Forrest's report rather

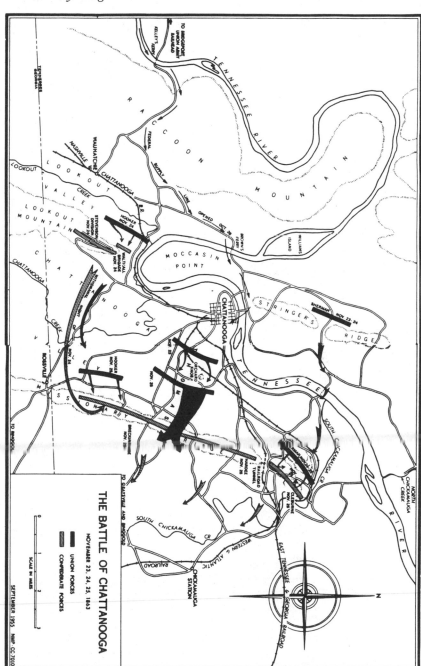

than Longstreet's suggestion. The victorious Confederate army moved slowly over the few miles to Chattanooga, where they found the enemy. The Yanks were *not* feverishly building bridges by which to escape north. They were instead strengthening the Confederate-built defenses of Chattanooga, and they seemed willing to stay. Bragg's troops settled down in a long curved line of works from Lookout Mountain below the city, across Chattanooga Valley, and along Missionary Ridge to the river above the city.

The Confederate soldiers in the Army of Tennessee could not understand why Bragg had not ordered an immediate pursuit on the morning after the battle along the Chickamauga. High-ranking officers were also incredulous. Bragg could not help noticing all the grumbling. He sought a scapegoat and he finally found, not one, but several.

Bragg wrote to General Polk requesting a reason why the right wing had been tardy in attacking on the second day of the battle. Polk did not reply immediately and when he did Bragg found his answer, that his courier had been unable to find General Hill to deliver the attack orders, totally unacceptable. Polk fell further out of favor with General Bragg when on September 26th he and General Hill met with General Longstreet to discuss their commander's poor performance during the recent battle. All three felt that Bragg was no longer fit to command and that this feeling should be made known in Richmond. Consequently, Polk wrote to the President and Longstreet wrote to General Lee and to Secretary of War James Seddon. In the latter missive Longstreet expressed the thought that with Bragg at the head of the Army of Tennessee only "the hand of God can save us or help us." [2] He further advocated the transfer of General Lee to temporary command of the western army.

On October 1st General Polk was relieved of his command and sent to Atlanta. He bitterly complained directly to President Davis about the curt dismissal. After pressure from the Chief Executive, Polk was ordered reinstated but he refused, saying he would not serve under Bragg again. The unhappy general was then transferred to Mississippi.

Another meeting was held on October 4th to discuss Bragg. At this meeting many of the top ranking officers of the army were in attendance. The outcome of this conference was a written recital of woes which was signed and sent to the President. "Two weeks ago this army, elated by a great victory which promised to prove the most fruitful of the war, was in readiness to pursue its defeated enemy. That enemy, driven in confusion from the field, was fleeing in disorder . . ." The Union army was allowed to strengthen its position at Chattanooga unmolested while "Whatever may have been accomplished heretofore, it is certain that the fruits of the victory of the Chickamauga have now escaped our grasp. The Army of Tennessee, stricken with a complete paralysis, will in a few days' time be thrown strictly on the defensive, and may deem itself fortunate if it escapes from its present position without disaster." [3] The petition went on to ask for the removal of Bragg as army commander. When this appeal reached Richmond, President Davis decided to visit the troubled command to see if he could mediate an acceptable solution to the problem.

When Davis arrived at Bragg's headquarters on October 9th, he brought Lieutenant General John C. Pemberton with him as a replacement for the now departed Leonidas Polk. The soldiers would not hear of such a thing. Pemberton was a Northerner by birth and many Southerners viewed him with distrust, especially since he had surrendered Vicksburg a few months before. Giving in to popular demand, Davis changed his plans and sent Pemberton elsewhere.

The President next attempted to solve the problems of the high command by calling a meeting with General Bragg and his four top subordinates — James Longstreet, Simon Buckner, Benjamin Cheatham, and D. H. Hill. Davis, with a surprising lack of tact, asked each of the four for his views on Bragg's ability to continue as commanding general. The generals all concurred that Bragg would be better employed at some other task. After this the meeting ended with no apparent solutions at hand. Bragg wasted little time in seeking revenge on his outspoken generals. He had already gotten rid of Polk and on October 11th he wrote Davis and asked for — and got — Hill's immediate transfer.

While all this turmoil swirled around Bragg's head another Confederate general got into the act. General Forrest had been sent on a raid toward Knoxville when Bragg, with no explanation, ordered him to turn over his troops to Brigadier General Joseph Wheeler. Forrest was furious. He wrote a strong letter of protest to Bragg and followed that up with a visit to headquarters. He accused Bragg of persecuting him and ended his tirade by saying: "You have played the part of a damned scoundrel, and are a coward, and if you were any part of a man I would slap your jaws and force you to resent it. You may as well not issue any more orders to me, for I will not obey them." [4] Bragg was wise enough not to accept Forrest's thinly veiled invitation to a duel and within a short time the famed cavalry leader was given an independent command far from Bragg.

Meanwhile there was some high level shuffling going on in the Union army as well. General Grant was summoned from Missis-

sippi, for a meeting with Secretary of War Edwin M. Stanton. They
met on a train en route from Indianapolis to Louisville. Stanton
placed Grant in command of all the western armies and gave him
two sets of orders. They were identical except for one point. One set
of orders provided that Rosecrans stay on as commander of the
Army of the Cumberland. The other set put General Thomas, "the
Rock of Chickamauga", in command. Grant had the option of issu-
ing either of the two orders. He chose to replace Rosecrans with
Thomas and ordered the latter to hold Chattanooga until help arrived.

The Union soldiers at Chattanooga were beset with logistical
difficulties from the outset. Supplies — food, clothing, ammunition
— could not be sent down the Tennessee River to them from the direction of Knoxville, because the Confederates controlled the river
above the city. The most logical source of supplies was the base
camp at Bridgeport, Alabama. From there, in normal times, provisions could be taken across Raccoon Mountain into Lookout Valley
and around the northern foot of Lookout Mountain and into Chattanooga. Confederate artillery on Lookout Mountain, however,
commanded this approach also. As a result, any supplies going to
the beleaguered garrison from Bridgeport, had to go through the Se-
quatchie Valley and up over Walden's Ridge emerging north of
Chattanooga. This route was a long, hard sixty miles, and the draft
animals were barely able to pull enough food over the mountains to
sustain themselves. Soldiers were reduced to half rations and then
quarter rations. Thousands of horses and mules starved to death.

While the Federal soldiers desperately held on, help was on the
way. General Sherman was marching his Fifteenth Corps up from
Mississippi. (The men of Deshler's brigade would soon face some of
the same soldiers who had overwhelmed them at Arkansas Post.)
Major General Joseph Hooker was bringing the Eleventh and
Twelfth Corps by rail from the Army of the Potomac. One division
of the Seventeenth Corps was on the way from Arkansas.

All of this maneuvering had little direct effect upon the soldiers
of Deshler's brigade. They had gone into camp near the center of the
army's line at the foot of Missionary Ridge. The opposing picket
lines there were only two hundred yards apart and much fraterniz-
ing went on. The pickets called informal truces of varying durations
and met each other between the lines. There they talked of home,
their loved ones, mutual friends, etc. A lively trade was also carried
on in such items as southern tobacco for northern coffee and southern newspapers for those from the North. When the truces were over
the men returned to their lines and made ready to kill each other

again. Not all of the pickets engaged in these friendly bartering sessions. The Texans did not seem able to get along well with the Yanks who had come from the Army of the Potomac. It seemed as if they "could always get along with Ohio and other western troops," but the "eastern troops always seemed to have a big red mad on." [5]

As the Army of Tennessee settled down to wait for the Union army to starve, the Confederates had a lot of free time on their hands. There was a limit to how much time could be spent visiting with enemy pickets and pulling "graybacks" out of the seams of their clothes so the men quite predictably turned to other forms of entertainment. Near where Deshler's men were camped was an area which became known as "Hell's Half Acre." Soldiers and civilians congregated there to engage in every imaginable game of chance from faro and monte to draw poker. Civilian sharpers came up from Atlanta to fleece the soldiers of their meager pay. Apparently the soldier-gamblers didn't mind. After all, what else was there to spend money on?

As the autumn days slowly dragged by, the Federal soldiers came ever closer to starvation. Many of them lingered where the horses were fed and scrambled for any kernels of corn that fell into the mud. When Grant arrived in Chattanooga, he immediately approved a plan to bring relief to the besieged men.

On the night of October 26th, Brigadier General William B. Hazen's brigade clambered aboard pontoon boats and floated down the river as noiselessly as they could. Their destination was the Confederate picket post at Brown's Ferry. In conjunction with this movement, Brigadier General John B. Turchin's brigade marched west across Moccasin Point, and the bulk of General Hooker's two corps marched east from Bridgeport, across Raccoon Mountain, and through Lookout Valley to Brown's Ferry. Turchin's men arrived on the east bank of the river before dawn. Shortly thereafter, Hazen's waterborne brigade hove into view and made an amphibious assault, scattering the Rebel pickets. Within a few hours a pontoon bridge was down and Turchin's men were across.

By October 28th, Bragg was finally aware of this threat against his left. He told Longstreet that he would send him two divisions with which to attack Hooker's rear guard at Wauhatchie. Instead only one Confederate division was committed and the resulting midnight attack was a failure. Bragg had once again waited too long and the Federal supply line from Bridgeport to Chattanooga — the "cracker line" — was open.

As Grant began to rejuvenate the Army of the Cumberland and received reinforcements from other commands, Bragg made a serious blunder. He divided his force in the face of the enemy. This tactic worked well for General Lee at Chancellorsville when he sent Stonewall Jackson with most of his army around the Federal right flank. This, however, was not Chancellorsville, and Bragg was not Lee. On November 5th, following Bragg's orders, General Longstreet took his Virginia troops and headed for Knoxville to confront Major General Ambrose Burnside. When General Grant learned of the departure of these fifteen thousand veteran troops he ordered General Thomas to attack Bragg's right flank without delay. Thomas was unable to do so because his horses were still not strong enough to pull the artillery that would be necessary for such an attack.

Grant was not one to sit idly by. He champed at the bit waiting for the arrival of General Sherman's troops and the strengthening of Thomas's horses. The head of Sherman's column arrived at Brown's Ferry on November 20th. These men were ordered to go north of Chattanooga, behind Stringer's Ridge, and cross the Tennessee River near the northern end of Missionary Ridge. The plan for the impending battle was for Sherman to hit the north end of the ridge while Hooker attacked over Lookout Mountain toward the south end of the ridge. General Thomas was to hold the Army of the Cumberland in readiness near the center of the Confederate line so that he could apply pressure there and keep Confederate troops from reinforcing either flank.

Once again Bragg depleted his force. On November 22 he dispatched General Buckner's troops to eastern Tennessee to aid Longstreet. The next day Cleburne's division, including the Texans of Deshler's brigade, was ordered to follow Buckner. By this time Sherman's men were preparing to cross the river and Bragg was finally awake to the situation. He recalled Cleburne's men, who had gotten as far as Chickamauga Station and were about to entrain. It was the Irishman's division, and in particular Deshler's brigade, that would turn in the best record in the battle for Missionary Ridge.

The makeup of this brigade had changed since the Battle of Chickamauga. After the death of General Deshler, the brigade was commanded for a time by Colonel Mills. In mid-October Brigadier General James A. Smith was given permanent command of the unit. General Smith was a graduate of West Point and had recently been promoted from the colonelcy of the Fifth Confederate Infantry Regiment. The division commander was still General Cleburne, but corps command was once again entrusted to Lieutenant General Hardee, who had returned from Mississippi to replace General Polk. General Smith's new command also became more than ever a

"Texas" brigade. The Arkansas regiment was split up and recombined with Arkansas units in another brigade. To fill the void created by this transfer, the Seventh Texas Infantry Regiment, under Colonel Hiram B. Granbury, was assigned to the brigade on November 12, 1863.

The Seventh Texas was raised by thirty-three-year-old John Gregg in 1861. The nine companies that formed the regiment were mustered into Confederate service at Marshall, Texas, during the first week of October 1861. They left Texas almost immediately for Hopkinsville, Kentucky, where the regiment was officially organized on November 9th. Gregg was elected colonel, Jeremiah Clough was elected lieutenant colonel, and Captain Granbury, of Company A, was elected major.

The regiment stayed near Hopkinsville for the next three months. While there nearly one hundred men died of disease before ever seeing the enemy. The Seventh Texas then marched down to Fort Donelson where it was captured in February 1862. Officers were sent to Camp Chase and Johnson's Island, and the enlisted men were imprisoned at Camp Douglas. By the time the regiment was exchanged in September, another sixty-five men had died. Company K formed in February 1863, as the tenth company and Company F was disbanded in May of the same year. During the Vicksburg Campaign the regiment took part in the Battle of Raymond, near Jackson, Mississippi, where casualties were very heavy. The men came east in time for the Battle of Chickamauga, and remained in the Army of Tennessee thereafter. Attrition had an effect on this unit just as in all others. By the time they were brigaded with the other Texans, the men of the Seventh Texas were commanded by Colonel Granbury.

On Monday, November 23, 1863, Confederate troops on Missionary Ridge viewed Federal preparations for what they assumed was to be a grand review as two divisions of troops began forming up. The Yanks, however, were preparing for a reconnaissance in force and not a parade. As Bragg watched in disbelief, the blue wave swept across the field and engulfed the Confederate advance lines at Orchard Knob. The Confederates thus lost a part of their first line of defense. This day's action was just a warmup for the fighting which would, within a few days, drive them back into Georgia.

The next day was spent by Thomas's men in looking to equipment and making ready for the major battle that was sure to follow. Hooker led an assault on Lookout Mountain that, because of the mist and fog that shrouded the peak, came to be known as the "Battle Above the Clouds." Only a token Confederate force had been left on the mountain since the establishment of the "cracker line" from Bridgeport, and Hooker succeeded in driving it off.

At the opposite end of Missionary Ridge the men under Sherman were getting ready to attack. They charged with only light resistance to the top of a hill, only to discover a discontinuity in the ridge. They had captured a little hill which was separated from the main ridge by a small valley. By this time it was late afternoon and Cleburne's division began arriving on the scene. Smith's Texans were the first to arrive and Cleburne ordered them to the top of the detached knoll. As they attempted to carry out this order they were fired upon by the Federals who had beaten them to the top. The Confederates fell back across the valley and continued skirmishing until nightfall.

After dark Cleburne sent to his wagon train for axes so that trees could be felled and breastworks erected. Having anticipated a retreat across the Chickamauga, he had earlier sent his artillery across and he now ordered the guns to rejoin him. During the night the Texas Brigade abandoned its original works and fell back to a prominent elevation known as Tunnel Hill. The brigade established temporary residence about one hundred and fifty yards north of the railroad tunnel. The Sixth, Tenth and Fifteenth Texas now occupied a position along the western face of the crest with Swett's Mississippi Battery on its right. The line bent back toward the east along the north slope of Tunnel Hill where the Seventh Texas was stationed with the Seventeenth, Eighteenth, Twenty-fourth and Twenty-fifth Texas on its right. Some Georgia troops were to the left of the brigade and Colonel Daniel Govan's Arkansans were to the right. As the Confederates labored to throw up some protection they were interrupted by a lunar eclipse which made it too dark to work. By dawn they were driven to cover by vigilant Federal pickets who could see them through the haze.

During the early morning hours of November 25th, skirmishers were active between the lines and Union artillery played along Tunnel Hill. At about 10:30 A.M., General Smith's skirmishers were forced back to the main works and Federal skirmishers occupied the Confederate works that had been deserted the night before. Large bodies of blue clad soldiers could also be seen moving south near the west face of Missionary Ridge as they positioned themselves for an attack on Tunnel Hill from that direction.

Heavy skirmishing continued until shortly after noon when a general advance was undertaken by the Federals near the apex of the Texas Brigade's line. Swett's Battery was very effective and the attackers made every effort to shoot down the gunners. There were no breastworks protecting the cannoneers and many fell as the enemy infantry crept to within fifty yards of the guns. In order to protect the cannons a counterattack was mounted by the left of the Seventh Texas and the right of the Sixth, Tenth and Fifteenth Texas. The Federals were effectively pushed back but not without cost to the Confederates. General Smith and Colonel Mills were both wounded and command of the brigade passed to Colonel Granbury of the Seventh Texas. The Yankees regrouped and came charging back up the hill. By this time all of the officers and many of the enlisted men in Swett's Battery had been killed or wounded and the guns were commanded by a corporal. Colonel Granbury detailed a number of infantrymen to help serve the guns and another enemy attack was turned back.

At this stage of the battle commanders on both sides were feverishly juggling bodies of troops so as to strengthen their respective positions. The combined Second, Fifteenth and Twenty-fourth Arkansas Infantry was brought up to help protect the cannons and soon the Thirty-sixth Georgia and the Fifty-sixth Georgia came up to support the Texas Brigade. Down in the valley, Brigadier General Charles L. Matthies brought his brigade up to support the Twenty-seventh Pennsylvania and the Seventy-third Pennsylvania of Colonel Adolphus Buschbeck's brigade, who were pinned down on the side of the hill opposite the Sixth, Tenth and Fifteenth Texas. Companies of the Fifth Iowa were gradually committed as skirmishers to the right of the Twenty-seventh Pennsylvania. On the other side of the Pennsylvanians were the Ninety-third Illinois, and the Twenty-sixth Missouri, and then the Tenth Iowa.

At one o'clock Sherman's men again moved forward up the steep sides of Tunnel Hill. Confederate artillerymen depressed the muzzles of their pieces as far as possible and swept the hillsides with shell and cannister. Still the Federals came. The Arkansans, in an effort to stem the blue tide, resorted to rolling large rocks down upon the attackers. The two Georgia regiments twice counterattacked but with no success. The third time the Georgians charged they were joined by the Arkansas regiment, the First and Twenty-seventh Tennessee Regiment, and part of the Sixth, Tenth and Fifteenth Texas. Colonel Holden Putnam of the Ninety-third Illinois grabbed his regiment's battle flag and attempted to rally his men until he was killed. Soon the men of the Twenty-seventh Pennsylvania were out of ammunition and were forced to retire. When they fell back the regiments on either side were left without support and they, too, retreated. The jubilant Rebels chased the Yanks down the hill and captured scores of prisoners and eight battle flags. Among the flags was the one that Colonel Putnam had so courageously tried to advance. Four of the flags were taken by the Sixth, Tenth and Fifteenth Texas. The rest of the fighting in this sector consisted of long range skirmishing and artillery fire.

The Texas Brigade had fought well and had lost many men through wounds in addition to General Smith and Colonel Mills. The ordeal experienced by a wounded man was quite often terrible. He might lay where he fell for hours before being given aid. He might then be carried on a stretcher to an ambulance which would take him to a hospital of sorts. The ambulances were quite often without springs and as they jounced along the well rutted roads or through plowed fields each bump was instantly felt by the injured men inside. The hospital might be set up in a nearby house or barn or it might be just a shady area in a field. The large, slow-moving musketballs that caused many of the wounds did a fearful amount of damage. A soldier with a shattered arm or leg bone would almost automatically have that limb amputated. The germ theory of disease transmission was not well-known yet and the surgeons, many of them with no more than a rudimentary knowledge of medicine, did not take the time to clean their hands or their instruments between patients. Consequently, many of the wounded who died would have survived had they not been subject to such unsterile conditions in the hospitals.

The experience of an officer of the Twenty-fourth Texas who was wounded in the leg at Missionary Ridge, serves to illustrate some of the prevalent medical procedures. This officer was lucky in that the bullet passed completely through the leg without hitting the bone. The surgeon who examined the man wanted to make sure that there was no foreign matter in the wound such as bullet fragments, pieces of cloth from the pant leg, or dirt. He probed the wound by sticking one finger into the hole caused by the entrance of the bullet and another finger into the exit hole. When his two fingers touched each other the doctor judged that the wound was not contaminated. The soldier undergoing this crude examination did so without the benefit of any anasthesia and, remarkably, healed well enough to eventually return to his unit.

While the Texas Brigade and the other Confederates at the northern end of Missionary Ridge were successfully holding General Sherman's army at bay, their comrades to the south were not faring as well. General Hooker led his men down from Lookout Mountain and into Chattanooga Valley. Then, instead of pushing his way onto Missionary Ridge near the southern end of the Confederate works as had been planned, he stalled. He could not cross Chattanooga Creek because the bridges had been burned and he consumed several precious hours building new ones. Grant's battle plan was not working very well but he still had Thomas's Army of the Cumberland itching for action. Finally, Grant ordered Thomas forward and the men reacted with a yell. Confederate skirmishers were easily driven in and the first line of trenches captured while the defenders scrambled up to a second line about halfway up the ridge.

The Yanks had fulfilled their orders. They had taken the enemy position at the base of the ridge. Having done so, they now began to be clobbered by Confederate artillery at the top of the ridge. Within a few minutes the Federals rose up as if of one will and began charging up the hill yelling, "Remember Chickamauga!" They meant to avenge themselves and avenge themselves they did. As they swept up the hill, Confederates on top rolled lighted cannonballs down on them. The Yanks would not be denied and as they gained the top of the ridge the Southerners began streaming down the other side.

CHAPTER SEVEN

Winter Quarters

As the disorganized Confederate army fled into northern Georgia, Cleburne's division took up the position of rear guard for Hardee's corps. General Cleburne further ordered the Texas Brigade to act as rear guard for the rest of his division. By 9:00 P.M. on November 25, 1863, the rest of Hardee's corps was across South Chickamauga Creek, and the Texans pulled out of their positions and followed. "Sadly, but not fearfully, this band of heroes left the hill they had held so well . . ." [1]

The next day was Thanksgiving Day but there was little for which to be thankful among the tired, retreating soldiers of the Texas Brigade. They marched all day listening for the sounds of pursuit and lamenting their fate: "If we can't hold such a line as this against those blasted Federals, where is the line or position between here and the coast of Georgia that we can hold!" [2] By nightfall they reached the bank of the East Chickamauga. The river would have to be forded but the night was cold. Cleburne determined to let his men wait until morning before plunging into the icy water. At 3:00 A.M., any sleep that General Cleburne may have been able to obtain that night was interrupted when he received a message from General Bragg urging him toward a gap in the mountains near the town of Ringgold, Georgia. The gap was a good defensive position from which to hold the Union army at bay until the bulk of the Confederate army could get safely away.

Cleburne crossed the river and rode on ahead to reconnoiter the suggested position while his men were aroused from their sleep.

Some of the men stripped down to their shirts before stepping into the cold, waist-deep water. Others merely stripped to the water line. When they reached the far side they were allowed to warm themselves and dry their clothes for a short time before resuming the march. The column passed through the sleepy town of Ringgold, to a point just east of there where the road, the river, and the railroad passed through a gap in Taylor's Ridge. Cleburne halted his troops at this gap and prepared to delay the enemy.

Ringgold Gap was about one hundred yards wide at its mouth. Cleburne posted a section of Napoleon guns from Semple's Alabama Battery in the gap and camouflaged it with tree branches and brush. Four Arkansas regiments provided infantry support for these guns. On the north side of the gap the Sixth, Tenth and Fifteenth Texas, and the Seventeenth, Eighteenth, Twenty-fourth and Twenty-fifth Texas took up positions which were partially hidden in a fringe of timber. The Seventh Texas was on top of the ridge on this side and on the south side of the gap were some Alabama and Arkansas troops. The Confederates were scarcely in position when skirmish fire broke out on the far side of town.

The Union soldiers under "Fighting Joe" Hooker had broken camp at 5:00 A.M., and started out after Bragg. Hooker's three divisions represented three different Federal armies. From the Army of the Cumberland came the First Division of the Fourth Corps under Brigadier General Charles Cruft. From the Army of the Potomac came the Second Division of the Twelfth Corps under Brigadier General John W. Geary, and from the Army of the Tennessee came Major General Peter J. Osterhaus's First Division of Sherman's old Fifteenth Corps. Some Confederate cavalry had been left behind at the ford, and at about eight o'clock they sighted the advance guard of the enemy. A few shots were exchanged before the Confederate horsemen retreated through Ringgold and on through the gap.

Hooker was anxious to pounce upon what he thought was a vulnerable Confederate rear guard. He therefore pressed forward with Brigadier General Charles Woods's brigade without waiting for any of his artillery to come up. Woods sent out the Seventeenth Missouri and the Thirty-first Missouri as skirmishers and they were soon heavily engaged with Company K of the Seventeenth, Eighteenth, Twenty-fourth and Twenty-fifth Texas and with Companies C, F, and L of the Sixth, Tenth and Fifteenth Texas. Skirmishing became general all along the line and General Woods ordered up the Twenty-ninth Missouri to support the two regiments already in action. The Missourians were no match for the Texans, and soon "the whole line of skirmishers and support was driven back upon the main line in confusion, and were not again entirely rallied until after the [Confederates] retired." [3] The Twenty-ninth Missouri left their battle flag and fifty to a hundred prisoners in the hands of Captain Bryan Marsh's Company I of the Seventeenth, Eighteenth, Twenty-fourth and Twenty-fifth Texas.

Hooker's command had tasted victory at Missionary Ridge, and the mere repulse of a skirmish line was certainly not enough to deter them for long. General Woods sent the Thirteenth Illinois to the right where they occupied some houses near the gap and tried in vain to silence the two fieldpieces which were belching cannister and solid shot at them. Two more Missouri regiments, the Third and the Twelfth, busied themselves with the Texans in the timber while the Seventy-sixth Ohio attempted to scale the ridge to the north and turn the Confederate right flank.

The movement against the right was quickly discovered by Generals Cleburne and Lucius Polk. Polk's brigade had been in reserve and he now dispatched the First Arkansas to the top of the hill to help the Seventh Texas repel the enemy. General Osterhaus observed the Confederate troop movements along the crest and ordered Colonel James A. Williamson to send one of his regiments to support the Ohioans. Williamson, in command of the Second Brigade, sent the Fourth Iowa. The Federals moved up the side of the ridge in a draw, or gully, by which they were shielded until near the top. As they approached the crest they were savagely met by the Texas and Arkansas troops. The Fourth Iowa quickly arrived and fought desperately alongside the Ohio regiment. After fifteen or twenty minutes of fierce fighting, both attacking regiments were pushed back down the hill a short distance. Here they were reinforced by four more Iowa regiments from Williamson's brigade. Together, the six regiments dug in and kept up a heavy skirmish fire playing all along the crest of the ridge.

The action in this area subsided briefly as both sides hurried additional troops forward. General Polk brought two more regiments up and Brigadier General Mark P. Lowrey brought up three more. At the same time four Ohio and Pennsylvania regiments from General Geary's corps started up the mountainside. As some of these soldiers from the Army of the Potomac passed through the Twenty-fifth Iowa, they were cautioned to advance more warily. The reply was something to the effect that the Eastern soldiers would soon show these Westerners how to fight. Within a few moments, however, the advice of the Iowans proved valid as the Confederates unleashed a devastating cross fire on these fresh troops which sent them reeling. Soon the Yanks on the hillside pulled back to lick their wounds. They had suffered greatly. The Seventy-sixth Ohio left its regimental battle flag and eight flag-bearers on the ridge and lost forty percent of its strength in killed and wounded. Losses in the Texas Brigade were light. The Seventh Texas, which had been engaged in the hottest fighting, had only five men wounded.

The sun was at its zenith when General Cleburne received word that Bragg's army had retreated far enough for him to abandon his position at the gap. The camouflage screen was rebuilt in front of the cannons and they were then withdrawn. A small force of skirmishers remained behind until mid-afternoon to keep an eye on the enemy. Six pieces of Federal artillery arrived at about the time that Cleburne's men were pulling back and they commenced to shell the gap and the ridge on either side. No Confederates were reported hit by these shots and Cleburne successfully retired his force a mile or two beyond Ringgold Gap. He then took up a position near where the railroad ran through another mountain range and waited for the Federals to advance once more. General Hooker, however, seemed satisfied to have chased the Rebels as far as he had, and instead of pursuing them farther, he led his men back to Chattanooga. The spirited defense of Ringgold Gap had prevented the Federal army from following up its victory at Missionary Ridge and crushing Bragg's army.

Thus the Army of Tennessee's campaigning ended for 1863. The Confederate Congress was duly impressed with the work of Cleburne's division at Ringgold Gap, and issued a formal vote of thanks to his men.[4]

> Resolved, That the thanks of Congress are due, and are hereby tendered, to Maj. Gen. Patrick R. Cleburne, and the officers and men under his command, for the victory obtained by them over superior forces of the enemy at Ringgold Gap . . . by which the advance of the enemy was impeded, our wagon train and most of our artillery saved, and a large number of the enemy killed and wounded.

On the evening of November 28th, Braxton Bragg wrote a preliminary report of the Chattanooga campaign and sent it to Richmond. He also finally decided that he could no longer effectively command his army and asked to be relieved. A couple of days later his request was honored and he turned the army over to General Hardee, who had agreed to accept temporary command. Bragg was not shuffled off to a minor assignment at some obscure post or relieved of all military duties and sent home. In spite of his lack of popularity with soldiers and civilians alike, he was still a close friend of President Davis. He was rewarded for his ineptitude by being "kicked upstairs." He was made Davis's military adviser — sort of a vice-commander-in-chief.

General Hardee did not feel qualified to command the Army of Tennessee permanently, nor did he want that responsibility. A successor was sought who would satisfy everybody, and of course no such person existed. After much debate among the Cabinet, General Joseph E. Johnston was selected. He was ordered on December 18, 1863, to turn over command of the Department of Mississippi to General Leonidas Polk and to report to Dalton, Georgia, for further instructions. Johnston arrived to a hearty reception by the soldiers a few days after Christmas. His instructions were little more than suggestions, however. He was encouraged to take the offensive and regain lost territory in Tennessee and Kentucky.

The Secretary of War was woefully misled as to the strength of the army in Georgia at this time. It was thought in Richmond, that the Army of Tennessee was the largest army ever fielded by the young government and that it was well clothed, well fed, and well armed. Johnston found that his army of thirty-six thousand men was none of these things. Six thousand men were without guns and probably at least that many were without shoes and/or blankets. These conditions all contributed to a growing feeling of frustration among the soldiers. When they lost a battle they retreated, and when they won they did not reap the full benefits of the victory. Desertions were frequent. Many members of the Texas Brigade walked away from the army and headed for the Trans-Mississippi. They did not look on this as desertion. They merely felt that they were returning to their rightful places west of the river, there to continue the fight against Lincoln's soldiers. When General Johnston arrived upon the scene, he was already more popular than his predecessor had been. He did what he could to bolster the sagging morale of his men. He started granting large numbers of furloughs and he proclaimed an amnesty whereby any deserter who returned to the army voluntarily would be received with open arms and no punishment would be meted out for the offense. This humane policy added materially to the manpower of the Confederate army at Dalton.

The Dalton area became winter quarters that year by chance. That was where Bragg's army was when the Yankees quit chasing it so that is where the winter would be spent. General Cleburne's infantry division and General Joe Wheeler's cavalry division were camped six or seven miles north of Dalton at Tunnel Hill, Georgia. As the men settled down for the winter, they erected huts in which to live that were quite similar to those the Texans had built at Arkansas Post. Usually between two and six men got together and constructed a shelter that would house them all. The degree of comfort obtained was a function of how hard the men wanted to work. Some dug shallow pits into the earth, spread pine boughs for roofs and called the result "home." Others built sturdy log huts with fireplaces and built-in bunks and storage shelves. Chimneys were fashioned from barrels with the tops and bottoms knocked out. These were stacked on top of one another and mortared together with mud and straw. The men of the Texas Brigade spent part of the time getting acquainted, or reacquainted, with the new addition to the brigade — the Seventh Texas.

Some time around the first of the year General Cleburne unveiled a plan which he felt would help offset the two-to-one manpower superiority enjoyed by the Federals in Chattanooga, over the Rebs at Dalton. He proposed recruiting slaves into the Confederate army. He made his idea known to General Johnston and other high army officials at a meeting at Johnston's headquarters. His audience was stunned by the proposal and shocked that anyone could ever think of arming the slaves. It must be explained that Cleburne was born and raised in Ireland and had no deep-seated conviction in the worth of the slave system as practiced in America. He grew up in a country where most of his countrymen were as oppressed by their English rulers as the black American slaves were by their white masters. He could empathize with the slaves and felt that, if his plan was adopted, blacks might win their freedom by serving honorably in the armies of the Confederacy until the war ended. None of the attendees at the meeting shared his views, so he withdrew them from further consideration. Major General William H. T. Walker, apparently motivated by patriotism, sent a copy of the proposal to Richmond where it was received with dismay. Officially, Cleburne's loyalty was never in doubt but it is interesting to note that this outstanding soldier was never again promoted.

In the early part of 1864, Confederate military authorities began to realize that there were a lot of soldiers whose enlistments were about to expire. The young men who had rushed to join the army in 1861 had almost completed their original three-year enlistments. Since a war obviously could not be fought without an army, a vigorous campaign was launched to obtain reenlistments. The men were urged to enlist "for the war." In other words, they would stay in the army for as long as the war lasted whether it was twelve more months or twelve more years. In later years many veterans would claim for their regiments the distinction of having been the first to reenlist. It is not clear now which unit deserves this honor but it is clear that virtually all of the men in the Texas Brigade signed up again. Feelings were mixed between an intense longing for wives and families at home and a strong desire to stay in the army and help win independence for the Confederacy. For most, national pride won out. Captain Bryan Marsh of the Seventeenth Texas wrote his wife in February that the troops were, "reinlisting [*sic*] for the War . . . I have not yet but expect too. You need not look for me at home until the war ends. . . ." [5]

All was not idleness in camp. General Cleburne conducted classes on military matters for his brigade commanders and they, in turn, instructed regimental leaders, and so on down to the soldiers in the ranks. Drill was also a common occurrence in the lives of the men under Cleburne. His Inspector-General, Major Dickson, was a stickler for adherence to orders and when this was not forthcoming he was very displeased. Once, while posting a picket, the major ordered the men to "Shoulder arms" while he issued instructions to the officers and noncommissioned officers. These instructions dragged on and a few of the men shuffled their feet a little to ease their discomfort. Major Dickson, on noticing this, ordered extra duty for the offenders. General Cleburne happened along at about this time unbeknownst to Dickson. "Major Dickson, bring the men to order arms [a much more comfortable stance than "shoulder arms"] while you give these instructions not in the book." This was greeted with a cheer and for a long time after that whenever the major appeared someone would call out, "Who gave the instructions not in the book?" The answer — "Major Dickson." [6]

While northern Georgia served as the winter home of the Army of Tennessee, the Union soldiers returned to Chattanooga for the winter. They were no longer afraid of being penned up there and starved to death. They had proven that they could break that stranglehold. Not all of the Federal troops remained in Tennessee. Sherman's command, for instance, had returned to Mississippi from whence it had come, but in early February these thirty-five thousand men headed east from Vicksburg. General Polk, the Confederate commander in Mississippi, immediately wired for reinforcements to meet this threat. President Davis requested General Johnston to send as many troops as he could spare without endangering his own army. Johnston did not wish to comply, claiming that any troops he might send could not reach Polk before Sherman reached Mobile — the assumed Federal goal. Finally, after much correspondence, Davis ordered Johnston to send Hardee's corps west.

As a result of this direct order the men of the Texas Brigade marched from their camps near Tunnel Hill down to Dalton where they boarded the trains for Atlanta on February 21st. When they arrived at Atlanta, they changed trains and started west. By the time the brigade reached the vicinity of Montgomery, Alabama, "the Cradle of the Confederacy," word was received that Sherman had turned back. His expedition sputtered when the cavalry force that he was expecting to hook up with had the misfortune to run into the Confederate cavalry of Nathan Bedford Forrest. Forrest chased the Federal horsemen back to Memphis, and Sherman returned to Vicksburg. Hardee's corps was ordered back to Dalton, and the Texans enjoyed the trip immensely. Many of them wrote their names and addresses down on slips of paper which they attached to rocks or sticks. Then when they passed through a village they tossed these toward young women who might be near the depot. In this way many of the soldiers acquired female correspondents to whom they wrote for many months thereafter.

On March 5, 1864, Colonel Granbury was promoted to brigadier general to rank from February 29th, and was formally given command of the Texas Brigade. One of his first acts was to reorganize his command. The consolidation of the regiments after their assignment to the Army of Tennessee had not been very popular with the troops. A natural sense of pride in his individual unit was very strong in the American soldier of the 1860s. These Texans did not want to belong to consolidated regiments. They wanted to belong to the regiments in which they had enlisted two to three years before. General Granbury was not able to return all of his regiments to individual status because there were not enough men left in some of them to allow that. He did the best he could. The Tenth Texas Infantry became a separate regiment. The Sixth and Fifteenth Regiments remained combined with members of the old Sixth Infantry forming six companies and former members of the Fifteenth comprising four. The combined Seventeenth, Eighteenth, Twenty-fourth and Twenty-fifth Texas was split into two regiments, the Seventeenth and Eighteenth, and the Twenty-fourth and Twenty-fifth. These combinations remained in effect until the closing days of the war.

Late in March an event took place which added a touch of levity to army life. During the night of March 21st and 22nd a late snow coated northern Georgia with five inches of the fluffy stuff. The soldiers, many of them not much older than schoolboys, began to throw snowballs at one another. After a time they tired of such small-scale antics and soon whole regiments were snowballing each other. This spread to brigade level and before long five thousand troops were involved. Officers took command of their units and led them into friendly combat with banners snapping in the wind and bugles blaring. The officers felt immune to the snowy missiles by virtue of rank. They were mistaken. It seems that the number of snowballs thrown at an officer was in direct proportion to his rank. Lieutenants and captains did not make nearly as desirable targets as majors and colonels. The Texas Brigade attacked Lowrey's Alabamians and Mississippians and ran them out of their camp. The sense of realism extended even unto the taking and exchanging of prisoners of war. Finally, after about five hours, the battle wound down to a close and the exhausted warriors returned to their quarters to nurse their wounds. Due to the somewhat less than scrupulous practice of packing snowballs around rocks or lead bullets there were many black eyes and bruised heads evident in camp for the next few days. The snowball battle was one of the last happy events in the history of the Army of Tennessee. The Campaign of 1864 was about to begin, and with it the gradual retrograde to Atlanta.

CHAPTER EIGHT

Dalton to Atlanta

On May 4, 1864, the campaign for Atlanta began as part of a coordinated Federal offensive on all fronts. On that date General Sherman — who had succeeded General Grant as commander of the Military Division of the Mississippi — started forward with his armies. The makeup of the Federal force invading Georgia had changed somewhat since the previous November. Major General James B. McPherson replaced Sherman as head of the Army of the Tennessee but George Thomas still commanded the Army of the Cumberland. John M. Schofield superceded Ambrose Burnside in command of the Army of the Ohio and this army, now that Knoxville was secure, soon joined Sherman's force.

While the Federals moved toward Dalton, the Texas Brigade moved to a new campsite some miles from where it had been situated. The site selected for the new camp was in some woods and it took the men all day to clear the area and erect breastworks. The next day, May 7th, they began settling into their new home. By this time the armies of Generals Thomas and Schofield began to menace the Confederate positions just north of Dalton, and the Texans were forced to abandon their new camp to meet the threat.

On May 8th at about 3:00 P.M., Brigadier General John Geary pushed the 119th New York Infantry forward as skirmishers while he tried to force a passage at Dug Gap. The gap lay about four miles southwest of Dalton, and was one of only a few openings in the mountain range known officially as Chattoogata Ridge. Dug Gap was defended by two regiments of dismounted Arkansas mounted ri-

101

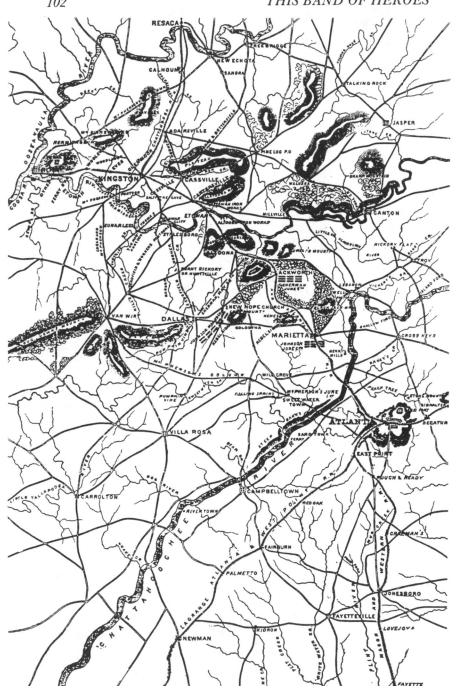

— This map of northern Georgia appeared in the July 2, 1864, issue of *Harper's Weekly.*

fles and a Kentucky cavalry brigade when the Union skirmish line came forth. The attackers left their knapsacks behind so that they could more easily climb over the rocks and up the steep sides of the ridge, which was popularly known as Rocky Face Ridge. The fighting went on until dark and some of the brave New York and Pennsylvania soldiers reached the crest where they met fierce hand-to-hand resistance. But time after time the Confederates forced the attackers back down the ridge.

While this fighting was going on Pat Cleburne hurried the men of his division toward the sounds of the guns. The Texas Brigade preceded the rest of the division to the base of the ridge on the eastern side of the gap. Some of the more spirited Texans seized the cavalry horses tethered there and raced to the crest. By the time the rest of the brigade was in position the Union attack was broken off. The Texas Brigade spent the night on the ridge and the next day details were sent down the western face to collect serviceable weapons that had been left by the enemy.

The Federal effort at Dug Gap was discontinued when General McPherson reached Snake Creek Gap farther to the south. There he was just west of Resaca, and in a good position from which to cut the Rebel army off from Atlanta. On the morning of May 9th, McPherson's troops moved through the gap and on toward Resaca. Unknown to the Federals, however, was the fact that Brigadier General James Cantey had arrived with his brigade from General Polk's command in Mississippi. Instead of facing minimal opposition from Georgia militia, McPherson was confronted by four thousand entrenched veterans. After probing the Confederate lines the bluecoats fell back to Snake Creek Gap to await further developments.

Early the next morning, the Texas Brigade was ordered to Resaca. It was a hard march and after many miles the men halted for a brief rest. Then, as so often happens in wars, they were ordered to countermarch back to their positions at Dug Gap. The men were tired after the long and apparently fruitless journey, and to add to their discomfort the leaden skies poured forth a heavy rain that soaked them to the skin. They left again on the 11th and marched only a short distance back toward Resaca before they halted for the night and threw up breastworks. The next day was spent in relative inactivity but before dawn of the 13th, the Texas Brigade, along with the rest of the Army of Tennessee, marched for Resaca in earnest. The heavy fighting for Atlanta was about to begin.

As General Johnston hurried his forces south from Dalton, General Sherman did the same. The Federal army moved in a parallel line with the Confederates but on the opposite side of Chattoogata Ridge. When Sherman's veterans began passing through Snake Creek Gap, they found their opponents well entrenched and waiting for them. Johnston's army was placed with its left resting on the Oostenaula River and its right upon the Connasauga River. The Texas Brigade took up a position near the center of the line and waited.

Although General McPherson had failed to cut the Confederate supply line near Resaca, the idea of doing so still appealed to Sherman. He planned to occupy the Confederates with strong demonstrations all along the line while at the same time sending a force across the Oostenaula to get between Johnston and Atlanta. The crossing would take place several miles downstream from Resaca at a place known as Lay's Ferry. There, on May 14, Federal soldiers from General Thomas Sweeny's division of the Sixteenth Corps began to cross the river. Confederate cavalry posted on the south side of the river unsuccessfully disputed the maneuver, and two Federal regiments were soon across. Before a pontoon bridge could be laid, word came that a large Confederate force was approaching and Sweeny quickly recalled his men.

Meanwhile, closer to Resaca, the main battle was being fought. It was a seesaw affair with the heaviest fighting taking place on the Confederate right. Major General John B. Hood's corps repulsed an attack in this sector and then launched a counterattack which was blunted by the timely arrival of Union reinforcements. The Texas Brigade saw only heavy skirmishing, and at dark, both sides settled down to prepare for a renewal of the contest the next day.

After nightfall a message arrived at General Johnston's headquarters which stated that two divisions of Union troops had crossed the Oostenaula. Fearing for his communications, Johnston cancelled Hood's attack orders for the next morning, ordered a pontoon bridge constructed across the river in case retreat became necessary, and sent W. H. T. Walker's division to face the enemy at Lay's Ferry. Of course by the time Walker's men arrived, the two regiments — not two divisions — of Yankees were not to be found. Walker sent a report to Johnston and left a few troops to picket the crossing while he took the bulk of his division to nearby Calhoun. Hood's attack order was then reinstated.

Sherman's battle plan for May 15th required General Sweeny to recross the Oostenaula, while Hooker's corps attacked the right center of the Confederate line. When the Federals began crossing the river, word was quickly relayed to Johnston who once again revoked his orders to Hood. Hooker's attack was turned back after some very spirited combat but Sweeny's men were soon across the river in force. Johnston felt he had no choice but to retreat toward Calhoun.

That night the sleeping men of the Texas Brigade were aroused a little before midnight and told to sleep with their weapons and accoutrements by their sides. They were awakened again a short while later and started for Calhoun. As they trudged across the pontoon bridge they were cautioned to be as quiet as they could lest Sherman's pickets learn of their departure. Many troops had already crossed and many others would follow. Both the pontoon bridge and a nearby railroad bridge were employed in the evacuation and when the last of the men had crossed the bridges were burned.

Cleburne's division stopped near Calhoun the next day where it linked up with Walker's division and prepared to protect the rear of the retreating army. The Texas Brigade formed a second battle line behind General Lucius Polk's brigade. By the time skirmishing began, and before either side was fully committed, General Cleburne learned that another large enemy force was approaching Calhoun from his right rear. He broke off the engagement and pulled his forces back to a more defensible location. The enemy did not attack and Cleburne was soon ordered to continue his withdrawal to Adairsville. Leaving the Texans as pickets, the rest of the division pulled out shortly after midnight.

The Union pursuit of the retiring Rebel army was more persistent than it had been after the Battle of Missionary Ridge. Soon after the Texas Brigade caught up with the rest of the army near Adairsville, the van of the enemy caught up too. The Confederates were now quite adept at throwing up breastworks and were well protected by them when the Yanks appeared. The skirmish fire eventually ignited a small engagement — it could hardly be termed a battle — in which the advantage of a good defensive position was again well illustrated. As one member of the Texas Brigade put it: "it is all one sided, that is we kill them and they can't hurt us." [1]

Johnston had hoped to make a stand at Adairsville. His maps indicated a narrow valley there — narrow enough for his army to deploy completely across it and up the hills on either side. This type of position would enable him to offset the advantage of numbers enjoyed by his antagonist. It would be the type of position held by Cleburne's division at Ringgold Gap, only on a much larger scale. Unfortunately, however, the maps were misleading. The valley was much too wide to accommodate the Army of Tennessee. So, once again, retreat!

Two roads led south out of Adairsville. One ran almost due south to Kingston and the other bore a little east of south to Cassville. While Polk and Hood led their troops along the road to Cassville, Granbury's Texans formed the rear guard of Hardee's corps as it moved out on the other road. Johnston was baiting a trap in which he hoped to catch General Schofield's command as it marched toward Cassville. Polk's corps was to delay the Yankee advance while Hood countermarched north on a road that was just east of, and parallel to, the one on which Schofield was approaching. While Polk engaged the head of the enemy column Hood would attack from the east and the jaws of the Confederate trap would slam shut before help could arrive.

The Texas Brigade was a few miles west of Cassville, skirmishing with the advance of General Thomas's army, when General Hood moved out. Reports soon reached Hood that Yankee troops were to the east of him. With this startling bit of information he immediately departed from the original battle plan and faced his corps around to confront this new threat. Schofield continued toward Cassville without any flank attack while Hood prepared to do battle with what turned out to be only a small enemy detachment. Johnston, dissatisfied with Hood's failure to attack, ordered him to fall back. The entire Confederate army took up a new position a couple of miles southeast of Cassville where the Southerners remained behind their hastily erected breastworks throughout the afternoon and evening of May 19th. At a council of war with his corps commanders Johnston decided that this new position was too weak to hold.

In the pre-dawn hours of May 20, 1864, therefore, the men of the Texas Brigade stumbled sleepily onto the road and headed south once more. They must have scratched their heads as they reflected upon this latest turn of events. General orders had been read to them only the day before in which General Johnston said: "Your communications are secure. You will now turn and march to meet his [Sherman's] advancing columns. . . . I lead you to battle." [2] The "battle" turned out to be another tiring march away from the enemy's "advancing columns." The Texans stopped near Cartersville to eat breakfast but were hurried along before some of them had a chance to eat. By noon they reached the Etowah River where they were able to rest for a couple of hours before crossing. When the march was resumed they traveled a few more miles until they reached Willford's Mill, on the banks of Pumpkinvine Creek. Here they stopped.

While the Confederates sat back and caught their breath, Sherman's men were resting near Kingston. Sherman did not want to risk a frontal assault so he started shifting his forces to the right. He hoped to be able to sidestep Johnston and move upon Atlanta by way of Dallas, but alert Rebel cavalry kept the Confederate commander fairly well posted with regard to enemy troop movements. The Army of Tennessee was ordered out to block the intended passage through Dallas and by May 25th the lines were drawn for what would become known as the Battle of New Hope Church.

The Confederates faced roughly northwest with Hardee's corps anchoring the left flank near Dallas. Hood's corps held the right near the little crossroads known as New Hope Church and Polk's corps occupied the center. Heavy fighting occurred in front of Hood when General Hooker's Twentieth Corps tried to overwhelm the entrenched Confederates. This first day's battle lasted all afternoon and into the evening before the Federals decided that they had had enough for one day. When they pulled back they left over a thousand dead and wounded lying in the rain (which had been falling all day). While all this was going on the men of the Texas Brigade were marching and countermarching and wondering just where they were going. They finally halted in a reserve position slightly removed from the battle area.

By the next day most of Sherman's army was on the scene. Sherman did not have an accurate picture of the Confederate troop disposition and feared having his left flank turned. To prevent this he brought most of his force to bear near the little country church. This, in turn, caused Johnston to juggle his troops again. Part of the redistribution of Southern strength was the sending of Cleburne's division to Hood's right. No general fighting took place that day but skirmishers on both sides stayed busy.

Sherman hoped to slide part of his army around the Confederate right flank and he therefore sent Major General Oliver O. Howard off to the northeast with troops from the Fourth, Fourteenth, and Twenty-third Corps. The Federal move started a little before noon. After marching a short distance, Howard halted his men and prepared for battle. Skirmishers returned with the news that they had not found the end of the Confederate line as they had thought. Howard got his troops under way again and marched them a little farther. By now the Federals were sure that they had arrived upon the relatively unprotected right flank of the Army of Tennessee. Events soon transpired that proved that they were only half right. They had arrived at the right flank, but it was far from unprotected.

As the Union skirmishers pressed through the thick woods they slowly pushed back the dismounted troopers of the Tenth Confederate Cavalry Regiment who were posted there. In the meantime, the men of Granbury's brigade hurried to their right along a little ridge. When they stopped they were right behind the slowly retiring skir-

mish line. An infantry skirmish line was put out and the tired cavalrymen of Brigadier General John H. Kelly's division passed through
to the rear. They had done their job. They had delayed the Yankee
push long enough for Granbury's men to arrive on the scene. The
Union skirmishers of General William B. Hazen's brigade were now
exchanging fire with fresh Confederate soldiers and the Texans soon
had the men in blue dropping at an alarming rate. Finally the Rebel
skirmishers were ordered back to the main line.

It was about five o'clock in the afternoon when the firing esca-
lated and General Hazen rushed his men forward. The Texans had
not had time to build log breastworks and some of the Yanks, upon
seeing this, came on with a yell. "Ah! damn you, we have caught you
without your logs now." [3] There was much natural cover along the
ridge, however, and as the Yanks appeared in their sights the Texans "slaughtered them with deliberate aim." [4] In addition to the
devastating effect of the point-blank fire of the Texans was a sweep-
ing cross fire from Brigadier General Daniel Govan's brigade just to
the right of Granbury. Casualties were heavy among the Federals
and after almost an hour they began to fall back. Hazen's tired brigade was relieved by Colonel William H. Gibson's six western regiments. These men were met by the same fierce defense as their pred-
ecessors and, though they fought tenaciously, they were forced to
retire. Colonel Frederick Knefler's brigade comprised the third and
final assault wave and by sundown it too had withdrawn.

Near the end of the day's fighting an event took place which
was not uncommon in the Civil War, but would never happen in a
modern war. An Indiana regiment, possibly the Thirty-seventh, was
vainly trying to dislodge the Sixth and Fifteenth Texas. On they
came through the deadly fire. The Federal color-bearer was seen to
fall but his flag was instantly snatched up and borne forward. The
second flag bearer was soon killed, and a third, and the fourth until
a total of six men had been shot down carrying the banner. By the
time the sixth man fell the Union battle line was beginning to fall
back and the flag lay in the dust within a few paces of the Confederate line. One of the retiring infantrymen saw the flag and ran to
recover it. He dropped his rifle and shook the flag defiantly at the
Texans. Confederate rifles were instantly trained on him but before
any triggers were pulled someone shouted, "Don't shoot him, he's
too brave." The man, whether brave or crazy, was allowed to retreat
with his flag. This episode illustrates quite well the nineteenth century notion of honorable warfare.

The story of the Indiana flag that was almost lost does not end
here. During the battle a young soldier from the Sixth and Fifteenth

Texas captured one of the Indiana infantrymen. The Confederate had been born in Indiana, and when he and his prisoner compared notes they found that they had several mutual acquaintances in that state. They had, in fact, lived in the same vicinity as one another, attended the same school, and sat at the same school desk! The chain of coincidence still does not end. The woman who sewed the Indiana battle flag and presented it to the regiment was the aunt of this young Confederate!

After the fighting subsided the slope in front of Granbury's men was carpeted in blue as dead and wounded Union soldiers lay everywhere. The undergrowth in the area, including many small trees, had been completely shot away by musketry. Some of the dead trees had been ignited by shell bursts and cast an eerie light over parts of the battlefield. Not all of the Yankees who lay in front of the Rebel position were casualties. Many had elected to stay where they were — hoping, perhaps, that another attack would be made, at which time they could rejoin their comrades. Others had returned to carry off the wounded under cover of darkness. About nine o'clock General Granbury ordered his brigade to prepare to attack. The men looked to their weapons, fixed bayonets, and waited. An hour later a bugle sounded the charge. Captain G. W. Lewis of the 124th Ohio had led a small party back to the battlefield to retrieve the body of a fellow officer. When the bugle sounded Captain Lewis remarked that it must be an artillery call. "It is certainly not an infantry call." Sergeant Orson Vanderhoef disagreed. "By God, it's the rebel forward, I've heard it many a time on picket, and we'd better be getting out of here pretty God damned quick." [5]

The Texans responded to the bugle call with a mighty rebel yell that rent the still night air as they sprang over their works and down the hillside. The Federals who were able to run did so but not all of them escaped. Over two hundred were captured including some seventy who were wounded. General Cleburne heaped praise upon the Texas Brigade in his official report of the battle. "It needed but the brilliance of this night attack to add luster to the achievements of Granbury and his brigade in the afternoon. I am deeply indebted to them both." [6]

After the Confederate counterattack ended, the skirmishers were posted well to the front while the rest of the brigade fell back to its original position on the ridge. A Confederate artillery battery continued to shell the Federal camp for about an hour before quiet again finally descended upon the countryside. Early the next morning the skirmishers were recalled. As they passed over the field of battle of the previous evening they were greeted by awful scenes of death. Confederate and Yankee dead were sprawled out in grotesque postures. Weapons and ammunition lay everywhere. The Confederates went through the knapsacks of their fallen foe searching for any little items that would make life more bearable. The original owners had no further use for the knapsacks and it was a proud Rebel indeed who happened to acquire a bit of coffee or sugar in this manner. The dead Union soldiers were buried near where they fell in large common graves. Some time later, after the Confederate army had moved on, some of these graves were opened so that the bodies might be sent north to families. By this time, however, identification had become almost impossible.

Thus ended the battle, part of the New Hope Church action, that was known as the Battle of Pickett's Mill or the Battle of Pumpkinvine Creek. The Federal loss was estimated at about fifteen hundred. Confederate losses were relatively light. Cleburne's entire division lost only four hundred and fifty-eight men, but of this number the Texas Brigade lost thirty-three killed and one hundred and fourteen wounded.

Both armies spent the next few weeks maneuvering for better positions. Sherman moved his armies to the northeast a few miles and allowed them a week to rest and refit near the town of Acworth. Johnston took up a line which ran from Brush Mountain southwest to Pine Mountain and thence to Lost Mountain. Granbury's brigade, after some marching and countermarching, finally settled down a little to the southwest of Pine Mountain near a tiny crossroads community known as Golgotha Church.

Throughout most of the month of June the skies over northern Georgia were gloomy with rain and the roads were bottomless rivers of mud. Marching was accomplished with the greatest of effort. Men and animals of the Texas Brigade were often knee-deep in the muck and the wagons and cannons sank in up to their wheel hubs. The men slept where they dropped, even if that might be in great puddles of water several inches deep. Even in these circumstances some of the soldiers looked for the proverbial silver lining. In spite of their discomfort they were reasonably sure that they were drowning scores of graybacks, the ever-present body lice.

On June 10, 1864, General Sherman's men began to advance once again. The three Federal armies approached the Confederate defense line in roughly parallel lines of march. McPherson's army moved south along the railroad from Acworth to Marietta. General Thomas moved the Army of the Cumberland on General McPherson's right while General Schofield's small Army of the Ohio took the westernmost route. Skirmish fire soon broke out all along the line.

During the fighting of the next few days the Confederates suffered a very high ranking casualty. On June 14, 1864, Lieutenant General Leonidas Polk, the Bishop-General, was killed by an enemy artillery shell. He and Generals Johnston and Hardee had ridden to the top of Pine Mountain to reconnoiter the surrounding countryside. An enemy artillery crew spotted them and opened fire hoping to disperse them. After the first shot Johnston and Hardee moved off out of sight of the Yankee gunners but Polk lingered and the second shot killed him.

The next day the pace of the fighting picked up near Golgotha, as all along the line the Union armies relentlessly pushed forward. Granbury's brigade waited patiently as the enemy approached. Late in the afternoon the Yanks were sighted. They were still several hundred yards away and some of them were seeking shelter behind the old log meeting house. Near the left side of the Texas Brigade a four-gun battery opened fire. Within fifteen minutes the little church was flattened and the gunners began loading grape and cannister into their pieces. At this time, too, Confederate rifles joined in. The fight was brisk but short-lived. By sundown the Federals had retired and only an occasional shot was fired.

The next couple of days were spent by both sides maneuvering and skirmishing. The left side of the Confederate line had been bent back until it faced west. Union artillery crews soon found that they could enfilade the line where it was bent, so during the night of June 18–19 Johnston's army fell back once more. The new position ran from Kennesaw Mountain on toward the south. Hood's corps anchored the right flank along the crest of the mountain. The center of the line was held by Polk's corps, which was now temporarily commanded by Major General William W. Loring, and Hardee's corps was on the left. As General Sherman shifted troops to the south it became necessary to transfer Hood's corps to the left of the Confederate line to keep it from becoming overlapped. This left Hardee's corps in the center of the line and Granbury's brigade near the center of the corps.

In the battle that followed, the Battle of Kennesaw Mountain, General Sherman stepped out of character for a short time. Instead of sidestepping the Confederate army and trying to cut the rail line to Atlanta, Sherman chose to commit his forces to a head-on assault against an entrenched enemy. Why he changed tactics at this time can only be guessed at. He might have felt that his troops were becoming lethargic. After all, hadn't the next step after a skirmish or battle always been to try to flank the Rebs out of their positions? Perhaps a pitched battle would wake them up. Sherman may also have felt that by this time General Johnston might be trying to out-guess him by shifting troops to the south to counter the expected flanking movement before it developed. If this was the case then the Confederate line would be stretched very thin in places. A third pos-sibility is that Sherman might have seen the spirit of the Southern fighting man and he might have realized that the only way to con-quer this spirit would be to crush the life out of the enemy army. The maneuvering that had been done by Sherman's armies up to this time had gotten them deep into Confederate territory but they were still faced with a powerful foe. Perhaps, with a little luck, a direct at-tack would prove successful and this army could be destroyed. For whatever reason, the three Federal armies attacked on June 27th.

At 8:00 A.M. the Union artillery began its attempt to soften up the Confederate works. By nine o'clock the barrage was lifted and the Northern infantry began to attack. Cleburne's division was posted north of a bend in the Confederate lines now known as the "Dead Angle." Troops from General John Newton's division of the Fourth Corps were assigned to take this particular piece of Georgia real estate and on they came. They approached the rugged slopes of Kennesaw in compact regimental formation. As they clambered over the rocks the leading regiments were cut to ribbons by rifle and artillery fire. In spite of the heavy losses the Union soldiers slowly inched their way forward. Although Granbury's men were not ac-tively engaged in this battle, their comrades in the other brigades of Cleburne's division fought gallantly.

At one point in the fighting the underbrush, which had finally dried out after weeks of wet weather, caught fire from the exploding shells and the muzzle flashes of the rifles. As at Chickamauga, many of the Federal wounded were in danger of burning to death. Lieuten-ant Colonel William H. Martin, who commanded the First and Fif-teenth Arkansas Regiment in Polk's brigade, tied a white handker-chief to a ramrod and leapt upon the breastworks frantically waving his makeshift flag of truce. A temporary cease-fire was effected so the wounded men could be removed. Some Confederates even joined in the rescue effort. As soon as the Yanks were safely evacuated the shooting resumed. By 11:30 A.M., it had ended.

General Sherman had been made to see the futility of attacking an enemy who occupied a position which was almost impregnable. General Johnston had seen that the Yankee soldiers could, and would, fight. Sherman lost about three thousand men that day and the Confederate losses were about seven hundred and fifty. Many men on both sides suffered from heat exhaustion as the sun had finally made an appearance and sent the mercury over the one hundred-degree mark.

Both armies remained in their respective positions for the next few days regaining their strength. The right of Schofield's army was now farther south than the left of Hood's corps. By July 2d McPherson's army was moving south and that night the Confederate army once again pulled out and headed deeper into its own territory. When Sherman discovered that the strong Kennesaw Line was vacant he ordered an immediate pursuit. He hoped to be able to catch the Rebels before they could reestablish a defense, but Johnston had planned ahead and retired only a few miles into previously erected works near Smyrna. After a day of skirmishing here, Sherman again threatened to get behind Johnston so the Smyrna works were abandoned and the Confederates retreated to the north bank of the Chattahoochee River just a few miles from Atlanta.

The Army of Tennessee again occupied a position that had been built in anticipation of its need. Slave labor had been employed, and the position was a strong one. In fact, it was too strong for Sherman to risk another bloodbath such as the one at Kennesaw Mountain. Instead he cast about for some way to maneuver the Confederates out of their works. This planning took a few days and the men of the Texas Brigade caught up on some badly needed rest. They were also able to bathe and wash their clothes in the river — two luxuries which they had not enjoyed for some time.

The Federal commander decided on a course of action and sent a cavalry force upriver to try to cross over at Roswell. On July 8th he also ordered Schofield's Army of the Ohio to cross the river a few miles above the Confederate right flank. A small force of Confederates disputed the passage but they were driven off, and by sundown a lodgement had been made on the south bank of the Chattahoochee. Once again the veteran Union soldiers were able to accomplish by marching what they could not achieve by fighting. During the night of July 9th the Confederate army crossed the last of the three main rivers between Dalton and Atlanta.

The Confederates established themselves along Peachtree Creek and waited while the Federal armies crossed the Chattahoochee and moved toward them. Granbury's men enjoyed a time of relative ease. They had time to play poker or bathe again. They feasted on vegetables along with their regular rations of beef and corn bread. Whenever the men had enough to fill their stomachs they regarded the occasion as a feast.

Johnston's army had fought only two major battles since leav-

ing Resaca, and had been quite successful in each of them. Yet Johnston had been continually forced to give up ground until now he was
at the very outskirts of Atlanta. President Davis had never been extremely fond of General Johnston and it is probable Davis thought
this general would not stand and fight if there was a chance to retreat. On July 17, 1864, he replaced Johnston with a fighter — John
Bell Hood.

The announcement of the change of commanders was met with
dismay by the rank and file of the Texas Brigade. They, along with
most of the rest of the soldiers, had grown very attached to General
Johnston. They trusted him. If he said fight, they would fight; and
if he said retreat, they would retreat. They knew that Johnston
would try to keep them clothed and fed. To many soldiers that was
at least as important as winning battles, perhaps more so. Throughout the army small knots of men gathered to talk of this latest development. General Hood was not popular, and some of the talk bor-
dered on mutiny. Men refused to do any duties and openly
threatened to desert. The men did not know what to expect of Hood.
They would not be long in finding out.

By July 19th Generals Schofield and McPherson were northeast of Atlanta, and General Thomas was directly north of the city.
Thomas was in the process of crossing his command over Peachtree
Creek, and was separated from the other two Federal armies by a
large gap. Hood wanted to fight and here was his chance. If he could
fall upon Thomas with the bulk of his army before the Army of the
Cumberland could get entirely across the creek, he might be able to
destroy, or so cripple that army that it would be out of action for
awhile. He could then turn his attention toward McPherson and
Schofield.

Battle plans were finalized and General Hardee's corps was to
initiate action by attacking at 1:00 P.M. on July 20th from right to
left. General Polk's old corps, now under the permanent command
of Lieutenant General Alexander P. Stewart, was to the left of Hardee and would join battle as soon as Hardee's left became engaged.
During the morning Hood became alarmed at the rapid approach
from the east of the other Federal armies. He ordered Stewart and
Hardee to shift a little to the right. This movement so deranged Hardee's corps that he could not begin his attack until almost four
o'clock. By that time Thomas had all of his men across the creek and
they started to entrench.

Cleburne's division, and thus Granbury's brigade, was held in
reserve as Hardee committed his other three divisions to battle.
General Walker's division in the center of Hardee's line was badly

mauled and Cleburne was ordered to the front to relieve him. At this time Hardee received an urgent dispatch from Hood. The right flank of the Confederate army was in danger of being turned and a fresh division of troops was required at once to stave off this danger. Hardee immediately cancelled Cleburne's attack orders and sent him to the trouble spot. Without the use of Cleburne's men, the Battle of Peachtree Creek drew to a close at great expense to the Confederates. They lost three times the number of men the Federals lost, and they gained no ground.

As darkness fell, Granbury's men marched into Atlanta, and then turned east. When they reached the main Confederate line they turned right and took up a position on the extreme right of the army along a ridge known as Bald Hill. Trenches were begun before turning in for the night. The Twenty-fourth and Twenty-fifth Texas was on the far right of the brigade. Next to them was the Seventeenth and Eighteenth Texas, and then the Tenth Texas with the Sixth and Fifteenth Texas on the left of the brigade. To the right of the Texans were some dismounted Alabama cavalrymen from Brigadier General William W. Allen's brigade and on their right were some more troopers from Brigadier General Alfred Iverson's Georgia cavalry brigade.

When the sun rose on the morning of July 21st, the men quickly set to work to improve their defenses. What they had not noticed in the dark but comprehended with horror in the light of day, was the fact that their line was immediately adjacent to an angle in the overall Confederate line. Their position was subject to enfilade fire from Union artillery and the enemy guns soon made their presence felt. Shells began exploding in and around the trenches with alarming frequency. Seventeen men in one company of the Eighteenth Texas were killed or wounded by a single shot, leaving only one man of the company still standing. A member of the same regiment, writing years later, described how an enemy "cannon ball hit the breastworks in front of us and struck a man on the head, his head struck me in the breast and knocked me down and covered me with his blood." [7]

Federal infantrymen were not long in making an appearance. Brigadier General Mortimer Leggett's division launched an attack on Bald Hill. As the Confederate skirmishers slowly fell back the dismounted cavalrymen opened fire upon the oncoming Yanks. Unfortunately, this put the skirmishers in a deadly cross fire. Their only chance for survival was to lie down and wait to be captured by the advancing enemy. The cavalry on Granbury's right soon broke toward the rear. With the right flank uncovered, the Twenty-fourth and Twenty-fifth Texas was forced to give ground. It swung back in an arc until it was at right angles to the rest of the brigade. Slowly the men of the Twenty-fourth and Twenty-fifth fought their way back — almost to the site of their original line. Losses in the Texas Brigade were heavy, even though they were protected to some extent by breastworks. The attackers fared worse, however, and one of the lead regiments, the Twelfth Wisconsin, lost over twenty percent of its men, including five color bearers. After dark the works, which had been so desperately defended, were abandoned.

Granbury's brigade pulled back into Atlanta, but there would be no rest this night. General Hood had decided to try some of Sherman's own tricks on him. He would send Hardee's corps on a roundabout march to the south and east so that it could fall upon McPherson's unsuspecting left flank and rear near Decatur. As the Texans passed through Atlanta they joined the rest of Hardee's corps as it made its way from the Peachtree Creek battlefield. They were hungry, thirsty, and very tired.

General Hood expected Hardee to be in position to attack by daybreak on July 22d, but the uncertain terrain and the lack of reliable maps delayed the start of the battle until after noon. When the Confederates reached the village of Akers, the road forked and two divisions were sent up each road. Cleburne's division took the left fork and before long was approaching Bald Hill from the southeast.

The three corps of General McPherson's army were surprised — but not stunned — by the appearance of four Confederate divisions bearing down upon them from their left rear. The Union soldiers of the Fifteenth and the Seventeenth Corps were in line facing west toward the city of Atlanta. The line of the Sixteenth Corps extended east from the southern end of the main line so that it faced south. Near midday the Confederate divisions of Generals William Bate and W. H. T. Walker finally arrived in position and attacked the left end of the Sixteenth Corps line. Thus, the Battle of Atlanta was begun.

CHAPTER NINE

Atlanta

On the morning of July 22, 1864, cautiously advancing Union skirmishers discovered that the Confederate trenches east of Atlanta were empty. The Confederates had evacuated their works and fallen back to another line of trenches some twelve hundred yards closer to the city. When this information was relayed back to the rear, the main Union battle line was put in motion. The men of the Fifteenth and Seventeenth Corps immediately got busy reversing the abandoned Confederate trenches so they could be held against an attack from the direction of the city. By mid-morning the array of Union forces east of Atlanta consisted of the Seventeenth Corps on the southwest — or left — end of the line with the Fifteenth Corps on its right and the Twenty-third Corps next in line. The Sixteenth Corps was held in reserve.

The Confederate divisions of Generals Bate and Walker had taken the right-hand fork at Akers. The men had had little rest since the night of the 20th and they were tired. They had advanced in line of battle through a thick woods and, by noon, were in position to begin the assault. The left wing of Major General Grenville M. Dodge's Sixteenth Corps had arrived at the left of the Union line shortly before, and these were the first Federal troops to become aware of the Confederate flanking movement. As the scattered shots of the opposing skirmishers broke the stillness of early afternoon, it became evident that both armies were surprised. Dodge's men had had no intimation that there were any Confederates in the immediate area, and General Bate had felt certain that he had passed com-

117

pletely around the left flank of the Union army — he was expecting to come in *behind* the enemy.

The three Federal brigades hastily entrenched themselves and the air was soon filled with whistling death. One brigade faced east and the other two looked south. As the Rebels advanced, two batteries of light artillery poured a constant torrent of shell and cannister into them. On the extreme right of the Confederate line the men of Bate's division fought their way nearly to the enemy works before being forced back by a countercharge. The Ohio and Illinois troops forced the attackers back toward the woods, capturing, as they went, two Confederate battle flags and hundreds of prisoners.

Walker's men were just to the left of Bate's division and they, too, were having a rough afternoon. They came out of the woods four ranks deep in front of Brigadier General John W. Fuller's brigade of the Sixteenth Corps. As they started across the field they were shocked by the intensity of the small arms fire being delivered into them. They halted momentarily and then retreated into the woods to regroup. As the Yanks lay in wait for the attack to be renewed, General Fuller issued some attack orders of his own. The Rebels were to be allowed to move well into the field separating the two forces. Then Fuller's left two regiments, with bayonets fixed, were to fire a volley and charge. The Federals were impatient, though, and as soon as the Southerners broke the cover of the woods the Twenty-seventh and the Thirty-ninth Ohio regiments charged. The counterattack struck Brigadier General C. H. Stevens's Georgia brigade. The Georgians halted, wavered, and then beat a hasty retreat.

While half of General Fuller's brigade was involved with Stevens's Georgians, the other half watched as the rest of the long Confederate battle line threatened to move past their right flank. Fuller quickly ordered his two Ohio regiments to break off their pursuit and wheel to the right. His other two regiments, the Nineteenth Missouri and the Sixty-fourth Illinois, had already pivoted back until the brigade battle line faced almost west. As General Walker rode forward, waving his hat and urging his men onward, a Yankee bullet found him. The combined flank fire of the four Federal infantry regiments and the almost point-blank fire of the Fourteenth Ohio Battery proved to be too much for the Confederates. Once again they retreated back into the trees.

Union General James B. McPherson had been observing the battle from a point in the rear of Fuller's brigade. Apparently satisfied with the progress of the fighting, he and two orderlies set out to see how the Seventeenth Corps was faring. There was a gap in the

Union lines of about a half mile between the Sixteenth and the Seventeenth Corps. As McPherson's small party rode through the woods between the two corps, it encountered a Confederate skirmish line from Cleburne's division. The Yanks were ordered to halt but the general decided to try to escape through the trees. He turned his horse and sank his spurs into its flanks. As he did so, several shots were fired and he fell from his horse. The fatal bullet passed through his heart and he was probably dead before he hit the ground. After the war there was much controversy concerning who had fired the shot that killed the general. Since a fusillade of shots was fired it is impossible to say whose bullet killed him. It seems certain, though, that the commander of the Federal Army of the Tennessee had run into the advance elements of Cleburne's division and, in particular, the Texas Brigade.

Cleburne advanced his command with Govan's brigade on the left and Granbury's on the right with Lowrey's in reserve. Govan's Arkansas brigade marched up the McDonough Road until it came upon the left end of the Seventeenth Corps. The Federal line, which ran roughly northeast to southwest, was refused sharply to the east and it was at this point that Govan struck. The Union soldiers were entrenched in two parallel lines with tangles of abatis protecting the approaches to each. A section of Napoleon guns from the Second Illinois Light Artillery swept the road near the right of the Federal position. Six more guns were posted on the left. As the left side of the Arkansas brigade fought its way up to the enemy line, the men found that their numbers had been drastically reduced, and they were unable to carry the works. Many were captured. The Confederates on the right of Govan's brigade overlapped the Union line and were soon turning to the left to roll up the Iowa regiments which opposed them. The fighting was sharp, and in some instances bayonets, clubbed muskets, and fists were used. At one point the colonel of the Fifteenth Iowa reached across the works and physically yanked the colonel of the Forty-fifth Alabama into the trenches as his prisoner. At about the same time most of the members of the Sixteenth Iowa were being captured by the Confederates.

Granbury's brigade was to the right of Govan and the Texans poured through the gap that existed there. In addition to General McPherson's fatal encounter, another high-ranking officer was surprised in the woods. Colonel Robert K. Scott, commanding a brigade in the Seventeenth Corps, was away from his troops when he fell captive to Granbury's men with scarcely a shot being fired.

As the battle intensified in the rear of the main Union line, concerned commanders swung their men around to meet the enemy. Two brigades of the Fifteenth Corps realigned themselves to face south and meet Granbury's oncoming men. The Confederates had moved so far into Union territory without any serious opposition that they had outdistanced their support. The individual regiments found themselves separated from each other in the thick woods and concerted action was almost impossible. Recognizing the need to regroup, General Smith — who was again in temporary command of the Texas Brigade while General Granbury recovered from illness — ordered his men to fall back. Again owing to the difficult terrain and circumstances, the order was not received by all of the regiments in the brigade. The Seventeenth and Eighteenth Texas and the Fifth Confederate, which had been temporarily assigned to the brigade, were almost entirely cut off when the Fifteenth Michigan and the Ninety-ninth Indiana launched a counterattack. The two Confederate regiments were captured, almost to a man, although many escaped in the ensuing confusion. Both regimental battle flags were lost.

There was a considerable amount of rivalry between the Fifteenth Michigan and the Ninety-ninth Indiana at this time. The animosity apparently stemmed from an effort on the part of brigade commander Colonel John M. Oliver — formerly of the Fifteenth Michigan — to obtain a promotion to the rank of brigadier general. He circulated a petition to that effect among the officers of his brigade. Lieutenant Colonel John M. Berkey, of the Ninety-ninth, reported that the officers of his regiment refused to sign it and ". . . after that we never captured a prisoner but what he [Colonel Oliver] added to his report that the 15th Michigan did it." [1] The Hoosiers asserted that one of their soldiers — from Company I — found the flag of the Seventeenth and Eighteenth Texas lying on the ground, and that Colonel Fred S. Hutchinson of the Fifteenth Michigan ordered it brought to him. Sergeant Major Andrew La Forge of the Michigan regiment, however, also claimed to have been the one who captured that flag. "With revolver in hand, I jumped upon the breastworks and demanded the surrender of the flag, at the same time reaching for the top of the flagstaff. In the meantime my regiment came to the rescue, and we captured the flag." [2] In spite of these conflicting reports the capture of the prisoners and flags was officially credited to the Fifteenth Michigan. Indeed, the flag of the Seventeenth and Eighteenth Texas, which is now in the Texas State Archives, has a handwritten inscription to that effect written on it in ink.

As the Texas Brigade tried to reorganize itself, part of Lowrey's brigade passed through it to the front. The individual regiments had become intermingled with each other and with other brigades. The

Sixth and Fifteenth Texas joined Govan's brigade for the rest of the day and assisted that brigade in capturing two enemy battle flags. The Twenty-fourth and Twenty-fifth Texas, fighting on the left of the brigade, captured the flag of the Third Iowa. Finally, after several assaults, the Texas Brigade retired to a position in the rear of Govan's brigade.

Meanwhile, General Hood finally initiated the second part of his battle plan. Major General Benjamin F. Cheatham had brought his corps from the Peachtree Creek battlefield into the interior defenses east of Atlanta, when Hardee started his flanking march. These fresh troops began an attack to the east about five o'clock in the afternoon. The Federal soldiers on the left side of the original line of battle had jumped over their breastworks and fought from in front of them when Hardee's corps had attacked their rear. Now they had to cross over again to repel Cheatham's men. In some places the defenders were under fire from front and rear simultaneously. Some of Cheatham's men broke through the lines of the Fifteenth Corps but were unable to sustain their advantage. By nightfall the battle was over.

General Hood's second major battle as an army commander thus ended in defeat. He lost thousands of irreplaceable men and failed in his attempt to crush the Union Army of the Tennessee. Had he committed Cheatham's corps a couple of hours earlier he might have been successful. By the same token, if Sherman had committed his entire force the result might have been even worse for the Confederacy. The Texas Brigade, already under strength, lost three hundred and twelve men killed, wounded, or missing, during the Battle of Atlanta.

Both armies spent the next few days resting and reorganizing. General Sherman named Major General Oliver O. Howard to succeed the slain McPherson as head of the Army of the Tennessee. Lieutenant General Stephen D. Lee was appointed to permanent command of Hood's old corps. W. H. T. Walker's division was disbanded and the troops distributed to the other divisions within Hardee's corps. Brigadier General Hugh W. Mercer's brigade of Georgians was added to Cleburne's division.

Sherman was up against a fighter in Hood. The new Confederate commander had fought two bloody battles in three days — although he lost both of them. Still, if Sherman could cut Atlanta off from the rest of the world, he might be able to capture the city without having to face Hood in another pitched battle. After all, Sherman might have reasoned, the next time the outcome might be different. Consequently, Sherman shifted his Army of the Tennessee from the extreme left of his command to the extreme right. By sundown of July 25th, General Howard's new command was west of Atlanta, and marching toward the Atlanta and West Point Railroad. If all of the rail lines into Atlanta could be controlled by the Union forces it would then only be a matter of time before the city would be forced to capitulate.

Hood learned of the sidewise movement of Federal troops and dispatched the corps of S. D. Lee and A. P. Stewart to stop it. The two forces met near Ezra Church, about two and a half miles west of Atlanta, on July 28th. The Confederates attacked repeatedly, but in a piecemeal fashion. After several hours they withdrew — badly bloodied. They lost in the neighborhood of five thousand men and only managed to inflict about six hundred casualties upon the Northerners. The men of the Texas Brigade were close enough to hear the rattle of small arms fire and the deep booming of the artillery but took no part in the battle.

Granbury's pickets were busy all day, every day, and it seemed as if the main body of the brigade was constantly within earshot of heavy skirmishing. On August 3d, the brigade moved a couple of miles southwest of Atlanta along the railroad to West Point where it stayed for the next four weeks. There was occasional skirmishing during this time and one very successful scouting expedition in which twenty beef cattle were captured without the loss of a single man. Of course it must be remembered that the cows were unarmed.

During the month of August both armies carried out numerous cavalry raids. Union cavalry tried to cut the rail line into Atlanta and Confederate cavalry tried once more to cut the Union supply lines from Tennessee. None of these forays were overly successful. The least successful, as far as General Sherman was concerned, began in late July. Brigadier General Edward M. McCook led one raiding party southwest of Atlanta and aimed at the Macon Railroad where he was to tear up track and put the road out of commission. At the same time, Major General George Stoneman's troopers were headed south from the other side of Atlanta. They had the same target in mind, but they had a secondary goal: to free the thousands of Federal prisoners being held at Macon and Andersonville. McCook was able to destroy some track near Lovejoy's Station, but Stoneman took it upon himself to juggle his assigned priorities and tried to free the prisoners first. The overall result of the two-pronged sortie was that the railroad was inoperable for only a few days and McCook lost nine hundred and fifty men captured while Stoneman and five hundred of his men wound up in the same prison camps they had attempted to liberate.

In view of the way the Union raid was bungled, General Hood felt confident in assigning Major General Joseph Wheeler to lead a raid of his own. President Davis agreed with the plan and Wheeler was soon heading north with half of the Confederate cavalry in Hood's command. The intent of this raid was to cut, if possible, Sherman's rail line to Chattanooga. If his supplies were suspended he would either have to retreat or attack the Rebels in their works and risk a disastrous defeat. Wheeler was unsuccessful in forcing a permanent stoppage, but he did disrupt things for a time. Hood felt that Sherman would have to retreat. When Union troops were observed filing out of their lines on August 25th, his conviction seemed justified.

General Sherman, far from contemplating retreat back to Tennessee, was instead sending his men farther to the southwest. As they moved, the Federals tore up more railroad track. The destruction of southern railroads approached assembly line precision. Gangs of men worked in close harmony. One group pried up the rails while another group gathered up the cross ties into a heap for burning. A roaring fire would soon be going and as the ties burned, the long rails were laid across the fire. When they were white hot they were taken from the flames by gangs of men and twisted around trees or telegraph poles. This procedure rendered the rails totally useless and the twisted remains came to be known as "Sherman's neckties."

By the time General Hood discovered that the enemy had advanced, rather than retreated, it was August 29th and Federal soldiers were camped along the railroad to West Point, about fifteen miles southwest of Atlanta. The Confederate commander still did not realize the extent of the problem he faced. He thought that a heavy raid was in progress and that only two enemy corps were involved. On August 30th General Hardee was sent with his corps and S. D. Lee's corps to check the advance of the "raiders." The Texas Brigade began the march at 10:00 P.M. and marched all night. By sunrise the men reached the village of Jonesboro.

The van of the Federal Army of the Tennessee crossed the Flint River west of Jonesboro on the night of the 30th. By noon the next day, the Fifteenth Corps was strongly entrenched about a half mile east of the river and facing Jonesboro. On its right was Brigadier General John M. Corse's Second Division of the Sixteenth Corps. The remainder of the Sixteenth Corps and all of the Seventeenth Corps were just west of the river. The Confederates were disposed with General Lee's corps on the right and Hardee's corps, temporarily commanded by General Cleburne, on the left. In Cleburne's absence his division was

led by General Lowrey, and it was placed on the left of the corps with
Granbury's brigade on the left of the division.

The Confederate battle plan called for the troops to be committed from left to right with Lee's corps advancing when they heard
Cleburne's men firing. Granbury's left regiment was the Twenty-
fourth and Twenty-fifth Texas, and that regiment had been designated as the battalion of direction. The entire Confederate battle
line was to base its movements on the motion of this regiment. At
about three–thirty in the afternoon, after a short Confederate artillery preparation, the line of gray clad infantry stepped forward.

The Texans advanced slowly for about four hundred yards before they came into enemy range. Then they charged. They had intended to hit the right end of the Union line and turn it onto the center. Instead, the entire division encountered some Yankee cavalry
who were fighting dismounted just to the right of the main line of
works. The horsemen were no match for the battle hardened Confederate foot soldiers. After emptying their carbines and revolvers,
they fled for the river. The Rebels chased them all the way and, as
one Texan put it: "They runing for life and we for fun, and the ob-
jects being so muck [much] in their favor that they out ran us by
odds and got away (except the killed and wounded)." [3] When the
Confederates reached the river they were supposed to halt but the
Tenth Texas splashed on across. When they finally returned to the
command their colonel explained to General Granbury that a Yankee battery posted on the west bank was in a position to do them
great harm if left to itself. Therefore the men of the Tenth had
crossed the river and chased the enemy gunners away.

Unfortunately for the Confederacy, the rest of the battle did not
go as well as that portion fought by Cleburne's division. Major General John C. Brown finally found the end of the Federal line and led
the other division of Hardee's corps against it in an unsuccessful assault. Lee's men heard the firing between Cleburne's division and
the Union cavalry and assumed that the main Federal force was engaged so they moved out to attack the Fifteenth Corps. They, too,
were thrown back and by 4:30, the battle was over for the day. Casualties were not exceedingly heavy. In the area in which the Texas
Brigade fought they were rather light. General Granbury reported a
loss of sixteen killed and sixty-two wounded and stated that the "enemy's loss must have been slight, as we passed over but few dead
bodies." [4]

During the same day General Schofield's Army of the Ohio
broke the rail line at Rough and Ready, about halfway between
Jonesboro and Atlanta. Hood finally began to grasp the gravity of

the situation. In fact, he was convinced that, not only was the entire Union army south of Atlanta, but that an attack upon the city from that direction was imminent. He sent a messenger to Jonesboro to tell Hardee to send Lee's corps back to Atlanta immediately. Hardee, meanwhile, was ordered to stay with his corps and try to protect the city of Macon. The reduction in manpower forced Hardee to redistribute his troops, and Cleburne's division was moved to the right flank during the night.

When the sun rose on September 1st the men of the Texas Brigade were northwest of Jonesboro. General Govan's brigade was on the extreme right of the Confederate line and on its left were the Texans. The line faced a little north of west with the right slightly refused — or bent back — toward the railroad. Enemy sharpshooters began sniping as soon as there was enough light to pick out targets, but it was mid-afternoon before the battle commenced.

Brigadier General Jefferson C. Davis's Fourteenth Corps, Army of the Cumberland, arrived on the scene during the morning and at three o'clock launched a series of attacks against the northern end of the Rebel works. The main Federal effort was directed at the angle in the line where Govan's brigade bent back toward the east. The first attack was turned back but the Yankees regrouped and came forward in a formation that was four or five lines deep. With bayonets glistening in the sun they hit the salient and powered their way through the defenses. The Arkansans fought gamely but almost before anyone realized what was happening, General Govan and most of his men were captured.

During this time the men on the right side of Granbury's brigade were doing all they could to help their comrades stem the tide. It became evident that as soon as the Federals were able to dispose of their prisoners they would attempt to crush the Texas Brigade. The Texans began taking heavy enfilade fire from the right and General Granbury ordered them to face around to meet the expected attack. By this time Geneal Hardee was rushing reinforcements to Govan's assistance. These fresh troops, along with Granbury's men and the uncaptured remnants of Govan's command, drove the Yanks back far enough to relieve the immediate pressure and before the Federals could mount another attack, blessed darkness fell. Govan's losses were the heaviest with seven hundred and twelve men listed as casualties — most of them captured. Granbury's losses were sustained mostly by the right side of his brigade and amounted to eighteen killed and eighty-nine wounded.

General Hardee notified General Hood in Atlanta, that he was grossly outnumbered and that he was moving south to avoid being surrounded. Hood saw that there was no longer any hope for Atlanta, and during the night of September 1, 1864, the city was evacuated. All military stores that could not be carried away were destroyed to prevent them from falling into Federal hands. The exploding railroad cars full of ammunition could be heard all the way to Jonesboro. Hardee's retreating soldiers could see on the skyline the flames from the burning depots. The next morning the mayor of Atlanta officially surrendered the city to the Federals.

Hardee's command travelled as far as Lovejoy's Station before the men again threw up breastworks and prepared for more fighting. The next few days saw much skirmishing but no serious fighting. Finally, on the morning of September 6, 1864, the Confederates at Lovejoy experienced something they had not known since mid-July — quiet! There was no picket firing to be heard. There were no enemy artillery shells bursting at random within their works. The Federals had gone back to Atlanta.

General Sherman had said that his goal was to defeat the Confederate Army of Tennessee. The capture of Atlanta was only incidental. His actions during the first week of September seemed to contradict this. Instead of sending his men to fall upon the divided segments of Hood's army while they could destroy it in detail, he brought all of his troops into the city. While it is true that the soldiers of both armies were weary of the constant marching and fighting, Sherman seems to have passed up a chance to shorten the war by several months. With the Army of Tennessee out of the picture, the thousands of Federal troops in Georgia could have been sent east. General Lee's valiant Army of Northern Virginia, holed up within the defenses of Petersburg, could not have held out very long against the combined forces of Grant and Sherman.

To this day General Sherman is held in something less than high regard by the citizenry of Atlanta. He began earning this contempt by one of his first official acts upon entering the city. He did not want to be bothered by nonmilitary problems such as feeding the impoverished inhabitants. In order to forestall any such problems Sherman ordered all of the civilians to leave the city. He proposed a two-day truce so that those citizens who wished to go south could be escorted by his troops as far as Rough and Ready, where they would be met by Confederate soldiers who would convey them to Lovejoy's Station. General Hood agreed to the temporary cessation of hostilities but protested Sherman's "unprecedented measure" of "studied and ingenious cruelty." [5] Over the next few days the two army commanders exchanged heated communications: Hood condemned

Sherman's actions and Sherman defended himself by saying that the citizens were being expelled for their own safety.

The Confederate army finally reunited and spent a few days resting just north of Jonesboro. While here, the Texas Brigade was visited by Miss Mary Gay of Decatur, Georgia. Her half brother was Lieutenant Thomas Stokes of the Tenth Texas. At the beginning of the spring campaign Lieutenant Stokes and some of his friends had visited Miss Gay and left their heavy winter overcoats with her for safekeeping. Now, with cool weather approaching, she was returning them. Miss Gay exhibited a considerable amount of ingenuity and daring in transporting these items through the Union lines. First, she approached the Federal provost marshall at Decatur with a request for an army wagon and driver to take her to her sister's home in Augusta with some bedding and some other items. Next, she begged a number of discarded grain sacks from the Federal camp. Then she hurried home to stuff the Confederate clothing into the sacks, which she then sewed shut. The next morning a Yankee soldier arrived with a wagon and loaded it with the innocent looking sacks. Miss Gay directed him to a friend's home in Atlanta, where she arrived in time to see her friends preparing to head south in compliance with Sherman's evacuation order. The carefully concealed gray overcoats, among them that of General Granbury, were thus transported by Federal soldiers as far as Rough and Ready with the rest of the refugees.

Sherman left the Confederates alone while his own men rested and recuperated from the long campaign. The Confederates enjoyed this respite, and spent most of September a few miles southwest of Atlanta. The army was visited there by President Jefferson Davis and other dignitaries. Some observers within the army viewed the president's visit as an ill omen. After all, he had visited the Army of Tennessee just before the Battle of Murfreesboro, and the army had been forced to retreat to Tullahoma after the battle. He had been a guest at army headquarters prior to the Battle of Missionary Ridge —that disastrous battle was followed by a retreat to Dalton. Now, after being forced to give up Atlanta after an arduous struggle, the president arrived for another visit to discuss strategy with General Hood. One of Granbury's men, exhibiting an unusual amount of foresight, wrote in his diary, "This army is going to do something wrong—or rather it will undertake something that will not be a success." He felt Davis had come "to concoct some other plan for our defeat and display of his Generalship."[6]

The reason for Davis's visit was to check on the morale of the men. The rank and file of the army had already become distrustful of General Hood. Many of his high ranking subordinates shared this feeling. Davis conferred with Hood's three corps commanders and they all felt that the best interests of the Confederacy would be served if the Army of Tennessee had a new commanding general. The two most likely replacements for Hood were Generals Joseph E. Johnston and Pierre G. T. Beauregard but neither of these men was in favor with the president. As a compromise, Davis appointed Beauregard to head the newly established Military Division of the West, composed of Hood's command and that of Lieutenant General Richard Taylor in Louisiana. At the same time, General Hardee was relieved and his corps was taken over by Lieutenant General Benjamin Cheatham.

While the president was at the front the troops were assembled for him to review. Among the president's party was Governor Francis R. Lubbock of Texas. As he came riding along in front of the long line of soldiers the governor stopped in front of the regiment just to the right of the Twenty-fourth and Twenty-fifth Texas. This regiment was made up primarily of Irishmen but the governor obviously thought he was addressing fellow Texans when he announced, "I am Governor Lubbock of Texas." Then, instead of hearing a loud cheer, the governor heard a thick Irish brogue say, "An who the bloody Hell is governor Lubbock?" [7] The governor apparently had no reply.

President Davis and his entourage departed, and General Hood settled down to the business at hand. He still felt that if he could put his army between Atlanta and Chattanooga, Sherman would have to come out of Atlanta and face him in battle. Furthermore, Hood was confident that he would be fighting this battle on ground of his own choosing and would thus be able to smash Sherman's army from behind carefully prepared breastworks. This being the general plan, the Army of Tennessee started north.

CHAPTER TEN

The Tennessee
Campaign

The Confederate army started its northward movement on the morning of September 29, 1864. The men of the Texas Brigade left their camp at Palmetto, Georgia, and were across the Chattahoochee River by the next morning. The march was slow and easy with frequent stops. On October 2d they formed a line of battle just west of Marietta. While the men were in this formation the regimental commanders addressed them and gave them the first inkling of General Hood's strategy for the coming campaign. The men were told that they would be required to do some hard marching and some heavy fighting in the days ahead and that they would quite probably be on short rations a good deal of the time. These hardships were nothing new to these veterans, so they responded with enthusiasm when told that they would attempt to flank Sherman out of Atlanta.

That evening as the Texas Brigade was relaxing in camp, a thunderstorm came up rather suddenly. A bolt of lightning struck so abruptly that the men thought that enemy artillery had opened up on them. The lightning bounced back and forth among the trees and hit a stack of muskets. The guns were bent and twisted and scattered about. One man was killed as a result of the lightning and several others suffered minor injuries. Almost every man in the Twenty-fourth Texas was temporarily stunned. Once again casualties were suffered that were not the result of hostile action.

General Hood's plan seemed to be working as Sherman and most of his troops left Atlanta and started out after the Rebels. The Union commander had grown worried about his line of communication with the North, which Hood now threatened. While most of the Confederate army stayed near Marietta, Major General Samuel G. French's division moved to tear up the railroad north of that place and to destroy the bridge across the Etowah River near Allatoona. Sherman had left detachments of men along the railroad as he moved south toward Atlanta; and French encountered some of these troops in a spirited skirmish. The Confederates had carried two Yankee positions and were investing the third when word came — later proving to be erroneous — that Federal reinforcements were rapidly approaching from Atlanta. As a result, General French broke off the engagement and fell back without being able to destroy the large Federal supply depot at Allatoona.

Early on October 6th the Army of Tennessee took up the march again. Rain fell throughout the morning and the men plodded along in the mud. They travelled west to Cedartown and then north toward Rome. They demanded the surrender of the Union garrison at Resaca, but when the Federals refused General Hood decided not to waste any more time with this relatively insignificant body of enemy troops. The Confederates bypassed the town and moved on Dalton. On October 13th Dalton surrendered and the destruction of the railroad commenced in earnest. The rails were heated and twisted just as enthusiastically by the Texans as by their foe on earlier occasions. The Confederates had a different name for these mangled rails. They called them "Jeff Davis neckties." After tearing up the railroad as far north as Tunnel Hill, the Confederates turned southwest and headed for the Alabama state line.

Hood's infantrymen marched into Gadsden, Alabama, on October 20th. The next day Sherman's men entered Gaylesville, thirty miles to the northeast. From there the Union commander could play a waiting game. If the Confederates attempted to march back to the relief of Atlanta, Sherman could cut them off. If the Federal supply depot at Bridgeport, Alabama, was the target, Sherman could also block that move. Up to this point Hood's plan was working. He had drawn most of the enemy soldiers out of Atlanta — indeed out of Georgia. He had not yet met Sherman in battle, however, and quite frankly, did not have enough confidence in his men to warrant risking battle. Meanwhile, Sherman decided not to wait for Hood's next move but gave up the chase and returned to Atlanta.

While the Army of Tennessee was at Gadsden, General Beauregard joined General Hood. Together they mulled over the recently hatched plan to invade Tennessee. Maps were studied and many of Hood's subordinate officers were consulted. The general plan that emerged was grandiose and far-reaching. Hood proposed to march his army into Tennessee where he would cut off Sherman's supplies, defeat any opposition he might encounter, receive hordes of recruits, and then go on into Kentucky from where he would threaten Cincinnati. If Sherman followed him, Hood would give battle on ground of his own choosing. (This idea was becoming a familiar part of all of Hood's campaign plans.) If Hood defeated Sherman he would then be in a position to send reinforcements to General Lee at Petersburg. If, on the other hand, Sherman elected to march through Georgia to the coast, Hood could march his entire army through the mountains and into Virginia. There he and Lee could team up to defeat Grant's army before Sherman could arrive by ship from the Georgia seacoast. General Beauregard insisted that before starting off on this expedition, Hood should leave all of his cavalry with General Wheeler south of the Tennessee River, so that Sherman could be observed and harassed. In Wheeler's stead, Hood would have the use of General Forrest's cavalry.

The Confederates left Gadsden on October 22d and headed northwest for Guntersville, seventy-five miles away, where Hood intended to cross the Tennessee River. After the first day's march he received word that General Forrest was near Jackson, Tennessee, and, because of high rivers, was unable to meet him at Guntersville, as previously planned. Hood altered his line of march accordingly and set out the next morning for Tuscumbia, Alabama, in the northwest corner of the state. The hard marching Rebels bypassed Decatur on the 29th, with only a token effort to capture the Federal garrison there. They arrived at Tuscumbia on October 31st.

At Tuscumbia, the soldiers rested while General Hood fumed. He had expected the railroad from Corinth, Mississippi, to have been repaired. He was planning to resupply his army at Tuscumbia and turn quickly north into Tennessee. Instead the army lay idle for three weeks. General Beauregard again visited the army and consulted with Hood. Meanwhile President Davis was having second thoughts about Hood's army going off into Tennessee and leaving Sherman free to do as he wished in Georgia.

Shortly after the arrival of the army at Tuscumbia, the Reverend J. B. McFerrin was preaching to a large assemblage of soldiers from Cleburne's division when a light rain began to fall. Since the preacher was not finished with his sermon and there was no shelter to which the gathering could adjourn, he put on his hat and overcoat and continued. Most of his audience did likewise. After the sermon was finished several soldiers were standing near their stacked arms when lightning struck a nearby tree. One man was killed and several were injured. The contemporary account of this event closely parallels that described as having happened a month earlier while the Texas Brigade was still in Georgia. (They may, in fact, represent different versions of the same event.)

On November 13th General Hood crossed the Tennessee River with part of S. D. Lee's corps and established a headquarters at Florence, Alabama. The next day General Forrest's tired troopers arrived, and on the 15th the Texas Brigade followed them across the pontoon bridge. Shoes, clothing, and other essential supplies had finally arrived, and on November 21st the next leg of the journey began. The weather turned cold and snow stung their faces as the Texans marched north. By the 26th they were within a few miles of Columbia, Tennessee, and their first opposition.

Most of the Union troops that hoped to stop the Confederate invasion had been in the Atlanta campaign. On September 28th General Sherman sent General Newton's division of the Fourth Corps, and General Morgan's division of the Fourteenth Corps, to Tennessee to defeat Forrest's cavalry. Three weeks later, when it became obvious to Sherman that Hood meant to march north, the rest of the Fourth Corps was dispatched toward Pulaski, Tennessee, under the command of General David Stanley. By November 14th the leading elements of General Schofield's Twenty-third Corps also reached Pulaski, where Schofield assumed command of all the troops at that place. When the Army of Tennessee passed some twenty miles to the west, Schofield hastened his men back to Columbia, on the Duck River.

General Schofield found that the size of his force was inadequate to defend Columbia. On the night of November 27th, he accompanied his troops to the north side of the river and burned the bridge behind him. General Forrest took his cavalry across the river a few miles east of Columbia on the 28th, and began forcing the Union horsemen back toward Nashville. Hood left two infantry divisions from Lee's corps and virtually all of his artillery in front of Schofield while he led the rest of his force to the right and across the river.

At daybreak on the 29th, General Hood accompanied the Texas Brigade as it waded the river at Davis Ford. Behind them, among the twenty thousand Confederates, came many Tennesseans who hoped that their stay in their native state would be a long one. General Schofield started part of his command north in order to avoid being surrounded. He left some men behind temporarily to prevent S. D. Lee's men from coming across the river and falling upon the rear of his army. By mid-day his troops were at various points between Columbia and Spring Hill. Other Federal soldiers were east of

Columbia, keeping an eye on Hood for fear that he might decide to turn and take Schofield's force in flank.

The Confederate commander made no attempt to roll up Schofield's left flank. He meant to get to Spring Hill as quickly as possible and thereby cut the Federals off entirely from Nashville. Were he able to accomplish this, Hood felt he could defeat Schofield and then turn toward Nashville and the continuation of his victorious campaign through Tennessee and Kentucky.

The Confederate cavalrymen drove their Union counterparts as far as Mount Carmel during the morning. The majority of the Southern horsemen then turned west to Spring Hill, leaving a force of sufficient size to keep Brigadier General James Wilson's Yankee cavalry out of the picture for a time. A small Federal force garrisoned Spring Hill, and when Forrest's men appeared east of town these soldiers were ready to meet them. The first Rebel advance was repulsed. By the time a second attack could be mounted, aid arrived in the form of two infantry brigades from the Fourth Corps. General Forrest was notified by Brigadier General James R. Chalmers that they now faced a large force of entrenched infantry. The Confederate cavalry commander scoffed at this notion and ordered Chalmers to make the charge. When this second attack was easily repelled, Forrest remarked to Chalmers: "They were in there, sure enough, weren't they Chalmers?" [1] The Confederate horsemen then spent the next few hours occupying the enemy with skirmish fire and waiting for the arrival of Hood and the rest of the army.

By about 3:00 P.M., the vanguard of the Confederate infantry was crossing Rutherford Creek some two and one-half miles south of Spring Hill. From this point the recollections of the participants became somewhat confusing and contradictory. General Hood, in later years, wrote that from the crossing at Rutherford Creek he could see Union wagons and men hurrying along the Franklin Pike toward Spring Hill. He ordered General Cheatham to send his troops to take possession of the road in question and prevent its further use by the enemy. Lieutenant General Stewart's corps, Hood added, would immediately be sent to support the movement. General Hood believed that he had outraced the bulk of Schofield's army to Spring Hill. Hood, however, must have known that there were Federal troops in the town because Forrest's cavalry had been skirmishing with them since early afternoon. Cheatham's orders, however, were to block the road. No mention was made of trying to overwhelm the defenders of the village. As events soon proved, it might have been wise to assign the capture of the town as the primary objective and the closing of the pike as a secondary goal.

As a component of Cheatham's corps, Cleburne's division turned left and advanced *en echelon* across the fields toward the Franklin Pike. Lowrey's brigade was on the right with Govan's brigade behind and to the left and Granbury's brigade on the extreme left of the division. As Cleburne's men passed out of view over a small rise Major General Bate's division arrived from Columbia. General Cheatham immediately ordered Bate to form his division with its right on Cleburne's left and to advance upon the Franklin Pike. By the time Bate's men formed a line of battle, however, they had lost sight of Cleburne's division.

There were more Federal troops in the neighborhood now but their exact whereabouts and strength were unknown. As Lowrey's men emerged from a small wooded area, they located the enemy — Major General Luther P. Bradley's brigade — which was posted south of the town and just to the right of a grove of trees. When the leading edge of the Confederate battle line passed through these trees it came under the sights of the Forty-second Illinois and the Sixty-fourth Ohio. For a few moments it was like a carnival shooting gallery as sheets of flame issued forth from the Union position and large gaps were ripped in the Rebel ranks. At about the same time two Union artillery pieces opened up from near the pike. The Confederates reeled for a moment in the face of this fierce and unexpected onslaught. Recovering quickly, the battle line wheeled to the right and resolutely attacked. A Union veteran of that battle later wrote that the Confederates,

> pulled down the rims of their old hats over their eyes, bent their heads to the storm of missiles pouring upon them, changed direction to their right on double-quick in a manner that excited our admiration, and a little later a long line came sweeping through the wide gaps between the right of the 42d and the pike, and swinging in towards our rear. Our line stood firm, holding back the enemy in front until the flank movement had progressed so far as to make it a question of legs to escape capture . . .[2]

The four Yankee regiments were overpowered by the well seasoned Confederate division. After a few minutes Cleburne's men began chasing their antagonists back toward the village. As the fleeing Federals crossed a branch of McCutcheon Creek, they unmasked a row of reserve artillery. Eight cannons opened fire over the heads of the Yanks and into the advancing Rebels. Cleburne probably thought that he had come up against a heavily reinforced enemy position and he quickly ordered his troops back out of range of the big guns. While all this was going on, Granbury's men were so far to the left that they didn't suffer much from the fire of Bradley's men. They were instead raked by the fire of the Thirty-sixth Illinois, which was in support of the two guns posted near the pike.

It was nearly dark when Cheatham's third division, that of Major General John C. Brown, was hurried into position on Cleburne's right with orders to attack immediately. When General Brown arrived at his assigned position, he observed that the enemy line extended far to his right and that to attack would be to invite annihilation. He informed General Cheatham of the situation and waited for further orders. Bate, by this time, had almost reached the Franklin Pike. He had never caught up with Cleburne and did not know that that general had turned to the right. Bate had pushed straight ahead, and his skirmishers were firing on Union soldiers hurrying up the road to Spring Hill when orders came to close up on Cleburne's left. General Brown was ordered to refuse his right brigade and make the attack as previously ordered. Brown balked, and all Confederate offensive action halted for the day.

General Stewart's corps, which Hood had promised would closely support Cheatham's movement, was held south of Rutherford Creek until after dark. When the Confederate commander finally sent Stewart across the creek he ordered him to pass around Cheatham's right and block the Franklin Pike north of the village. Stewart started out over the dark and unfamiliar roads when a later order from Hood directed him to form on Cheatham's right. Stewart was perplexed by the two orders so he halted his men and rode to Hood's headquarters for clarification. It was nearly midnight, and Hood told Stewart to let his men camp for the night where they were. The movement could continue in the morning.

During the night the men of the Texas Brigade slept within about a hundred yards of the Franklin Pike. Some of the men occasionally heard movement along the road but assumed that it was caused by Bate's men moving up. Captain Richard H. English, of General Granbury's staff, went over to investigate and got himself captured by members of the Twenty-third Michigan, who were quietly hastening northward. It seems incredible that none of English's friends raised the alarm when he failed to come back. At about midnight it was reported to General Hood that Union troops were using the pike. What happened next is subject to dispute.

Hood claimed that he ordered General Cheatham to send some men to obstruct the pike so that the Confederates could attack in the morning. Cheatham claimed that he sent men to cover the pike but that they found everything quiet and returned to their camp. The intriguing piece of the puzzle was supplied by Hood's adjutant, Major

Mason. He confessed that Hood's order to Cheatham, which he himself was to have written and sent, was never delivered. No matter which of these versions is correct it appears that some Confederate soldiers from Major General Edward Johnson's division entered the pike and found nothing to alarm them. Almost certainly they reached the road between elements of Schofield's column. It must always remain a mystery why someone — Hood, Cheatham, Cleburne, *anyone* — did not post troops so as to deny the use of the Franklin Pike to the enemy army.

General Hood was extremely upset when he awoke the next morning to find Spring Hill empty and Schofield's army well on its way to Franklin. He felt that he had been cheated of the best opportunity he had ever had to strike a decisive blow in this campaign — perhaps in the entire war. He tried to lay the blame for his failure on General Cheatham, whom he had only recently recommended for promotion to lieutenant general. Cheatham was partially at fault — but only partially — as were Generals Cleburne, Granbury, Bate, and Hood himself. Hood even attempted to blame the very backbone of his army — the infantrymen. He wrote that his army seemed "unwilling to accept battle unless under the protection of breastworks. . . ." [3] By the end of the day Hood's veterans would disprove his lowly regard for them.

It was about eighteen miles to Franklin, and the Army of Tennessee wasted no time in getting underway. Hood still felt that he could crush Schofield's army if he could catch it before it got too close to Nashville. A. P. Stewart's corps led the way, followed by Cheatham. S. D. Lee's men arrived at Spring Hill from Columbia about 9:00 A.M., and, after a short rest, set out after Cheatham. By the middle of the afternoon Stewart and Cheatham arrived in the vicinity of Franklin.

The village of Franklin lies bounded on the north and east by the Harpeth River. General Schofield's men occupied a line of earthworks that completed the enclosure of the town on the south and the west. Schofield had hoped to get his army across the Harpeth and on the road to Nashville before the Confederates caught up with him. As his men hastily repaired the only remaining bridge to make it serviceable for wagons and artillery, he had the remainder of his force man the aforementioned defenses.

Stewart's vanguard dispersed some far-flung Union pickets and the Confederates began to deploy for battle. Stewart's corps peeled off to the right while Cheatham's men stayed on the main Columbia–Franklin pike. About three miles south of Franklin lies a low range of hills known as Winstead Hill. It was here that the Confed-

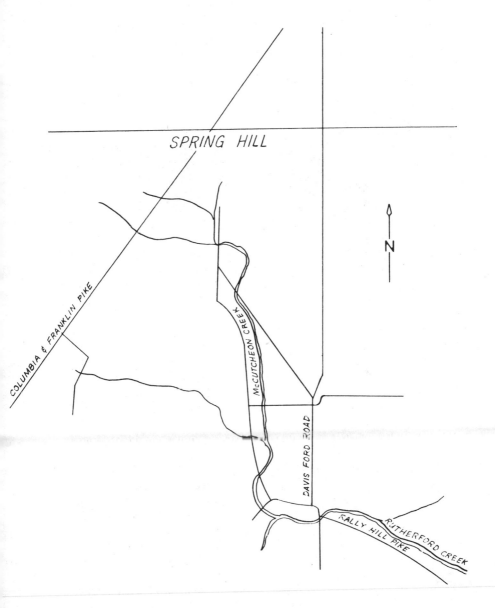

The Battle of Spring Hill

erate battle lines began forming. Cleburne's left brigade, Granbury's, formed with its left resting on the pike. Just across the pike to
the left were the men of Brown's division.

Veterans of the charge that was about to be made would later
recall it as being closer to the picture book image of a military attack
than any others they ever experienced. At about four o'clock on that
unseasonably warm afternoon, the bands started playing patriotic
airs. The long lines of men moved forward to the strains of *Dixie*, and
the *Bonnie Blue Flag*. The skirmishers who had been sent out earlier,
had stopped after advancing two or three hundred yards and were
exchanging shots with the nearest enemy line. As the Rebel battle
line swept forward it caught up with the skirmishers and kept on
going. On the other side of the field, and in the direct path of the
Texas Brigade, was the brigade of Colonel Joseph Conrad. The men
of Conrad's brigade belonged to Brigadier General George Wagner's division of the Fourth Corps. They had been posted about a
quarter of a mile in advance of the main line of Union works. They
had orders to remain in this position as long as they could.

Granbury's men continued across the open field, holding their
fire. Colonel Conrad ordered his sergeants to stand in the rear of his
line with fixed bayonets to discourage any of his men from running
away. He received new instructions about this time telling him to
fall back to the main line of works if the Confederate attack was too
heavy. Conrad had many new recruits in his brigade and he feared
that an order to retreat with the enemy so close would cause the new
men to panic. If this happened their terror might communicate itself
to the veteran troops and a wholesale rout would be the result. The
Union commander resolved, therefore, to stay where he was for as
long as he could.

Finally the two lines of combatants were close enough and both
sides opened fire. The Confederates paused for a brief moment and
then came on with renewed anticipation of a victory. The defenders
had time to fire seven or eight shots each before they were overwhelmed. As orders were issued to fall back, a footrace began. The
Federals were running for their very lives. The Confederates continued to pour forth a destructive fire as they chased after the Yankees.
The Yanks in the main line behind Conrad's brigade held their fire
for fear of hitting some of Conrad's men.

As the last of the retiring Federals cleared the breastworks, the
men who had been waiting there opened fire. In some instances,
Confederate soldiers were so close behind their quarry that they
crossed the works with them and were quickly captured or killed.
Federal artillery, triple shotted with cannister, cut huge swaths in

the Rebel ranks. The fighting on the east side of the pike was frenzied as bayonets and rifle butts were freely wielded. Within the Union trenches pandemonium held brief reign. The recent arrivals got in the way of the men of the Twenty-third Corps who were already there. In an effort to alleviate the confusion, Lieutenant Colonel Edwin L. Hayes of the 100th Ohio ordered the Fourth Corps men in his sector to fall back to a second line of works where they could regroup. Some of Hayes's men thought the order was for them too and they started for the rear.

Colonel Hayes was able to rally his men before they had gone too far. With the help of the Twelfth and the Sixteenth Kentucky, as well as the reserve troops of Colonel Emerson Opdyke's brigade, they fought their way back toward the breach in the line. Hand-to-hand combat was fierce, but the Federals were finally able to force the Southerners out of the trenches. Some of the Confederates made their way to the rear but most of them stayed against the forward slope of the Union earthworks. It was soon dark but for the next few hours the fighting continued. Soldiers of both sides held their rifles as far over the works as they could without exposing themselves and fired into the enemy huddled below. Finally it grew still. The Battle of Franklin was over.

The battle had lasted only a few hours, but the human destruction was frightful. Bodies of soldiers killed at the beginning of the contest were hit again and again and were found literally riddled with bullets. Blood flowed like water in the drainage ditches along the sides of the pike. The Army of Tennessee had lost almost six thousand men — men for whom there were no replacements — in killed, wounded, and captured. Also among the casualties were twelve general officers Major General Patrick R. Cleburne was killed there — as was Brigadier General Hiram B. Granbury. Three other generals were killed, one was captured and six were wounded — one mortally. General Hood would not easily find high quality replacements for Cleburne, Granbury, and the other generals who were lost that day. Worse for the nation, there were no replacements at all for the six thousand brave soldiers who were lost.

Who won the Battle of Franklin? The Confederates had attempted to drive Schofield's command into the river and they had been stopped. They were not the winners. The Union army retreated during the night and left the field of battle in the hands of the Confederates. They were not the winners either. Looking at the battle as a single disconnected military contest, it would appear to have been a Confederate victory. The Confederates had, after all, forced the eventual retreat of the enemy. Looking at the battle as a part of

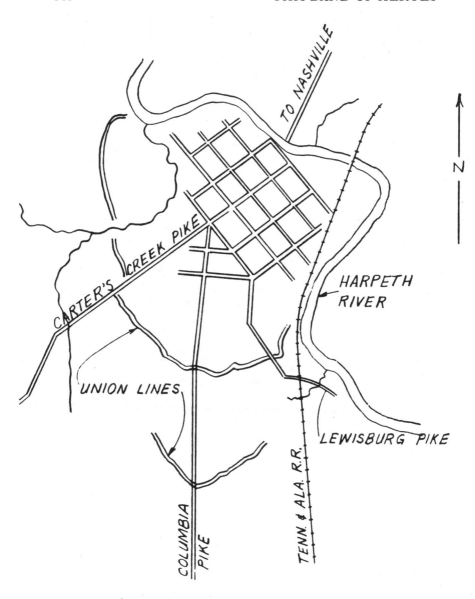

The Battle of Franklin

— After the *Official Records*

the Southern war effort, however, shows it to have been a tragic loss for the South. Hood's losses were almost triple those of Schofield. In addition, the North still had vast manpower reserves upon which to draw to replace the men she lost. There were no more reserves for the Army of Tennessee.

At this point General Hood should have seen the proverbial handwriting on the wall. His army had suffered a severe beating at Franklin by an opponent who then fell back to a fortified city, Nashville, where reinforcements waited. The Confederates were demoralized. The men of the Texas Brigade felt that they had been betrayed by General Hood. The recent battle had not been the type of fighting that had been promised them. It had certainly not been fought on ground of Hood's choosing. Some of the men had stronger feelings and cursed Hood for a murderer.—

> The wails and cries of widows and orphans made at Franklin . . .
> will heat up the fires at the bottomless pit to burn the soul of Gen
> J B Hood for Murdering their husbands and fathers at that place
> that day. It can't be called anything else but cold blooded Murder.
> . . . 'Vengeance is mine Sayeth the Lord' and it will surely over-
> take him.[4]

On the morning of December 1, 1864, the crippled Army of Tennessee, after burying the dead of both sides, set out for Nashville. The vacancies in the command structure created by the fearful losses at Franklin had to be filled. Brigadier General James A. Smith, one-time commander of the Texas Brigade, replaced the fallen Cleburne as division commander and Captain Edward T. Broughton of the Seventh Texas assumed command of the brigade. These changes illustrate the conditions of all the Confederate armies at this stage of the war. A captain filled a position normally held by a brigadier general.

Nashville lay, for the most part, within a bend of the Cumberland River. The city had been in Federal hands for over two years and in that time its defenses had been constantly improved. The lines of works described irregular and somewhat concentric arcs, with each end resting on the river and completely enclosing the city. Major General George Thomas was in command of all Union troops here. In addition to the men already at Nashville, and Schofield's recently arrived command, there were two divisions fresh from Missouri, about five thousand men from Chattanooga, and several Negro regiments. Hood was badly outnumbered.

The Confederate army took up a position along the hills south of Nashville and began to dig in. General Hood knew that a direct

attack on the city would be suicidal. The only chance for Confederate success, he felt, would be to wait for Thomas to attack "and, if
favored by success, to follow him into his works." [5] This was the
same sort of strategy employed by Braxton Bragg at Chattanooga
the year before but the unfortunate results of that campaign do not
seem to have impressed the Confederate high command enough to
caution Hood. The situation at Nashville was, in fact, less favorable
to Southern hopes than had been the case at Chattanooga. At Chattanooga, the Confederate lines overlapped the Union defenses and a
relative state of siege existed. At Nashville, the number of Confederate soldiers present was so pitifully reduced that only about half of
the Yankee line was covered. There was no shortage of food or clothing for the men in the city this time, but out along the hills to the
south were cold, hungry soldiers, many of whom were barefoot.

Hood arrayed his troops with Cheatham's corps on the right,
S. D. Lee's corps in the center, and Stewart's corps on the left. On
the right side of Cheatham's corps the Texas Brigade was assigned
to a position slightly in advance of the rest of the line. The Texans
worked hard to make their position as secure and as comfortable as
they could. They dug a small ditch in front of their works and also
made use of stout head logs. Their sleeping quarters were anything
but elegant. Some of the men built small huts with fence rails covered with dirt and others improvised shelters from cornstalks. Some
of the men who were without shoes wrapped their feet in rags or
pieces of blankets. Brigade shoe shops were established, but because
of the scarcity of leather about all that could be done was repair
work. No new shoes were made. A soldier with worn-out shoes could
go to the cobblers and have pieces of green cowhide stretched over
the shoes with the hair to the inside. The soldier would then be
forced to wear the shoes until the hide cured somewhat and shrank
tightly to his foot. Another reason for leaving the shoes on all the
time was so some less fortunate fellow soldier wouldn't steal them.
Rations were typically poor and firewood rapidly became scarce.
The men of the Army of Tennessee had little to be optimistic about.

Meanwhile, in Washington, President Lincoln and Secretary of
War Stanton were worried about what General Hood would do
next. Throughout the first week in December there was a steady
stream of messages back and forth between Washington and Nashville. General Thomas was urged to take the offensive and drive
Hood back out of Tennessee. Thomas, on the other hand, was never
known for making a move before he was ready. He patiently wired
Washington that he could not move until he had more horses for his
cavalry and artillery. The countryside was scoured for serviceable

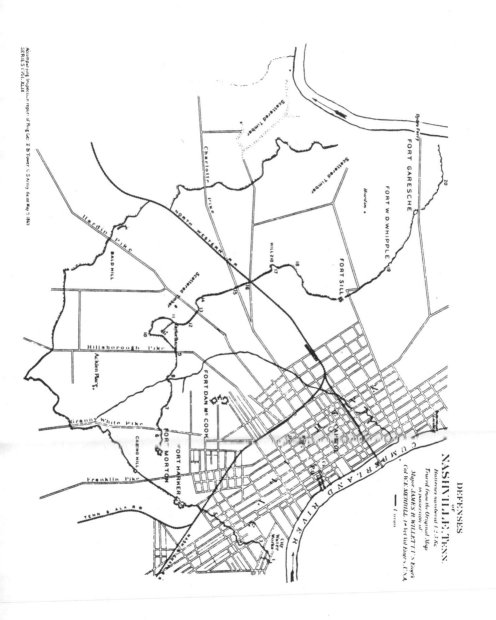

DEFENSES
OF
NASHVILLE, TENN.
Batteries numbered 1-2 &c
Traced from the Original Map
in possession of
Major JAMES R WILLETT, U.S. Rivers
Col W.E. MERRILL, 1st Vet Vol Engrs, U.S.A.
—— *Union*

animals. Farm horses, carriage horses, and even circus horses were pressed into service.

While Thomas was collecting horses, General Hood was repeating another phase of the siege of Chattanooga. Just as General Bragg had sent a large portion of his force off to Knoxville, Hood now sent General Forrest with most of his cavalry, along with General Bate's division of infantry, to operate against the Federal garrison at Murfreesboro.

On December 9th the weather took a turn for the worse. The temperature plummeted and a sleet storm covered everything with ice. Firewood was, by this time, almost all gone and the suffering was intense. General Grant ordered Thomas replaced but countermanded the order pending a break in the weather. Thomas was almost ready to move. The ice melted on the 14th, and that evening General Thomas called his corps commanders together for a final briefing. The attack would be made the next morning with the Union left keeping the enemy busy in its front while the right made a giant wheeling movement and attempted to roll up the Rebel left flank. The Federal troops were up before the sun on the 15th and anxiously waiting for orders to get under way. A heavy fog finally lifted about eight o'clock and the battle for Nashville began.

The Union troops on the left were members of Major General James B. Steedman's Provisional Division. This command was made up of two brigades of Negro troops along with detachments from General Sherman's army who had been unable to rejoin their proper commands. As the battle lines advanced and firing became general the heat of battle warmed the soldiers of both sides.

The earthworks thrown up by the Texans did not look very formidable to the oncoming Federal infantry. When the position was stormed, however, it became apparent how strong both the fortification and the defenders really were. The Eighteenth Ohio and the Second Battalion of the Fourteenth Corps attacked side by side. The Confederates greeted them with a hail of bullets. About a hundred members of the Ohio regiment managed to gain a temporary lodgement within Confederate lines but they received no support. The men of the Second Battalion,[6]

> . . . were mostly new conscripts, convalescents, and bounty jumpers, and on this occasion, with but few honorable exceptions, behaved in the most cowardly and disgraceful manner. The enemy, seeing the men hesitating and wavering, fired a heavy volley and stampeded the whole line.

With the Second Battalion in full retreat, the Ohioans could not hold out in the face of the fire now brought to bear upon them. They too withdrew. After that there were no more serious attempts to overrun the right side of the Confederate line. The Yanks were content to keep the Rebs occupied just enough so that they could not send troops to other, more threatened, parts of the line.

Although the Texans and the rest of the men on the right of the Confederate line were able to turn back the enemy attack, the battle was not going well on the left. The Federal turning movement got under way with the pivot point at about where the Confederate line bent back along the Hillsboro Pike. This part of the line was covered by five unfinished forts, or redoubts, which had each been designed to accommodate an artillery battery and its infantry support. As the huge blue spoke swung around from the northwest the undermanned redoubts began to fall. Redoubt #5 fell first and then, after three hours of intense fighting, Redoubt #4 was also captured. Each of these forts had been stoutly defended and the attackers were made to pay a price for their capture.

General Stewart, in charge of the Confederate left, urgently requested that Hood reinforce his position against the massive Federal attack. Since Lee's corps had been practically idle all day, Hood drew troops from there and hurried them to the left. A short time later most of Cheatham's corps, including the Texas Brigade, was also sent to the aid of Stewart. By this time three of the redoubts had been captured and the other two had been abandoned. Soon a blessed nightfall put an end to the fighting for the day.

The Confederates were roughly handled during the first day's battle and Hood was forced to consolidate his force even more. The Union army had pushed the Rebels about two miles, and General Thomas felt that Hood would use the cover of darkness to begin a full scale retreat. For all of Hood's other faults he was not a quitter. When daylight broke on the morning of December 16th, the Army of Tennessee was still in the trenches. The new line of defense ran from Peach Orchard Hill on the right to a hill approximately two and a half miles to the west which has since come to be known as Shy's Hill. Both ends of the line were refused to the south and the Texans took up a position at the west end of the line just south of Shy's Hill.

By 6:00 A.M. the Federal infantry was on the move all along the line. Brigadier General James Wilson's twelve thousand man cavalry corps had played a major role in the previous day's fighting and by mid-morning it, too, began to move. The dismounted Union cavalrymen were behind Hood's main line facing north. Opposite them, defending a fishhook in the Confederate line, was Cleburne's old division. Wilson's repeating carbines crackled viciously but the Confederates stood firm. In fact, the defense was so stubborn that it caused General Wilson to have second thoughts about his effectiveness. He suggested to General Thomas that his men might be better employed on the left end of the Federal battle line but Thomas turned down his request.

Early that morning General Steedman finally realized that the Confederate troops in his front had been withdrawn. He cautiously advanced until he reached Peach Orchard Hill and then launched a series of unsuccessful assaults on the men of Lee's corps. Throughout the morning these attacks were successfully turned back, but General Hood grew increasingly concerned. Was it possible that Thomas had reversed his earlier battle plan — and now meant to turn the Confederate right? To counter such a possibility, Hood withdrew the Texas Brigade and two others shortly after noon and ordered them back to the right. It began raining as the Texans took up the march, but this was probably no more than a minor irritation to men in the midst of a battle. When they reached the extreme right of the army they were put into line and helped stave off another Union attack.

If Hood still entertained any doubts about Thomas's battle plan these doubts were soon disspelled. When Cleburne's three brigades were pulled out of their positions near Shy's Hill, the remaining men had to stretch their line even thinner to try to make up the difference. By now the superiority in firepower and numbers enjoyed by the Federals could no longer be denied. The bluecoated soldiers must have sensed that one of the two remaining Confederate armies of any size had been knocked to its knees. While Granbury's brigade helped keep Steedman's Negro troops at bay on the right, the left crumbled. Just as at Chattanooga, the battle seemed to be going well on the Confederate right when the left and center broke.

By three–thirty in the afternoon the Texas Brigade was on the road toward Franklin. Soon the entire Army of Tennessee was streaming to the rear. Troops from Lee's corps formed the rear guard along with General Chalmers's Confederate cavalry. These troops were able to hold off pursuit until the army had had a chance to reform itself into recognizable units. For the next ten days the army hurried south. Union cavalry constantly harassed the rear guard as the rest of the army struggled onward through the mud and slush of a cold Tennessee December.

On Christmas morning, the head of the gray column reached the Tennessee River near Bainbridge, Alabama. Artillery was posted to discourage patrolling gunboats and a pontoon bridge was thrown across. Early the next morning the men began to cross. As the tired and barefoot soldiers trudged across the bridge they sang a parody of the *Yellow Rose of Texas:*[7]

> *So now we're going to leave you, our hearts*
> *are full of woe;*
> *We're going back to Georgia, to see our*
> *Uncle Joe.*
> *You may talk about your Beauregard, and sing*
> *of General Lee,*
> *But the gallant Hood of Texas, played hell*
> *in Tennessee.*

The Tennessee campaign was over. General Hood estimated that it had cost him ten thousand casualties. Worse than that — it had cost the Confederacy an army. The once proud Army of Tennessee was reduced to about the size of one full strength division. Had Hood bypassed Nashville and gone on north there might have been different results. The people in the North were tired of war. If Hood could have made it into Kentucky — and threatened Louisville or Cincinnati — the Federal government might have been forced to sue for peace, recognizing the independence of the Confederacy. Hindsight is always better than foresight, however, and Hood undoubtedly felt that the course he followed was the best one.

CHAPTER ELEVEN

The End of the War

The shattered Army of Tennessee marched through Tuscumbia, Alabama, and on into Mississippi. On New Year's Day, 1865, the men camped near Corinth. Most of the soldiers of the Texas Brigade devoted at least a few minutes that day to wondering what the new year would bring. Peace would finally come, it now seemed certain, but at a tremendous price. The dreams of independence were gone except in the hearts of a very few. Peace would come but it would be under Yankee rule — a bitter pill to swallow for men who had spent three or more years trying to overthrow that rule. Thoughts also turned to New Year's Days of the past. On New Year's Day of 1864, the Texans had been snug in their winter camp near Dalton, Georgia. In 1863, they had been comfortably ensconced in their winter huts at Arkansas Post. In 1862, most of them had been home with families. Would they ever see their loved ones again?

By January 10, 1865, the army reached Tupelo, Mississippi, where it was to rest and refit. General Hood had never been as popular with the rank and file as Joe Johnston had been and now his stock had fallen to a new low. With the results of his disastrous Tennessee campaign weighing heavily upon him, Hood requested that he be relieved of command on January 13th. His request was quickly granted and the Army of Tennessee was put under the command of Lieutenant General Richard Taylor.

General Taylor, son of former president Zachary Taylor, had prior military service in the War with Mexico. When the Civil War broke out he was a senator in the Louisiana legislature. He went to war as colonel of the Ninth Louisiana Infantry and quickly rose in rank. After successfully turning back Union Major General Nathaniel P. Banks's Red River Expedition in April of 1864, Major General Taylor was promoted to the rank of lieutenant general. He was a stranger to the Army of Tennessee but he would not be around long enough to get very well acquainted.

Many soldiers, evidently seeing the handwriting on the wall, began to desert and head for home. It was evident to them that the war was lost. They had done their best but Southern independence was not to be. They did not feel that there was anything left from which to desert. They were merely going home to see to their families and to try to get a crop planted. In an effort to bolster morale and hold his new army together, General Taylor ordered every fifth man to be furloughed. In the Texas Brigade the lucky men were selected by drawing lots. It is not known how this move affected the overall morale of the army but the twenty percent who were sent home certainly had their spirits lifted. In addition to the attrition caused by desertion and furloughs, some four thousand men were sent to aid in the defense of Mobile, Alabama.

On January 23d, General Hood issued his farewell address to the army and officially turned over the command to General Taylor. He expressed his "thanks for the patience with which you have endured your many hardships during the recent campaign. I am alone responsible for its inception. . . . I urge upon you the importance of giving your entire support to the distinguished soldier who assumes command . . ." [1] By the time this was written, Taylor's days as army commander were already numbered. One of the three corps of the army had already left for the Carolinas, another left two days later, and the third would depart within a week. General Taylor, having inherited two army corps, ordered them both to the east within a week and was then an army commander without an army.

The Texas Brigade left Tupelo by train on January 25th headed for Mobile. The decrepit old boxcars and flatcars were crowded with soldiers. Immediately upon reaching Mobile the troops were put aboard a riverboat and started up the Tensaw River. They disembarked at Tensaw Landing and were transported by rail to Montgomery, Alabama.

Either the troops were ready for a drinking spree of gigantic proportions, or for some unknown reason the city of Montgomery and its inhabitants had incurred the wrath of the Texas and Arkansas troops camped nearby. After dark, contrary to orders, these soldiers began slipping into town. The first stops, as always, were the saloons. Before long most of the men were in advanced stages of intoxication. At one point a barrel of whiskey was rolled out into the street and opened up. A crowd of soldiers quickly gathered and while some of them undoubtedly used cups to dip out the brew, many were reported to have drunk out of the barrel like horses at a watering trough. Tempers flared and fistfights were frequent. One member of the Texas Brigade wrote years later that,

> Some made it into camp that night, some came in in time for roll-call after daylight. Some had one eye in a sling and some had two. Some didn't have as many ears nor as much hair as they took to town with them.[2]

The people of Montgomery were probably glad that the soldiers left the next day for Columbus, Georgia.

The train reached Columbus about dark. Banners of welcome were stretched overhead and tables laden with food were laid out at the depot. The people here were either sincerely glad to see the soldiers or were hoping to ward off a Montgomery-type incident with the bribing effects of good food, freely given. It didn't work. After the men were full of meats, cakes, pies, coffee, and other relative delicacies, they headed for the business district and the grogshops. After another night of revelry the troops were again put on the train and hurried eastward.

By noon the next day the Texas Brigade reached the village of Fort Valley, about sixty miles east of Columbus. The train stopped here and the women of the village were on hand with baskets of food for the soldiers. This brief stopover was marked by nothing more serious than some scattered incidents of rudeness, and the men were soon on their way to Macon. By this time the officers in charge of transportation for these troops seem to have caught on to the rowdy mood of the men. The train roared through Macon without even slowing down and headed for Milledgeville. The men camped in the woods outside of town and set out on foot the next day for Augusta.

As the soldiers marched, they crossed the path of Sherman's army. The sight of such utter desolation was hard to comprehend. There were no animals around, crops had been burned in the fields, and many stately Georgia plantation homes had been reduced to smoke-blackened chimneys and piles of rubble. The troops reached Augusta late one evening and most of them marched on through the city, crossed the Savannah River, and camped in the piney woods of South Carolina. There was some rambunctious merrymaking in Augusta that night, but most of the men were quiet and stayed in camp. Perhaps they reflected upon their own recent behavior in comparison with the havoc wrought by Sherman's bummers.

By early March 1865, the military situation in the Carolinas was truly desperate. General Sherman had burned his way from Atlanta to Savannah, and then started north toward Virginia. By now the Federal army was in North Carolina, headed for Goldsboro. General Hardee commanded various state guard and militia units. He was doing all he could with his pitiful force to hinder Sherman's progress. General Bragg, who had recently been in command of the garrison at Wilmington, was hurrying his men to join Hardee. The remnants of the Army of Tennessee were moving across the state from the west in an effort to link up with the rest of the Confederate troops in the area. General Joseph E. Johnston was resurrected from military limbo and given command of all the Confederate forces in Sherman's path.

The victorious Union soldiers of Sherman's command, some sixty thousand strong, were divided into two separate wings. The Left Wing was under the command of Major General Henry W. Slocum and consisted of the Fourteenth and Twentieth Corps. The Right Wing was made up of the Fifteenth and Seventeenth Corps and was led by Major General Oliver O. Howard. The Tenth and Twenty-third Corps were marching in from the seacoast and would give Sherman a total strength of about one hundred thousand men when they linked up. General Johnston still held out some hope that this immense army could be defeated. The only way this could be accomplished was for Johnston to attack and defeat the enemy in detail, and that is just what he intended to do.

On the morning of March 19, 1865, Johnston's small army, which continued to be known as the Army of Tennessee even though it was actually made up of remnants of several commands, lay in wait for Sherman's Left Wing near the town of Bentonville, North Carolina. As the men of the Fourteenth Corps moved along the road to Goldsboro, they ran into some Confederate cavalry skirmishers. Confederate artillery soon joined in but it was thought to be only a token effort at resistance. A message was quickly sent to General Sherman informing him of the action and assuring him that probably only a small force of Rebels was involved. Before much longer General Slocum would realize that he had underestimated the size of the opposition.

Slowly the Confederate cavalry gave way. They allowed themselves to be driven through the ranks of the patiently waiting infantrymen of General Bragg on the Confederate left. As the Union infantry hit Bragg's line they were momentarily stunned by the savagery of its defense. This was no mere scouting party! Sherman's men had come to blows with veteran Rebel troops. The Yanks soon retreated and began to throw up defensive works.

In mid-afternoon Johnston launched his counterattack and quickly developed a breach in the Union lines. As the Southerners poured through the gap the battle took on a semblance of the Battle of Chickamauga eighteen months earlier. At Chickamauga, the Confederates had rolled up the Federals after they got through the break. At Bentonville, this was not to be. The men of the Fourteenth Corps fell back when they saw that they were in danger of being cut off. The ragged gray army pushed the Yanks about a mile to where the Twentieth Corps was trying to deploy, and toward the end of the day this new Federal position was attacked. The fresh troops proved to be too much for Johnston's men, and the fighting slowly dwindled away as darkness fell. The Confederates gathered their dead and wounded and retired to the lines they had held that morning.

During the course of the battle, General Slocum had again sent a report to Sherman. This time, however, he urged the commanding general to hasten the Right Wing of the army to a junction with him at Bentonville, Sherman immediately ordered the requested movement. The men of the Right Wing were already tired from the day's march but off they went. After having marched all night, Major General Hazen's division arrived at the scene of conflict early the next morning.

The Battle of Bentonville was, for all practical purposes, over. Only skirmish fire punctuated the stillness on March 20th, as both sides realigned their works in preparation for more action. The left side of the Confederate line was forced to draw back away from the Goldsboro road when the Union reinforcements began to come along behind them. The Texas Brigade did not participate in the fighting as it was still en route from Raleigh. The Texans arrived in the middle of the morning and immediately went to work strengthening their part of the line.

By March 21st, both wings of Sherman's army were present and Johnston was tremendously outnumbered. The Confederate line was in the shape of a horseshoe with Mill Creek at its back and only one bridge across which they might retreat. Late in the afternoon, Major General Joseph A. Mower advanced his division on the Union right in a bid to capture the bridge. He pushed forward for a time with some success. In passing around a swampy area his three brigades became separated, and it was at this time that Confederate infantry and cavalry combined in a spirited counterattack. This assault was successful and Mower's men withdrew.

This last Confederate charge had a particularly sad side effect for General Hardee, who helped lead it. His sixteen-year-old son had begged him for years to be allowed to join the army. The general finally consented and permitted his son to enlist in the Eighth Texas Cavalry, the renowned Terry's Texas Rangers. A few hours later young Hardee was dead. His brief military career had consisted of one cavalry charge which, though successful, only delayed the inevitable for a few weeks.

The weary men of the Army of Tennessee fell back during the night. They crossed the bridge in the rain and retreated to Smithfield, where they set up camp. Sherman was content to let them go. He moved his troops to Goldsboro, where they found the Tenth and the Twenty-third Corps already encamped. The Confederates were now outnumbered by about five to one. Sherman could see that the end was near. He left his troops and hurried to City Point, Virginia, to confer with President Lincoln and General Grant as to the terms of surrender he should offer General Johnston. Lincoln was more concerned with the cessation of hostilities than he was about the actual terms. Almost any terms would satisfy him as long as the fighting stopped.

Early April 1865, found both armies reorganizing their command structures again. Sherman divided his men into four separate parts: the Army of Georgia under General Slocum; the Army of the Ohio under General Schofield; the Army of the Tennessee under General Howard; and the cavalry under Major General Judson Kilpatrick. On April 9th Johnston also restructured his army. The change that most affected the Texans was that they ceased to exist as a brigade. All eight Texas regiments were combined, renamed the First Consolidated Texas Regiment, and assigned to General Govan's brigade. The only other regiment in this new brigade was a similarly reconstituted Arkansas unit which included the Texans' old comrades of the Nineteenth and Twenty-fourth Arkansas regiments.

April saw other drastic changes in the war picture. On April 2d Richmond fell. Lee's army left its trenches at Petersburg, and headed west hoping to be able to escape into North Carolina, and join Johnston's army. Sherman left Goldsboro on April 10th and began to apply pressure to Johnston in order to delay any proposed junction of the two Rebel armies. Shortly thereafter word was received in both camps that General Lee had surrendered his army at Appomattox Court House, Virginia. Johnston now realized that there was no point in continuing to fight. He sent a message to Sherman on the 14th requesting a temporary armistice so that terms of surrender might be discussed.

The main Union force was located near Raleigh by this time,

while the Confederates were in the vicinity of Greensboro. The meeting between the two commanders and some of their aides took place between these locations in the home of a Mrs. Bennett at Durham Station, on April 17, 1865. Sherman had received word just before leaving for the conference that President Lincoln had been murdered. He broke the news to Johnston who was visibly moved. Sherman assured him that the president's death would not jeopardize their impending peace talks and a tentative agreement was arrived at the next day and sent to Washington for presidential approval.

The terms of this pact were generous. The Army of Tennessee would disband. The soldiers would return to their home states where they would turn in their arms to the state arsenals. Civil rights would be restored and respected and life would go on with a minimum amount of disturbance by the Federal government. These terms were immediately rejected by the vengeful authorities in Washington. Sherman was rebuked for being soft on the Rebels and General Grant insisted that the same terms be offered Johnston as had been offered General Lee.

While these high level discussions were going on the men of the Texas Brigade enjoyed a brief respite from the physical rigors of active campaigning. Emotionally, however, there was much agitation. They now admitted that the war was over and they would never have an independent southern government. They spent the idle days discussing their postwar plans and deciding the routes by which they would return home. This routine was broken by the discovery of two barrels of apple brandy buried beneath an old oak tree. The tree had blown down and left its treasure available for discovery by the ever thirsty soldiers. Almost everyone in the brigade partook of this treat, from the lowliest private on up to the officers, including chaplains. Many of the men got so drunk that when it started to rain late that afternoon they were either unable or unwilling to seek shelter. They slept wherever they happened to fall.

On April 26th the terms of surrender were finalized. All of the men would turn in their weapons and be paroled at Greensboro. Privately owned horses and mules could be retained and officers could keep their side arms. Transportation to their home states would be furnished to the Confederates by the Federal government wherever possible. In order to furnish protection to the defeated soldiers and to allow them to hunt game on their way home they were allowed to keep one rifle for every seven men (modified the next day to one rifle for every five men). It took several days for the paperwork to be completed regarding paroles so the soldiers of the late Confederacy lounged in their camps discussing their futures.

General Johnston issued an eloquent farewell address to the army in which he urged the men:

> ... to observe faithfully the terms of pacification agreed upon, and to discharge the obligations of good and peaceful citizens as well as you have performed the duties of thorough soldiers in the field. By such a course you will best secure the comfort of your families . . . and restore tranquility to our country. . . . You will return to your homes with the admiration of our people, won by the courage and noble devotion you have displayed in this long war. I shall always remember with pride the loyal support and generous confidence you have given me.[3]

On April 28th, perhaps in response to Johnston's farewell, he received a message reassuring him of the continued support of the Texas Brigade.

> We . . . respectfully desire to assure General Johnston of our un-diminished confidence and esteem; and fully sympathizing with him in the present issue of our affairs, do most cordially tender him the hospitality of our State and our homes (such as the future may provide for us.) [4]

The message was signed by Lieutenant Colonel William A. Ryan, the highest ranking officer remaining in the Texas Brigade, and seventeen other officers.

When the officials of the Confederate government fled Richmond, they had taken with them the little bit of money that remained in the Treasury. Now, with Richmond in enemy hands and the two largest armies surrendered, it seemed pointless to maintain the funds of a government that had ceased to exist. A large part of the money was therefore distributed to the men of the Army of Tennessee. It didn't go far. Each officer and man received about a dollar and a quarter. It was the first hard money that many of them had seen in years.

The surrender of an army is a novel experience for those being surrendered. The Texans had all been through this before at Arkansas Post, and in the case of the Seventh Texas, at Fort Donelson. Here, as in the other instances, the men were required to surrender their weapons. Even though there would be little use for the thousands and thousands of muskets that already filled government warehouses in the North, many bitter Rebels resolved that they would not add to the largess. Some swung their rifles by the barrels and splintered the stocks against trees and rocks. Others used the crotches of trees as makeshift vices. With the rifle barrel wedged between the tree branches and body weight applied to the stock, the gun soon had a barrel so twisted as to be beyond repair. This was all well and good and the Confederates doubtless felt that they were depriving the Yankees of a small portion of the traditional fruits of victory. A rumor soon cropped up, however, that no soldier would be paroled until he turned in his gun in serviceable condition. The rumor proved to be false but for a short time there were a lot of Confederates frantically trying to straighten their rifle barrels in the crotches of the same trees that were used earlier.

General Sherman kept his troops out of the Confederate camps, thereby sparing the Southern soldiers further humiliation. On May 1st Reverend J. B. McFerrin preached a farewell sermon to the Texas Brigade and on May 2d, paroles were issued. Four hundred and forty Texans from Granbury's old brigade signed paroles. They were all that was left of the over eleven thousand men who had served in the Texas regiments comprising the brigade (although there were quite a few men, not captured at Arkansas Post, who were still serving in the Trans-Mississippi Department). Early on the morning of May 3d, the Texans headed west with mixed emotions. They were relieved that at last the war was over. They were filled with regret at having lost. Veterans from Lee's army were already passing through the area on their way home, and some of the men from Granbury's brigade linked up with old friends from Hood's old Texas brigade for the return trip. They marched southwest to Salisbury, and then most of the men from Texas turned west toward Asheville, North Carolina, and the mountains of eastern Tennessee.

The men broke up into small groups of three or four to make travelling easier. They headed for Greenville, Tennessee, where they expected to board trains for Nashville. There were no schedules to meet, but still the men usually made about twenty miles per day. People living along the route were quite generous with their foodstuffs and gladly fed all who stopped at their homes. It didn't take long for the men to realize this — some of them would stop for meals every hour or so. They had not eaten that well in a long time!

After about two weeks the small squads of ex-soldiers began arriving in the vicinity of Greenville. A large contingent of Negro troops was camped near the city and relations between the two groups of former enemies were strained at best. As one group of Texans walked along a road near the Federal camp the ex-slaves lined both sides of the road and hurled insults at the Confederates. A white Federal officer, attempting to defuse this potentially dangerous situation, accompanied the Texans with his pistol drawn. Another group of Confederates had a similar experience but with much lighter overtones. Both sides traded insults in a somewhat good-natured vein. As the Texans neared the end of the blue gauntlet, an older black corporal gently chided his brothers in arms: "You'd better mind what you'se about, if one of dem dar white men gits hold on yer — dey will wear you off to a frazzle. One o' dem will whip 5 or 6 of you if he catch you out o' sight." [5] The experience with the black soldiers gave pause for reflection. Although they had faced black troops at Nashville, the Texans were still not quite used to seeing black men in any role other than one of subservience.

On May 22d, two trainloads of ex-Confederates left Greenville, headed for Nashville. The roundabout route took them through Knoxville and Chattanooga. Finally, three days and three or four minor train wrecks later, they reached Nashville. After spending a day there they boarded a steamer that took them down the Cumberland River to the Ohio, down the Ohio to the Mississippi, and down the Mississippi to New Orleans. Most of the Arkansas troops in the group were put ashore at Memphis. A lot of men headed for the eastern part of Texas changed boats at the mouth of the Red River, and headed up that river toward Shreveport. The remaining men reached New Orleans on the afternoon of June 1st and remained in the Crescent City about ten days before taking ship for Galveston.

This trip home was, of course, not the same for all members of the Texas Brigade. Many of them were still recovering from sickness or wounds when General Johnston surrendered. For them the journey home was often much slower and more difficult. Joseph McClure, for instance, of the Eighteenth Texas, was badly wounded in the fighting east of Atlanta on July 21, 1864. He spent almost a year convalescing before he felt able to travel. He started home from Georgia on July 15, 1865, riding the trains as much as he could, but hobbling along on crutches much of the way to Vicksburg, Mississippi. After a few days rest he walked on to Mount Prairie, Texas, where a friend loaned him a mule for the rest of his trip to Alvarado. The mule was a little friskier than McClure cared for and he wrote later that "to control the mule I had to leave one crutch. That ride almost wore me out." [6] In spite of all the difficulties encountered on his trek, McClure reached home August 15, 1865.

CHAPTER TWELVE

Aftermath

Texas was not as badly scarred by war as some of her sister states of the late Confederacy. There were no great campaigns within her borders, and no major battles were fought there. The soldiers of the Texas Brigade did not come home to total physical devastation of the countryside as did fellow Confederates from Virginia, Georgia, and the Carolinas. What the Texas veterans faced was emotional, psychological, and political devastation.

These men had done everything in their power to gain independence for the South. They had suffered untold hardships over the last three to four years. They had been starved, frozen, imprisoned, wounded, and forced to wage war with, in many cases, substandard equipment. Many of the men came home with wounds or illnesses that would measurably shorten their life spans. Some didn't come home at all. Had the goal they sought been attained, however, these nuisances would have been bearable. But they had lost. The South was not free. A feeling of futility must have filled these men. They had given every ounce of their courage at places like Arkansas Post, Chickamauga, and Franklin. They returned home to a grateful, but defeated, civilian population and tried to pick up the threads of their lives.

Adding to the emotional trauma, perhaps not even separable from it, was the psychological effect of the defeat. The victorious government in Washington lost no time in making certain that all rebellious spirit was forever crushed. Former Confederate soldiers and government officials were made to feel like second class citizens.

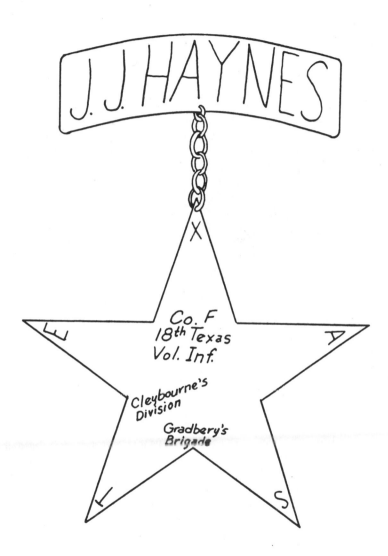

This reunion type badge has the names of both Generals Cleburne and Granbury misspelled. (Drawn from memory by the author after having seen it.)

The Freedmen's Bureau was established to secure newly granted rights to the former slaves. Slavery had never become as deeply entrenched in Texas as it had in other Southern states. Still, the sudden change in status of the Negroes was a bitter pill to swallow for the proud ex-Confederates.

Some semblance of stability finally began to emerge from the political chaos Texas experienced immediately after the war. A convention was called to revamp the state constitution so that the state could be readmitted to the Union. This activity was attended by much bickering between the Unionist and Secessionist delegates. The election for state government offices which followed in the summer of 1866, was also bitterly contested. The legislature was finally seated and they set about selecting two men to represent Texas in the U.S. Senate. One of the men thus chosen was Oran M. Roberts, former colonel of the Eleventh Texas Infantry Regiment, and the other was David G. Burnet, who had been President of the Republic of Texas. Both men had supported the Confederacy and were, therefore, refused admittance to the halls of Congress when they arrived in Washington. This incident illustrates the political frustration forced upon the people of Texas.

As the years rolled by, various restrictions were lifted, and life in Texas became endurable again. It would never be the same as it was before the war — but by the mid-1870s many of the old wounds were beginning to heal. Across the country veterans began to meet at regular intervals to mourn fallen comrades and to relive their exciting war experiences. Probably the first formal organization of ex-soldiers was the Military Order of the Loyal Legion of the United States. This group was formed before the war was even over, and its membership was restricted to Union officers. About a year later the largest of the Union veterans' groups was formed — the Grand Army of the Republic. National veterans' organizations for former Confederates were slower to form. The main reason for this was probably a fear that any such gatherings would be looked upon in the North as nothing more than collections of Rebel diehards trying to foment another insurrection. In spite of this, ex-Confederates across the South did gather on local levels just a few years after the war and the men of the Texas Brigade were no different.

The men of Granbury's brigade began holding reunions as early as 1872, and an actual brigade reunion association was formed in 1877, under the presidency of Congressman (and former colonel of the Tenth Texas Infantry Regiment) Roger Q. Mills. The first "official" reunion of this organization was scheduled to take place at Corsicana, Texas, in July of the following year, in conjunction with the annual reunion of Hood's Brigade Association. Information about these early reunions is scarce but by the mid-1880s these events had become very regular. Granbury's veterans formed a sort of reunion alliance with the survivors of Sul Ross's brigade (the Third, Sixth, Ninth, and Twenty-seventh Texas Cavalry Regiments), Mathew Ector's brigade (the Tenth, Fourteenth, and Thirty-second Texas Cavalry Regiments), and the Good–Douglas Texas Battery. These brigade associations met every year in a different town — usually in August. Then, for two or three days, the old soldiers would eat, sing songs, trade reminiscences, mourn departed friends, and listen to speeches.*

National veterans' conventions began to be held at different points throughout the South. There was a big gathering at Houston in 1895, which was attended by many former soldiers of Granbury's brigade. The 1901 reunion at Memphis, drew twenty members of the brigade, representing every Texas regiment in the brigade except the Fifteenth. (The Arkansans who had fought alongside the Texans do not appear to have attended any of these brigade reunions. It is not known whether they were not invited or whether the distance involved was too great.) Attendance at the reunions — whether at a national or brigade level — fluctuated over the years. In the early years many men were too busy raising families to take time out for reunions. In later years sickness and old age kept a lot of the former soldiers at home. At the 1884 reunion, which was held at Dallas, ninety-six men showed up. Every Texas regiment of the old brigade was represented except the Sixth. Seven years later only five men were present at the reunion at Fort Worth. This decline in attendance was not a trend, however, as there were fifteen men at the 1905 get-together at Tyler. The only regiments represented at that gathering were the Seventh, the Seventeenth, and the Eighteenth. There was a reunion at Terrell in 1921, but by that time most of Granbury's survivors were in their eighties. Not much information has been unearthed about the 1921 affair. It is not known how many veterans attended, but there cannot have been many.

The three main business items transacted at the reunions were the election of officers for the coming year, the preparation of a resolution of thanks to the citizens of the host community, and the selection of a meeting site for the following year's event. These things

---

* The official proceedings of the reunions of 1884, 1899, and 1900, can be found in the Texas State Archives. The proceedings of the 1905 reunion were reprinted in *Chronicles of Smith County, Texas* [Volume VIII, No. 1]. Contemporary local newspapers also devoted much space to these events.

were usually taken care of in short order so the veterans could get on
with their socializing. There were always plenty of fine things to eat,
patriotic old Southern songs were sung for and by the old soldiers,
and various dignitaries from within the brigade and elsewhere addressed the gatherings. An underlying theme of most of these
speeches was one of pride in having been Confederate soldiers.

A story is told of how General Robert E. Lee felt about having
fought for the South. After the war he was president of Washington
College — now Washington and Lee University — in Lexington,
Virginia. One of his students, a former soldier named Humphreys,
appeared to be overworking himself, and Lee asked him why he was
in such a hurry to finish his education. The young man replied that
he was trying to make up for the time he lost in the army. At this
point Lee told him, "Mr. Humphreys, however long you live and
whatever you accomplish, you will find that the time you spent in
the Confederate army was the most profitably spent portion of your
life. Never again speak of having lost time in the army." [1] This same
pride of having served the South was echoed and reechoed throughout the postwar Confederate reunions. At the 1891 reunion of Granbury's brigade, the aging veterans heard Judge A. J. Booty tell them
that "every Confederate soldier . . . was a hero and fought for a
cause of which none need be ashamed." [2] Many were the references
to the "grand old cause" and sometimes the speakers went a little
too far. One of the orators at the 1899 gathering at Garland heatedly
defended the right of the states to secede. The local newspaper de-
clared that his address, "while very commendable in some respects
was of rather inflammatory character; and calculated to stir up feelings and memories that should not be aroused." [3]

By the 1890s most of the old soldiers had gotten over any feelings of bitterness and hate. One of the speakers at the 1891 reunion
was a former Union soldier. He described how things had looked
from his side of the various battlefields during the war and praised
his former enemies for their courage and chivalry. The former Confederates thoroughly appreciated his remarks. Others from the
Union army sometimes attended the reunions of Ross's, Ector's and
Granbury's brigades. Many were present at the gathering at Weatherford in 1892, some wearing newly made blue uniforms. The former
enemies were described as having "the kindest of feeling for one another." [4]

As the years passed, the ranks of surviving veterans of both
armies were thinned by death. The men of Granbury's brigade are

all gone now. Some rest in well-kept family plots. Some lie in unmarked graves in Georgia and Tennessee. Some lie in northern cemeteries in Illinois and Ohio. Many of these men died before having had a chance to leave families, and now they lie forgotten. Their deeds, however, must never be forgotten.

Men of the Texas Brigade, Rest in Peace.

Appendix A

THE FLAGS OF GRANBURY'S BRIGADE

Confederate battle flags came in many designs, shapes, and colors. When the words "Confederate Flag" or "Confederate Battle Flag" are mentioned today most people think of the type of flag carried in the Army of Northern Virginia. This was the familiar red flag with blue Saint Andrew's cross bearing thirteen white stars. But there were many others. The battle flags carried by Major General Earl Van Dorn's corps in the Army of the West (and later in the Army of Tennessee) were red with single white or gold crescent moons in the upper left corners and thirteen white or gold stars sprinkled across the rest of the field. The regiments in Major General Leonidas Polk's corps, in the same army, carried different flags. Some were blue with white crosses, either upright or Saint Andrew's. Others were blue with upright red cross upon which were thirteen white stars. The flags of Major General William J. Hardee's corps were blue with a white disc in the center upon which the unit designation was painted.

Very few battle flags of Granbury's Texas Brigade survive today. One well preserved example is in the Texas State Archives. It is the flag of the Seventeenth and Eighteenth Texas that was captured at Atlanta. This cotton flannel flag is of the Hardee pattern and measures $31^1/_2$-by-$38^1/_2$-inches. The names of four battles are painted in white upon the badly faded blue field. It is interesting to note that the Texans chose the name "Tunnel Hill, Tenn." instead of "Missionary Ridge" to designate that particular battle. The flag was returned to the State of Texas in 1914.

Another Hardee pattern battle flag is in the collection of the United Daughters of the Confederacy Museum in Austin, Texas. It was carried by the Sixth and Fifteenth Texas in the later stages of the war. It, too, is of cotton flannel and it measures approximately 30-by-38-inches. It has a slightly different device in the center and carries no battle honors. This flag was presented to the State of Texas on November 25, 1885, by William J. Oliphant who had served in Company G of the Sixth Texas. Mr. Oliphant stated that the

. . . flag that was carried through the battles of the Georgia Campaign having become unrecognizable from being so badly shot-

165

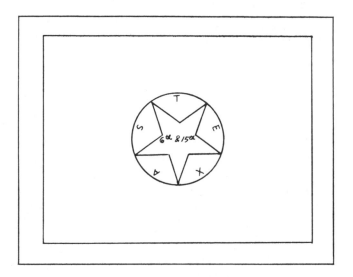

Flag of the Sixth and Fifteenth Texas.

torn and blood stained, another flag of which this tattered relic alone remains, was presented to the regiment and was borne through all the engagements that followed to the close of the war, including the fearful slaughter at Franklin, Tennessee.

The flag that was replaced may have had the designation of the Sixth, Tenth and Fifteenth Texas, rather than just the Sixth and Fifteenth. Oliphant went on to describe the flag as having

> . . . been the mute witness of many heroic deeds. . . . Many splendid specimens of Texas youth and manhood have gone down to their deaths beneath its folds, and it is the wish of those who have preserved it, that this flag should become the property of the State.[1]

Another regimental flag may be described with some degree of accuracy even though its whereabouts (if it still survives) is unknown. It is the flag surrendered by the Sixth Texas Infantry Regiment at Arkansas Post. A Galveston newspaper carried an article in 1885, which stated that this flag was in the possession of a Union veterans' organization in Williamsport, Pennsylvania. The article went on to describe the flag as having a representation of a hand pointing at a cluster of stars in the upper corner. Former members of the Sixth Texas living in Victoria, agreed that the flag that was described was not the one that they remembered being carried some twenty-three years earlier. Mrs. Richard Owens, who had sewn the original flag of the Sixth Texas, still lived in Victoria. It was decided to ask her if she could recall exactly what it had looked like.

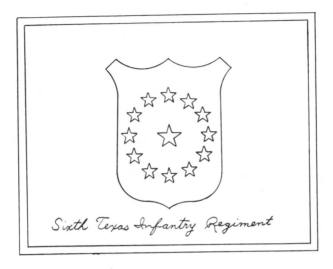

Flag of the Sixth Texas Infantry Regiment (author's interpretation of written description).

Mrs. Owens did better than to rely on her memory for she produced the patterns from which she had made the flag!

The flag was larger than most, although the exact dimensions are not now known. It was made of red merino and had a white silk fringe border. In the center of the flag was a 28-by-36-inch blue shield. A large Texas star was in the middle of the shield and twelve smaller stars were along the sides. Beneath the shield were the words SIXTH TEXAS INFANTRY REGIMENT sewn in white silk.

Colonel Garland had asked the ladies of Victoria to make a flag for his regiment while it was at Camp McCulloch, but due to a shortage of proper material the ladies were unable to comply with this request. Mrs. Owens was able to obtain some fabric through her husband's mercantile store, however, and she and her daughters commenced work on the flag. The regiment left Victoria before the flag was completed so it was sent on later. The men were in northern Texas when the flag arrived and they carried it proudly until forced to surrender it at Arkansas Post.

No other regimental flags are known by this author to exist, but a few company flags may be described. As stated in the text of this work most of the companies that went off to war carried some sort of flag. The use of company flags was so common, in fact, that when white surrender flags appeared among the ranks of the Twenty-fourth Texas at Arkansas Post, Colonel Deshler mistook them for the "small company flags, such as are frequently carried by volunteer companies." [2] The variations in design were probably more pronounced than among the regimental flags. Some of the descriptions given here are sketchy, at best, but serve to illustrate the diversity in design.

Sergeant W. W. Heartsill described the flag presented to his company as follows:

> It is formed of three bars, two feet in width, and fifteen feet long; the centre [*sic*] bar white, the other two red; at the upper left-hand corner, is a deep blue square to the depth of two bars; on one side of this square eight stars, (emblematical of the eight States that have seceded.) On the opposite side is the emblem of our State, the "LONE STAR." On one side of the Flag is painted in plain neat style, (by Mr N S Allen) the following; "SEMPER PARATUS." W. P. LANE RANGERS. by the ladies of Marshall, April 20th 1861.[3]

It is not known whether this flag was carried at Arkansas Post, since this company had existed as Company F of the Second Texas Mounted Rifles for over a year. The company was then remustered as an independent cavalry company under the command of Captain Sam Richardson. After the reorganization in Tennessee in the summer of 1863, the men of this company were assigned to Company L of the Sixth, Tenth and Fifteenth Texas.

Official reports of the Battle of Arkansas Post mention the capture of a Confederate flag bearing the inscription, *McCulloch Avengers*. Unfortunately no further description of this flag is available. Almost certainly it was carried by some company of the Twenty-fourth or Twenty-fifth Texas Cavalry Regiments. There are two fairly good reasons for suspecting this. First, these two regiments shared the right side of the breastworks — where the flag was captured — with the Sixth Texas. Second, the name "McCulloch Avengers," almost certainly refers to some wish to avenge the death of the Texan Ben McCulloch who was killed at the Battle of Elk Horn Tavern (or Pea Ridge), in early March of 1862. By this time all of the Confederate regiments who were at Arkansas Post had formed except the Twenty-fourth and the Twenty-fifth. It seems quite likely, therefore, that one of the companies in these regiments chose the name that later appeared on the captured banner.

The men of the Fifty-seventh Ohio captured a large cotton flag at Arkansas Post that was a variant of the First National Flag. It measures $37\frac{1}{2}$-by-$68\frac{1}{2}$-inches, and has a silk border. The name WILSON GUARDS appears in red letters on the center stripe, but the significance of the name is not definitely known. It may refer to a company from Wilson County, Texas. Wilson County, formed in 1860, lies just to the southeast of San Antonio, and this general area furnished a large number of men to the Sixth Texas Infantry Regiment. Another possibility is that this was the company flag of Captain William C. Wilson's Company D of the Tenth Texas Infantry Regiment. This flag was retained by Colonel William Mungen, commander of the Fifty-seventh Ohio, and has remained in his family.

Mention has been found of the company flags of Companies B and G of

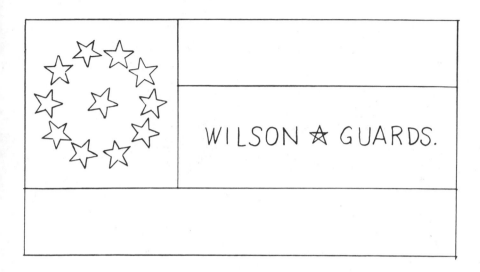

Flag of the Wilson Guards (possibly Company D, Tenth Texas Infantry Regiment).

the Sixth Texas. On the day that Company B left Belton for Camp Mc-Culloch, Captain Henry E. Bradford was presented a flag by Miss Kate Ludlow on behalf of the ladies of the town. Its description, however, is not known. Similarly, on the day that Company G left Austin, it was presented with "a beautiful silk flag, the Stars and Bars of the Confederacy." [4] Many people think of the familiar red battle flag with the blue Saint Andrew's cross when reference is made to the "Stars and Bars," but this inference is incorrect. The Stars and Bars was the First National Flag of the Confederate States of America, having three bars of red, white, and red respectively, and a blue union with white stars in a circle representing the seceded states. The battle flag was not officially adopted until 1863.

The flag presented to Company G of the Fifteenth Texas Cavalry was, as mentioned in the text, a "Bonnie Blue Flag" made of silk. The flag commonly referred to as the *Bonnie Blue Flag,* was a solid blue flag with a large white star in the center, but there were undoubtedly variations of this design.

The Goodman Museum in Tyler, Texas, has a Confederate flag in its collection that has been attributed to Company A of the Seventeenth Texas Cavalry. The flag, a Second National Flag, measures 46-by-69³/₄-inches, and is made of silk with red silk fringe on three sides. This flag was saved from capture at Arkansas Post by Ed Parker of Company A. There is a discrepancy in the story of this flag. The Confederate Congress did not adopt this flag pattern until almost four months after the fall of Arkansas Post. That leaves two possibilities for the origin of this flag. It might have merely

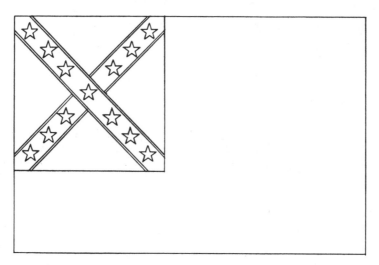

Flag said to have belonged to Company A, Seventeenth Texas Cavalry Regiment.

been an unofficial version of the flag that was to be adopted, but the likelihood of this is rather remote. More likely, it might have been carried later in the war by Company A of the Seventeenth Texas Consolidated Regiment Cavalry (Dismounted), which was composed of soldiers — including Ed Parker — who had escaped capture at Arkansas Post.

The ladies of Starrsville, a small community near Tyler, Texas, presented a flag to Captain Jonathan C. Robertson of Company C, Seventeenth Texas Cavalry. Although Captain Robertson was discharged before the Battle of Arkansas Post, his successor, Captain Bryan Marsh, made sure that the flag was well cared for. At the fall of Arkansas Post, Captain Marsh carefully hid the flag in the lining of his overcoat. Then, after Marsh was released from prison, he returned the flag to the ladies of Starrsville. Unfortunately, the location of this flag is not known.

There are certainly other flags in existence that were carried by the men of Granbury's Texas Brigade. If one assumes that each company of each regiment had a banner then there would have been almost a hundred flags in the eight Texas regiments. Those that are available for study, however, cannot help but stir strong emotions in anyone who has the good fortune to examine them. Perhaps others will come to light someday.

Appendix B

THE WEAPONS OF GRANBURY'S BRIGADE

The weapons carried by the men of Granbury's Texas Brigade were varied. Contemporary recruiting posters urged each prospective cavalry-man to furnish himself with a double-barreled shotgun, a large knife, and one or two pistols. Some soldiers undoubtedly came equipped with all of the ordnance mentioned in the recruiting posters while others probably rode off to war with antiquated flintlock squirrel rifles as their only weaponry. The double-barreled shotguns were preferred to the single shot rifles. Since a good deal of fighting on horseback was expected to be at very close range it was felt that two quick charges of buckshot would do more damage than a single rifle ball. The members of the Fifteenth Texas Cavalry who were en-gaged with the Fifth Kansas Cavalry at Orient Ferry found, however, that their shotguns were not very effective at long range.

Probably the most popular pistol on either side during the Civil War was the .36 caliber Model 1851 Colt. Called by its inventor the Navy model, this pistol was used by tens of thousands of cavalrymen. Colt had also pro-duced a bigger pistol since 1848, called the Dragoon model. These large re-volvers each weighed about four pounds and fired a .44 caliber bullet. Each of these guns had been in production for ten years or more when the war started, and there were many Texans who owned one or two of them. It can also be reasonably surmised that most other revolvers in production before the war, such as the Model 1858 Remingtons and the Whitney revolvers, were used by members of Granbury's brigade. For example, a photograph of John Scott Pickle of the Eighteenth Texas Cavalry shows him holding what appears to be a Whitney revolver.

Southern armsmakers also went into production and in most cases their weapons were copies of the popular Colts. In Texas, the pistol works of Tucker and Sherrard at Lancaster, near Dallas, built a small number of large Dragoon-type guns. At least one or two of these Texas-made handguns found their way into the possession of soldiers of Granbury's brigade before they left the state. Later, in 1864, several of the officers of the Seventh Texas Infantry Regiment purchased .36 caliber pistols from the Confederate gov-ernment arsenal at Macon, Georgia. These guns were probably the brass framed copies of the Whitney revolver, and are known as Spiller and Burr revolvers.

Knives were popular side arms early in the war on both sides, although much more so in the South. The sizes and descriptions of these items were even more varied than those of the guns. Everything from small dirks to huge Bowie knives were used. Some of the larger knives had their blades fashioned from old blacksmiths' files. These blades might be up to two inches wide and fourteen inches long. Some were fitted with D-shaped knuckle guards and resembled small swords. The percentage of these knives which drew Yankee blood is minute. Their main uses were for cooking, camp chores, and for adding to the fierceness of soldiers' photographs, and they were soon discarded.

The infantrymen who became part of Granbury's Brigade were also armed with whatever weapons they could find. Members of the Seventh Texas, for instance, entered the service with double-barreled shotguns, sporting rifles, and even a few Model 1841 (or Mississippi) Rifles. By 1863, most of the infantrymen were armed with rifles or muskets, although there were still a few shotguns in evidence. (The dismounted cavalry regiments at Arkansas Post retained a large number of shotguns from the time when they had been mounted.) Not all of the infantry regiments carried the same type weapons. Contemporary records of the Sixth Texas bear this out. These records show a total of seven hundred twenty-seven long arms issued to the various companies between December 1861, and August 1862. Within this quantity are at least four different variations. Most common, at four hundred twenty-six, are "muskets" or "smooth muskets." These were probably all unrifled .69 caliber arms. Some were undoubtedly of the Model 1842 configuration that were used in the Mexican War. Others were older models that had been converted from flintlock to percussion. Some of these, however, still retained the earlier form of ignition (as a receipt for "175 Musket flints" dated August 18, 1862, shows.) The second most popular arm, listed at two hundred and fifteen, was the Mississippi Rifle. Originally a .54 caliber rifle, most of these were bored out and re-rifled to .58 caliber in the 1850s. Forty-seven weapons were identified as either "Enfields" or "Minié muskets." The two terms were often used interchangeably to refer to the Model 1853 Enfield rifles that were the standard arms of the British army. They were imported in huge numbers by both sides during the war and were as well made and as accurate as any of the military rifles being manufactured in America at that time. Last on the list were thirty-nine "Rifle muskets." These were probably Model 1855 Rifle Muskets which, with only a few minor changes, were produced by the thousands in the North throughout the war.

All of these weapons were, of course, surrendered at Arkansas Post. After the men of Granbury's brigade were assigned to the Army of Tennessee, they were all furnished with infantry weapons. These consisted primarily of captured Springfields, English Enfields, or any of a variety of other European arms imported from Austria, Belgium, or France. At least some of the men in the Sixth, Tenth and Fifteenth Texas carried .54 caliber Austrian rifles. We know a little bit about the types of weapons used by the Texans but just how accurate were they?

In the July 1971 issue of *American Rifleman*, Jac Weller compared the relative accuracies of several original Civil War firearms. Among the tested weapons were several types used in the Texas Brigade. These included the Model 1863 Springfield, the Model 1853 Enfield, the Model 1854 Austrian musket, the Model 1841 U.S. Rifle, and the Model 1842 U.S. Musket. Mr. Weller conducted his tests by firing five shots in a row at each target from a bench rest and then measuring the size of the group. The least accurate gun, not surprisingly, was the Model 1842 smoothbore. Its group size on the one hundred-yard target measured thirty-six inches. The four rifles were able to keep their five shots in groups ranging from seven and one-half inches to thirteen inches, with the best results being turned in by the Enfield.

The elite among the shoulder arms were the sniper rifles. Some of these weapons were monstrous twenty- or thirty-pound rifles made expressly for pinpoint accuracy. Others were imported English Kerr or Whitworth rifles. Some members of the Texas Brigade were detailed as sharpshooters at different times during the war and at least some of them used telescopic-sighted Whitworths. A former user, not a Texan, wrote that the kick of these guns was so great that the telescope would quickly black the eye of the person firing it. These .45 caliber weapons were extremely accurate. Union Major General John Sedgewick, who was killed at the Battle of Spotsylvania Courthouse in Virginia, was allegedly picked off by a Confederate sharpshooter at a range of eight hundred yards. General Cleburne is also said to have witnessed, through field glasses, a fifteen hundred-yard hit by one of his snipers. During Mr. Weller's field tests he also evaluated three Whitworths. His best one hundred-yard group size was a remarkable four and three-quarter inches! Then, firing at a six-by-six-foot target at one thousand yards, Mr. Weller hit fifteen in a row!

While the arms used by the Texans seem rather primitive by modern standards, it seems that they were armed about as well as their Union adversaries.

Appendix C

THE MEN OF GRANBURY'S BRIGADE

Not all of the men in the regiments which comprised Granbury's Texas Brigade actually ever served under General Granbury. For instance, even though almost five thousand men from these regiments were captured at Arkansas Post in January 1863, there were several hundred who were not. Some were absent on sick furlough, some were detached on temporary duty at other locations, and a few escaped from the Post amid all the confusion surrounding the surrender. Some of these "refugees" were temporarily attached to the Fourteenth Texas Infantry Regiment for a few months. Then, in the spring of 1863, these men and most of the others who had avoided capture were formed into the Seventeenth Consolidated Regiment of Texas Cavalry (Dismounted). This regiment eventually became a part of General Camille J. Polignac's brigade and fought with distinction in the Trans-Mississippi Department. Some members of the Fifteenth Texas Cavalry formed a small detachment under their old regimental designation as did remnants of the Twenty-fourth, and the Twenty-fifth Texas Cavalries.

The National Archives in Washington, D.C., contains the compiled service records of all the men who served in the Texas regiments which comprised Granbury's Brigade. (Unfortunately, the records in the Texas State Archives are not nearly as extensive.) A review of these records — contained on forty-five rolls of microfilm — has yielded the following rosters.

In the case of each regiment, the names of the men who served on the commissioned staff are presented first. When a man is listed in more than one place it means that he held more than one position on the regimental staff. For instance, Hiram Granbury is listed under three offices — major,

175

lieutenant colonel, and colonel. This simply means that he held each of these ranks at some time. And since he served as captain of Company A before his election to the regimental staff, his name will also be found listed with that company.

Following the commissioned staff of each regiment are alphabetical rosters of the men in Companies A through K. The names and ranks of company officers and noncoms are not listed separately but their names are given in their alphabetical sequence. If a man transferred from one company to another his name is shown in both places. After Company K of each regiment is a list of names of men who served in that particular regiment but about whom information is so scarce in the records consulted that even their companies cannot now be determined.

After all of the regiments is a list of the members of Captain Sam Richardson's independent company of Texas Cavalry — the W. P. Lane Rangers — which was compiled exclusively from W. W. Heartsill's *Fourteen Hundred and 91 Days in the Confederate Army.*

An asterick (*) indicates that that particular soldier was present with his command at the last surrender at Greensboro, North Carolina, on April 26, 1865.

Commissioned Staff, Sixth Texas Infantry Regiment

Colonel:
    Robert R. Garland
Lieutenant Colonel:
    Thomas Scott Anderson
Major:
    Rhoads H. Fisher
    Alex M. Haskell
    Alex H. Phillips Jr.
Adjutant:
    Samuel J. Garland
    W. W. Phillips
    Sebron G. Sneed
Surgeon:
    Jonathan H. Lyons
    David McKnight
Assistant Surgeon:
    S. E. Goss
    J. Pervis Jenkins
    Alex Jones
    R. A. Smith
    George W. Tribble
Assistant Commissary of Subsistence:
    James K. P. Campbell
    George W. Sampson
Assistant Quartermaster:
    Jonathan E. Garey
    Udolpho Wolfe
Chaplain:
    Buckner H. Harris
    R. McCoy
Ensign:
    A. E.———ce

Company A, Sixth Texas Infantry Regiment

Allison, S. George	Davis, Lewis C.	Holland, J. F.
Barber, D. A.	Debroh, Isham	Holland, T. J.
Barton, S. H.	Dehroh, J. M.	Holt, James
Bendon, J. W. H.	Dial, H.	Holt, Thomas J.
Benedict, George B.	Drake, James A.	Hornburg, Henry
Blossman, F. E.	Ebner, Frederick	Johnson, George M.
Bosworth, J. H.	Fink, Christian	Johnson, James P.
Bradford, Samuel S.	Fowler, A. W.	Johnson, M. R.
Breeden, David F.	Gisler, Jacob	Kell, George
Brimingham, Charles	Goodall, John	Kleas, Philip *
Britton, George W.	Hampil, Charles W.	Knopp, John J.
Burley, Sylvester *	Hanna, Albert	Knopp, Peter
Butts, John W.	Harless, J. H.	Kuhlenthal, Ed. C. T.
Cantwell, William J.	Harless, William D.	Landell, Edmond H.
Carlyle, William T.	Harmes, Casper	Lewis, Josiah
Carpenter, Jeff B.	Harrell, John E.	Lindsay, John
Carpenter, W.	Harris, Henry H.	Lindsay, Thomas
Casey, John	Haynes, Christopher C.	London, Max H.
Cherry, Robert W.	Haynes, James H.	Longnecker, Simon K.
Coleman, Thomas	Hazle, William	Lowther, N. B.
Couper, William C.	Henry, J. R.	Mahan, John
Cox, John H.	Hogan, John W.	Martin, Augustus

Martin, Robert
Martin, Sebastian
Martin, William
Maxwell, James
Maxwell, William W.
Miller, John
Moore, Bede
McDonald, Lewis
McDonald, William R.
McNamara, William
Newport, James A.
Nichols, John
Nimmo, Joseph W. *
Pearce, James H.
Phillips, Alex H. Jr.
Phillips, William W.

Poston, William
Power, John
Ragland, James
Randall, Oliver P. *
Riley, George J.
Riley, T. W.
Rose, George W.
Rose, John
Samuels, B.
Seaman, Charles
Seery, Peter
Sims, Henry H.
Smith, Edwin R.
Snider, William
Squyres, Lemuel
Stanton, William E. *

Stapp, Christopher
Stehr, August
Surlan, Frederick
Sutton, R. E.
Taylor, Adolphus
Threlkeld, J. B.
Traber, Joseph
Walker, E. H.
Waters, William D.
Watters, Gilbert D.
Wetherell, James E.
Whelan, Charles
Williams, Samuel
Wilson, E. T.
Wilson, J. W.

Company B, Sixth Texas Infantry Regiment

Adcock, Alexander
Adcock, James
Adcock, Lewis *
Albert, J.
Alexander, L.
Alexander, Samuel
Auster, J.
Beck, F.
Beck, Louis
Biedermann, P. G.
Brown, Stanley
Carter, William H.
Clark, H.
Connery, James
Couturier, Louis
Cunningham, Andrew P.
Curran, T.
Davidsburg, D.
Davidsburg, D. H.
Dietz, John
Ernst, Joseph *
Fiedler, William
Fox, Jacob
Franz, H.
Gabel, Joseph
Gensch, F.
Gibson, John
Gilbert, R. R.
Hahn, John *
Hanne, J. F.
Hans, Jacob
Heck, Christian
Hermanns, H.

Hilf, Charles
Hiller, Adam
Hoenes, Peter
Hoffman, Sebastian
Homan, A. B.
Jones, Anson B.
Kaiser, Balthaser
Kern, Jacob
Klein, A.
Kolle, Frederick
Kroschel, Louis
Langner, Oscar
Leischner, Charles
Levy, S.
Lewis, G. S.
Lewis, John M.
Lobman, Samuel
Marks, Ernest
Mehnert, Edward
Meyer, Sebastian
Mitchell, J. S.
McCarty, John
Netter, J.
Pela, Victor
Piekert, Joseph
Pilgram, John
Ponton, A. J.
Rider, William
Rieger, Benjamin
Robinson, William
Rupley, James A.
Sanders, James
Sasse, F.

Schiewitz, Michael
Schott, Sebastian
Schraeder, Henry E.
Schubert, Francis
Schuchert, Ludwig
Schuppe, August
Silverstine, L.
Silverstine, S.
Sinner, S.
Spaith, D.
Spencer, J. A.
Spencer, William H.
Stehr, August
Steinmetz, Louis
Stewart, James *
Strauss, Frank
Upstett, F.
Vermillion, R. A.
Voight, A.
Voit, J.
Wagner, August
Walter, Charles
Waters, William D.
Weiss, Otto
Wertheimer, W.
Westly, J. H.
Whellin, Edward
Wilburn, T. L.
Woelffel, R.
Wurz, A. N.
Wurz, Joseph
Zahn, Hermann
Zmuda, M.

Company C, Sixth Texas Infantry Regiment

Alsup, Ludy C.
Alsup, R. J.
Alsup, William R.
Anderson, A. R.
Baker, A.
Baker, Jesse *
Baker, J. L.
Baker, Thomas

Barnett, James A.
Barnett, J. P. *
Bass, Alonzo T.
Batling, Henry
Bellinger, W. R.
Benham, Lee
Bloomberg, J.
Botts, H. C.

Bowerman, William
Branch, James L.
Britton, Cornelius
Bryan, James W.
Burns, W.
Clark, F. B.
Connally, C.
Conway, John

Cross, S. F.
Crozier, W. A.
Cummings, John F.
Day, James R.
Deitch, Solomon
Derozier, Alex
Dick, T. A.
Dunlop, Colin
Finch, R.
Flynt, Thomas L.
Frank, B.
Gipson, Samuel *
Hahn, Alex B.
Halfin, Eli
Halliburton, Meldrum M.
Harrison, Charles
Henriquez, George
Henson, W. H.
Hilliard, G. W.
Hurley, William R.
Jones, A. W.
Kelley, William

Lewis, Harvey A.
Light, Michael L.
Light, V. D.
Light, W. R.
Malone, J.
Martin, Thomas J.
Murphy, David
McCaughan, John D.
McCorkle, Eli A.
McDonald, D.
McGinnis, Patrick
McVea, James A.
McVea, J. G.
McVea, John J.
McVea, Martin
Nations, L. B.
Nations, W. A.
Norfleet, J. M.
O'Neill, David
Ramsay, James *
Ramsay, Texas O.
Reese, Charles

Roebuck, R
Sharp, Thomas C.
Shefsky, Henry
Shoemaker, David *
Steiner, L.
Stevenson, John
Stroope, Isaac P.
Stroope, John P.
Stroope, S. C.
Suton, J. L.
Taylor, Daniel *
Taylor, Thomas R. *
Thetford, T. C.
Tumlison, J. L.
Tumlison, John H.
Turner, John
Tuton, James L.
Tyler, William G.
Wallace, E. M.
Wilson, W.
Wolfe, J. A.
Wooten, J. F. M.
Wooten, S. M.

Company D, Sixth Texas Infantry Regiment

Ballinger, Green
Bates, Thomas Frank
Baxter, William H.
Benson, Isaac
Bernard, Frederick
Bernard, Louis
Brandis, Charles
Bridges, John
Brown, John
Brown, Lewis
Brown, William
Bruce, Arthur
Bryant, Wolfred N.
Cheesman, Arthur
Clouder, George
Coveney, John
Crill, Joseph
Gulici, David
Dale, John F.
Davis, Thomas
Demonet, John
Dietrich, Sebastian
Dressy, Alexander
Duffy, Augustus
Dunbar, Adam
Dunbar, William *
Dyson, Robert
Edgar, Edward *
Eidelbach, John *
Flood, Richard
Funk, Martin *
Gibson, William Henry
Golden, W. M. *
Guthrie, Charles S.

Hasbrook, Robert A.
Hill, John W.
Hill, Thomas
Hines, Morris
Holmes, William
Holt, Jonathan F.
Hunt, Wheeler D.
Inglehart, Edward T.
James, Sidney
Jones, Henry
Keller, Frederick
Kimball, Thomas
Kuykendall, Robert
Lehman, Samuel
Lewis, D.
Lewis, George S.
Ludwig, Conrad
Maihaivier, Antonio
Meyers, Jacob
Mylius, Herman
McCue, Thomas D. *
McLeod, Daniel
McNabb, John
Nolte, Joseph
Nye, Thomas C.
Nye, William
Ohlendorff, John G.
Pairon, John *
Pearezon, E. A.
Pearezon, Philip E.
Peden, Lewis
Phillips, John *
Plagge, Richard H.
Price, John

Quedans, Barney
Raiman, John
Rierden, Lawrence
Rodgers, Martin
Salzeger, Godfried *
Savary, Wiley P.
Savery, Harvey T.
Schubert, John
Schwerburger, Wendelin
Selkirk, James
Serrill, Richard O.
Shafer, Henry *
Sheppard, W. D.
Shortridge, John H.
Smith, Francis *
Smith, Henry
Smith, John
Smith, Thomas
Soper, Peter
Sterling, Rudolphus D.
Sterling, William
Sterry, James
Stewart, Greenberry L.
Stewart, John A.
Stewart, W. Scott *
Stickles, Peter D.
Van Bremer, Samuel
Vogg, Charles
Wadsworth, William B.
Waldman, Charles
Watrous, F. A.
Wilkinson, Jonathan Gid *
Woodward, William H.
Yeamans, Erastus
Zipprian, Christian *
Zipprian, John

Company E, Sixth Texas Infantry Regiment

Alexander, Alfred A.
Anderson, Henry M.
Barnes, S. M.
Barry, John
Bohsle, John
Bollini, Charles
Brook, John R.
Brothers, Thomas J.
Bulger, Philip
Bulger, Samuel B.
Campbell, Alexander
Clemensen, W. Henry *
Cockrum, Andrew J.
Cocks, Hardy D.
Cocreham, Sylvester K.
Cogswell, William T.
Combs, James H.
Cowey, Charles W.
Crenshaw, Henry L.
Crenshaw, Nicholas
Donegan, John R.
Ducrois, Eli
Eckols, David W.
Eckols, Thomas J.
Glosson, W. M.
Hamlin, Vincent B.
Higgins, William
Hoke, Berlin A.
Hubert, William G.
Ingram, Robert
Karnes, John
Kincaid, James M. *

Lancaster, James A. L.
Lopez, Isaac
Maddox, Amos H.
Maddox, Levi
Malone, William L.
Mathews, Samuel R. *
Mayfield, John W.
Mayfield, Luke
Medlin, William
Miller, James W.
Miller, John R.
Molz, John M.
Molz, Peter *
Molz, William
Moore, Mark
Morse, John
McAnelly, Martin V.
McGuffey, William J.
McKinney, Frederick A.
McLelland, Andrew
Nance, Lewis H. *
Neill, Henry C. *
Newton, Lemuel F.
Noel, Henry T.
Ochletree, Alexander
Owen, William H.
Park, John H.
Ratcliff, Samuel
Rea, Edward G.
Robertson, James A.
Robinson, Calvin F.
Rochelle, J. W.

Roemmell, Henry
Rose, Asa S.
Rose, Joshua
Sanders, Adams
Sanders, Stewart M.
Simmons, Martin
Smith, Albert G.
Smith, Daniel F.
Smith, James I.
Smith, Lewis
Smith, William
Snell, William W.
Stanley, E. J.
Suchart, Fritz
Sullivan, Seaburn J.
Swann, Thomas H.
Taylor, Thomas R.
Thompson, Edward
Tiner, William W.
Tom, Houston
Vickers, William R. *
Wagner, John M.
Wakefield, John J.
Wallace, John R.
White, Abraham M.
White, James A.
White, Jeptha N.
White, John P.
Williams, Andrew
Williams, George W.
Wilson, Joseph
Young, Henry C.
Zorn, Peter

Company F, Sixth Texas Infantry Regiment

Aiken, Bartley
Anderson, James
Anderson, Michael
Ashford, James P.
Atwood, Cornelius M. *
Baker, Jackson
Bawcom, William H.
Berry, Christopher A.
Bigham, Samuel W.
Birch, Benjamin J.
Blackburn, Richard T.
Blodget, James D.
Bond, Francis E.
Bonner, George A.
Boyd, Roland R.
Boyd, Willis W.
Bradford, Hennry Ed
Brown, John W.
Burley, Sylvester *
Cearnel, Henry S
Cearnel, W. P.
Chalk, Robert L.
Chambers, James M.
Chapman, John D.

Church, Benjamin F.
Cowan, James W.
Crow, Reuben
Davis, John B.
Denton, William B.
Dodson, William T.
Dollar, D. W.
Doss, Christopher C.
Doss, Harmon W.
Drake, Francis M.
Ellis, Porter L.
Elms, Henry
Everett, William R.
Evetts, William C.
Fewel, Louis L.
Fleming, Charles *
Francesco, Juan
Glowner, David
Griffith, Amos B.
Haggerton, Charles
Hall, Josiah A.
Hamilton, Woodie T.
Hampton, Wade W.
Hannon, Robert S.

Hartrick, William T. J.
Holmes, A. S.
Hulsey, Green E.
Kellen, William
Kelton, Mark A. *
Kinman, Collins L.
Leonard, Martin
Mayes, Daniel
Merchant, David B.
Meredith, William H.
Methvin, Albert
Methvin, Alford
Methvin, Levi T.
Murray, William D.
McKenzie, Harvey
McLaughlin, Alonzo F.
Oakley, Pleasant A.
Oliphant, Aaron E.
Oliphant, James M.
O'Neal, Stephen
Pace, Joseph A.
Parks, Hamilton
Parks, Henry T.
Petty, Isom S.

Petty, James E.
Polk, Josiah L.
Reed, Warren *
Royal, Jesse
Scott, James B.
Scott, Jesse G.
Seay, Gerrett W.
Shelton, Dred D.

Shelton, James J.
Shelton, John
Shelton, Thomas B.
Sinclair, James A.
Sinclair, William W.
Smith, Gabriel W.
Smith, Peter
Smith, William W.

Snodgrass, James A.
Standley, Sidney
St. Clair, Stephen A.
Stone, John A.
Supple, John B. B.
Sutton, Andy
Sutton, Jesse
Vaughn, Nathan
Williamson, Thomas T.

Company G, Sixth Texas Infantry Regiment

Alexander, Newton
Alexander, W. A.
Alford, H. M.
Amidon, Dwight
Baldwin, James S.
Bird, William H.
Brown, James F.
Burleson, Ichabod Cabron
Burleson, John T.
Carrington, Robert Emmet
Condell, Robert W.
Costa, Joseph A.
Crosthwait, Richard H. L.
Daugherty, John S.
DeHority, E.
Dinkins, J. H.
Dobbs, J. E.
Dukes, James *
Dunson, William M. *
Fisher, Rhoads H.
Gatlin, N. M.
Giles, W. L.
Glasscock, Frank
Glasscock, L. P. *
Grumbles, J. W.
Grumbles, Samuel H.
Grumbles, T. A.
Hamilton, James W. N.
Hill, Abel W.
Hill, G. I. *

Hudson, Green
Jenkins, Samuel L.
Jernigan, Albert J.
Johnson, John
Jourdan, George W.
Jourdan, William A.
Kelley, Jacob *
Kline, J. H.
Labenski, Charles Carroll *
Loevell, D. W.
Lowery, Albert M.
Lowery, Ransom
Malitzky, Lewis *
Marsh, Darius
Meeks, M.
Meeks, Robert
Mellenger, Ross B.
Millett, Emery E.
Morris, S. W.
Murphy, Peter
McClure, H. M.
Oldham, William H.
Oliphant, William James
Patterson, Robert
Peck, S. R.
Peel, J. Wesley
Pickens, Israel
Piper, B. F.
Raston, James
Robertson, Benoni

Roundtree, H. C.
Rutledge, W. P.
Sampson, George W.
Sever, Jefferson
Simms, Francis M.
Simms, James
Smith, James W. *
Sneed, Sebron G.
Sneed, William J.
Stanley, George W.
Stephenson, A. B. *
Stephenson, J. T.
Sweem, J. M.
Taylor, James
Teaff, N. F.
Teague, G. M.
Terrell, C. D.
Tinnin, William
Tucker, J. T.
Turner, James M.
Turner, J. M. V.
Walker, Benjamin F.
Walker, J. M.
Wilkes, Benjamin F.
Williams, Samuel
Wilson, A. J.
Wilson, David W.
Wilson, Don W.
Wilson, Merit D.
Woodward, Josiah P. *
Yates, Henry W.

Company H, Sixth Texas Infantry Regiment

Andrews, Lafayette
Atchison, William J.
Atwell, James
Barwold, Edward
Bindrick, George
Black, Augustus
Brightwell, Charles R.
Brightwell, John A. *
Bums, John
Carden, Joseph W.
Chichester, William G.
Cocke, S. F.
Coller, Frank
Cox, Charles W.
Cox, Harvey H.
Cox, John H.
Cox, Joseph H.
Crenshaw, Moses

Cromwell, Alex G.
Delaney, Philip
Fagan, Joseph
Finlay, George P.
French, James A.
Gaylord, Edward H.
Gisler, Jacob
Harvey, Henry B.
Harvey, Robert B.
Hensoldt, Arno
Hiershery, August
Hogan, Granville
Hogan, J. F.
Hogan, Robert
Hughes, James
Ingram, Jasper
Johnson, George M.
Kay, John W. *

Kinsella, Edward
Kuhlenthal, Ed. C. T.
Linkenhoker, William P.
Longnecker, Albert
Manes, John *
Moore, Samuel Jr.
Moses, E. M.
Muckey, Bill
McCord, James A.
McLeod, Alexander
McLeod, Angus
McLeod, Murdock
McLoud, Malcolm
McNamara, William
Neal, James H.
Newport, James A.
Nimmo, Joseph W. *
O'Riley, Edward

Patton, John
Pettus, John P.
Polte, S. R.
Power, John
Ray, William L.
Rice, Stephen E.
Romero, Louis *

Roovy, John
Ross, W. J. M.
Rowland, J. G.
Sampson, James A.
Sanchez, Marion
Seamen, Charles
Sessions, Henri W.

Sims, Henry H.
Sims, John M.
Spencer, William N. *
Stapp, Hugh S.
Tanner, John
Traylor, Pascal M.
Venables, William L.
Wilburn, George M.

Company I, Sixth Texas Infantry Regiment

Arnold, M.
Barton, O. P.
Bayer, Chr.
Bishop, William
Brysh, Anton
Burkhard, J.
Crill, Joseph
Dlugosh, Joseph
Frey, Alfred
Gibs, F.
Gohlki, John
Golla, John
Gomert, William
Gregorzyck, F.
Hensoldt, Arno
Huttig, G.
Joska, Joseph
Katzmark, John
Kielbassa, Ignetz

Kolozey, Simon
Kosielsky, Anton
Kuhl, Julius
Lesse, Albert
Lunzin, George
Mertens, H.
Naunheim, C. P.
Nobis, William
Opiella, John
Poetter, G.
Potter, Henry
Prutz, William
Reid, Patrick
Reis, Gustaf
Reuser, Louis
Riedel, C.
Riedel, E.
Riedel, F.
Riedel, M.

Rummel, F.
Sauermilch, C.
Schroeder, Fred
Schroeder, Gottlieb
Shefsky, Henry
Sheppa, J.
Sheridan, Francis
Shwurz, Thomas
Spremberg, Robert
Stephan, Charles A.
Strieber, Adolph
Sturmer, G.
Thea, John
Volst, Gustav
Warzecha, John
Zimon, V.
Zowada, Vincent
Zuch, L.

Company K, Sixth Texas Infantry Regiment

Andrews, ——
Braden, Adam
Braden, Edward
Braden, Martin
Burns, Henry
Burtschell, Henry
Bustillos, Antonio *
Cannon, James
Cardena, Joseph
Christless, Michael
Copeland, Thomas
Cotton, Andrew E.
Craft, John M.
Derr, Henry
Despres, John M.
DeYturri, Manuel
Dignowity, Albert W.
Dilman, Charles
Dirr, John
Doyle, Thomas L.

Duby, Alexander
Foga, William
Fooke, William
Fremon, Leon A.
Frick, Claus Henry
Garner, W. S.
Garza, Joseph R.
Garza, Simon
Gordon, Jerre
Grell, John Otto
Griffin, Charles
Hawkins, Ambrose *
Hessler, Ernest
Hoever, Charles
Hoever, Frederick
Hogan, Andrew
Horl, George
Hudsler, Henry
Mainze, Charles
Marquerd, Edward

Marquerd, Gustav
Megill, Andrew
Miller, Armsted
Musiol, James
McAllister, Samuel W.
Navarro, Eugenio
O'Donoghue, Mortimer
Oswald, Carl
Ponsley, John
Riley, James
San Miguel, Andrew
Sarats, Peter V.
Schlunz, Dedlef
Schmidt, Albert
Schmidt, Gustav
Schoenen, Henry
Scofield, Joseph
Sheppard, Woodworth V.
Suniga, Antonio
Williams, S.
Woodworth, V. S.

Miscellaneous, Sixth Texas Infantry Regiment

Antonia, S.
Fiddler, M. (laundress)
Hanser, Benjamin D.
Hanser, Wiley N.

Harris, William
Halsey, James W.
Henderson, Isaac E.
Jones, M. (hospital matron)

McNill, O. (laundress)
Napier, O. (matron)
Welch, W. P.

Commissioned Staff, Seventh Texas Infantry Regiment

Colonel:
J. William Brown
Hiram Bronson Granbury
John Gregg
William L. Moody
Lieutenant Colonel:
Jeremiah M. Clough
Hiram Bronson Granbury
William L. Moody
Major:
Hiram Bronson Granbury
William L. Moody
K. M. Van Zandt
Adjutant:
George A. Blair
William D. Douglas
Richard H. English
Surgeon:
Jonathan Alston
John R. Crain
Robert A. Felton
Assistant Surgeon:
Robert A. Felton
Davis T. Richardson
Assistant Commissary of Subsistence:
S. T. Bridges
William W. West
Assistant Quartermaster:
William Bradfield
Quentin D. Horr
Chaplain:
Stokley Chaddick
Ensign:
Ira B. Saddler

Company A, Seventh Texas Infantry Regiment

Abernathy, D. F. *
Abernathy, Martin V.
Alexander, C. N.
Arnold, W. F.
Barton, J. W.
Bennett, W.
Bentley, George W.
Bland, John V.
Blankenbaker, David W.
Bowen, Leonidas S.
Brooks, J. W. G.
Brown, C. J.
Brown, T. J. Sr.
Bryan, A. H. *
Bryan, Allen H.
Caldwell, F. M. *
Callaway, J. N.
Cantrell, John L.
Carroll, N. H.
Carter, Milton
Cawthon, John O.
Cheek, Richard M.
Dechard, H. B.
Estes, Edward B.
Evans, W. W.
Fowler, Tilman

Galloway, Robert V. *
Galloway, James L.
Gill, William A.
Goff, A. L.
Granbury, Hiram Bronson
Gray, Robert W.
Hardin, Julius A.
Hardin, J. D.
Harris, R. W.
Harrison, John A.
Hicks, H. D.
Hofeckert, Philips
Hoggans, Thomas W.
Holloway, John
Holloway, J. V.
Holloway, P. L.
Hooks, David
Houston, A. M.
Jackson, Edward S.
Jones, R. B.
Kendall, Benjamin F.
Kidd, John C.
Leonard, Malcolm M.
Longineau, J. B.
Marshall, William W.
Matthews, J. M.

Moffitt, Benjamin F.
Murry, J. H.
McCary, J. W.
Norvell, J. Sam
Nowlin, J. W.
Pilkinton, F.
Price, Goolsbury W. *
Prior, James
Quinn, Michael
Riddle, Dr. J. J.
Roberts, John D.
Rogers, Joseph Franklin
Rogers, William E.
Roper, Andrew M.
Rosson, E. B.
Royall, A. J.
Rozell, W. W.
Ruyle, William A.
Sadler, Ira B.
Shead, Charles B.
Shirk, Henry
Shook, Thomas W.
Slavin, Newton C.
Sparks, James H.
Sparks, R. W.
Speagles, H. W.

Strand, Christian O.
Trice, C. W.
Trice, J. D.
Watters, John
Webster, D. B.
Webster, M. M.

Wilie, T. W.
Williams, George W.
Williams, L. H.
Williams, Leonard S. *
Wood, J. F.
Wood, William R.

Company B, Seventh Texas Infantry Regiment

Anderson, Samuel
Appleton, A. H.
Arden, David
Babb, Peter
Baulknight, D. H.
Bivens, James K.
Bivens, W.
Boothe, Julius C. B.
Boren, Robert A.
Boyce, William
Brooks, B.
Brooks, T. R.
Bussey, William
Camp, R. S.
Camp, Thomas B.
Chapman, B. P. *
Christian, W. F.
Covin, John H.
Crigler, Edward V.
Crosby, Charles B.
Crosby, J. E.
Derrick, William B.
Devany, George P.
Duckworth, A.
Dudley, James
Duffey, Thomas J. *
Duffy, John W.
Earp, R. M.
Echols, George *
Eley, William
Ensinger, J. G.
Fincher, T. M.
Floyd, Adolphus
Ford, Alexander
Ford, George F.
Ford, Richard W.
George, James A.
Gillespie, John T. Jr.
Gillespie, John T. Sr.
Gillespie, William H.
Glass, William T.

Green, Jessie R. *
Hale, G. T.
Hale, J. W.
Hammet, George W.
Hanner, J. W.
Hardey, William
Harkey, L. William
Harris, Jonathan C.
Harrison, William J. *
Hart, William A. *
Henry, George W.
Howard, A. H.
Humphreys, U.
Johnson, George W.
Johnson H. H.
Johnson, J. M.
Johnson, John
Johnson, Smith M.
Johnson, William B.
Jones, Crawford T.
King, Luke L. *
Kolb, C. J.
Lansdale, P. W.
Lewis, William B.
Lowe, Thomas J.
Maples, John T.
Mapp, B. H. *
Marshall, Edward P.
Martin, L.
Martin, P. B.
Moncrief, Austin
Montgomery, J. A.
Moseley, W. P.
Niblock, J. C.
Niblet, Caleb J.
Owens, Stephen
Palmer, W. D.
Parham, E. B.
Perry, S. C.
Poteet, S. D.
Potts, David M.

Rape, J. H.
Richardson, J. A.
Riley, M. W.
Robinson, Benjamin F.
Robinson, J. W.
Rogers, Asberry C.
Rogers, Benjamin F.
Rogers, Edward B.
Scott, John
Scott, T. J.
Silas, John
Smith, James E.
Smith, James L. Jr.
Smith, John L. Sr.
Smith, William E.
Stephens, E. T.
Stone, Elias M.
Stone, William H.
Strong, J. B.
Sudduth, D. B.
Swords, J. K.
Talley, S. G.
Thomas, James
Thompson, William C.
Thompson, W. F.
Tucker, Charles M.
Utley, William H. *
Walker, Augustine
Walworth, H. B.
Watkins, M.
Watkins, Thomas O.
Whiting, W. D. G.
Wilkerson, D. C.
Wilkerson, Jessie M.
Williams, D. F. *
Williams, T. J.
Wilson, Jasper M. *
Wilson, J. W.
Wilson, William R.
Young, J. L.
Youngblood, J. A.

Company C, Seventh Texas Infantry Regiment

Allen, Charles
Atkins, W. A.
Boykin, John H.
Bridges, S. T.
Brinley, M. F.
Britton, Henry B.
Britton, James D.
Broughton, Edward T.
Broughton, N. W.
Brown, J. F.

Bryan, A. B.
Bryan, D. B.
Bryan, S.
Bush, William C.
Cantrell, G. P.
.Cantrell, N. T.
Carriger, Ira
Cravey, R. Z. G.
Davidson, A.
Davidson, A. J.

Davidson, J. F.
Donnell, Daniel
Donnell, Irvine
Douglas, William D.
Easter, John J.
Elkins, M. J.
Elkins, Thomas
English, Charles E.
English, Richard H. *
Featherston, Martin A.

Fisher, James P.
Frazier, Thomas
Freeman, J. W.
Furrh, Alexander
Furrh, G. Washington
Gray, L.
Grisham, James N.
Grisham, W. O.
Guthrie, Edward J.
Hammock, John
Harr, Charles L.
Harris, Henry
Henderson, J. D.
Henderson, James F.
Herring, Stephen
Hinds, A. G.
Holtz, S.
Jarmon, John M.
Jarmon, Robert
Jones, John W.

Lewter, Peter H.
Mills, John
Moon, J. C.
Morgan, Lovless D.
Morgan, Moses A.
Morris, J. E.
Mosely, W. M.
Murdock, James H.
McDonald, J. W. J.
McInvail, James
Netherlain, J. B.
O'Quinn, C. H.
Pace, John T.
Payne, James L.
Pinson, A. G.
Ray, James Y.
Reagor, L. S.
Robertson, Samuel
Rogers, Albert G.
Rogers, Allen

Rogers, E. M.
Rogers, Pinckney
Rose, Dwelley H.
Ross, Ewler, H.
Scott, Jack W.
Shields, John C.
Shumake, G. W.
Simmons, George
　　Washington
Snipes, G. J.
Stalcup, John W.
Stanley, W. H.
Taylor, John T.
Vercher, L. H.
Walker, Robert J.
Warner, Stanley M.
Wells, Joseph L.
Williams, John
Wilson, G. H.

Company D, Seventh Texas Infantry Regiment

Acree, F. H. J.
Adams, Archibald G. *
Alexander, Robert H.
Alford, Joseph P.
Allen, William S.
Bailey, Marion *
Beall, Thomas J.
Bedell, Charles E.
Bedell, John L.
Bradfield, John A.
Brantley, Louis W.
Brawner, Joseph S.
Brigs, Thomas E.
Brown, R. C. S.
Bruckmiller, Joseph P.
Burnett, Samuel
Callaway, Joshua S.
Carr, Benjamin F.
Cave, John M.
Clough, Jeremiah M.
Crawford, J. D.
Doppelmeyer, Daniel
Duke, Julius C.
Duncan, Benjamin A.
Edwards, William G.
Feehan, Patrick
Feller, August
Finley, John H.'
Finley, Wilber F.
Fisher, Conrad
Ford, Luther R.
Franks, Augustus
Fyffe, Jacob M.
Fyffe, James R.
Fyffe, William
Gerould, John G.
Grier, Robert A.
Hall, Jesse
Hall, William K.

Hardin, A. J.
Harris, John C.
Hauenstine, Cornelius
Hawley, Theodore P.
Haynes, Robert Reid
Henrich, Charles *
Hicks, Jacob
Holbert, Marvel
Horr, Quentin D.
Hudson, James R.
Huggins, George W.
Hunter, James B.
Hynson, John Ringgold
Hynson, Noland
Jennings, Thomas S.
Johnson, Felix H.
Johnson, Thomas W.
Johnson, Westley B.
Jones, J. P.
Jones, Robert
Jones, W. B.
Joyce, Billington S.
Karch, Michael
Lipscomb, Cuvier *
Lipscomb, G. B.
Lipscomb, Joseph P.
Long, Robert H.
Maddox, William
Manson, Benjamin F.
Mason, William H.
Mills, Henry Y.
Mills, Thomas A.
McCaskill, Alexander S.
McCulloch, James
McKay, Thomas
McPhail, William H.
Otis, Thomas
Owen, O. F.
Peaks, Marcus D. L.

Percival, Joseph
Pickett, Greg W. *
Pierce, William C.
Ram, Henry C.
Sanders, Lee
Sanders, William P.
Scogin, Benjamin T.
Scrivner, Joseph M. W.
Shelburne, Andrew J.
Simmons, William W.
Smith, Fred A.
Stafford, Richard
Stansbury, Robert N.
Stevens, James M.
Talley, Charles E.
Talley, James L.
Taylor, James L. *
Taylor, John W.
Taylor, Joseph William
Taylor, Wiley O.
Terry, J. H.
Thetford, Andrew Jackson
Thompson, Larry
Thompson, William B.
Thompson, William S.
Tucker, George D.
Van Zandt, Isaac L.
Van Zandt, K. M.
Wade, J. A.
Ward, Lee G.
Ward, Virgil V.
Watson, D. M.
Weathersby, C. Richard
Weathersby, J. F.
Weaver, Daniel P.
Weiler, John
Welch, C. R.
West, William W.
Willard, William

Wilson, Edward O.
Wilson, Jason H.
Womack, O. J.
Woodson, Lucian
Woodson, William Jr.

Company E, Seventh Texas Infantry Regiment

Allen, Adoniram J.
Allen, R. T.
Alvis, T. J.
Arnold, W.
Atwood, Isaac Y. B. *
Bagley, William S.
Barron, John W.
Baty, J. B.
Bradshaw, K. D.
Butler, Hezekiah
Butler, Thomas
Byrd, W. L.
Campbell, James C.
Chisum, George W.
Coke, S.
Collier, Green A.
Coupland, Andrew A.
Craft, Jesse
Criswell, James G.
Davis, Jack
Donley, S. P.
Elkins, David
Fowler, John W.
Frederick W. C.
Fry, Leberton *
Galliger, Barney
Garner, J.
Garner, W. J.
Goodwin, S. H.
Gorney, Aron N.
Granberry, John

Green, T. W.
Greer, Wade H.
Grissom, John
Harrison, John
Harrison, W. H.
Haynes, Benjamin L.
Hearn, James F.
Higgins, Pat A.
Hill, A. W.
Holt, W. J.
Horton, J. W.
Hoyt, Wait S.
Ireson, Andrew B.
Irving, P. R.
Jack, A. N.
Johnson, Alfred A.
Johnson, F. M.
Johnson, R. A.
Johnson, S. M.
King, P. B.
Landers, John
Lawrence, Richard
Leadbetter, James R.
Martin, A. H.
Martin, Calvin F.
Martin, James J.
Martin, J. M.
Martin, S. C.
Martin, William Richard
Martin, W. R.
Mathews, J. E.

Middleton, Jackson V. B.
Middleton, S. Thomas B.
Miller, A. L.
Morgan, Edmond D.
Murphy, Robert F.
McKinley, John N.
Nicholson, James D.
Nixon, Calvin S.
Norton, Martin F.
Pearson, Alfred H.
Pearson, William H. *
Phillips, Arthur B.
Priest, Henry M.
Priest, William H.
Rankin, James C.
Shockler, Thomas H.
Singletary, Thomas H.
Stewart, William H.
Stone, Adolphus W.
Stone, H. M.
Stone, Wesley A.
Timmons, J. L.
Townsend, Thomas S.
Trimble, James M.
Vining, B. F.
Ward, Silas M.
Webb, Joseph
White, Florens J.
Williams, James M.
Woodall, Benjamin F.
Wynn, W. H.

Company F, Seventh Texas Infantry Regiment

Baswell, John P.
Bayless, Robert
Beavers, E. A.
Bledsoe, J. K.
Boren, B. N.
Brown, Thomas J. Jr.
Cantrell, John L.
Carroll, N. H. *
Carter, James M.
Carter, Milton
Davis, H. W.
Dean, M. J.
Delay, C. C.
Elliott, John
Ellison, William
Epperson, T. J.
Evans, John L.
Featherston, Charles H.
Felton, Robert A.
Golden, John A.
Hardin, Julius A.

Harden, M. G.
Harrison, Thomas
Jefferson *
Hays, I. N.
Hicks, E. C.
Hicks, John M.
Hill, A. W.
Howe, M. N.
Huckaby, William
Johnson, Felix H.
Jones, Henry L.
Jones, J. T.
Jones, T. H.
Kelly, A. R.
Kelly, E. A.
Kidd, F. C.
Kinsey, Daniel
Knowles, James M.
Moore, C. F.
Moore, John H.
Moore, Thaddeus M.

More, T. O.
Murry, J. H. *
Naylor, P. J.
Naylor, W. L.
Newman, J. M.
Parmer, F. M.
Parmer, G. W.
Potter, John B.
Potter, John C.
Potter, R. L.
Ray, Bryant H.
Ray, James Y. *
Reid, C. F.
Rice, H. F.
Roberts, N. L. *
Roberts, W. J.
Sensabaugh, William
Sewell, James H.
Shackleford, A. R.
Shackleford, S. S.
Shackleford, William P.

Shelton, M. R.
Smith, R. E.
Smith, William H.
Smyre, J. A. *
Taylor, J. W.
Thompson, W. H.
Thorn, James T.

Valentine, J. S.
Watters, John
Watters, T. Y.
Wimberley, W. C.
Wood, J. F.
Wood, William R.
Yarbrough, Burke

Company G, Seventh Texas Infantry Regiment

Anderson, Asa G.
Anderson, George K.
Anderson, Zachariah J.
Archibald, A. B.
Archibald, Robert
Balch, John T. *
Ballard, Evans
Bigger, Robert F.
Bigger, William A.
Blain, George A.
Blythe, William H.
Bradley, F. M.
Bradley, George T.
Bryan, Joseph H.
Burleson, John *
Burleson, Oliver
Burlison, Augustus
Burlison, Isaac
Busby, John W.
Cason, B. L.
Chambers, Bryant L.
Chambers, Henry
Clanton, Thomas
Claypool, James
Clough, M. J.
Coleman, H.
Collett, James H.
David, J. W.
Day, Francis M.
Dunbar, R. C.
Eskridge, T. P.
Fuller, Milton *
Goza, J. J.
Grann, Helge J.
Gregg, John

Groover, William L.
Harris, William T.
Henderson, John M.
Henderson, Simion T.
Henderson, William H.
Hertert, John Q.
High, Robert A.
Hobbs, Elijah
Holt, Robert
Huckaby, William S.
Humber, Jonathan T.
Indamon, Mick
Jordan, T. A.
Lee, J. B.
Lewis, V. L.
Lewis, W. W.
Love, A. C. Jr.
Love, C. W.
Love, Jonathan W.
Manning, Joseph N.
Mayo, J. N.
Means, Jonathan L.
Miles, James D. *
Miller, George Alexander
Mims, Benjamin F.
Mims, John
Moody, G. M.
Moody, Leroy F. *
Moody, William L.
Murray, P. K.
Murray, Robert
McCarty, Ira C.
McIlveen, W. A.
Neal, Robert E.
Neal, W. L.

Oliver, John E.
Oliver, Robert L.
Oliver, W. A.
Paxton, William F.
Petty, M.
Powell, Robert H.
Purtell, Charles J. *
Rakestraw, G. A.
Riley, Ed. D.
Roark, John A.
Robinson, James
Robinson, Jonathan F.
Sims, W. F.
Smith, Joshua C.
Smith, Stephen H.
Steele, E. R. G.
Steele, J. Warren
Steele, Robert S.
Stegall, Jeremiah
Stewart, George W.
Stewart, Hewitt B.
Story, H. M.
Story, Thomas S.
Strain, J. A.
Streety, S. J.
Surraville, J. B.
Tidwell, F. L.
Trawick, C. C.
Tull, Lemuel G. S. J.
Walker, S. A.
Whitley, Josiah
Williams, J. P.
Williams, J. R.
Womack, John A.
Yarbro, Franklin L. *

Company H, Seventh Texas Infantry Regiment

Austin, Hiram G.
Bailey, John H.
Beck, Elias Frank
Blackburn, R. A.
Board, Stephen
Boss, F. M.
Breazeale, C. J.
Brittain, George H. *
Broom, Henry J.
Broom, John P.
Brown, Charles W.
Burk, William H. B.
Burns, William M.
Campbell, R. M.
Campbell, W. E.

Cattenhead, W. C.
Clark, James H. *
Clark, William Tandy
Collier, E. G.
Cooper, D. Y.
Coore, J. W.
Coyle, William A.
Craig, James M.
Craig, Thomas H.
Crawford, Joy S.
Davis, L. A.
Dugan, Thomas W.
Ellis, C. C.
Everett, R. C.
Everett, William L.

Fields, Wallace W.
Fisher, George K.
Ford, William T.
Forrest, Elisha K.
Forrest, Oren P.
Forrest, R. O.
Foscue, Ben D. *
Foscue, J. S. *
Fowlkes, E. B.
Frazor, E. B.
Freeman, Matterson
Gibson, William J.
Grisham, Richard W.
Gupton, Marcey H.
Hagen, Patrick

Hall, John A.
Hamilton, Richard S.
Harvey, J. J.
Harvey, M.
Hearne, John P.
Hearne, LaFayette (Negro)
Henderson, Preston
Hill, Samuel (Negro)
Hill, William B.
James, B. Frank
Jones, J. B.
Jones, Joseph M.
Jones, R. B.
Jones, W. F.
Kennedy, D.
Key, J. M.
Lewis, Benjamin F. *
Lockett, William
Logan, A.
Ludolph, Francis
Martin, Ira L.
Meadows, J. A. *
Mebane, W. B.
Melton, Robert N.
Modrall, W. B.
Moore, J. M.
Munden, Andrew J.
Munden, Jonathan P.
Murray, William
McAdams, H. D.
McClaran, D. F.

McCrackin, Isaac O.
McMillan, J. Y.
McMills, John H.
McMills, William
Nance, Andrew J.
Nathan (Slave of T. H. Craig)
Peavy, Henry
Perkins, I.
Phillips, Zach
Pleasant, B. B.
Powell, Charles W.
Powell, Jesse (Colored)
Powell, W. D.
Richardson, William Mills *
Riley, James F.
Roberts, Chillian R.
Roberts, John P.
Roberts, William D.
Rogers, H. J. C.
Rogers, J. W.
Rogers, L. J. W.
Rush, James K.
Russell, Palesteen
Russell, Valentine
Russell, W. T. *
Sam (Contraband-Property of J. S. Crawford)
Schwabenland, H.
Sharp, J. H.
Shepherd, R. O.

Shepherd, William W.
Skyles, Vol
Skyles, Charles
Skyles, F. M.
Smith, B. F.
Smith, R. B.
Stewart, M. H.
Sypert, A. A.
Sypert, B. P.
Sypert, J. W.
Summers, John
Terry, J. H.
Thomas, John
Tillery, James B.
Tubbs, J.
Turner, C. A.
Vance, A. J.
Vanderslice, T. F.
Vanderslice, W. J.
Vincent, A. P.
Wakeland, F. M.
Walker, R. H.
Wells, C. W. *
Williams, C. C.
Williams, James A.
Williams, Joseph R.
Winfrey, H. J.
Winn, George
Woodley, J. C.
Woods, W. J.
Wynn, James P.
Young, J. B. D.

Company I, Seventh Texas Infantry Regiment

Airheart, Moses C.
Akin, J. M.
Arnold, James
Arnold, John C.
Arnold, William
Ballinger, Edward
Ballenger, John L.
Barnwell, S. J.
Beard, James
Beard, William
Beard, Willis
Berry, J. T.
Berry, L. D. *
Blackwelder, J. A.
Bledsoe, William J.
Brown, John William
Buckner, J. T.
Burt, O. E.
Cole, Harris T.
Cole, S. C.
Copeland, Wiley F.
Crocker, James
Duke, J. D. *
Duke, L. H.
Fambrough, D. F.
Fetherston, Charles
Foscue, J. S. *

Freeman, Matterson R. *
Furgerson, Isaac
Gallahar, Charles
Glover, L. T.
Goodlett, Jessie H.
Graham, Dr. Robert H.
Haburn, T. H.
Haddox, Wilson H.
Hall, Dixon B.
Harper, T. J.
Harrison, G. R.
Havery, Brown
Higginbotham, Jasper N.
Holloway, P. L.
Hudson, Robert
Hudson, W. H.
Irrin, James N.
Jordan, Henry
Kavenaugh, Charles
Keener, Linson M.
Lambeth, H. F.
Land, Robert F.
Langston, Americus
Latham, Starling
Laws, Thomas G.
Lummus, J. G. *
Lynch, J. G.

Maddon, T. R.
Manning, James
Mathews, T. R.
Mercer, J. B.
Mills, James A.
Montgomery, Benjamin L. *
Montgomery, R. Scott
McAllister, M. L.
McDavid, James E.
McDavid, Robert J.
McGehee, J. A.
McKinley, D. M.
McKinley, Thomas R. *
Neal, John C. *
Nichols, L. M.
Parmer, James S.
Pearson, Ben W.
Pegues, G. W.
Pegues, J. A.
Power, George T.
Pridgen, L. R. *
Riddle, Jasper M.
Riddle, Sylvanus W.
Roberts, James M.
Robertson, P. P.
Roquemore, Henry A. D.
Rush, Leonard

Rush, Uriah W.
Scarbrough, C. F.
Stanton, F. W.
Strong, George S.
Strong, S. W.
Tierce, J. P.
Utzman, Frank

Vaughan, J. C.
Vaughan, James W. *
Waller, J. T.
Watson, J. E.
White, A. H.
White, James D.
White, James R.

White, William K.
Whitley, J.
Williams, Presley D.
Williamson, William H.
Wilson, John
Wilson, William R.

Company K, Seventh Texas Infantry Regiment

Alvis, T. J.
Arnold, W.
Ball, James A.
Bennett, Solomon
Bevil, J. W.
Boney, Henry W.
Boyd, John
Casey, Elsbury B.
Chapman, J. H.
Claunch, John C.
Claunch, T. J.
Clausel, Richard H.
Cochran, Martin C.
Colley, John C.
Collier, W. A.
Coppedge, William L.
Coy, Mitchell H.
Crockerell, William M.
Danley, Andrew J.
Dotson, J. B.
Dudley, Austin
Dudley, James
Duncan, James M. *
Duncan, James M. C.
East, William
Ellison, Thomas K.
Fight, James O.
Fitzgerald, John
Freeman, H. J.

French, J. P.
French, Mike K.
Garner, J.
Garner, W. J.
Greer, Wade H.
Grissom, John
Haclin, J. A.
Hamill, James O.
Hartley, John
Hightower, Isaac O. *
Hill, G. H. B.
Hobbs, C. C.
Hogan, William H.
Hooks, William T.
Hoot, George W.
Hoot, Robert B.
Hurley, William C.
Jones, Crawford T.
Jones, James J.
Justice, John M.
Mapes, Jeremiah N.
Martin, James
Mezzles, Jesse
Monin, Joseph N.
Moore, John *
Mosley, Jefferson
McGriffe, James
McLaughlin, David N.
Oden, James

Oliver, James B.
Orr, A. J.
Orr, John
Plummer, A.
Poore, John F.
Price, J. G.
Purcell, James D.
Reid, Caloway
Reid, William H. *
Richardson, R. C.
Roberts, Ira G. *
Robinson, G. W.
Robinson, J. K.
Ryan, John
Saratt, John M.
Schooler, William T.
Simpson, Thomas P.
Slatter, Thomas R.
Smith, J. L.
Smithson, Allen F.
Smithson, H. M. *
Stewart, Robert A.
Taylor, James L.
Terry, Lafayette F.
Trimble, Isaac Preston
Tutt, James B.
Voyles, Elijah
Walker, Robert W.
Wall, Jesse J.
Wilks, Robert F.
Willingham, W. R.

Miscellaneous, Seventh Texas Infantry Regiment

Colton, W. B.
Fort, Clinton
Johnson, Samuel A.
Levy, J.

Parthenay, Charles
Riggle, John D.
Robinson, John J.
Rudd, J. F.

Sledge, B. F.
Young, J. K. P.

Commissioned Staff, Tenth Texas infantry Regiment

Colonel:
    Roger Q. Mills
    Allison Nelson
Lieutenant Colonel:
    Roger Q. Mills
    Robert Butler Young
Major:
    Seborn C. Brasher
    Jonathan R. Kennard
    Robert Butler Young
Adjutant:
    Joseph T. Hearne
    Jackson L. Leonard
    Jonathan A. Willingham

Surgeon:
William H. Gantt
A. C. Love
David F. Stewart
Assistant Surgeon:
T. C. Foster
James H. Kerr
A. C. Love
R. A. Smith
David F. Stewart
Assistant Commissary of Subsistence:
T. C. Alexander
Isham H. Earle
Assistant Quartermaster:
Sam Barnes
A. Banks
Jonathan R. McDonald
Charles Stewart
Chaplain:
Joseph Dial
Hosea Garrett

Company A, Tenth Texas Infantry Regiment

Alford, John P.
Allen, George W.
Ashcraft, William D.
Baker, Enos H.
Barry, Thomas A.
Beaver, Albert
Berryman, William
Blackshear, Edward T.
Bookman, James F.
Bookman, Joseph F.
Bookman, Paul E. *
Brewer, Samuel B.
Brooks, James J.
Brown, Pinckney B.
Choice, James J.
Coody, James H.
Cook, Samuel M.
Coot, Thomas
Day, John W.
Dearman, D. D.
DeBerry, William E. *
Dedmon, John
Dodson, William G.
Driscol, John J.
Driscol, William B.
Driscol, William Y.
Duckworth, George H.
Edmondson, John W.
Edmondson, Kinchen C.
Edwards, Thomas J.
Edwards, William
Ehrenpfort, George
Faris, Cannon B.
Ford, Jackson
Foster, John E.
Foster, Thomas C.
Franklin, William L.

Gailbreath, James R.
Gardner, Joseph H.
Goodrum, Seaborn
Gregg, James
Haddon, Nicholas G.
Hambright, Robert L.
Harper, Benjamin E.
Harper, Jordan J. *
Hibbits, James E.
Hibbits, Robert R. *
Hill, Stephen H.
Hoke, William W.
Horn, John W.
Howard, Robert W.
Howard, William H.
Hurst, James H.
Hyden, James A.
Jackson, Lewis
Johnson, Benjamin
Johnson, Henry H.
Johnson, William
Kelley, Powell V.
Kennard, Jonathan R.
Kirkling, Robert Thomas M.
Lewis, Thomas J.
Lockett, John M.
Loftin, Henderson
Martin, Joseph L.
Mendenhall, James C. D.
Miller, Benjamin F.
Montgomery, Benjamin F.
Montgomery, John A.
Morgan, G. W.
Morrison, James H.
Morrison, Robert
McCargo, James R. *
McCoy, John H.

McFarland, George W.
McFarland, John
McIntyre, Franklin
McKee, Archibald D.
McKee, Patrick C.
Neale, Joseph R.
Nesbitt, Joseph B.
Newton, Benjamin
Parnall, James C.
Pierson, Benjamin A. *
Polk, Lewis T.
Post, John Allen
Post, Wiley G.
Sandell, Henry C. P.
Scott, Samuel L.
Sheffield, Thomas J.
Sherrell, Simpson L.
Shull, S. L.
Sloan, Thomas
Smith, Edwin D.
Smith, Jackson B.
Smith, James G.
Smith, James T.
Spencer, James H.
Spencer, William B.
Stifflemire, J. P.
Stifflemire, Enoch J.
Stifflemire, Jacob
Stones, Henry N.
Thames, William T.
Tidwell, Lewis G.
Tillman, J. E.
Upchurch, Oliver H. P.
Weatherford, Sion C.
Weeks, Cornelius
West, Harrison
Wheeler, William H.
Willis, Alexander L.

Company B, Tenth Texas Infantry Regiment

Anglin, Elisha
Anglin, John T. *
Anglin, Seth B.
Barber, Silas H.
Bates, John E.
Bates, Seth H.
Bates, William A.
Bennett, Hugh C.
Bennett, James W.
Bennett, William H.
Billington, Allison
Black, Elisha
Black, John
Bower, Christopher C.
Brewer, Greenberry
Burditt, W. R.
Butler, G. B.
Campbell, John P.
Cargile, John
Cargile, William H.
Caruthers, Ewing
Chaffin, Christopher C.
Clayton, W.
Clendenen, Richard
Clendenen, Andrew J.
Clendenen, George W.
Clendenen, James A. *
Clendenen, William P.
Cleveland, William
Clopton, Benjamin M.
Cohron, John W.
Crabb, Jackson L.
Davis, Allen G. *
Dewey, Reuben
Doughty, John
Doughty, Van S.
Eagler, James
Estes, Aaron
Foster, George W.
Fullerton, William A.
Gardenhire, George G.
Garrett, Benjamin

Garten, Harrison R.
Gary, John
Gilley, George P.
Gilley, James M.
Gray, Job C.
Hammett, Thomas B.
Hammett, William
Hemphill, James
Henry, John R.
Hogan, Henry D.
Hogan, James G.
Holeman, Wesley
Hume, Prue B.
Hunter, William M.
Ivy, William B.
Jack (Negro S'v't of Capt.
   Bennett)
Jones, Hardy
Jones, Hiram R.
Jordan, John W.
Jordan, William F.
Justice, William
Key, Samuel H.
Knight, Henry C.
Lasswell, William J.
Lewis, John S.
Lofland, Benjamin B.
Lynn, John M.
Magee, DeWitt C.
Matthews, Joseph K.
Matthews, Wilson R.
Miller, Richard G.
Mills, Coleman
McCuiston, John C.
McDonald, Alexander M.
McDonald, Benjamin F.
McFall, Leonidas M.
Neil, William H.
Packwood, Travis C.
Parker, James
Parr, William A.
Patterson, Duke H.

Patterson, St. John
Peck, Monroe
Porter, William B.
Prendergast, Davis M.
Prendergast, Harvy D.
Richardson, Alexander
Ridge, James H.
Rucker, George W.
Sasser, William M.
Scruggs, Edward Y.
Seawright, William M.
Sharp, James E.
Sharp, Nathaniel H.
Sharp, Thomas H.
Sims, John
Smallwood, George
Smith, David C.
Stanley, William F.
Steele, Alvarado *
Stewart, Columbus
Tharp, John
Tharp, William D.
Tidwell, Seaborn S.
Tidwell, William H.
Tucker, Milton A.
Tucker, Newman
Walker, Stephen D.
Waller, John T.
Weaver, Joseph T.
Webb, George W.
Webb, Jacob C. *
Webb, Robert W.
Webster, William R.
Wheeler, Edward D.
Wickie, Lewis *
Wilder, William M. *
Williams, Benjamin F.
Williams, Leander M.
Wilson, David A.
Wilson, John A.
Wolverton, John W.
Wood, James H.
Wood, Thomas M.
Wood, William E.

Company C, Tenth Texas Infantry Regiment

Able, Ezekiel
Anderson, Amzi D.
Baldwin, William H.
Banks, James L.
Beaver, Andrew J.
Bell, James M.
Berry, Columbus
Berry, Milton H. M.
Berry, Samuel
Billingsley, Burrell
Billingsley, John J.
Billingsly, Christopher
Birdwell, William G.
Blanton, Isaac *
Bransom, James W.

Buckaloo, Joseph
Burditt, W. R.
Burlingame, Hiram
Carter, Edmund
Carter, John W.
Carter, Thomas A.
Chaney, James C.
Chaney, John W.
Chaney, Mathew D.
Chaney, Reese D.
Clark, Dutton M.
Clark, James L.
Clark, James W.
Conley, Thompson
Criner, James I.

Earnest, George L.
Eddlemon, Asbury F. *
Eddlemon, David
Edgar, Alexander *
Edgar, Thomas S.
Fairley, Augustus
Farrell, Thomas
Farris, John A. *
Fisher, William
Formwalt, John A. *
Franklin, Robert L.
Gentry, William P.
George, John C.
Graham, Matthew *
Graves, Hiram P.

Gregory, Francis M.
Griffin, William P.
Griffith, George M.
Hadley, William B.
Halpin, Joseph
Harrell, Washington W.
Harris, Samuel N.
Harris, Thomas R.
Harris, William H.
Hillyer, Simon
Huett, John M.
Hurst, Carter H.
Hurst, David J.
Inmon, Johnson
Jackson, James A. E.
Jackson, William G.
Jewell, George B.
Johnson, H. C.
Johnson, James M.
Johnson, James S.
Jones, James W.
Jordan, Lovel
Kennard, David S.
Key, Columbus M.
Killough, Albert W.
Killough, John H.
Laudy, Robert M.

Law, Peyton J.
Ligon, James J.
Linthicomb, William T.
Manley, Collin J.
Marshall, Louis P
Massey, Nathan A.
Mills, John B.
Morris, Burrell
Morrison, Jesse P.
Morrison, James Preston
Morrison, William M.
Murphy, Wiley
McAdoo, James S.
McKensey, William M.
McNeal, George W.
McPherson, John H.
Noll, Ernest
Patton, William
Patton, Robert C.
Petri, Frederick L.
Quick, John C.
Randle, George W. L. *
Reader, William J.
Renfro, John W.
Renfro, William S.
Riddle, Alexander
Sexton, James A.

Shannon, William J.
Shannon, William R.
Shaw, James D. *
Simer, Mitchell M.
Spraigue, Lycurgus D.
Stephens, George W.
Stephens, John W.
Stephens, Merril W.
Stephens, William Hezekiah
Stewart, Joshua D.
Stewart, Thomas B.
Stokes, Thomas J.
Torbett, James H.
Twillegar, George E.
Varnon, William M.
Weir, Columbus C. *
Weir, Newton Jasper
White, Benjamin F.
White, Martin V.
Whitsett, Joseph W.
Whitsett, Thomas W. *
Willingham, Edmond A.
Wilshire, James M.
Wilshire, John T.
Woodson, Lowery W.
Wright, William M.
Wynn, William O.

Company D, Tenth Texas Infantry Regiment

Adams, Peter L.
Adams, William L.
Augustine, Joseph
Awalt, Isaac R.
Aycock, William
Aycock, Yancy
Balderee, Sterling
Barrington, Thomas B.
Bass, John W.
Baty, John A.
Baty, Thomas F.
Beam, George
Beam, William
Beaver, Hugh K.
Beaver, Thomas H.
Beene, William P.
Betts, Isaac R.
Betts, Joseph
Betts, William A.
Bonner, Andrew S.
Bonner, Irvin H.
Bonner, John L.
Bonner, Oliver A.
Boswell, William O.
Bowles, Dawson
Brooks, William
Busby, David
Busby, Milton
Campbell, Charles C.
Campbell, Jefferson G.
Campbell, Robert B.
Carter, David L.

Clark, Lawrence
Colgin, Charles
Colgin, Richard E.
Colgin, Saladin E.
Craig, Samuel R.
DeBorde, John J. *
Drake, Mathew M.
Drake, Thomas M.
Driver, Marion
Echols, Benjamin R.
Ferrell, James L.
Ferrell, William H.
Fife, James H.
Ford, John W.
George, Gaius
Glenn, Jacob W.
Glenn, William M.
Goodwin, John F.
Gray, Zebulon
Gregg, John
Hagan, Jesse
Harris, Charles H.
Harris, Moses C.
Hogue, Josiah F.
Hogue, William A.
Jobe, Moses
Kendrick, Joseph J. *
Kennedy, Reuben D. *
Lee, Jerry W.
Lee, Jesse G.
Lee, John
Lee, John

Lee, John
Lee, John T.
Lee, Levi
Lee, Robert
Manley, M. D.
Mathis, W. N.
Mayo, George W.
Mayo, William R. *
Miller, Amanuel M.
Moreland, Lucius L.
McChord, Erasmus D.
McCullogh, W.
McSwain, John W.
McSwain, Peter R.
Newby, Uriah E.
Overstreet, Daniel S.
Overstreet, James
Overstreet, Thomas
Overstreet, William
Owen, James J.
Patton, William T.
Praul, Joseph C.
Pruitt, John H.
Pruitt, Francis M.
Quimby, Hance R.
Roark, Barney P. *
Robertson, Abe
Shanks, James H.
Shanks, Robert J.
Shelton, Thomas
Simmons, W. F.
Sims, Thomas W.

Slaughter, George W.
Small, John K.
Smith, Presley E.
Smith, William L.
Spillers, William A.
Tacker, John B.
Tacker, Joshua E.
Tacker, John Robert

Tacker, Wesley S.
Taylor, William L. *
Tull, Isaac W.
Walker, James
Watson, Charles L.
Watson, John C.
Welch, Henry B.
Whaley, Elijah M. *

Whitestone, W. D.
Williams, David H.
Wills, Simon W.
Wilson, William C.
Wooley, John W.
Wortham, James W.
Wortham, John Lee

Company E, Tenth Texas Infantry Regiment

Allen, Eason R.
Allen, Harrison
Allen, Reuben
Anderson, William H.
Barker, Enoch W.
Barker, Jesse G.
Barker, Pleasant G.
Binion, James B.
Brown, Anderson
Brown, James S.
Brown, Simeon W.
Burrow, David E.
Burrow, James W.
Burrow, Levi C.
Burrows, William H.
Clark, Nimrod M.
Clifton, Epaminondas W.
Clifton, James M.
Clifton, Jesse R. *
Clingman, Adam C.
Clingman, Eli P.
Coats, Edmund
Coats, William
Cockburn, Clark T.
Colly, Jacob C.
Cook, William G.
Copelan, John
Copeland, Samuel
Cowser, John F.
Crain, Joel
Cruse, Noble
Culwell, Andrew J.
Culwell, Thomas M.
Denton, Abram L.
Dixon, James J.
Dixon, William B.
Dockery, George W.
Driver, George D.
Earp, Thomas E.
Ellis, Joseph
Enders, Fred W.
Ensey, Ezekiel
Ensey, Rodom A.
Ensey, William H.

Farrer, William H.
Fletcher, George W.
Fletcher, William *
Fletcher, William K.
Followell, Francis
Gore, Andrew J.
Gore, John T.
Guerrin, Thomas
Hale, Henry M.
Hanna, John M.
Hargess, James A.
Hawkins, George W.
Hefner, Francis M.
Higgins, Fountain P.
Hill, John H. *
Hoggard, James
Hoggard, William C.
Houston, Thomas
Hughes, George S.
Inlich, James P.
Johnston, Martin H.
Jones, Charles P. *
Julian, Joseph P.
Kra, J. L.
Leonard, Jackson L.
Lewis, Francis M.
Lewis, George W.
Lewis, Pleasant F.
Lex, Coonrht
Long, George W.
Long, Robert G.
Lovel, William Frank
Lovel, John H. *
Lucky, Timothy H.
Mackey, Francis M.
Mantle, William M.
Matlock, Samuel
Miller, George E.
Mooney, Sampson
Mooney, William L.
Moore, Crosby
Morris, Thomas A.
Morris, W. E.
Mosley, James F.

McCarty, John
McCoy, William
McCulla, John C.
McKamy, William N.
McKnight, Andrew A.
McKnight, John C.
McLarty, Charles B.
McMurry, William
Newsom, William S.
Newsome, John A.
Nichols, William H.
Norrell, Thomas J.
Nowell, Washington H.
Paschal, John J.
Paschal, Henry A.
Patterson, Arthur F.
Pearson, Dudley F.
Pointer, John
Prince, Albert A.
Prince, Thomas M.
Prince, William C.
Redwine, James W.
Reynolds, Grouchy G.
Reynolds, William T.
Richie, James S.
Rowden, Ezekiel
Sessions, John N.
Smith, Charles W.
Smith, Hugh P.
Smith, Joseph R.
Smith, Lewis G.
Smith, William R.
Strickland, Daniel
Sullivan, J. J.
Thomas, James Madison
Thompson, Berlin M.
Thompson, Robert
Towles, John C.
Tucker, Elijah
Watkins, George
Woodall, Joseph A.
Wright, David S.
Wright, Jackson Joseph
Wyette, Hickman D.
Young, Bailey P.

Company F, Tenth Texas Infantry Regiment

Atkins, Samuel H.
Batts, Charles L.
Benson, Pruit C.
Berry, William W.

Boyett, James J.
Boyett, John R.
Brasher, Semore C.
Brasher, William M.

Carey, John J.
Carey, William C.
Carter, George
Carter, James *

Clark, Alexander M.
Clark, George W.
Crow, John B.
Darr, William T.
Dickerson, William A. W.
Donovan, John
Duffee, Michael
Duncan, James A.
Edminston, James C.
Edminston, Joseph E.
Edwards, Elisha T.
Edwards, Rufus K.
Ellis, Elbert K.
Ellis, Richard
Evetts, Samuel G.
Fagan, James
Farquhar, William E. *
Farris, John P.
Finn, Dennis
Fisher, James Wesley
Fisher, William
Fuller, Isaiah D.
Greer, Henry D.
Hanaman, Albert
Harris, James M.
Hill, William W. *
Hinnber, Gerhard H.
Hood, James S.

Howell, William D.
Hurley, Perry A.
Hurston, Johu R.
Jackson, James
Jaques, Stephen T.
Johnson, Lemuel
Johnson, Presly R.
Jones, James M.
Keogh, John
Landrum, Joseph H. *
Langford, George W.
Lee, William T.
Loden, Cantrill W.
Lovett, John Westley
Malone, Jasper
Martin, Charles
Marr, Erasmus E.
Mason, Robert R.
Mathis, Andrew W.
Mosley, Robert W.
Murray, Joshua W.
McDavitt, Edward
McMichael, John B.
McMichael, William A. *
Nevills, William W.
Newsom, Jesse B.
Newsom, William H.
Norton, William A.

Palmer, Martin
Patterson, Charles P.
Perry, Alvin P.
Perry, James S.
Perry, Preston W.
Peyton, John R.
Phelps, Elisha T.
Phelps, James N.
Pollock, James R. *
Price, Morgan
Ragsdale, William H.
Rector, William G.
Reeves, Samuel J.
Reynolds, John
Ridens, John H.
Ryan, Daniel *
Seale, Thomas
Smith, Thomas
Taylor, Samuel A.
Tidwell, Franklin J.
Victor, Alfred
Vivion, Thomas M. *
Walker, David C. *
Walker, William J.
Walls, Timothy L.
Wamble, John E.
Weaver, Jesse W.
White, John P.
Willingham, John A. *

Company G, Tenth Texas Infantry Regiment

Atkinson, Alonzo
Atkinson, Moscow B.
Baine, William R.
Barker, Simeon T.
Barton, Thomas M.
Barton, William B.
Bomgart, Ernst
Booth, Joseph *
Brackin, James A.
Bradford, Charles W.
Brown, Samuel W.
Bruce, Eli W.
Buster, John V.
Cale, James E.
Chase, Oscar P. *
Clark, John L.
Cleveland, Thomas J.
Cook, Daniel L.
Cotton, Benjamin H.
Cotton, Jasper C.
Crow, John A.
Crozier, Robert R. *
Dailey, James P.
Daily, Calvin P. (Col'd S'v't)
Dickerson, Achilles G. *
Espire, Frederick
Fordtran, Eugene H.
Fuqua, John W.
Gage, James
Gage, Marion *

Garrett, Hosea
Gill, Thomas J.
Gillerland, Haney A.
Givens, William H.
Gray, Jesse G.
Greenhouse, Andrew J.
Griffey, Robert
Guthrie, Thomas B.
Guthrie, Ulysses *
Harlan, Isaiah
Harris, Elihu W.
Harris, Hendrix P.
Henderson, Henry A.
Hill, James M. *
Hopkins, James K.
Houston, John H.
Houston, William
Hunt, John H.
Joiner, William
Jones, Jasper N.
Kies, John G. *
Lauderdale, James S.
Lewis, John H.
Linn, Rankin M.
Lipscomb, Abner S.
Lockridge, John B.
Lockridge, William J.
Longley, Alexander C.
Longley, George W.
Longley, Marion L.

Malone, Hal D.
Marshall, Isaac
Martin, Oliver H. P.
Massengale, Harris M. *
Massengale, William S.
Meek, James D.
Meek, William J.
Momie, F. W.
Moran, Peter
Morriss, Richard O.
Morriss, Thomas W.
Mundine, John C.
Myers, David R. *
McBride, Robert N.
McDonald, Jonathan R.
McGregor, Daniel
McGregor, John D.
McGregor, Malcolm C.
McKnight, James H.
Phears, Marion
Phears, McDonald D.
Picture, Alfred
Purcell, John
Raines, Jeremiah
Rial, Walter D.
Roberts, Dr. Thomas L.
Rucker, Edmond T.
Sanders, George P.
Schmidt, Fredrick
Seales, James S. *

Seaton, Benjamin M.
Sharp, Valerius P.
Sherlock, Richard W.
Smith, Charles T.
Smith, Hamilton
Snider, Joseph L. *
Sparks, Hugh S.
Speight, Simon E.

Stanley, George R.
Steele, Abner L. *
Stevenson, William
Stokes, George (Col'd S'v't)
Stokes, William E.
Stricklin, Matthew
Tabor, George W.
Taylor, James

Verdan, Robert J.
White, Patrick Y.
Williams, Alonzo J.
Williams, George W.
Williams, Lloyd B. *
Wood, Abraham R.
Woods, James S.

Company H, Tenth Texas Infantry Regiment

Alexander, Leonidas A.
Alexander, Thomas C.
Armstrong, William M.
Arrowood, McDonald
Ashby, Edward L.
Barnes, Samuel
Bassel, Benjamin
Bassel, Byron J.
Beard, William
Beard, Willis
Beaty, Richard S.
Bell, Anderson M.
Bell, Robert A.
Bellomy, T. Jefferson
Bellomy, Marion
Bishop, John H.
Bivens, Elijah
Branner, Charles
Brewer, William
Burch, Ellison
Burnam, George B.
Burnam, James H.
Bushman, Henry
Carson, James T.
Casey, Richard F.
Cassel, Daniel W.
Click, James M.
Collard, Felix
Collard, William E.
Crawford, Samuel A.
Crow, Benjamin F.
Davenport, J. . A. *
Davenport, Overton F.
Dawson, Wilburn A.
Dean, William R.
Decordova, Joshua R.
Draper, Jasper
Draper, Joseph L.
Durnett, Charles A.
Echols, Smith E.

Edwards, Joshua H.
Everett, Thomas
Fine, James P.
Fine, John C.
Flanigan, John W.
Franks, David R.
Green, Albert G.
Hall, Amasa M.
Hall, David E.
Handy, B. S.
Hanna, Samuel A.
Hartgraves, Brice
Henderson, Thomas *
Hoghland, Henry J.
Holloway, Jasper N.
Holt, Thomas J.
Jones, James P.
Jones, James W. *
Jones, John F.
Jones, Martin A. *
Judah, William B.
Killingsworth, Peter L.
Leach, Richard Martin
Leatherman, Daniel W.
Lee, Baldwin P.
Lee, Timothy
Lefevre, Curatious M.
Lenihen, Patterson S.
Lindsey, Albert
Lindsey, Thomas R.
Logan, Jasper N.
Logan, Joel H. *
Logan, Robert S.
Logan, Wyatt L.
Lollar, William
Low, William A.
Mabray, Henry L.
Manly, Bohannon
Marr, Henry W.
Mathews, William A.

Mayfield, John T.
Mefford, Samuel A.
Miller, Thomas G.
Moss, Samuel R.
McAlister, Wilson *
McClain, William B.
McIlhaney, Henry C.
McIlhaney, Randle H.
McIlhaney, William J. G.
Oglesby, Charles F.
Oglesby, William
Oglesby, Willis
Phillips, Wesley J.
Porter, Franklin L.
Price, Lee
Prowse, George W.
Prowse, Joseph
Pugh, James W.
Randal, Thomas J.
Robinson, Asa
Robinson, Solomon H. *
Ross, Thomas B.
Sanders, Earby
Sanders, James M. *
Sanders, William T.
Scott, John W. *
Scott, Robert S.
Sedberry, John S.
Simpson, Kaufman
Smith, Edward M.
Smith, James D.
Smith, James K.
Smith, John A.
Snoutz, Phillip *
Taylor, Robert A.
Waters, William D.
Webb, Thomas M.
Williamson, Asa C. *
Wilson, George I.
Wilson, John R.
Wood, George B.
Wright, Willis D.

Company I, Tenth Texas Infantry Regiment

Adams, John H.
Allison, James H.
Barnett, David A.
Benge, Thomas O.
Benge, Ware
Birdwell, Samuel
Bowman, Lewis
Brock, Hugh

Calhoun, John H,
Calhoun, Kimbrough O.
Chambers, Asa
Chambers, John R.
Chambers, William T.
Chapman, Isaac S.
Clardy, Norman S.
Cottrell, William

Crabtree, Alexander
Deaver, John C.
Deaver, Levi N.
Edwards, John P. *
Elam, Andrew M.
Evans, William N.
Fanning, Nathan
Gafford, William R.

Garrett, Robert A.
Gibson, Emanuel
Goodwin, Josiah C.
Gregory, William J.
Hamby, Harvey N.
Hamby, William M.
Huffstuttle, Adam *
Hull, Elijah W.
Johnson, Jerry M.
Lambert, Amon
Landreth, William
Ledbetter, Andrew J.
Ledbetter, Archibald B.
Lewis, John
Lockridge, Laton
Long, Samuel
Manly, Henry B.
Manly, William C.
Moran, William H. *
Morris, Roberson
McCoy, James C.
McCoy, John
McCoy, William N.

McCrary, Absalom M.
McCrary, Austin M.
McCrary, James A. *
McKenzie, David C. *
McWhorter, James S.
Nolen, William P.
Powell, Joseph M.
Radford, William
Randal, Joseph W.
Roberson, Benjamin
Roberson, Hiram R.
Roberson, Isaac J.
Roberson, Jacob
Rose, John
Sikes, Andrew J.
Sikes, Martin L.
Stephens, Peter
Stokes, Thomas J.
Tabor, John Henry
Taylor, John W.
Thompson, David L.
Thompson, John F. C.
Trimble, James L.

Tuggle, Henry P.
Vanover, Samuel
Vickers, A. Newton
Vickers, David P.
Vickers, Eli M.
Vickers, Henry P.
Vinson, Armistead W.
Wakefield, George N.
Walker, Henry H.
Ward, William A. R. D.
Westbrooks, William G.
Wheeler, Andrew J.
Wilkerson, Joseph E.
Williams, ———
Willingham, Isaac Y.
Willingham, John A.
Willingham, Thomas B.
Wilson, David G.
Wright, James W.
Wright, Spencer
Wyatt, Flemon J.
Yates, Austin N.
Zorn, James C.

Company K, Tenth Texas Infantry Regiment

Bassel, Andrew J.
Bassel, Byron J.
Blair, Jasper G. W.
Blair, John F. *
Boatright, Daniel T.
Campbell, Etson *
Childers, William
Collard, Felix
Costs, Uriah
Crawford, Jasper J.
Crews, Thomas C. C.
Crow, Benjamin F.
Daniel, James
Davenport, John A. *
Davenport, Overton F.
Decker, Isaiah
Denmark, George W.
Derrick, Archibald D.
Dial, Andrew Jackson
Dial, James R.
Dixon, Montgomery
Dodson, George W.
Dukes, Berry
Edington, Edmond J.
Embry, Enoch J.
Embry, Henry W.
Embry, William T.
Force, Samuel F.
Gailey, Asa L.
Garrison, Levi

Green Albert G.
Green, Elias
Grigsby, Emmons
Haley, David C.
Hall, Aralza
Hatton, William C.
Hill, Harrison D.
Hollingsworth, Aaron H.
Hoover, Abraham
House, Brinkley S.
Howard, Harvey
Hughes, Henry W.
Hughes, James A. *
Hughes, James G.
Hughes, Nathaniel S.
Keen, Elijah J. *
Keen, Joseph
Kincaid, William G. W.
Leach, Richard Martin
Lee, Francis M.
Lewis, William H.
Little, George
Logan, Lewis
Milton, Morgan J.
McClain, William B.
McClain, William R.
McCoy, Francis M.
McCoy, Reuben M.
McCutchen, William P.
McGary, Edward O. H.

McGary, Joseph W.
McGary, Marcellus
Nichols, Thomas N.
Nichols, Wesley
Pennington, Asa
pennington, James
Pennington, John
Pennington, Riggs
Pennington, Simeon
Roberson, James E.
Roberson, James M. M.
Roberson, Mathew N.
Roberson, William
Rucker, Jeremiah T.
Shelmadine, Hiram J.
Shipman, William
Smith, Benjamin F.
Smith, Edwin R.
Smith, Elbert S.
Smith, Joseph B.
Smith, Sterrett A.
Snider, Noah
Tudor, Nicholas F. M.
Upshaw, George A.
Wade, Ebenezer
Wade, William M.
Wallace, William M.
Wheeler, Charles
Whitehead, Charles F.
Wilkerson, John
Wooton, James

Miscellaneous, Tenth Texas Infantry Regiment

Gibson, Daniel D.
Johnson, J. D.
Leer, Lewis G.

Moore, Henry
Smith, Solomon (Negro)
Swain, Wilson

Taylor, G. W.
Thompson, Dock R. M.

Commissioned Staff, Fifteenth Texas Cavalry Regiment

Colonel:
George H. Sweet
Lieutenant Colonel:
William K. Masten
George Bible Pickett
Major
William H. Cathey
George Bible Pickett
Valerius P. Sanders
Adjutant:
M. Shelby Kennard
Stephen C. Thompson
Surgeon:
Elias J. Beall
Thomas M. Matthews
Carroll M. Peak
Assistant Surgeon:
Thomas M. Matthews
Thomas Stewart
Nathan H. Wynkoop
Assistant Commissary of Subsistence:
Thomas E. Sherwood
Assistant Quartermaster:
Thomas Cox
Julian T. Fields
Thomas J. Johnson
W. R. Story
Chaplain:
William Harris
A. L. Hay
John Johnson
Samuel Johnson
Thomas Woodfield

Company A, Fifteenth Texas Cavalry Regiment

Allen, Daniel P.
Avant, Durmer
Avant, William
Beason, Richard J.
Birdwell, James M.
Birdwell, Joseph
Bishop, William G.
Bishop, William H.
Burns, Robert M.
Cannon, Seamon B.
Carson, John P.
Cochrehan, S. K.
Collum, Perry P. R.
Combs, J. W.
Corben, E. J.
Cox, Aaron W.
Cox, Andrew J.
Evans, Edward D.
Foler, John T.
George, J. W. A.
Good, Isham J.
Gordon, William T.
Harper, Marquis L.
Harrell, John E.

Harris, Marion D.
Harris, William L.
Harrison, William J.
Hathaway, Gilbert B.
Hill, James T. C.
Inmann, Carrol
Isaacs, John A.
Johnson, John
Johnson, John Jr.
Johnson, John Sr.
Johnson, Samuel
Kincaid, David G.
Kincaid, James M.
Kincaid, James M.
Kincaid, William M.
Laddington, James H.
Laddington, John
Landon, Asa
Linley, Henry
Lockwood, Theodore
Logan, Henry C.
Marsh, John W.
McCann, James
McCann, William C.

McFarland, John W.
McGary, Daniel L.
McMinn, Valentine
McNally, Joseph
Nolen, Benjamin F.
Nolen, Francis M.
Obarr, Robert
Obarr, Thomas
Odell, John L.
Page, James K.
Page, John T.
Park, Daniel
Park, Woodson
Patten, James M.
Patten, William M.
Payne, Richmond
Perry, Napoleon B.
Roberts, William T.
Robertson, Doc F.
Robertson, Pinkney C.
Robinson, Joel T.
Robinson, Joseph
Robinson, William A.
Rozell, Jacob F. W.

Rozell, James N.
Rozell, William G.
Ruddell, John L.
Rutledge, Jamison C.
Sanders, Thomas W.
Sanders, Valerius P.
Schneider, Gustavus A.
Self, William B.
Shott, William F. *
Shropshire, Benjamin N.
Smith, James H.

Smithson, William
Spear, George W.
Speer, Joseph
Steel, Charles
Stevens, William D.
Sweet, George H.
Taylor, William
Thompson, Henry C.
Thompson, Marcus A.
Thompson, Stephen C.
Thompson, Stephen T.

Toler, John T.
Trainer, David J.
Trainer, Samuel E.
Wadkins, John A.
Walters, Richard
Ward, George W.
Welch, James
Welsh, John R.
Woolridge, William
Young, William *
Youngblood, Jesse

Company B, Fifteenth Texas Cavalry Regiment

Anderson, Adam C.
Anderson, Francis M.
Anderson, Hiram F.
Anderson, John
Anderson, William
Ball, Scott
Barnett, Thomas C.
Barrett, John William
Barrett, Flavius J.
Bradford, William H. H.
Braham, William
Brandon, Walter W. *
Brown, Adam S.
Brown, Robert J.
Bryan, Allen A.
Bryan, William
Burk, W. L.
Burrus, William C.
Cameron, John
Carson, William T.
Cartright, Thomas Jefferson
Cartwright, George W.
Cartwright, Lemuel
Carver, William F.
Cates, Robert
Coleman, Thomas B.
Collins, Christopher C.
Collins, Robert M. *
Collum, Perry P. R.
Cook, Marion D.
Cook, William B. F.
Cook, William D.
Counterman, Daniel
Crier, Daniel W.
Crimer, Joseph J.
Crutchfield, Leroy S.
Darnell, William J.
Davenport, Thomas W.
Davenport, William J.
Dawson, John T.
Dean, George P.
Derrick, William V. *
Edmonson, Richard C.
Eldridge, Joel
English, W. J.
Evans, Thomas
Finley, John
Finly, Francis M.

Flint, John
Floyd, Robert W.
Ford, F. F.
Fullingim, Jesse P.
Gallop, William E.
Gaston, Robert E.
George, Washington M.
Gilliland, A.
Goff, Isaiah
Gose, Christopher C.
Goutier, George R.
Grantham J. W,
Grider, John W.
Grider, Joseph M.
Grider, Thomas
Haley, James C.
Harding, James L. *
Harkreader, John F.
Harris, McCamey A. *
Hart, John J.
Hart, John M.
Hendricks, P. P.
Hines, James E.
Hopkins, Moses B.
Howell, Riley
Howell, Zachariah
Hudson, Irby
Isbell, Marvin T.
Jones, John E.
Jones, J. W.
King, Isaiah W.
King, William A.
Kirby, Thomas W.
Lackey, Oliver
Lawrence, J. E.
Lee, James
Leutz, Thomas B.
Lipsey, Samuel F.
Lux, John T.
Lynch, Solomon M.
Mahaffy, Alexander
Mahaffy, H. T.
Mapes, James H.
Meeks, Alex
Mershon, James H.
Miller, Eli R.
Miller, Francis M.
Miller, Joshua

Miller, S. D.
Millhollon, Isaac Newton *
Mills, George M.
Mills, Jesse
Mills, William Perry
Mount, Frederick M.
Mounts, William T.
McCulloch, John M
McKinney, James Henry
McLemore, William H.
McMahan, John W.
Neal, Shepherd
Osteen, James W.
Osteen, Sylvester
Owens, S. B.
Parsons, J. P.
Paschal, L. S.
Patton, J. H.
Payne, Richmond
Pennington, Green B.
Phillips, William T.
Pickett, George Bible
Priddy, William T.
Qualls, Merideth
Qualls, William R.
Rankin, Berry
Reed, Solomon S.
Reed, William S.
Renfro, William
Roberts, James
Roberts, Leonard *
Robertson, C. F.
Robertson, Isaac N.
Robertson, Thomas D.
Rogers, Columbus
Rogers, George W.
Rogers, J. M.
Rozell, James P.
Sanders, H. D.
Sanders, S. H.
Sheets, Samuel N.
Shoemaker, Milton M.
Smith, Jesse
Smith, John
Stewart, Thomas
Stricklin, Amos
Taylor, Thomas D.
Thomas, H. B.

Thomas, John W.
Thomas, William
Tipton, William w.
Tucker, Milton A.
Uhr, Mathew
Van Vickle, John
Wade, Richard M.

Wagoner, John
Walling, Daniel
Warson, John W.
Watson, John J.
Wheeler, George
Whitley, Joseph
Whittington, Jasper

Williams, H. B.
Williams, William
Wilson, Alexander
Wilton, Henry Hawkins
Winneford, Joseph
Woods, Samuel A.
Wright, Harbin

Company C, Fifteenth Texas Cavalry Regiment

Able, Thomas S.
Ables, Ezekiel
Ables, James
Adams, John D.
Aiken, Michael C.
Allen, John R.
Armstrong, William P.
Barnes, George B.
Bectal, Daniel
Benizon, Solomon
Boisseau, Richard H.
Borneau, William H.
Bourn, James E.
Bridges, Ellison W.
Brown, John S.
Buntin, Barnabas S.
Buntin, Bembal W.
Buntin, Benjamin F.
Burns, George B. *
Calloway, Sam
Campbell, Samuel R.
Campbell, William A.
Casstephens, Joshua W.
Carmack, James
Chandler, James E.
Chinaworth, James F.
Choat, Calvin S.
Christopher, Benjamin F.
Christopher, John D.
Christopher, John S.
Clanton, William H.
Coleman, William F.
Conley, William R.
Ovilington, James M.
Crawford, Alfred H.
Criswell, James
Dodds, James D.
Dougherty, N. N.
Douglas, James
Duke, John J.
Earley, D. T.
Earley, J. P.
Ellet, Casper P.
Elliot, Daniel W.
Elliott, Samuel V.
Ellis, C. P.
Ellis, George L.
Ellis, Richard N.
Fathree, Hilliard H.
Ferril, S. L.
Fields, Julian T.
Ford, W. S.

Frame, James P.
Gibson, Andrew J.
Glass, Samuel B.
Goodwin, Thomas J.
Greathouse, John C.
Green, W. H.
Harless, Charles D.
Harris, P. S.
Hartgraves, Charles A. W.
Henson, Henry
Hook, Samuel W. A. *
House, Samuel C.
Hudman, Joseph J.
Huff, Arthur D.
Hughes, Andrew G.
Hughes, William M.
Ivey, Green C.
Jacobs, J. T.
Johnson, Mathew
Johnson, Pascal M.
Johnson, Robert
Jones, Alexander
Jones, David C.
Jones, H. R.
Jones, Richard J.
Jones, Roberts
Jones, Samuel
Knoy, George
Lamb, George
Lamb, Nathan
Landers, J. C.
Landry, John
Lee, James H.
Lewis, Riley M.
Lewis, Robert
Lowe, Thomas K.
Murry, John
Martin, Francis M.
Martin, Jonathan
Martin, William K.
Miller, William B.
Mitchell, Ezekiel A.
Mitchell, George W.
Mooney, Charles S.
Moore, W. S.
Morris, William J.
Morrison, Jesse P.
Morrison, Samuel P.
Murry, Elam J.
McBride, John W. *
McCorkle, John
McCorkle, Archibald K.

McCorkle, George W.
McCorkle, William A.
McCreary, Alexander M.
McCreary, Moses A. *
McCutchan, A. D.
McDaniel, J.
McFadden, William R.
McGowen, Benagar
McVey, Aaron B.
Neely, Charles
Newly, John F.
Newman, James
Nichols, J. B.
Norris, James E.
Nunn, Newton N.
Owens, James H.
Parish, Harvey
Parker, Charles P.
Parker, Samuel V.
Parsons, Warren D.
Peterson, Charles
Posey, B. B.
Ramsey, John J.
Raney, Wyatt
Ray, John A.
Richardson, John
Roberts, Raymon H.
Robinson, John B.
Roper, John H.
Roy, Joel
Saylor, Abraham
Sherwood, Thomas E.
Sisson, John
Smith, C. T.
Smith, John
Spain, Wiley J.
Spradling, Robert Wilson
Steel, Hampton
Stewart, Jonathan W. *
Stiles, James S.
Sullivan, John W.
Sullivan, Milton
Sumberland, James T.
Sutherland, William H.
Tate, Martin V. *
Taylor, James C. *
Taylor, Mathew T.
Terry, J. N.
Thrasher, John B.
Titus, James E.
Triplett, A. H.
Tubbs, R. C.

Tucker, James
Turner, Daniel
Turner, Elisha
Wagoner, James
Wakefield, H. F.
Wallis, W. L.

Warren, Robert W.
Weaver, William C.
White, F.
Wiggins, David
Wilkins, Charles S.
Williams, Benjamin F.

Williams, Hugh M.
Williams, James
Williams, William H.
Williams, William W.
Winneford, N. R.
Woodberry, Jonathan D.

Company D, Fifteenth Texas Cavalry Regiment

Adams, Andrew J.
Adams, John B.
Adams, Samuel
Alston, Richard
Angeline, John B.
Arrington, C. T.
Arrington, Ed. D.
Arrington, James C.
Arrington, John M.
Arrington, T. H. T.
Avery, Toby
Baker, W. H.
Banister, Lawrence
Bargely, John
Barker, William H. H.
Barrett, John W.
Barrie, Samuel F.
Berryhill, M.
Bond, Henry
Branch, Elihu
Brinkley, William
Browder, William
Brown, Chatham E.
Brown, Youn
Bryan, Thomas J. *
Bryant, Thaddeus Y. *
Campbell, Squire C.
Carmack, James C.
Clanton, Wiley R.
Clark, William B.
Climer, John
Coen, Samuel
Connit, James C.
Crawford, Alfred H.
Criswell, David P.
Cummings, Alfred
Dalcern, M.
Dalcon, C.
Daws, John J.
Day, William M.
Dennis, Barnet H.
Dennis, William M.
Dickey, John W. *
Dickey, Samuel L.
Durham, James M.
Evans, R. B.
Ford, Howell E.
Frame, James P.
Frizzell, A. J.
Frizzell, John W.
Gage, James M.

Galbreth, A. J.
Goforth, John L.
Gotcher, James A.
Green, John
Gregory, John M.
Hardin, John
Harris, Holden
Harris, Timothy
Hart, John M.
Harvey, George
Havens, Harvy T.
Havens, Thomas J.
Hayes, John M.
Hennagin, Samuel A.
Herron, John
Herron, Silas
High, John
Hobbs, Timothy
Holt, Sherm
Homes, Henry T.
Homes, Thomas J.
Houston, Louis
Huffstutler, Caleb *
Huffstutler, Henry *
Isaacs, Alfred C. *
Isaacs, John A.
Isaacs, William M.
Ivey, James
Johnson, John H.
Kinman, Lee *
Kirby, Jesse
Landers, Able R.
Landers, Henry A.
Landers, Levi G.
Landers, William M.
Lewis, James J.
Liday, William H. *
Martin, Marcellus M.
Mathews, James S.
Mathews, Jeremiah B.
Mattocks, George
Messer, John A.
Middleton, James A.
Middleton, Nathan R.
Morrison, Jesse P.
McClain, James W.
McClane, Charles F.
McClane, Francis M.
McDaniel, William
McKenzie, J. D.
McLane, John

Naylor, C. H.
Neely, Isaac N.
Newman, Harvey
Norris, Martin C.
Nutt, Abel
Paschal, A. J.
Paul, Cason
Pearson, P. E.
Peters, Amon L.
Pheonix, James R.
Pierson, Leroy
Porter, Laban P.
Powel, Wiley J.
Powell, Jackson V.
Price, Merideth
Ray, John A.
Richardson, James F.
Roberts, McNeil
Robertson, James F.
Robinson, William H.
Rolling, John W.
Rose, Louis
Runnels, Harvey
Scarborough, Silas
Scarbrough, John
Sherwood, Jonathan E.
Smith, C. L.
Smith, J. M.
Smith, Jonathan N.
Smith, John
Smith, Mathew D.
Stephens, S. P.
Stewart, William
Tankersley, William H.
Tankersly, Daniel B.
Tankersly, James R.
Tankersly, John W.
Tankersly, Larkin
Taylor, Thomas
Thomas, John H.
Thomas, R. B.
Thomas, William
Thompson, Dempsy D.
Thornton, Daniel R.
Thornton, Philip
Toby, Avery
Toby, Samuel
Trainer, Samuel
Truitt, James
Truitt, P. M.
Vickers, Henry P.

Wade, T. V.
Waite, Thomas
Walls, John
Washburn, Josiah
Washburn, Samuel S. B.
Wells, John
Wilson, William H.
Wood, S. G.
Work, Robert F.
Wright, William

Company E, Fifteenth Texas Cavalry Regiment

Adams, William Frank
Alford, Wiley G.
Anderson, B.
Anderson, Dandridge
Anderson, H. L.
Applewhite, W. A.
Asberry, John
Beal, Robert T.
Boaz, William J.
Booth, John
Bowls, J. W.
Brandon, Richard D.
Breeding, B. W.
Burk, Aaron R.
Burson, James D. *
Camplain, J. S.
Chambers, Job C.
Chapman, William C.
Clark, William J.
Coley, F. J.
Craig, Jonathan B.
Crawford, Robert B.
Crimer, Samuel G.
Crouch, John A. *
Curry, Alexander
Davis, John W.
Davis, Peter G.
Dickson, Albert E.
Douglass, John D.
Dowell, J. T.
Eddy, Ezra
Eggleston, Irvin
Ellis, James F.
Ellis, William J.
Escu, R.
Fletcher, Martin D.
Flowers, Isaac
Flowers, William D.
Foley, Samuel
Fore, J. A.
Forsythe, Newton
Fort, James C.
Gibson, R. C.
Gillespie, Charles B.
Gillespie, James H.

Gothall, Phillip
Gregory, James M.
Grimsley, Charles
Grimsley, John
Guyer, George W.
Hampton, John
Harris, Stephen L.
Hart, B. B.
Haworth, William
Henderson, J. P.
Henderson, Robert W.
Herrol, Charles
Hood, Onslow M.
Holt, William L.
Howard, Asa
Howard, J. D.
Huffaker, James P.
Isaacks, William M.
James, Thomas L.
Jasper, Andrew J.
Jay, James M.
Johnson, Benjamin F.
Jones, Henry E.
Keller, Robert
Kelly, S. D.
Kennedy, Michael D.
Kimble, Charles B.
Kinslow, James T.
Knaar, Francis
Lurden, H. G.
Mahan, David
Marchbanks, Lafayette
Martin, Carr
Martin, Charles
Mathews, Robert N.
Mathews, Thomas M.
Moore, William H.
Mount, James
Mugg, James K. *
Mugg, W. H. H.
McCann, A. C.
McClure, John J.
McCormick, John R.
McCracken, James L. *
McDonald, Arch

McEwin, John F.
McGuire, Andrew
McGuire, Nelson W.
McMillan, William R.
McMurray, W. N.
Nance, James M.
Newton, John
Norred, John O.
O'Kelly, F. M.
Overton, Alonzo W.
Patrick, Ezekiel
Perryman, James M.
Pinkston, Albert G.
Poindexter, J. F.
Ray, Robert J.
Richardson, Jonathan
Roby, Singleton
Russell, E.
Russell, S. J.
Seely, Samuel
Shackleford, Charles A.
Smith, David H.
Southerland, E. A.
Sprinkle, James S.
Stewart, Benjamin F.
Stiles, Benton
Taylor, Benjamin F.
Taylor, Thomas L.
Teague, General M.
Terrill, James W.
Thomas, Robert J. *
Thomas, William
Thornton, L. B.
Trammell, Daniel J.
Vannoy, William O.
Waites, Jacob B.
Walker, William H.
Whaley, James C.
White, Meredith
Williams, J. A.
Williams, Joseph O.
Wilson, James
Wright, W. T.
Yantis, William O.
Young, Joseph S.

Company F, Fifteenth Texas Cavalry Regiment

Alston, Edward M.
Anglin, Silas K. *
Anglin, William A.
Archer, John M.
Archer, Kilgore
Arlage, William M.
Babb, George W.
Bates, John A.
Beall, Elias J.
Bennett, Elson G.
Bennett, John T.
Bennett, William H.
Bennett, W. J.
Billington, John L.
Bowden, James K. P.
Brady, William A.
Burney, William A.
Burrows, David L.
Chism, William E.
Choate, Richard C.
Cook, Silas K.
Corbin, Drew H.
Corbin, Johnson W.
Crist, George W.
Crouch, James E.
Dabney, Nathan E.
Daniel, Matthew S.
Davis, Thomas J.
Davis, William
Dyer, Madison
Evans, Jasper E.
Evans, Joel E.
Evans, John E.
Evans, Joseph E.
Flannegan, Samuel H.
Gilbreath, Benson
Hanks, Elijah F.
Hanna, Robert
Harmon, George W.

Harper, Cyrus A.
Hawkins, Pinckney H.
Herod, James
Herring, Edwin R.
Hodge, W. L.
Holloway, William H.
Holt, Nathan T.
Hopper, Lofton C.
Kennedy, Clement P.
Lee, Brooks, W.
Manks, Elijah F.
Middleton, William R.
Miller, Meredith N.
McCaig, William
McCorkle, James
McDonald, William M. *
Ogden, Elias D.
Owen, Benjamin
Parker, John
Parker, Ransom
Peeples, Joseph R.
Perry, Marcus L.
Persons, Alfred T.
Persons, Lewis R. *
Plummer, James Pratt
Reives, W. J.
Roberts, Hiram M.
Rogers, Moses Columbus
Rogers, William F.
Runnels, James A.
Sanders, Hampton S.
Sanders, Henry G.
Sanders, John
Schinault, Andrew J.
Seawright, John H.
Sharpe, Ezekial M.
Sharpe, William A.
Sharpe, William V.
Simon, Alexander

Slaughter, John
Slaughter, Wesley W.
Sorelle, Seaborne J.
South, William H.
Speers, William M.
Steel, Hampton
Steele, Alonzo L.
Strickle, George W.
Stryker, Dennis W.
Stryker, John B.
Swain, Robert H. *
Thomas, William M.
Thompson, William M.
Tidwell, James C.
Tipton, Samuel Houston *
Tucker, Milton A.
Tun, John G.
Turner, David D.
Turner, Thomas A.
Tyus, Benjamin R.
Tyus, Joseph B.
Usry, Benjamin
Valentine, James
Valentine, Tilman
Wadley, Joseph G.
Wallace, Benjamin F. *
Wheeler, Duncan C.
Wheeler, Edward D. C. *
Whitt, Eli J.
Williams, Brooks W.
Williams, Leander M.
Williams, Thomas
Williams, Thomas M.
Wilson, Hilliard J.
Wood, Christopher H. T. *
Wood, Ira
Wood, Joseph
Woods, Joseph H.
Woolverton, Tilman
Wright, John C.
Wynekoope, Nathan H.

Company G, Fifteenth Texas Cavalry Regiment

Archibald, Thomas M.
Arnold, William A
Bacon, George W. L.
Baker, Edwin B.
Baker, George W.
Baker, Samuel J.
Ball, James M.
Beck, James L.
Beck, Samuel J.
Bell, James N.
Boydston, Joseph E.
Bradley, Milton
Bristow, William M.
Burn, John Milton
Burnham, Joshua
Cannon, Isaac J.
Cantwell, James

Cantwell, Stephen
Cash, George C.
Cook, Andrew B.
Daugherty, John Q.
Eldridge, Joel
Elliot, John
Elliott, Stephen K.
Ellis, Milford
Fannin, John A.
Faulkner, Alsdorf
Flannery, Thomas B.
Foster, Henry C.
Fulsom, Joseph
Furst, Samuel
Hannon, Stephen A.
Hardwick, Samuel H.
Harper, George

Harper, James R.
Hart, John H.
Hill, Eli A.
Holland, Milton
Hunt, Lewis A.
Hurst, L. W.
Jackson, Calvin F.
Johnson, James L.
Kale, Richard D.
Keeney, Thomas
Kidd, William H. A.
King, James B.
Knight, Martin V.
Landers, Able W.
Lawrence, John H.
Lockard, John H.
Long, Ira

Lynch, James M.
Lynch, Solomon
Lynch, William W.
Martin, Benjamin F.
Martin, David S.
Mathews, George W.
Mathews, Merritt
Maxwell, Charles *
Miller, Joshua
Miller, Stephen
Miller, Thomas F.
Millwee, William Harvey
Minniken, John M.
Mounts, Daniel M.
McMurray, Hiram
Nance, Andrew J.
Norris, John G.
Parker, James H.

Parker, J. R.
Parson, James M.
Patterson, J.
Pickle, Joseph
Roach, Mike
Roberts, Benjamin
Rodgers, G. C.
Ross, George W. *
Sallyers, Daniel
Sego, Thomas
Sego, William
Selby, Isaiah
Selby, William
Shirley, Stillwell
Smith, Chester B.
Smith, Chilton L. *
Smith, Francis M.
Smith, Samuel K.

Sorars, H.
Starkey, Lorenzo D.
Street, David H.
Stroud, George W.
Sullivan, William R.
Teague, King D.
Teague, Thomas A.
Tillery, Samuel
Truss, Charles E.
Van Vickle, John
Violette, William A.
Walker, James M.
Welch, Thomas
Williamson, Thomas
Willis, Benjamin
Wilson, Richard J.
Woolery, John M.
Woolsey, Z.

Company H, Fifteenth Texas Cavalry Regiment

Abernathy, Holbert
Abernathy, Milton
Able, Joseph B.
Alteway, James E.
Armstrong, Aaron
Balthrop, Wiley R.
Been, William W.
Black, Hiram
Black, William P.
Blackwell, Levi G.
Blackwell, William H.
Blankenship, James
Boyle, Patrick
Burden, John
Burden, Joseph
Burris, George
Burrows, John
Burrow, Samuel
Byars, Alexander
Byars, Samuel
Cissna, John R.
Cox, James M.
Cozby, Robert M.
Crunk, Charles
Daniel, Enoch *
Drake, George W.
Dunaway, James
Dupree, Thomas D.
Elier, William
English, Elisha B.
English, W. Denton
English, William C.
Franklin, John H.
Fry, James T.

Fulfer, Joseph
Fulfer, Thomas
Fulfer, Zachariah
Garrard, Thomas S.
Garret, William
Gibson, J. D.
Guice, Jonathan L.
Hart, John M.
Harvey, R. B.
Hensley, Andrew J.
Herrin, Berry O.
Herrin, Louis H.
Hodges, James P.
Holloway, James R.
Holloway, Sidney
Jenks, Seth
Johnson, Barncy L.
Johnson, Isaac G.
Johnson, William M.
Jones, David J.
Jones, Thomas
King, Abraham B.
Long, James
Long, Martin V.
Long, William
Lynn, William
Madison, Benjamin L.
Malony, John P.
Miller, Pleasant
McCowen, John J.
Napier, Thomas
Paris, Solomon C.
Parker, David
Pyle, Barney B.

Ramsey, John A.
Reeves, John H.
Renkle, A. D.
Riddle, Henry A.
Roberts, Eli
Roberts, Paschal
Rolling, John W.
Sanders, Manuel W.
Settle, William H.
Shields, Joseph
Shook, Wiley A.
Simmons, George W.
Simmons, John N.
Smith, John H.
Spradling, Edwin J.
Spradling, James
Spradling, Oliver W.
Spurlock, John
Still, Jacob
Tomlinson, George
Turley, Allen
Turley, George W.
Vanbiber, Sandy
Vandiver, Thomas E.
Wallins, William R.
Walls, John E. L.
Williams, Bradley
Williams, Thomas J.
Williams, Thomas S.
Williams, William R.
Wings, John L.
Wood, John W.
Word, Charles J.
Worton, William
Wynn, George W.
Wynn, Hiram G.

Company I, Fifteenth Texas Cavalry Regiment

Adcock, James M.
Adkins, William A.
Alexander, Wiley B.
Anderson, Isaac

Anthony, Meredith G.
Bivins, Thomas C.
Black, Joseph L.
Blackwell, Henry F.

Casso, H.
Carter, Reuben T.
Chalk, Newton F.
Christman, Thomas J.

Christman, William
Clark, John
Clark, Thomas
Clewis, Louis
Collins, Andrew J.
Corley, John W.
Dean, Isham R.
Douglas, John
Eskew, Enoch
Evans, John
Evans, William
Finley, James H.
Ford, Howell E.
Franks, Francis M.
Franks, Thomas J.
Freeman, William M.
George, Orne
Gibbs, Elhanan A.
Graham, Calvin B.
Greer, Andrew J.
Greer, Edward P.
Greer, James M.
Haley, William A.
Hambrick, George B.
Hammock, Elijah

High, Henry H.
High, John W.
James, John A.
Johnson, James A.
Johnson, James F.
Johnson, Jerry M.
King, John
Marshall, William T.
Massey, Samuel R.
Meadow, Inman
Mirack, Abraham
Mitchell, L. W.
Moore, Edwin P.
Moore, James E.
Moore, Levi
Norman, Mathew M.
Parker, Louis B.
Pointer, John *
Potter, John
Rawkin, L. R.
Reeder, Thomas
Reese, A. H.
Rowen, Philip H.
Sartain, Charles J.
Sewell, Jacob L.

Shamblin, John A.
Sheppard, Jack
Shepperd, John
Shipman, Jacob
Shipman, Lucas A.
Simpson, Freelin
Smith, James
Smith, James M.
Smith, Paton
Smith, William C.
Speers, John
Spencer, George W.
Talley, Leonard
Tankersley, Richard C.
Trammell, John W.
Tull, George W.
White, Andrew M.
White, Mabern
White, Thomas V.
Williams, Brice M.
Wise, Hugh
Wise, Isaac N.
Wright, Benjamin G.
Wright, Edward L.
Wright, William C.

Company K, Fifteenth Texas Cavalry Regiment

Alford, Wiley G.
Ball, L. G.
Barker, Wash
Bell, Anderson W.
Bell, C. C. T.
Bell, James M.
Benson, S.
Benson, W.
Blevins, Richard
Blythe, James M.
Bond, Benjamin
Bond, Edward
Boothe, William
Boyle, Martin V.
Boyles, M. Q.
Boyles, William M.
Brooks, Francis
Bryan, John L.
Bryan, Thomas J.
Campbell, Henry
Casey, John
Casey, Uriah
Cathey, William H.
Chambers, James
Chambers, Job C.
Chambers, William
Chambers, William J.
Clingan, William David
Cooper, William
Davenport, O. F.
Dennis, H.
Denny, Alfred W.
Desmith, Louis
Dilahunty, Green B.

Dillaha, John
Elam, Jesse
Elam, Martin
Fanning, Andrew
Field, Robert M.
Fleming, A.
Frazier, William S.
Freeland, George W.
Halford, M. L.
Hamilton, William
Harald, John J.
Harp, Jo
Harper, Joseph C.
Hays, J. M.
Hays, S. A.
Hays, William C.
Hennagin, Samuel A.
Hightower, Henry
Houston, Mathew M.
Huffstutler, John
Jackson, James
Jackson, Jesse
Jackson, John W.
Jackson, William B.
James, P. H.
Karnes, William A.
Landers, Frank M
Landers, J. L.
Lattimore, George W.
Lewis, William A.
Long, John
Long, Solomon S.
Luster, J. C.
Luster, W.

Manly, William C.
Marshall, Robert F.
Marshall, Samuel E.
Middleton, James A.
Middleton, W. G.
Mills, John H.
Morris, William E.
McClain, James H.
McCreight, Thomas M.
McGee, J. F.
Patton, William W.
Pell, Robert D.
Penn, Theodore
Peters, Robert G.
Pheonix, Theodore
Porter, Gilbert
Renfro, William
Rucker, A. J.
Sheffield, James C.
Snider, William W.
Stewart, J.
Stewart, William
Turner, G. M.
Turner, James
Vickers, Henry P.
Waite, Thomas
Walford, M. T.
Walker, Gideon
Walker, M. B.
Walker, R. G.
Ward, F.
Ward, John
Ward, Samuel S.
Wilson, James M.

Wilson, Martin V.
Woodward, Augustus
Wright, W. O.

Miscellaneous, Fifteenth Texas Cavalry Regiment

Andrews, Henry
Hiller, J. M.
Laird, A. F.

Soney, T. S.
Turner, Marion

Commissioned Staff, Seventeenth Texas Cavalry Regiment

Colonel:
    George F. Moore
    James R. Taylor
Lieutenant Colonel:
    Sterling B. Hendricks
    John McClarty
    Sebron M. Noble
Major:
    John McClarty
    Sebron M. Noble
    William A. Ryan
    Thomas F. Tucker
Adjutant:
    Nathaniel R. Gibson
    James T. Russell
    J. A. Shaw
    L. S. Taylor
    Charles A. Webb
Surgeon:
    William H. Park
    Angus G. Shaw
Assistant Surgeon:
    James R. McDow
    R. L. Smith
    William H. Swindell
Assistant Commissary of Subsistence:
    James P. Ford
Assistant Quartermaster:
    James P. Ford
    Asa M. Wright
Chaplain:
    R. W. Thompson
    Jonathan C. Woolam

Company A, Seventeenth Texas Cavalry Regiment

Acosta, Francisco
Acosta, Juan Feliciana
Anderson, James M.
Arriola, Juan Guadalupe
Baker, Alexander
Balch, Joseph E.
Barnes, John J.
Barrett, William W.
Beaman, Josiah
Bigham, Mather S. H.
Billingsley, John P.
Blackwell, Thomas J.
Blanton, Malvin G.
Boyd, John M.
Brimberry, William A.

Brown, Bennett R.
Brown, James B.
Burrett, John
Burrows, Elijah M.
Burrows, William M.
Capell, Thomas
Carroll, L. J.
Castles, John E.
Chapman, William T.
Cherino, Jose M.
Chorn, W. W.
Christopher, Edward P.
Christopher, Pettus L.
Christopher, W. R. T.
Cleveland, James M.

Collins, William T.
Crain, A. H.
Crawford, James T.
Crouch, William
Cundiff, Samuel H. B.
Curl, Henry T.
Curl, James W.
Daniel, William L.
Davis, John L.
Edwards, Peyton F.
Elliott, Pinckney
Ellis, James W.
Engledow, Creed S.
Fears, William P.
Flournoy, Warner M.

Fulgham, James A.
Garrett, Felix J.
Garrett, John T.
Gilbert, Benjamin F.
Gilbert, John F.
Gilkerson, Robert L.
Goen, Jackson
Graham, Fines W.
Gunning, James E.
Halton, James H.
Hancock, Henry C.
Hardiman, Blackstone Jr.
Hardiman, Bunch
Hardiman, John B.
Haries, William H.
Harrell, David C.
Harrington, William S.
Hayter, William P.
Higginbotham, James D.
Hightower, James
Hobbs, Eli B.
Hooks, William D.
Hunter, Hugh M.
Hyde, Anthony G.
Ingledon, Credes
Jones, Aaron F.
Jones, Jehiel
Keppell, Thomas
King, Andrew A.

King, John M.
King, Richard J.
King, Rufus P.
Lambert, Hamilton
Lawson, Benjamin W.
Lee, James M.
Mackleroy, Alexander J.
Mansola, Lorenzo
Meeks, Isaac
Molton, Joel
Montes, Jose M.
Moore, Augustin J.
Moore, George F.
Moore, Nicholas J.
Moore, Rufus C.
Morris, William
Muckleroy, David Jr.
Muckleroy, Henderson
McCathern, Sebern S.
McClure, Henry S.
Noble, Sebron M.
Norris, James C.
Parish, William
Parker, Ed. W. H.
Parker, Jeremiah H.
Parmley, Carlisle
Partin, George W.
Patterson, John L.
Patton, Ellis L.

Perry, Flavius W.
Pike, James R.
Pleasant, Monroe
Pleasant, Thomas R.
Reid, John W.
Riddle, Harmon W.
Rusk, John C.
Rusk, Thomas D.
Sanders, John T.
Scoggin, Joshua Y.
Sellers, Williamson
Simpson, Victor J.
Smith, Alvin D.
Smith, James L.
Smith, Richard L.
Speaks, Frank A.
Steagall, A. H.
Stegall, Porter C.
Stephens, Augustus P.
Swift, James H.
Swift, William H.
Swinborn, Alva C.
Swinborn, Edwin N.
Taylor, Lawrence S.
Thomason, James H.
Thorn, Charles
Towson, William J. M
Turnbow, James
Ward, London B.
Weeden, James M.
Whittaker, Edward

Company B, Seventeenth Texas Cavalry Regiment

Alexander, J. J.
Alexander, Johnson
Arnold, Wilford
Atkins, John
Baker, William L.
Barber, Allen F.
Baugh, William C.
Bearden, John W. *
Bedford, Joseph
Bingham, Albert G.
Bobbett, John B.
Broom, Henry D.
Broyles, Benjamin G.
Butler, John S.
Cheek, J. W.
Click, Harrison
Click, Henry
Click, Henry T. *
Click, James
Click, William E. *
Cole, William T.
Crouch, Lawson W.
Crunk, Bird
Crunk, William C.
Davis, Samuel B.
Demint, James
Denton, William
Embry, William O.
Ferrill, Turner

Ferrill, William C.
Foust, William C.
Fry, Joseph O.
Gaither, Henry H.
Garner, Joseph
Gray, Mathew A.
Griffin, Andrew J. *
Griffin, Brantly
Grimes, Daniel J.
Grimes, Robert S.
Grisham, John T.
Hardgrave, Felix G.
Harris, Thomas A.
Harrison, Robert W.
Harvey, James H.
Harvey, Nehemiah
Harvey, William T.
Hendon, James H.
Higgins, Jefferson J. *
Hill, David C. *
Holbert, Charles P.
Holbert, John H.
Holbert, Joshua L. M.
Holbert, Stephen M.
Howard, Henry T.
Jenkins, William A.
Johnson, Samuel M.
Johnson, William
Kesterson, William

Lang, Thomas B.
Lang, William D.
Lindsey, Samuel
Long, Anderson
Long, George C.
Long, John F.
Long, William A.
Love, John R.
Mahan, Alexander
Mankin, Willis W.
Moore, Milton
Morris, Samuel H.
McGowen, Patrick
Nelson, Martin V.
Odom, Benjamin F.
Odom, Simeon M.
Odom, Simeon R.
Patrick, Samuel G.
Pearson, Martin V.
Phillips, Jack C. *
Phillips, John T.
Phillips, John M.
Pierce, Hughey J.
Pierce, Joseph W.
Pierce, Larkin L.
Pierce, Thomas W.
Pinkston, John M.
Prestidge, John Wesley
Reid, Josiah

Reynolds, Edward J.
Robertson, John
Rodgers, William M.
Rogers, F. M.
Self, Asa J.
Self, Ebenezer H.
Self, William E.
Shelton, Obadiah N.
Slover, James Z.
Slover, Theodrick
Smith, Israel Oliver
Smith, Joseph A.

Speir, J. P.
Tankersley, Thomas R.
Taylor, Charles W.
Taylor, James R.
Taylor, Levi J.
Taylor, Oliver C.
Teeter, George T.
Thomason, George W.
Thurman, Singleton J.
Townsen, Ed.
Trimble, Thomas J.
Wallace, Addison S.

Wallace, Joseph B.
Wallace, Robert R.
Wallace, Thomas K.
Wallace, William A.
Walter, Nathan
Williams, Francis M.
Williams, James D.
Williams, John W.
Williams, John W.
Woodall, Oliver G.
Yoakum, Wilson H.

Company C, Seventeenth Texas Cavalry Regiment

Allen, Abner C.
Allen, Elijah S.
Allen, John C.
Allen, William C.
Altman, Nathan
Ansley, Benjamin Thomas
Ansley, Joseph C.
Barbee, Thomas W.
Bates, George W.
Bates, James W.
Boatner, Elijah
Brown, Abner G.
Buckner, James B.
Buckner, Moses M.
Cade, David H.
Capps, William M.
Caswell, James R.
Choat, william
Clark, A. H.
Clary, Joseph M.
Cable, John F.
Collins, Christopher C.
Crawford, Thomas A.
Crawford, William H.
Crow, William
Crow, Zachariah H.
Day, Ballard N.
Day, James M.
Denberry, Thomas
Eberhart, Harrison
Echelson, Thomas
Fowler, Daniel R.
Galbraith, James
Gilchrist, Angus J.
Gilchrist, Gilbert S.
Gilliam, Arthur R.
Goodman, Alexander H.
Goodman, Benjamin Louis
Grier, John A.
Grier, Moses G.

Grier, Robert M.
Hall, Henry
Hall, Isaac S.
Hardin, Andrew H. *
Hastings, John R.
Hawkins, William F.
Herrin, John W.
Hughes, John A. L.
Hynson, James C.
Kay, James H.
Lawrence, William F.
Lee, Jackson C.
Lindsay, Elijah
Lindsay, Joel C.
Litchfield, William B.
Little, Louis W. *
Little, Robert J.
Loften, William P.
Louis, James D.
Lowery, Alfred P.
Lybrand, John J.
Mace, Solomon V.
Marsh, Bryan
Marsh, Peter
Massey, Benjamin F.
Matthews, James Clinton
Myers, Joel H.
McCasland, John D. F.
McClure, James M.
McClure, William J.
McDonald, William
McDougall, James R.
McFarland, William J.
O'Neal, James
Pace, Bartley N.
Pendergast, Newton M.
Person, Robert A.
Pierson, James M.
Pierson, Marshall L.
Pierson, William C.

Price, Benjamin F.
Price, George J.
Price, Marcus D. L.
Rains, John G.
Renneau, James
Roan, Marion
Robertson, John C.
Seastrunk, James W.
Seastrunk, Toler
Singleton, J. C.
Smith, William E.
Starr, James N.
Stiefer, George M.
Story, Joshua C.
Struck, Wallace C.
Taylor, Jonathan
Teague, Absalom F.
Thomas, Oliver H. P.
Thompson, John W.
Thompson, Samuel N.
Thompson, Wiley M.
Thompson, William H
Thurman, Thomas H.
Truelove, Timothy
Vance, William J. C.
Walters, William B.
Weeks, William S.
Wells, Bias A. *
Wells, Edward P.
West, William
Whitehorn, James E.
Wiggins, Thomas
Wiley, Thomas J.
Wilfong, Henry
Williams, Duff G.
Wilson, Francis M.
Wilson, James M. *
Wilson, Thomas J.
Worrell, Kintchen C.
Yarbrough, Wiley

Company D, Seventeenth Texas Cavalry Regiment

Able, John M.
Adkins, George E.
Alexander, Nathaniel C.
Alvis, Thomas J.
Ballard, Mathew M.

Ballard, M. M.
Barfield, Henry M.
Barfield, J. H.
Barfield, John F. *
Barfield, Stephen H.

Barfield, William J.
Beard, John
Bidwell, Elias B.
Boles, J. D.
Bradley, Bass A.

Bradley, John W.
Braley, James P.
Brock, Hardin V.
Brock, Joel M.
Brown, John
Browning, Cornelius
Byers, Isaac
Caison, Dan
Caison, William C.
Campbell, William B.
Carmichael, J. M.
Chandler, Crittenden
Coker, John
Cole, William F.
Dean, Charles
Dunbar, Thomas J.
Embry, J. D.
Evans, Henry R.
Ewing, Robert A.
Faulk, John
Ferguson, Robert A.
Fulton, William
Griffin, William
Gossett, James P.
Gossett, Rufus C.
Grimes, George K.
Hames, Edward P.
Haneman, Albert
Harris, Eli
Hasty, B. W.
Hatmaker, Henderson
Hays, James G.
Henderson, Newton
Hendon, Thomas B.
Holmes, Green W.
Hood, Rufus B.

Horton, William W.
James, George W.
Jones, Jesse R.
Jones, William L.
Jorum, Jacob
Kelly, John R.
Killingsworth, Andrew J.
Killough, William B.
Kirkland, William H. H.
Lamden, John F.
Lane, Drury H.
Lattimore, B. D.
Lattimore, D. H.
Lattimore, John H. *
Ledbetter, John B.
Leonard, Michael
Love, Jacob W.
Manuel, J. M.
Manuel, O. L.
Martin, John D.
Merrett, Hiram E.
Milton, Rose
Mitchell, Jacob K.
Moore, B. W.
Moore, James H.
Mullins, William H.
McCarter, David
McGee, James A.
McKinley, Leonidas L.
Newton, Samuel M.
Park, William H.
Parker, Jesse E.
Parks, A. D.
Parks, John M.
Pennington, John E.
Phelps, Ezekiel D.

Renfro, Virgil C.
Rhine, John
Rose, John H.
Rose, Zachariah M.
Ross, Franklin S.
Sides, L. R.
Slaughter, Lemuel P.
Smith, Abner J.
Smith, Henry B.
Smith, James M.
Smith, John T.
Steer, John
Stephens, William W.
Stewart, John S.
Sullivan, William H.
Taylor, W. J.
Thompson, William F.
Tilley, Brittain S.
Tindell, Henry C.
Tiney, H. C.
Wade, William
Wade, Woodson O.
Wagner, William M.
Wallace Theophilus S.
Walling, Richard
Walters, Lycurgus
Walters, Wade
Warren, Neal S.
Watson, Newton
Webb, John T.
Webb, Stephen L.
Whorton, W. M.
Williams, John C.
Yarbrough, Alfred
Yarbrough, Samuel E.
Yarbrough, Theophilus T.

Company E, Seventeenth Texas Cavalry Regiment

Abernathy, John W.
Agurs, William C.
Aiken, Joseph B. *
Anderson, Archibald E.
Anderson, Garrison
Anderson, Henderson
Anderson, Jefferson B.
Anderson, Matthew H.
Anderson, Wyatt
Bateman, Thomas L.
Baxter, George W.
Beekman, Harmon F.
Black, Asa R.
Boisseau, James R.
Boynton, Francis M. *
Boynton, McW.
Brantly, Robert
Brawner, William H. Jr.
Brawner, William H. Sr.
Brice, John C.
Brimer, William H. H. *
Cabiness, Tandy R.
Campbell, Elias L.

Cargill, Henry
Carstarphen, Joseph J.
Carter, William H.
Caste, Joseph
Coleman, Henry F.
Coleman, James N.
Coleman, Wyatt A.
Cook, Samuel A.
Coward, James M.
Coyle, Luther J.
Davis, Nathan
Davis, Thomas L. *
Dodson, James R.
Dry, Julius A.
Eakin, Joeph W.
English, William W.
Foy, James M.
Fustin, Martin W.
Garrett, William H.
Garrett, William M.
Gibson, Drayton
Hamilton, Milton M.
Harvey, William D.

Henderson, Elijah L.
Hendricks, Sterling B.
Hill, Dennis C.
Hill, Thomas S.
Hodges, Robert C.
Holden, George W.
Horton, James W.
Horton, Stephen J.
Horton, Thomas M.
Honston, Martin W.
Ivy, Jeremiah
Ivy, Thomas F.
Jarnagin, Eppy A.
Jarnagin, William A.
Jones, John E.
Jones, Orison T.
Lacey, Thomas
Long, George
Longshore, Larkin W.
Lovell, Teat
Martin, Alfred M.
Martin, Bennett M.
Martin, Lequilian W.

Matthews, William D.
May, John N.
Mays, Daniel *
Mays, Henry
Miller, Francis M.
Mims, James P.
Mims, Joseph B.
Moore, Riley M.
McGee, John C.
McMahan, Samuel W. *
Neil, William S.
Oden, G. Washington
Parham, Lucius P.
Patch, John H.
Peacock, Henry T.
Potter, James

Prince, Joseph W.
Rhodes, Bennett
Richmond, James M.
Richmond, Washington
Robinson, James
Robinson, William
Rogers, Daniel *
Roper, John H.
Rutherford, Lorenzo M.
Sanders, J. A.
Schumpert, John J.
Shadoin, Benjamin
Shadoin, Holl C.
Shadoin, John
Smith, Thomas H.
Soape, Joseph J.

Stroude, James W.
Stroude, John L.
Studdard, Thenny M.
Taylor, Absalom H.
Taylor, Joseph
Taylor, William M.
Terry, Thomas
Thompson, Joseph
Tillery, William J.
Tucker, Thomas F.
Tuttle, William A.
Vance, William L.
Westmoreland, James A. *
Wilkerson, William J.
Woodley, James C.
Woods, John M.

Company F, Seventeenth Texas Cavalry Regiment

Abbott, James
Agerton, Holloway
Attaway, Augustus F.
Attwood, Julius C.
Bagley, James J.
Bateman, John
Baton, William F.
Baxter, Wilburn M.
Blackburn, John M.
Blair, John A.
Bohanan, James M.
Brooks, DeWitt C.
Burnett, Charles G.
Christie, John
Chorn, W. W.
Cole, William H.
Colley, John
Collins, William A.
Collins, William L.
Copeland, Francis M.
Culpepper, William J.
Cunningham, William K.
Curry, George W.
Davis, Thomas Jefferson
Durkee, James A.
Eddington, James
Elliott, Edward F.
Fambrough, Anderson
Few, Caleb A.
Flanagan, Webster
Fowler, James W.
Galloway, Joseph
Galloway, Levi C.
Galloway, Robinson H.
Gibson, Benjamin H.
Gibson, Berrian W.
Gibson, Churchill C.
Gibson, James C.
Gibson, John T.
Gibson, William C.
Gillespie, John C.
Gould, George W.
Gray, Zachariah

Greathouse, H. P.
Greenwood, George H.
Hale, George W.
Harper, James B.
Harris, Wyley
Haynes, Joseph P.
Hearin, Elijah B.
Hicks, C. V.
Hicks, Gain
Hicks, William L.
Higginbotham, Seaton
Hill, Richard T.
Jackson, Mark L.
Johns, Thomas E.
Johnson, Emery
Johnson, Thomas J.
Jones, George
Jones, Stephen
Jones, William W.
Judge, John
King, George
Landrum, Edw. B.
Landrum, Willis W.
Lard, Robert H.
Lawrence, Ed
Laws, John W.
Lawson, Henry M.
Lee, Thomas L.
Loyd, Elijah W.
Marshall, William M.
Moore, John A.
Moore, Thomas
Moore, William
Morton, William
Motley, James W.
McClarty, John
Oliver, James R.
Payne, Thomas
Penn, William
Perry, James W.
Perry, William A.
Prather, Joseph
Preston, Duncan

Price, Calvin R.
Prior, William C.
Prothro, James M.
Pruitt, William J.
Robertson, William A.
Rowland, David G.
Russell, James T.
Sanders, R. C.
Simmons, William F.
Smith, James H.
Smith, John M.
Smith, Samuel
Smith, Stephen H.
Soap, Peyton
Still, Charles A.
Talley, William H.
Terry, John W.
Thomson, James F.
Tippett, Seburn T.
Tomlinson, Osburn G.
Turner, Memory C.
Vinson, Wash G.
Vinson, Young A.
Walker, David A.
Warrick, John W. W.
Watkins, Joel P.
Watson, Henry L.
Welch, Joseph
Wells, William
Whatley, William J.
Wilbanks, William A.
Wilkins, Mortimer
Williams, Charles D.
Williams, John L. W.
Wood, Eli
Wood, Jonathan O.
Wynne, James H.
Wynne, Joel J.
Wynne, William R.
Young, James R.
Young, Russell *
Young, William

Company G, Seventeenth Texas Cavalry Regiment

Aldridge, Jesse F.
Alexander, James R.
Bartlett, Oliver O.
Barton, Alfred
Beck, James R.
Bell, John Z.
Berg, Gilbert
Birdsong, William F.
Bonner, William B. *
Boyce, Newdigats C.
Boyd, Hezekiah
Buie, Gilbert Jr.
Chaffin, John T.
Christian, John
Clinton, Rice
Congo, William
Corard, Joseph S.
Couch, William J. *
Cox, Asberry G.
Cox, Columbus W.
Cox, Ira M.
Croley, George T.
Crosby, Augustus T.
Culberson, James H.
Darden, George W.
Darden, Robert S.
Day, Joseph N.
Day, Nathan R.
Deamore, John C.
Dodd, William R.
Dodson, Elijah R.
Dodson, Francis M.
Drennan, Isaac A.
Dudley, Ephraim T.
Dunn, Charles H.

Edwards, Paulding H.
Fenlaw, John A.
Flemming, Edward B.
Florence, Wiley E.
Foster, A. A.
Fowler, William
Fox, John
Gage, Henry
Gay, John R.
Glasco, Jesse M.
Harrison, William A.
Hart, Joseph B.
Hester, Henry W.
Holluns, Fair K.
Houghton, James A.
Ingram, John T.
James, David B.
Johnson, G. W.
Johnson, Henry P.
Johnson, James E.
Johnson, W. T.
Kennard, James W.
Kennard, Joseph G.
King, James N. G.
King, John W.
Kitchen, Wilson
Knight, Thomas J.
Lane, John
Lewis, Howell *
Little, Thomas B.
Lord, J. W.
Miller, William L. Y.
Montgomery, Stewart R.
Moore, Henry S.
Morgan, William

Morgan, William H.
Music, George W.
McCright, Quinton A.
McKinney, James S.
McWaters, Hubard M.
Newton, Fleming
Norris, John A.
Norton, Varnell
Partridge, John L.
Patrick, Lewis J.
Peteete, Richard
Petty, Henry *
Price, Charles T.
Pritchard, Joshua A.
Randolph, James R.
Redfield, Festus S.
Reeves, William
Sanders, Richard H. *
Scoggin, Jonathan
Shettlesworth, Jackson J.
Shrum, Jacob *
Simpson, Hugh J. M.
Simpson, William E.
Smith, James F.
Smith, John A.
Smith, John C.
Smith, Thomas M.
Spencer, William M.
Wagoner, Andrew C.
Watkins, Samuel Y.
Watkins, Thomas J.
Webb, Charles A.
Wilkerson, Archibald D.
Williams, Paschal K.
Wilson, John
Witcher, Charles S.
Yale, William S.

Company H, Seventeenth Texas Cavalry Regiment

Absher, Elijah
Bell, Oscar F.
Birdwell, John C.
Birdwell, William R.
Bone, James F.
Boyd, Benjamin F.
Branch, Lafayette
Brewer, John
Bruton, Joseph H.
Bruton, Thomas A.
Burke, Joshua G.
Butcher, James Y.
Cartwright, Leonidas M. *
Clifton, Isaac S.
Cobb, Henry
Coleman, Benjamin
Coltharp, Thaddeus C.
Conner, Thomas J.
Cornelius, Joseph D.
Cornelius, William F.
Cornelius, James L.

Darrett, William H.
Dixon, Edw. B.
Easley, Andrew J.
Enlow, James D.
Evans, Thomas J.
Evans, William H.
Fenley, William H.
Ferguson, John
Gibbons, Emmett N.
Green, Jefferson
Hamilton, Green B.
Hayter, John J.
Hearn, James F.
Hillion, Rice
Hughes, Roland E.
Hughes, William H.
Jenkins, William M.
Johnson, Hezekiah
Jones, George W.
Keys, Thomas
King, Albert G.

King, James M.
King, Thomas L.
Lawrence, Sextus P. P.
Lawson, Jeremiah
Ledbetter, Buckner H. T.
Manuel, William H.
Massey, William S.
Miller, James M.
Miller, Mason
Mongo, Sanda
Moody, Thomas B.
Morrow, Andrew J.
Moseley, James A.
Moseley, Sebron M.
Murphey, William H.
Murphy, Andrew J.
Murphy, John L.
McKey, George W.
McKey, william O.
McKnight, Felix L.
McMillen, William

McNab, John F.
Oates, John A. *
Park, Thomas L.
Power, Stephen M.
Ray, John C.
Richardson, Armistead
Richmond, Drayton G.
Richmond, John D.
Rider, Henry W.
Roberts, William J.
Rogers, Augustus W.
Russell, Newton
San Domingo, ———
Sanchez, Massaline
Sanchez, Stephen
Sanders, P. B.
Sanders, W.

Seelbach, Henry
Seelback, William
Simpson, Samuel T.
Skates, James M.
Slay, William
Smith, Monroe
Sprayberry, Uriah
Stanfield, James M.
Statum, James N.
Sutphen, William
Thomas, Allen F.
Thomas, James W.
Thomas, Joseph H.
Treadwell, Benjamin F.
Treadwell, Gustavus A.
Vernon, William
Vondersmith, James F.

Wade, Norvell G.
Wallace, Calvin B.
Wallace, James H.
Watkins, Jesse J.
Weatherley, Jobe P.
Weatherley, John
Weatherley, James M.
Weaver, George W.
Weaver, William H.
Whitaker, V. C.
White, Hardy H.
White, Harley C.
Whittaker, John H.
Whittaker, John P.
Whittaker, William C.
Wilborn, William E.
Wright, James O.

Company I, Seventeenth Texas Cavalry Regiment

Ables, Ezekiel
Abney, Nathaniel A.
Abshire, William
Aldridge, Joel H.
Allen, Frank B.
Allen, George W.
Allen, T. P.
Atkinson, Thomas M.
Bailey, Bryan W.
Bell, Alpheus H.
Bell, Asa S.
Bell, Durgin H.
Bird, Isaac C.
Blackburn, LaFayette
Boyd, Oliver H. P.
Brewer, William K.
Burks, James L.
Cannon, Charles
Cannon, James H.
Chandler, William R.
Clark, James E.

Clorch, John
Conway, James F.
Cook, John D.
Cooper, John
Cornelison, Jesse P.
Cox, Henry W.
Evans, John A.
Heifferman, William
Hill, Thomas M.
Hussey, James J.
Johnson, John W.
Jones, Moses R.
Jones, Samuel T.
Jones, William C.
Jones, William
Kennedy, Alfred
Kilgore, William R.
Leer, James
Lusk, Burton
Moffett, John W.
Myneer, Robert W.

McKnight, James G.
Parks, William L.
Price, Lazarus
Russel, Henry W. *
Smith, Abner O.
Smith, Benjamin F.
Smith, Edward
Smith, Everett
Swan, Harvy R.
Swan, Joseph
Swiney, J. B.
Tucker, Samuel
Underwood, Frank M.
Underwood, John G.
Underwood, Joseph W.
Walker, Thomas J.
Warren, Noah
Wilcox, Joseph J. *
Wilcox, Thomas R. *
Winn, Charles H.
Woods, Abraham *

Company K, Seventeenth Texas Cavalry Regiment

Adkins, George B.
Adkins, John
Barr, A.
Bass, Benjamin R.
Bass, Benjamin S.
Beard, J.
Bell, William S.
Blackwell, Reuben B.
Blalock, Charles S.
Brazealle, Charles J.
Bunch, John J.
Burress, Erastus S.
Cadehead, William C.
Coit, George W.
Coit, Joseph H.
Coleman, Thomas J.
Copeland, William H.
Craig, Jonathan L.
Crain, Giles B.

Cranberry, Richard H.
Crowson, William S.
Denson, Isaac N.
Ellis, Francis M.
Ferrell, Hezekiah F.
Ford, William C.
Foy, James M.
Garrett, J. M.
Gibson, Nathaniel R.
Graham, Matthew F. *
Granberry, Charles H.
Granberry, Richard C.
Green, Ephraim H.
Green, John W.
Green, Thomas A.
Hall, Clement C.
Hall, John W.
Hall, Rufus C.
Hall, William W.

Havis, Leroy G.
Hill, James T.
Hope, James Y.
Johnson, Kellis W.
Jones, Andrew J.
Jones, John S.
Keesler, Joseph
Kennedy, John J.
Kennedy, Joseph F.
Key, Claiborne
King, Fred
Lang, Edward B.
Laury, R. W.
Lawrence, F.
Livingston, James T. *
Livingston, William A.
Martin, George W.
Melton, Robert C.
Munden John P.

Munden, William
Murrell, Robert W.
Murrell, William
McKay, Dushee
McKay, Gill
McLellan, James
Perry, Edw. C.
Ramsey, J.
Richardson, John
Roberts, John C.
Rogers, Edw. J.
Rogers, Hily J. C.
Rogers, James C.

Roseborough, Franklin S.
Rowsel, William S.
Sanders, Thomas H. *
Sewell, Octavius A.
Shaw, Angus G.
Shaw, James A.
Skiles, David K.
Skiles, Samuel H.
Slaughter, John R.
Smith, Richard H.
Starkey, Andrew J.
Stephens, Henry
Stephens, Lewis H.

Stephens, William H.
Stone, Field
Stringer, Ralph
Swindells, James H.
Taylor, Charles M.
Taylor, Wiley O.
Turner, Albert G.
Vanderslice, Benjamin
Walker, Alfred T.
Walls, John L.
Ward, Leonidas G.
Whaley, Thomas J.
Williams, Joseph A.
Wood, Oliver H. P.

Commissioned Staff, Eighteenth Texas Cavalry Regiment

Colonel:
Nicholas H. Darnell
Lieutenant Colonel:
Jonathan T. Coit
Major:
Charles C. Morgan
William A. Ryan
Adjutant:
Nicholas Henderson Darnell Jr.
William A. Ryan
Surgeon:
—— Embry
William C. Warthen
Assistant Surgeon:
Francis D. Cash
A. H. Graham
J. K. Smyrl
Robert Stewart
William C. Warthen
Assistant Commissary of Subsistence:
Walter Caruth
Henderson Darnell
Assistant Quartermaster:
Chauncy Johnson
F. M. Wigginton
Chaplain:
A. B. Manion
Thomas Woodlief

Company A, Eighteenth Texas Cavalry Regiment

Abbott, Elijah
Allen, John
Balch, John B.
Bales, John B.
Ballew, Thomas L.
Barnett, William F. D.
Bartlett, William Henry
Benge, Samuel T.
Billingsley, Elbert G.
Billinglsy, Wardimer
Black, John A.
Blevins, Calvin W.
Boatwright, Claiborn
Boatwright, John H.
Boatwright, William C.

Brown, John S.
Burdit, Williamson
Burk, James M.
Burk, Jonathan
Burk, William Franklin
Cahill, William D.
Cappleiner, Samuel
Carter, John W.
Cason, Levi J.
Childress, Hiram A.
Chitwood, John A.
Chorn, William W.
Clements, Barton B.
Clements, James T.
Clements, Luther

Colgon, James
Conway, Gideon
Cooper, Elisha F.
Cooper, John B.
Cooper, Merriman L.
Criner, Granville W.
Crockett, Charles E. R.
Culberhouse, William J.
Daugherty, William
Davis, Pleasant J.
Dunford, James
Eastham, Samuel
Eaton, John M.
Evertt, Elijah
Farris, Thomas James

Feazel, DeWitt C.
Foley, Robert
Gebhard, Lewis H.
Gentry, John M.
Gentry, Wesley W.
Gibson, J. D.
Gibson, Samuel
Gilleland, John R.
Glasscock, Thomas W.
Goen, William
Goodgeon, Luther S.
Graham, Joseph *
Green, Alexander
Green, George William
Harrell, Thomas B.
Harris, James T.
Harrison, Jeremiah R.
Hart, Isidell H.
Hart, John H.
Hix, George
Hodges, Claborn J.
Hodges, Nathaniel Green *
Hodges, Thomas M.
Hoffman, Francis M.
Hood, Andrew M.
House, G. W.
Howell, Thomas A. *
Inmon, Isaiah
Jacobs, John M.

Jones, Alexander H.
Jones, Francis M.
Jones, W. B.
Kemp, Barnett B.
Kirkland, Thomas J.
Lancaster, James
Lawrence, Alanthus M.
Latimer, Alexander H.
Lee, Able
Michell, E. L.
Mills, William A.
Morrow, Jacob S.
Munfort, John D.
Myrick, Samuel
McAnear, Daniel
McAnear, John N.
McClure, Joseph
McClure, Samuel J.
McGhee, James M.
Nelson, James W.
Nelson, Samuel K.
New, George F.
New, William J.
Patrick, Erasmus
Perkey, Barnabas *
Polk, Benjamin G.
Reynolds, William M.
Rhods, Jacob
Rice, Jonathan W.

Richards, John W.
Richards, Stratford H.
Richards, Rily D.
Robertson, Elijah A.
Rogers, Robert C. C.
Scurlock, Alonzo C.
Scurlock, Malcolm V.
Simpson, Caswell C.
Smith, George W.
Solomon, Samuel
Starky, Benjamin L.
St. Clair, Thomas
Steen, John B.
Stubblefield, Beverly D.
Thomason, James M.
Thrash, John W. *
Tindell, Augustus S.
Voss, John B.
Voss, Wiley
Watts, Joseph M.
Watts, Thomas S.
Wheeler, John
Wheeler, Rufus K.
White, Marcus D.
Whitmeyer, William H. H.
Wilkerson, Fletcher
Wilkerson, Wesly
Wise, William T.
Wood, William J.
Woodson, Thomas M.

Company B, Eighteenth Texas Cavalry Regiment

Alexander, Alferd D. *
Allen, James T.
Atwood, Rufus T.
Avery, William Thomas
Barnhart, James Monroe
Batts, A. J.
Bennett, John
Berry, W. W.
Billingsley, Carrol
Black, Leonard W.
Boyd, William E.
Braman, John
Breeze, James
Brooks, Thomas J.
Buchanan, John C.
Burleson, John C.
Cain, William J.
Caldwell, H. C.
Campbell, Alexander C.
Campbell, A. J.
Carlin, Thomas J.
Carter, R. M.
Carter, William L.
Carter, W. J. S.
Castleman, R. A.
Castleman, R. M.
Castro, Jacob
Chambers, John H.
Clanton, James H.

Clanton, J. G.
Clanton, William H.
Cole, William C.
Corlin, William D.
Cowling, Thomas J.
Cowling, William D.
Crawford, E. S.
Davis, B. H.
Davis, Richard M.
Davis, William J.
Dechert, William H.
Deicher, Angus *
Delashaw, Marcus G.
Denny, Charles A.
Dixon, William H.
Dobson, Henry
Duty, Milton T.
Earle, William Henry
England, James W.
Erhard, A. A.
Erwin, J. P.
Fisher, John H.
Fisk, Josiah
Fore, Alfred M.
Fore, Robert D.
Forehand, Thomas H.
Garrett, Beverly
Garwood, Calvin B.
Glass, William G. *

Green, Joseph M.
Harmon, J. F.
Hill, Thomas J.
Hornsby, Malcomb M.
House, William G.
Hyde, Newton J.
Hyde, W. J. *
Jackson, John
Jackson, Robert
Johnson, Chauncy
Lane, Bast
Lane, David H.
Lanier, W. Riley
Mason, Abner A.
Maxwell, James C.
Meeks, Ambrose H.
Miller, Thomas H.
Montgomery, Lewis
Morgan, Hiram S.
Moore, A. E.
Moore, Nathan J. *
Murchison, Peter *
McDaniel, William A.
McInnis, Miles M. *
McLaurin, D. D.
McLaurin, James M.
McMahan, Michael M.
Nolen, William
Norwood, A. C.

Norwood, Joseph B.
Nowlin, Peyton D.
Owens, Ezekiel
Owens, William E.
Page, George L. *
Parks, Samuel
Patton, William B.
Pearson, Joseph
Perkins, J. W.
Perkins, William H.
Peyton, George L.
Peyton, W. W. *
Pickle, John Scott
Prewitt, James R.
Ranch, Joseph

Richards, W. B.
Riggle, Reuben S.
Romines, Thomas H.
Rowe, J. R.
Saunders, J. Ellison
Scott, George W.
Sims, Thomas
Smith, Lewis S. *
Stewart, Robert
Stroud, Reuben
Summers, Thomas J.
Summers, William M.
Summers, William N.
Swisher, John H.
Thomas, W.

Toney, Ed
Turner, James M.
Turner, Paschal R.
Vanderberg, W. J.
Vorin, Alfred
Vorin, Charles
Warren, Charles
Whitley, D. J.
Williams, John
Williams, John W.
Williamson, John B.
Wilson, William
Winfrey, John P.
Woods, J. E.

Company C, Eighteenth Texas Cavalry Regiment

Armstrong, John B.
Bass, Abraham
Bass, Nathan W. *
Beckner, Henry C.
Bennett, Hiram Columbus
Bradshaw, David A.
Brent, J. M. C.
Brock, John
Brooks, James B.
Browder, James M.
Browder, Ed. C.
Brown, Thomas J. *
Bryant, Silas R.
Bummers, John M.
Burkett, Henry
Byron, Val T.
Campbell, Jerry
Caruthers, John D.
Chesier, Eldridge D.
Chesier, William S.
Coats, James A.
Coats, John H. *
Coats, John W.
Coats, Samuel
Cochran, Archibald H.
Cole, Green A.
Combs, Robert
Compton, Hiram J.
Compton, William Robert
Cornett, Aug. A.
Cornett, Flavius J.
Cruse, Grandison
Cruse, William
Curby, Ben
Custard, William
Davis, Lafayette
Davis, William D.
Davis, William H.
Davlin, George W.
Dial, Thomas C.
Dickson, Charles
Dowd, Monroe

Dufour, Charles
Dunlap, Thomas A.
Durrett, Rice W.
Dye, George W.
Edmondson, John W.
Edmondson, Richard W.
Ewing, John
Farrar, Abram P.
Futrell, Daniel J.
Gordon, Thomas
Gradwohl, Morris
Grove, Isham A.
Haden, James H.
Hamilton, James A.
Harrison, D.
Haws, Thomas J.
Henderson, James P.
Irby, Stephen
Jones, Jesse
Jordan, David J.
Jordan, John William
Kirby, Benjamin C.
Knopfly, Jacob
Lamb, Martin
Lane, John W.
Lane, Stephen S.
Lanham, Thomas B.
Leonard, Thomas S.
Little, Riley T.
Loving, Henry D.
Luck, John
Luck, Thomas L.
Lucus, Thomas
Manning, Robert
Manning, Samuel W.
Manning, William B.
Montgomery, Oscar
Moon, Jesse
Myers, William
McDaniel, Benjamin F.
McDaniel, Isaac
McDaniel, John J. *

McDaniel, John S.
McDermitt, William A.
McDowell, Marion
McLane, Robert N.
Needham, James
Nelson, Daniel H.
Nelson, John Wesley
Nichols, Silas D.
Owen, James A.
Pickens, Mathew J.
Pike, John
Pike, William H.
Pounds, Balas O. C.
Pruitt, Willis Jackson *
Pugh, Jesse M.
Pugh, Prendo C.
Ramsey, Charles L.
Reedy, Benjamin F.
Reedy, David W.
Reedy, George W.
Rice, George W.
Riley, James W.
Rogers, Samuel J.
Royer, Julius
Rush, Sashel A.
Scurlock, Reuben J.
Sheppard, John M.
Simmons, William H. P.
Smith, Thomas D.
Smith, William H.
Spillers, John G.
Stockton, James P.
Stockton, William W.
Story, William
Strader, Robert
Straton, Warner W.
Stults, William
Summers, John M.
Swindells, Jonathan W.
Tallant, Jackson
Taylor, Thomas Henry
Thomas, Woodlief

Thompson, Aaron C.
Thompson, William B.
Upchurch, James A.
Walker, Benjamin H.
Wallace, Henry C.
Wallace, J. W.
West, William W.
Whitsel, William H.
Woodlief, Thomas J. *
Wright, Arminius

Company D, Eighteenth Texas Cavalry Regiment

Allen, Albert J.
Allen, Benjamin F.
Allen, Elisha W.
Anderson, Alfred
Anderson, Henry
Anderson, John C.
Bailey, Merritt J.
Baker, William R.
Bates, Thomas j.
Bates, Wilson
Berry, Thomas L.
Bevins, Samuel
Bigham, Robert B.
Bishop, Samuel W.
Blackwell, Amos J.
Blackwell, Joel
Blair, Joel D.
Blair, William B.
Blankinship, Francis M.
Blevins, George W.
Bock, William
Boren, Isaac S.
Boren, John
Brimer, David
Brown, John
Bryant, John N.
Bryant, N. L.
Burk, William A.
Burks, Jacob W. *
Burks, John
Burks, Samuel
Burks, William M.
Carroll, Thomas H.
Carter, William J.
Cares, Hiram B.
Cloer, George W.
Cox, Andrew P.
Cox, John J.
Cox, Samuel H.

Craighead, Allen
Cross, James W.
Cross, Virgil A. S.
Cross, William B.
Dallas, James W.
Damron, Milton W.
Day, Orlton A.
Denson, James Harvey
Draper, Edward H.
Draper, Thomas P.
Drorecus, Jose M.
Dyke, Pendleton
Early, J.
Early, Thomas
Early, William M.
Eaton, Samuel N.
Edrington, Henry C.
Elliott, H. W.
Elliott, T. W.
Ellis, Benjamin S.
Epps, James T.
Fisher, George
Fisher, James *
Fleming, Andrew J.
Foster, Wiley W.
Fulcher, Francis Theodore
Fulcher, Nathaniel P.
Gage, Robert
Garrison, William M. *
Graves, James H. *
Graves, Thomas B.
Gray, William F.
Griffin, James A.
Hamilton, William
Haynes, William P.
Holcome, Charles C.
Holcome, James M.
Holcome, William T.
Horrell, William

Jordan, William D.
Karnes, William E.
Kendrick, Albert A.
Leatherman, Marshall F.
Lee, James Y.
Martin, William M.
Meeks, Joseph J.
Miers, Isaac
Morris, Andrew
Murrill, Joseph W.
McCray, Elisha F.
McDowell, Hamilton
McDowell, John
Nimmo, George T.
Pennington, John
Reed, Alexander
Roberts, Cornelius B.
Roberts, James T.
Robinson, Thomas W.
Rodriguez, Jose M.
Scott, Jeremiah D.
Shipman, George W.
Shipman, William B.
Slaughter, James H.
Sneed, Richey
Sparks, Daniel
Spence, George M.
Spurlin, William R.
Stallcup, Edward
Stanley, Willis
Sutton, Anderson
Thompson, Doctor P.
Townsend, William M.
Trentham, John
Vanwinkle, Andrew J.
Wheat, Samuel D.
Wheat, William J.
Wilkins, Andrew J.
Willis, George A. C.
Wood, Joseph P.
Wood, William

Company E, Eighteenth Texas Cavalry Regiment

Allison, William M.
Barrett, Roswell B.
Basye, William F. T.
Bates, James William
Beeler, Miles
Billingsly, Marion H.

Bostic, John William
Bowser, Benjamin F. *
Bowser, Oliver P. *
Bramlett, Elkaner C.
Broad, William H.
Brown, W.

Buchanan, Alexander A.
Buchanan, E. P.
Butler, John
Butler, Richard M.
Byrd, Jasper
Caldwell, Nathniel H.

Caldwell, O. B.
Caldwell, Perry C.
Campbell, Archibald D.
Campbell, James W.
Campbell, W. L.
Caruth, Hiram L.
Chawning, Martin B.
Chawning, R. H.
Chenault, John
Chowning, Uriah J.
Coit, Jonathan T.
Collier, Joseph F.
Collier, Pierson W.
Collins, James
Collins, John F.
Cooper, Lee William
Cox, Marion
Cox, Orill B.
Craig, Frank H.
Crane, Benjamin F.
Curlee, Nicholas B.
Davis, James
Drake, Robert R.
Drake, William H. *
Eakins, Edmond
Emberland, George William
Emberland, John
Evans, Henry
Falkner, G. T.
Floyd, John S.
Floyd, Nat S.
Foster, Samuel J.
Foster, Taswell C.
Fowler, Bayley B.
Fowler, John S.
Good, George William
Grant, Wesley M.
Green, Charles H.
Green, William H.

Grooms, Alexander
Harman, Wyatt
Hays, Robert
Higgins, Elias
Higgins, Samuel T.
Hodges, Calloway
Hosa, John B.
Housley, William M.
Howard, Samuel T.
Huffman, John
Huskey, William
Husted, Joseph
Hyde, John W.
Jackson, William
Jenkins, John T. *
Jennings, John J.
Johnston, John A.
Johnston, William L.
Jones, Benjamin F.
Jordan, J. T.
Keen, Abner N.
Keen, James N.
Keen, Marion
Keenan, Marion F.
Lapole, James M.
Lively, Mark C.
Lovely, Joseph
Lyles, Robert H.
Malone, George H.
Mathis, James H.
Miller, William G.
Moonyham, Josiah
Mosely, Early A.
Moss, Josiah
Murphy, Samuel B.
McCauley, James W.
McCoats John T.
McCowan, John
Nask, Joseph J.

Nix, William H.
Parker, Oliver M.
Patell, Newton M.
Patterson, Allen T.
Patterson, William B.
Perry, William F.
Pettitt, William H.
Redington, Hiram F.
Redington, Obediah H.
Roark, Williamson H.
Row, William
Scott, Osceola P.
Scott, Walter M.
Shepherd, William H.
Sidwell, Gab Baker
Sims, Samuel
Smith, Jehu C.
Smith, Jesse M.
Smith, John J.
Smith, Luther A.
Sparks, Isaac
Sparks, James L.
Sparks, William
Strait, Enoch
Strait, Gray B.
Strait, Jesse H.
Thomas, James Pinckney
Thomas, John R.
Tucker, John William
Turner, George A.
Turner, Junius
Waggoner, Stephen
Walker, Benjamin H.
Waller, Benjamin H.
Ware, James B.
Warner, William
Wells, William
White, Charles F. B.
Williams, John H.
Witt, John T.
Wolf, Egbert L.

Company F, Eighteenth Texas Cavalry Regiment

Adams, Wiley
Alexander, O. W.
Beckner, John A.
Bochus, Michael
Boulware, David W.
Boyce, Aaron F.
Boyce, Albert G.
Boyce, William
Boyd, George W.
Bradley, Mark M.
Braker, Fred
Brewer, Thomas
Burnett, William S.
Caddle, Michael
Calhoun, R. N.
Carr, Patrick C.
Chapman, Ben L.
Chapman, Henry C.
Cherry, Noah

Cherryhomes, Henry S.
Clemons, John W.
Clifton, William M.
Cloud, John W.
Cloud, William J.
Cox, Jacob W.
Crunk, Felix F.
Custard, William
Dalton, Carter F.
Dalton, William M.
Flint, John
Forrest, George W.
Forrest, Henry C.
Gaines, James S.
Garrison, James B.
Gibson, William W. *
Gregg, William
Hall, David L.
Haynes, Henry P.

Haynes, John C.
Haynes, John J.
Hibler, Fuldon P.
Hord, Maury
Johnson, Thomas S.
Johnson, William
Jones, John J.
Jones, Richard C.
Kavanaugh, Charles A.
Kimbro, Crawford M.
Kirk, Jonah W.
Kobb, Joseph A.
Lackey, Green B.
Lackey, Henry L.
Larremore, Samuel H.
Lensing, Julius J.
Lewis, Elijah T.
Martin, John H.
Martin, William A.

Martindale, Robert M.
Moore, John H.
Moulthrop, Samuel E.
Murry, Ward
McCrocklin, John A.
McGee, Josiah
Nelly, Henry *
Nowlin, Peyton D.
Nowlin, William M.
Oatman, Clement
Oatman, Oval A.
Odom, Hugh S.
Owens, Thomas J.

Perry, William H.
Peters, David
Pound, Joseph M.
Powell, Elijah T.
Reeves, Amos Marion
Rice, George W.
Ridgeway, Spencer W.
Rigg, G. W.
Riggs, William A.
Robinson, Peter
Rowls, Richard H.
Samuel, Snowden D.
Scott, Erastus N.

Sellers, Benjamin F.
Seymour, Jonathan S.
Slater, Dawson
Smith, John J.
Stiles, Joseph W.
Stiles, Seborn E.
Styles, Jesse
Sweet, Henry Clay
Thompson, George
Thompson, George M.
Thompson, John R.
Thompson, William B.
Warren, Seab S.
Webber, Henry J.

Company G, Eighteenth Texas Cavalry Regiment

Actkinson, Henry D.
Allen, George B
Allen, John P.
Allen, William P. *
Bellyea, Elbridge
Berry, Thomas H.
Birdsong, William O.
Brewster, John C.
Brown, James M.
Brown, Robert
Brown, William B.
Bull, Tarleton D.
Burleson, William R.
Burnett, William L.
Cash, Francis D.
Castleberry, John R.
Clark, William T.
Cook, Jacob H.
Courton, John N.
Craft, Jesse
Craft, Thomas J. *
Crawford, Andrew
Crawford, Joseph
Crawford, William H.
Daugherty, Boone
Davis, David
Derrick, Fleming V.
Dollar, Ambrose
Dunham, William D.
Eads, James
Eads, Perry W.
Elder, John S.
Farris, Ambrose P. H.
Farris, Francis M.
Farris, Jasper
Fitzhugh, Samuel E.

Fry, Jepsey L.
Furgerson, John P.
George, Isaac
Gibbs, Allison
Gibbs, James
Gibbs, John *
Gillis, William D.
Graham, Spencer
Green, Joseph M.
Harris, Michajah W. *
Hopkins, Robert H.
Hunter, Jonathan D.
Jasper, William H.
Kelsey, Curtis W.
Killen, William M.
Lawler, William F.
Laxton, David B.
Long, Edward A.
Long, John W.
Loving, Joseph D.
Loving, William P.
Mahan, John J. W.
Martin, John
Martin, Samuel
Mason, David J.
Mayes, Samuel
Medin, Robert J.
Medlin, William O.
Myers, Noah
McCaslin, John W.
McCombs, David J.
McCombs, John M.
McKee, William
McKenzie, Hugh
McKittrick, Felix
McQuinn, Braxton

Neal, Joseph
Nowlin, James
Paine, Murrel
Paine, William M.
Peters, Emory B.
Petty, John G.
Pinckney, William H.
Pinnell, Benjamin F.
Reynolds, John C.
Reynolds, Joseph M.
Reynolds, Samuel N.
Reynolds, William J. *
Roberts, Soloman
Robinson, Anthony G.
Robinson, Charles M.
Robinson, Josiah D.
Robinson, Michael J.
Rodgers, L. H.
Sigler, George W.
Sigler, Jacob L.
Smith, James
Smith, Jasper J.
Stepper, George
Stevens, David
Stroud, Levi L.
Terry, Thomas J.
Triplett, William L.
Wakefield, J. Henry T.
Wakefield, Thomas A.
West, Thomas H.
Whitlow, Charles
Williams, Charles A.
Williams, Samuel A.
Williamson, Ashton
Yeakley, Martin Van
   Buren *
Young, Samuel

Company H, Eighteenth Texas Cavalry Regiment

Adams, James T.
Adams, Samuel
Alexander, Joseph
Anderson, Jefferson
Anderson, Thomas S.
Anthony, William B.
Baker, Jackson

Ball, Benjamin F.
Bennett, John W.
Bitticks, Henry W. C.
Boyd, John
Boyd, Martin A.
Boyd, Samuel D.
Boyd, William Y.

Brock, Lewelen
Brock, Tubar C.
Brown, Benjamin F.
Brown, William N.
Burch, David A.
Buttler, Ahira
Buttler, Felix H.

Cagle, Francis M.
Clifton, Eli
Clifton, J. M.
Coggins, Wilson J.
Cotrell, John
Crowford, Robert F.
Davidson, George W.
Davis, Moses A.
Davis, Orlando P.
Davis, Martin L.
Davis, Vincen Z.
Denney, William H.
Dennick, R. C.
Dennis, Thomas Joseph
Dobbs, John
Dun, J. E.
Dunlop, John
Ellis, Robert P.
Farrar, Alexander L.
Farrar, Frank Lewis
Farrar, Robert W.
Farrar, Thomas J.
Geaslin, James P.
Geaslin, William D.
Gibbons, William F.
Gibbs, James P.
Glandon, Isaac J.
Gober, Franklin A.
Gunterman, William S.
Hancock, William L.

Henderson, William H.
Hill, Henry
Hill, William C.
Hues, Richard P.
Hull, Samuel
Hurt, William
Johnson, James M.
Johnson, William A.
Kuster, Frederick
Langston, John C.
Larry, Jeremiah E.
Love, Thomas
Mayo, Samuel W.
Mayo, William
Morgan, James
Morgan, William
Moris, Volney T.
Morris, John
Mullican, George W.
Mullican, James M.
Mullican, Thomas J.
Murphy, William E.
McCandless, William W.
McCown, Franklin A.
Nabors, William H.
Neely, James M.
Nipp, Henry
Nowlin, William
Owens, John
Phipps, Charles K.

Phipps, Willis W.
Pool, James M.
Robinson, William D.
Rodrigues, Narcisso
Rushing, Elijah W.
Rutherford, M. S.
Scott, Samuel
Shepherd, David A.
Shoffer, C. F.
Simmions, Simon
Simmons, Samuel A.
Skaggs, William A.
Smith, Abraham M.
Smith, C. C.
Smith, William H.
Smith, William P.
Snow, Richard G.
Stevens, Holsten N.
Stout, Samuel D.
Tam, James
Thompson, George J.
Thompson, John W.
Tubbs, Robert
Tubbs, John
Vardeman, James
Westbrook, David T.
Whitlock, G. W.
Woods, Fleming B.
Wright, John
Wright, Thomas W. P.

Company I, Eighteenth Texas Cavalry Regiment

Bandy, R. T.
Banty, George W.
Barnett, Wyatt
Bledsoe, Fleming G.
Bledsoe, William A.
Bolton, Walker
Breeding, P. C.
Brown, William M.
Chapman, James M.
Chappell, J. P.
Clanton, M. M.
Clark, G. F.
Cox, John B.
Cox, William M.
Crabtree, R. D.
Crum, William H.
Darr, Henry L.
Davidson, J.
Dawdy, A.
Dawdy, W. C.
Dixon, W. H.
Dupree, Robert L.
Durrett, William H.
Ealey, John W.
Epler, William
George, William S.
Green, A. P.
Green, Hardin
Greyham, S. W.

Halford, W. S. C.
Hamilton, James N.
Hamilton, John S.
Hamlin, Joseph
Hargus, Thomas H.
Harrington, John T.
Harrington, William
Harris, Lycurgus
Harvin, W. W.
Hawthorn, Alf
Heand, J. H.
Heath, Zebedee
Howard, Newton
Humphries, T. J.
Hunnycutt, M. C. *
Inglot, John
Jackson, Kinney
Johnson, Caswell
Keightley, Edmond
Lacy, Joseph H.
Lavender, William T.
Love, Jonah
Love, William M.
Lovitt, James Franklin
Lovitt, Thomas J.
Lowery, Dudley B.
Mayers, Lewis C.
Miller, Elijah
Miller, Frank

Morgan, George Washington
Moore, G. W.
Moore, Hartwell H.
Moore, Hugh
Mosier, Harrison
McClanahan, James
McDaniel, Andrew
McDaniel, William H.
McFadden, J. P.
McKinney, Thomas M.
Orr, Alexander L.
Orr, James N.
Parker, Joseph
Patrick, C. H.
Pease, William H.
Penny, A. H.
Perry, Middleton
Perry, Nathan
Phipps, Joseph
Porter, John
Porter, Thomas A.
Renfro, William
Robinson, Yancy
Ross, D. T.
Samuels, Gabe
See, D. J.
Sewell, Andrew J.
Sewell, G. W.
Smith, John J. *

Snow, Jeremiah
Sorrels, John H.
Sorrels, Noah S.
Spencer, C. G.
Spencer, W. M.
Stadden, John

Stanford, Newton B.
Stubbs, J. E.
Taylor, Lewis H.
Teasley, William W.
Thomas, D. K.
Walker, Marcus L.

Weatherford, B. B.
Weatherford, T. Jeff
Weatherford, John
Weaver, James M.
White, Frank M.
White, George
White, Louis

Company K, Eighteenth Texas Cavalry Regiment

Adams, J. R.
Amos, Thomas H.
Armes, John
Bass, Algernon J.
Bell, F. M.
Blackwell, Martin P.
Blackwell, William H.
Blakely, James A.
Bobbitt, James P.
Bowles, John
Boyd, Robert T.
Bradley, Malvin M.
Bryan, J. H.
Bucher, William S.
Burton, Charles
Burton, James M.
Campbell, William A.
Carlisle, John T.
Clay, William W.
Coker, James J.
Collins, George S.
Collins, James L.
Collins, Jesse G.
Collins, Samuel B.
Cox, Joseph
Darden Herndon J.
Davis, Asbury M.
Davis, Osburn N.
Derden, James M. *
Dodd, Gerome H.
East, Joseph B.
Fane, J. M.
Featherston, William H.
Files, Adam E.
Files, T. J.
Gantt, Jacob M.
Goodwin, G. H.
Graham, Jesse M. *
Graham, William H. *
Green, William
Griffith, W. W.
Hardwick, D. J.
Herrell, William J.

Hines, Newton M.
Hodge, Darion
Hodge, Hardin A.
Horton, Ben Jeff
Howard, Nathan
Howett, Frank A.
Hudson, Thomas H. *
Ily, William G.
King, Isaiah
King, Z. H.
Knight, James A.
Knight, William C. *
Laurance, John
Lovelace, T. J.
Manion, Alfred B.
Manion, George D.
Mayfield, William H.
Micham, Asbury G.
Mills, Thomas
Mitcham, Elijah M.
Montgomery, R. C.
Moody, W. R.
Moorehead, Erastus M.
Moorehead, Jordan M.
Moorehead, W. H.
Morgan, William James
Murrill, John T. *
McBride, Littleton B.
McClane, C. W.
McElhaney, John F.
McLane, Cornelius
McMurchuson, D. M.
McNeeley, George
McNeeley, Martin C.
McNeeley, Thomas G.
McSpaden, Thomas S.
Nunley, Joseph N.
Oldham, William P.
Oldham, Jesse C.
O'Neal, Joseph N. *
Oneal, Wiley J.
Owen, Francis M.
Owen, John S.

Owen, Randolph
Owen, Samuel H.
Owen, William B.
Pate, John M.
Pate, Richard P.
Percivel, Constantine
Percivel, William H.
Pippin, Benjamin G.
Prewitt, Doctor Franklin
Price, James
Price, Jesse B.
Price, Joseph H.
Price, Thomas B.
Pugh, William M.
Ratliff, John D.
Ratliff, Richard M.
Reece, J. T.
Rhodes, Joseph C.
Rosinbum, James
Rounsavall, A. M.
Royall, William W.
Scott, Ashly W.
Scott, Oliver
Sessions, Jesse H.
Sessions, Joseph B.
Shefter, Antone
Simms, William
Spivy, Elias
Staley, Sampson
Stephens, John F.
Swift, W. H.
Tate, Dudley W.
Tibbs, James A.
Walker, James C.
Wallace, J. W.
Walthien, William C.
Weeks, James
Weeks, W. M.
Wiley, W. G.
Wilkinson, William H.
Williams, P.
Williamson, George B.
Winn, Pinkney T.
York, James L.

Commissioned Staff, Twenty-fourth Texas Cavalry Regiment

Colonel:
William A. Taylor
Francis C. Wilkes
Lieutenant Colonel:
Robert R. Neyland
Patrick H. Swearingen

Major:
    Patrick H. Swearingen
    William A. Taylor
Adjutant:
    B. D. Griffin
Surgeon:
    A. A. Laurence
    A. N. Perkins
Assistant Surgeon:
    C. M. S. Gayle
    A. C. Neyland
    R. J. Young
Assistant Commissary of Subsistence:
    M. N. Shive
Assistant Quartermaster:
    Dan A. Connor
Chaplain:
    J. B. A. Ahrens
    D. W. Fly

Company A, Twenty-fourth Texas Cavalry Regiment

Adcock, William H.	Fisher, Henry	Morris, J. S.
Allen, John	Fisher, Horton F.	Morrison, H. L.
Alston, George W.	Fisher, T. J.	Muldrow, S. W.
Bishop, B. F.	Freestone, J. B.	Myers, S.
Bishop, P.	Froidvaux, J. F.	McGahan, C.
Blocker, T. P.	Greer, J. C.	McGuire, Richard M.
Bridges, L. M.	Greer, John	McMahan, William C.
Bridges, C. A.	Greer, O.	McPeters, Samuel
Brooks, Winfield S.	Griffith, L. A.	Nicholson, Richard L.
Brownlow, J. W.	Hall, C. C.	Nugent, J. S.
Burkett, James	Hall, T. B.	Orman, Robert
Byrum, E.	Hazel, John	Parker, A. R.
Byrum, S. E.	Hensley, William H.	Patterson, John T.
Campbell, A. J.	Hope, C. C.	Patterson, William
Cartwright, P. L.	James, B. A.	Patton, W. T.
Cole, George W.	Johnson, T. B.	Pelham, J.
Cowan, Thomas J.	Jones, M. D.	Poole, Robert S.
Cowan, W. B.	Kegebehn, Henry	Pratt, Albert
Crozier, R. B.	Kenny, G. B.	Rawls, George C.
Dafford, Alfred	Kirksey, J. B.	Rickhow, G. Havorson
Dean, Henry	Kron, Fred W. *	Robinson, T. F.
Dean, R. R.	Lary, Levi	Roco, A. G. *
Dean, R. T.	Little, Samuel	Roco, Rufus H.
Deats, F. W.	Maddox, J. W.	Rucker, Nelson A.
Dorwin, W. H. C.	Mains, Henry	Sandel, D. C.
Durham, Robert M.	Marx, William	Shaw, John
Elam, Robert	May, Nathaniel R.	Sivils, John R.
Ellison, Jonathan W.	Miller, A. R.	Stone, C. L.
Ellison, L. W.	Miller, Henry	Tressam, John
Ely, J. W.	Miller, J. V.	Uzzell, M. M.
Ely, L.	Monk, Benjamin	Watson, John D.
Evans, Joseph	Monk, Silas	Williams, J. M.

Company B, Twenty-fourth Texas Cavalry Regiment

Adams, W. G.	Brooks, A. J.	Chambers, O. P. *
Alexander (Negro)	Burgess, I. J.	Chambers, Thomas
Bauguss, J. R.	Burgess, J. B.	Childers, J. P.
Bell, Henry Ellsworth	Chambers, D. L.	Childers, R.
Boulton, John T.	Chambers, J. F.	Collard, John S.
Brake, W. B.	Chambers, J. H.	Conn, J. L.

Copeland, A. C.
Cude, T.
Elam, M. L.
Estill, George (Negro)
Estill, C. B.
Estill, Milton
Forrest, W. W. *
Fowler, C. A.
Gayle, Julius
Golding, Henry R.
Golding, Thomas
Gooch, G. J. *
Graham, Moses
Green (Negro)
Green, Wiley
Grissett, John D.
Guyne, John A.
Gwynn, William J.
Hayden, Samuel
Hewitt, Israel
Hoskins, John C.
Hoskins, Thomas J.
Hulon, William *
Irvine, P. B.
King, Adam M. *
King, H. C.
King, Thomas A.
Lawrence, Charles

Lawrence, William B.
Lewis, Eldon
Lewis, John M.
Lindley, James
Lindley, John
Lindley, Elijah
Little, Jonathan
Malone, H. F.
Malone, T. M.
Martin, F. M.
Milburn, M. J.
Moore, William C.
McCann, James M. *
McCarley, James
McCrory, M. A.
McGary, J. T.
McGilvary, S. M.
McIntyre, James R.
McIntyre, Jesse
McKinney, A. W. *
Nelson (Negro)
Nichols, George J.
Nichols, Walter W.
Nobles, J. W.
Norsworthy, James H.
O'Banion, John R.
Pace, J. P.
Parker, David Henry

Quick, G. J.
Reding, J. B.
Rogers, W. D.
Rotten, L. J.
Rotten, W. W.
Sandell, Peter *
Sandell, Oliver
Sell, Worthy (Negro)
Smith, John
Spear, T. J.
Tarpley, Barbee
Terry, Samuel
Thomason, F. M.
Thomason, James B.
Thomason, J. S.
Walker, S. T.
Walker, William
Westmoreland, John T.
White, R. B.
Whittin, J. D. *
Williams, L. (Negro)
Wilson, James E.
Wilson, T. Alexander
Wilson, Thomas J.
Wood, R. L.
Woodson, William H.
Wooldridge, S. D.
Worthey, A. V.

Company C, Twenty-fourth Texas Cavalry Regiment

Alexander, Peter E.
Aynesworth, G. L.
Aynesworth, William C.
Barcroft, Joshua T.
Bare, Nathan
Bibles, Ave
Bradshaw, Fields M.
Burton, Wiley W.
Caison, James M.
Caraway, Bryant
Carraway, Louis J.
Carden, Joseph W.
Carnes, John Jr.
Carter, William M.
Coggins, Andrew J.
Coggins, John R.
Cole, Hugh
Collins, Albert G.
Cooksey, Woodson
Coop, George Y.
Cox, George W.
Cox, Josiah G.
Cox, Thomas T.
Crane, Hezekiah B.
Crass, Jasper N.
Crowel, D. M.
Cunningham, Robert
Darter, James I.
Dawson, James H.
Dorsey, Thomas
Dowdy, John A.

Dunn, John B.
Fitch, Thomas
Flemons, James C.
Fowler, George W. *
Frazier, Isaac F.
Frazier, William W.
Freeman, Francis M.
Ginity, John
Gooch, William H.
Grant, John T.
Haggard, Williamson
Hanna, Robert H.
Harbin, C. L.
Harbin, James
Harbin, W. C.
Harris, James T.
Harris, John C.
Hedgepath, J. W.
Herrington, J. A.
Hill, John B.
Hughes, James B.
Hughes, William L.
Jackson, Robert L.
Jeffreys, Isaac B.
Johnson, C. P.
Johnson, Jesse J.
Jones, Aguilla
Jones, Claiborne E.
Jones, Matthew L.
Jones, S. W.
Jones, W. C.

Kelly, Andrew J.
Kelly, Cyrus A.
Kelly, Napoleon L.
King, Crockett M.
Latham, James L.
Lindsey, Joseph L.
Manning, Thomas J.
Martin, Calvin L.
Martin, George W. H.
Martin, T. G.
Matthews, Joseph M.
Morgan, Thomas F.
Morrison, Byron
Moss, Thomas J.
McCarty, Thomas H.
McGee, D. C.
Neal, Robert N.
Newberry, Melvin A.
Nicholson, J. K. P
Nicholson, Richard L.
Owens, William L.
Oxford, A. B.
Parks, Porter
Patterson, Pat
Peters, Andrew
Pippin, Andrew J.
Pippin, Charles A.
Pippin, William C.
Prewitt, James
Prewitt, John S.
Prigmore, Joseph D.

Reed, James
Reed, Pleasant
Reneau, James M.
Renfro, George D. *
Richards, Charles S.
Richardson, Isaac
Robinson, Benjamin
Robinson, M. McD.
Rogers, Levi L.
Rogers, Moses
Rogers, William E.
Short, Martin L.
Snell, William
Sockwell, Thomas L.

Spann, Charles R.
Stone, Andrew L.
Sutten, John W.
Taylor, George W. *
Taylor, William A.
Tedford, A. M.
Toliver, Andrew B.
Underhill, Robert
Vickers, F. E.
Walsh, Charles R.
Welch, John
Welch, Michael G.
Welch, William
White, Harrison H.

Whitfield, William
Whitten, E. W.
Wicker, Claiborne W.
Wicker, E. J.
Willis, Jesse B.
Windham, David W. *
Woodward, Henry
Wright, James M.
Wynn, Andrew
Yarbrough, James M.
Yarbrough, Thomas C.
Young, William A.
Young, J. G.

Company D, Twenty-fourth Texas Cavalry Regiment

Adair, Leander B.
Ahrens, J. B. A.
Allen, Newton
Anderson, Robert J.
Arnes, John B.
Barrier, George Janson
Bobbitt, George R.
Box, William L.
Brewer, William M.
Burnes, Christopher C.
Cade, James C.
Cade, John R.
Carruth, James A.
Carruth, Harvey G.
Crockett, William R. D.
Cunerth, Otto *
Cuney, Philip M. *
Davis, Joseph H.
Davis, Stephen M.
Deggs, James R.
Donathan, Wiley F.
Donovan, James
Dorsett, William A.
Dunaway, William L.
Easley, Edward W. *
Eldred, John
Elliott, Thomas A.
Falk, Heiniard A.
Fisher, Preston
Ford, James D.
Glass, Hiram M.

Glenn, A. H.
Goodwin, Archibald T.
Graber, Henry W.
Grant, William F.
Grote, Frederick A.
Hargrove, Stephen P.
Henderson, Jerome W. G. D.
Hill, George
Huffman, Andrew J.
Huffman, John H. *
Hunter, David T.
Johnson, John H.
Johnson, Robert
Keesee, Walstein *
Keesee, William
Landrum, Nevil
Lard, Thomas
Lewis, Thomas J.
Lipscomb, M. Q.
Lipscomb, Robert A.
Lloyd, James A.
Lloyd, John L.
Locke, Maurice L.
Lott, Jesse R.
Mahon, Felix G.
Maier, Valentine
Martin, James O.
Matthews, Benjamin E.
Matthews, John F.
Medlock, Charles
Moore, John

Murphy, James H.
Murray, Thomas
McNorton, Lucian
Pankey, John B.
Rabier, Alexander
Raspberry, Logan L.
Reese, W.
Richardson, Z. F.
Short, Alphonso M.
Short, Clinton L.
Short, Thomas J.
Springer, Greenberry B.
Stafford, R. L.
Stafford, W. A.
Stephens, Thomas H.
Swearingen, John T.
Swearingen, Patrick H.
Sykes, Henry A.
Taylor, Charles L.
Taylor, Israel S.
Thompson, William O.
Tittle, George
Vincent, George S.
Walker, Robert A.
Walker, Samuel P.
Wallney, Otto
Wilborn, John D.
Wilks, W. C.
Womack, John C.
Womack. Daniel H.
Woodson, Miller A.
Wyatt, William
Young, William H.

Company E, Twenty-fourth Texas Cavalry Regiment

Atwell, Augustus
Baker, John C.
Bean, J. E. B.
Bean, Jesse M.
Berry, Calvin C.
Brooks, John N.
Butler, John
Calhoun, Charles J.
Cartney, L. H.
Clark, Jacob
Cochran, Adam E.

Collier, Charles B.
Corderry, James A.
Cravy, James H. H.
Davis, Green B.
Davis, William
Dickerson, William
Dickerson, William A.
Ferrell, Joseph E.
Floyd, Alonzo B.
Floyd, C. C.
Floyd, Preston R.

Foster, George R.
Frazer, William A.
Gandy, Isaiah W. *
Goolsbee, Z. R.
Gregory, John Q.
Harrison, Benjamin W.
Hawkins, Benjamin F.
Hawthorn, William L.
Hickman, Gustavus A.
Hill, B. F.
Hill, James H.

Holt, Isaac
Holton, Nathaniel
Holton, Reuben R.
Hosey, Marie Telles *
Howard, Francis M.
Humphreys, Gustavus A.
James, Henry S.
Kelly, Elisha
Kelly, Green
King, Benjamin F.
King, William L.
Landrum, William
Lewis, John
Lowe, Eli
Mandorsey, Freeman
Milner, William
Moore, John H.
Morgan, Daniel D.
Morgan, George W.
Morgan, Joseph N.
Morrison, John T.
Morse, Ellzey
McCartney, William H.

McDonald, James H.
McDonald, William L.
McFaddin, William J. P.
McLelland, Angus W.
Nantz, John T.
Oglesby, E. H.
Payne, J. M.
Perkins, W. J.
Phillips, Thomas
Pickett, Joseph T.
Powell, John Fletcher
Rainwater, Lemuel
Reader, William F.
Reese, John T.
Reese, Jordan
Reese, William
Rice, William T.
Rucker, G. F.
Rucker, G. W.
Rucker, James M.
Scarbrough, L. D.
Shepherd, John H.
Smith, George W.

Smith, J. F.
Smith, John W.
Sutherland, Hector
Wagner, William S.
Walkers, John M.
Ward, Elisha Patrick
Ward, M. B. *
Webb, Benjamin D.
Webb, John J.
Welborn, DeW. C.
Williams, Hezekiah
Williams, James *
Williams, Milton W.
Williams, Simon
Williams, William
Wilson, Francis
Wilson, William
Wood, Elbert
Woolridge, Henry H.
Woolridge, James E.
Wright, Abraham
Wright, James
Wright, Rayburn
Wright, William
York, R. A.

Company F, Twenty-fourth Texas Cavalry Regiment

Allison, Skeelton
Bains, William W.
Baker, John C.
Beard, Travis R.
Bleeker, J.
Boyer, W. V.
Briscoe, Robert P.
Brookshire, J. C.
Busby, D. H.
Callahan, Peter
Carey, A. T.
Childress, J. P.
Clanton, S. M.
Compton, H. T.
Corbitt, J. T.
Curry, W. D.
Dagnell, J. E.
Duncan, J. L.
Eason, J. C.
Foster, A. H.
Foster, R. G.
Fox, C. L.
Fulshear, J. C.
Fulshear, J. R.
Garner, H. P.
Gibson, Dudley *
Gibson, Thomas H.
Gorbitt, E. B.
Gray, F. K.
Griffin, S. F.
Hagan, C. R.
Hagan, H. A.
Hill, R. E.
Hodges, Robert Jr.
Houseworth, W. L.

Howard, J. V.
Hudspeth, A. R.
Iselt, Andrew
Janes, C. C.
Jones, J. A.
Kellough, T. W.
Kuykendall, J. B.
Latterner, C.
Latterner, W.
Lauraine, J. A.
Lietsch, Henry
Lawther, W. D.
Ludwig, Albert *
Ludwig, H. *
Lum, Albert J. *
Lum, L. H.
Mardis, T. H. B.
Mason, Samuel S.
Mayes, George E.
Mayes, John S.
Mayes, Mason G.
Millican, R. P.
Milstead, R. C.
Mitchell, John C.
Mitchell, Thomas W.
Mitchell, T. W.
McConnell, Henry F. *
McGaw, Thomas
McGee, Thomas
McGee, Thomas *
McLeod, James Jr.
Nelson, Alexander B. *
Newel, John E.
Newman, D. P. *
Nibbs, A. B.

Otte, Wiley
Pentecost, W. W.
Perry, Bryant O. H.
Perry, D. R.
Perry, William M.
Pharr, Jasper
Pharr, Walter
Phillips, Thomas *
Phillips, W. R.
Pickens, J. H.
Quarles, W. J.
Reed, William L.
Roach, M. *
Roberts, Thomas J.
Robertson, Alex L.
Robertson, H. C.
Rogan, Richard
Roper, D.
Rundell, John
Russell, W. H.
Ryan, D. S.
Setton, T. J.
Sherwood, William M.
Smith, John C.
Stevens, W. H.
Tenely, Samuel
Thornton, John W. *
Wade, Alex
Wade, P. T.
Walker, E. L.
Weatherford, James
Weatherford, S.
Weaver, C. H. *
Weaver, J. J.
Wessendorf, A.

Weyman, John
White, V. M.
Williams, J. C.
Williams, J. S.
Worthington, O.
Wright, D. W.
Wright, J. H.

Company G, Twenty-fourth Texas Cavalry Regiment

Abby, John (Indian)
Alexander, G. (Indian)
Allison, John M.
Anderson, Jack
Anesta, Manuel
Baker, John A.
Bane, Hiram
Beaty, John
Ben (Indian)
Berryhill, A. J.
Bevel, W. J. S.
Bob (Indian)
Booth, Charles J.
Brown, John F.
Brown, W. O.
Buchanon, G. M.
Buckner, James G. C.
Bullock, Charles W.
Caddell, B. F.
Caddell, William
Calloway, John (Indian)
Causey, Bob (Indian)
Chambers, J. M.
Chambliss, Eph C.
Chambliss, Van
Cheeves, Joseph
Chesher, W. C.
Connor, Dick (Indian)
Crawford, William
Cunningham, William B.
Dean, E. A.
Dick, Big (Indian)
Durham, M. L.
Edmondson, M. D.
Emanuel, ——— (Mexican)

Fuller, Joseph
George, Jesse (Indian)
Gibbs, G. H.
Goolsbee, Z. R.
Hanner, William
Harper, A.
Harris, L. T.
Henderson, James (Indian)
Humble, Thomas L.
Ike (Indian)
Jack (Indian)
Jackson, J. W.
Jacob (Indian)
James (Indian)
Jennings, E. L. M.
John (Indian)
Johnson (Indian)
Jolly, W. J.
Jones, J. A.
Kerr, C. D.
Kidd, Henry S.
King, A. M.
Lewis, Howel
Lewis, Irby
Lilly, H. L. *
Lindsay, D. S.
Maquirk, W. D.
Middleton, E.
Milner, William
Moore, Joseph
McKenzie, Daniel J.
Norden, Andrew J.
Phillips, Thomas
Poncheo, Sam (Indian)
Poncho, John (Indian)

Poncho, Tom (Indian)
Powell, John
Rand, G. W.
Reed, Thomas C.
Reeves, Joseph C.
Rich, George L.
Richardson, F. R.
Richardson, R. M.
Risinger, David
Risinger, J. B.
Risinger, Jordan J.
Risinger, L. J.
Risinger, Mack
Risinger, Willis
Sam (Indian)
Sampson, Billy (Indian)
Scott, John (Indian)
Silestine, Alex (Indian)
Slater, F. A. M.
Smelly, J. E. *
Smith, Thomas G.
Snider, Sanford
Snider, William
Suttle, John A.
Suttle, W.
Terry, Francis M.
Terry, William
Thompson (Indian)
Tucker, Jerry
Walker, Robert
Ward, Joseph
Watson, J. R. *
Whitehead, J. K.
Whittlesey, John R.
Wilkerson, S. W.
Wooten, Oscar L.

Company H, Twenty-fourth Texas Cavalry Regiment

Andrews, Cullen
Anesta, Manuel
Averell, William James
Baker, George Allen
Baker, Thomas Anderson
Bartlett, Nathan
Bartlett, William
Bates, John C.
Bawcom, Newton C.
Bratton, Robert Porter
Bringhurst, John Henry
Burrell, John Henry
Butler, William G.
Caviness, Joel F.

Caviness, William
Chesney, Thomas Perry
Cincere, Anthony
Coker, Alexander J.
Cole, Andrew Jackson
Conner, David
Conner, John
Conner, John H.
Cook, Andrew Jackson
Cook, Obed
Cowan, Henry H.
Cullen, Edwin Chipman
Cullen, Thomas J. *
Deakins, Joseph Warren

Dellis, John Wiley
Dickson, William
Doran, Thomas Lafayette
Eastman, Jacob Homer
Fisher, Samuel
Fisher, Thomas
Florida, William L.
Foster, Samuel Thompson *
Foster, William Jasper
Frazee, Edward
Freeman, George
    Washington
Gonzales, Rafael
Green, Charles

Green, James Jefferson
Gregg, John Henry
Guinn, John Peterson
Hall, James M.
Harrison, Joel
Hickox, Alfred
Holland, Daniel Oglestead
Hooper, Jerome
Hubbert, George Washington
Hubbert, Robert Henry
Hutchison, Samuel Tyson Moore
Iles, Thomas
James, Nathan Henry
Jones, Daniel Thomas
Jones, Richard A.
Kendall, Albert
Kirkpatrick, James William G.
Kitcham, W. P.
Lambdin, Robert B.
Lapeyre, Auguste
Lee, Randolph

Love, Oglethorpe
Lune, Jesus
Maddox, William Jefferson
Magill, Eugene Jefferson
Mitchel, James Lakoch
Moore, Benjamin
Moran, James A.
McMurry, William Marion
Neatherly, Thomas Jefferson
Neighbors, Albert W.
Neil, Alfred Claiborn *
Neil, John Hankins
Nooner, Joseph Whitsett
Norfleet, Edward Lomax
Norfleet, Nathaniel Munroe
Orrick, Henry Clinton
Pankey, Joseph
Pierce, Tilghman Weaver
Poe, James R.
Poe, John Asbury
Puckett, Thomas H.
Reid, Edward Monroe
Richards, Thomas Didimus
Richards, William Lawrence

Robinson, Jeremiah Kirklin
Rodgers, Hiram Runnels
Sanders, Jefferson
Sharwick, Peter Raiser
Shrewsberry, Simeon
Sloan, Archibald Overton
Stewart, George Washington
St. Onge, Godbrie
Templeton, John
Thomas, Charles
Thomas, Charles H.
Thompson, Edgar W.
Thompson, Robert Terlune
Votaw, Thomas F.
Warren, Benjamin Goodwin
Wendland, Frederick
Willborn, John Lewis
Winters, James Hampton
Woodall, Jarred Watson
Woodall, Kinney Bryan
Woods, George Wilson
Woods, John E.
Woods, Robert Evans
Wynns, George Thomas

Company I, Twenty-fourth Texas Cavalry Regiment

Alford, William H.
Alley, L.
Allison, Skeelton
Amerlan, Aubrey
Arman, Ferdinan
Balock, Frank
Bardin, D. C.
Barnett, John A.
Bates, T. J.
Bean, R. R.
Binkey, August
Blair, F.
Blair, G. W.
Bond, H.
Booth, John A.
Borrum, J. K.
Bouldin, E. S.
Bowers, D. W.
Brashear, J. H.
Brown, C.
Brysh, John
Burkett, Bart
Burkett, I.
Burkett, John
Burlin, P. L.
Burris, J. B. *
Burtrell, J. W.
Busley, P. M.
Chambliss, Samuel L.
Chandler, M. A.
Childress, Jeff
Clark, James
Clauswitz, Fred
Comford, F. H.
Compton, R. D.

Daniels, O. A.
Dean, Frederick C.
Dichnan, E.
Dickinson, John S.
Donalson, J. M.
Donelson, J. A.
Ellison, J. E.
Fisher, S.
Fly, B. F.
Fly, E. M.
Forhand, J. W.
Frietag, C. H.
Fulshead, J. B.
Gaither, A. B.
Garther, John
Giles, J. S.
Giles, M. C.
Glenn, William N.
Goddett, R.
Godfrey, John *
Green, J. G.
Green, L. B.
Haliburton, R.
Hanson, T. J. *
Harrell, E. M.
Harrell, J. C.
Hill, James H.
Holland, G. B.
Holland, James B.
Howington, E. M.
Hudspeth, A. R.
Hull, Jacob
Humphreys, J. A.
Husar, Alex
Inman, William B.

James, A. B.
Jasko, Joseph
Jesse, Mare
Joiner, R. H.
Jones, Andrew T.
Jones, E. T.
Jones, James H.
Jones, T. H.
Jones, W. H.
Kaczmarch, Joseph
Kay, F.
King, Benjamin F.
Kiolbassa, Peter
Klinger, Charles Jr.
Kolodeycryk, Joseph
Lancaster, William W.
Lawhorn, William
Liles, T. E.
Little, R. A.
Love, William
Lyesey, Albert
Malone, Thomas B.
Marier, Hosea
Martin, F. E.
Matthews, William M.
Matushak, John
Mayes, George E.
Moczyjsba, Frank
Moore, Thomas
Munch, C. A.
Munson, Edwin W.
McCauley, Lemuel Alexander
McCauley, R. L.
McCommon, J. A.

McConnel, Joseph
McFadin, J. C. B.
McIntyre, J. C.
Neuhaus, Frederick
Neuhaus, Heinrich August
   Hermann
Novock, John
O'Neal, J. J.
Opickley, J.
Pace, James N.
Parton, William
Pearson, W. S.
Penick, Jeff
Pharr, ———
Pheland, Jesse
Poland, G. B.
Pollard, Samuel H.
Pouncy, W. F. *
Powell, John
Preston, Samuel A.
Price, L. F.
Quinn, William

Radford, Jonathan W.
Radford, John P.
Radford, W. N.
Reaves, M. C.
Reissner, J.
Reynolds, W. F.
Roberts, David C.
Ross, W. B.
Rouly, J. W.
Rousch, Jonathan
Randell, John
Rusing, R. L.
Rutledge, E. B.
Rutledge, John L.
Scogin, Y. L.
Scronce, S. E.
Seal, Daniel
Sell, P. (Negro)
Sharp, H. *
Sherwood, William M.
Short, F.
Sims, Marion G.

Smith, C. E. *
Smith, J. V.
Spann, W. J.
Stein, John
Sutton, John
Sutton, W.
Swarting, William
Tidwell, R. T. *
Ursry, L. F.
Vogelsang, Herman
Walker, E. L.
Walker, James
Ware, J. J.
Weber, Bazel
Weeman, William
Whattley, E. W.
Wilburn, D. C.
Williamson, A. N.
Williamson, Charles A.
Wilson, D. C.
Wilson, William S.
Wood, Jasper
Woodford, E. S.

Company K, Twenty-fourth Texas Cavalry Regiment

Aaron, William
Ainsworth, J. P.
Anderson, Wyatt
Andrews, Harvey
Andrews, John
Asbury, John W. *
Baxter, James T.
Bobit, Peter
Bolt, Robert
Bowman, Robert M.
Box, William M.
Brantley, John D.
Brown, Andrew
Brown, Cyrus W.
Brown, Frid
Brown, James W.
Brown, Joseph H.
Brown, Sylvanus
Bryan, Mordecai A.
Callahan, Young
Callahan, J. H.
Campbell, John D.
Callaway, F. W.
Chandler, Thomas
Chon, Charles
Couch, Simon
Critz, John
Critz, Sebastian
Cupples, Charles
Doulain, John
Drake, Melzar
Duerr, Caesar

Eckhardt, William
Edwards, E. M.
Elson, William N.
Fort, Wesley D.
Frazier, Andrew Jackson
Frazier, John N.
Friar, William S.
Friar, J. H.
Gaebler, Ernst
Garey, Benjamin W.
Gehrin, Frederick
Golke, August
Graves, J. T.
Hanks, Wyatt
Hardt, Valentine W.
Hardt, William A.
Hardy, D. N.
Harrell, William N.
Harrington, Joseph
Harris, E. F.
Hartman, C.
Hethcock, Asa
Hester, S. F.
Hill, Christopher T.
Hill, Samuel M.
House, Christopher
House, Frederick
Humphreys, George W.
Jones, Hartwell K.
Lacknor, Conrad
Lawley, Mason
Longoria, Cedro

Lyons, George W.
Machost, Heinrich
Machost, John
Martinez, Prudencia
Messinger, Julius
Messinger, William
Miles, Joel S.
Moin, John M.
Moore, Thomas F.
McConnell, William
McFarland, George W.
McFarland, Jerry D.
McFarland, William
Parago, John
Pettit, Malone
Pool, Alfred C.
Rankin, James B.
Rankin, Samuel S.
Ruston, John M.
Sasse, Carl
Sasse, Frederic
Schley, Franz
Shive, M. N.
Sommerville, Samuel E.
Souermilch, Andreas
Stringfield, James M.
Tate, William C.
Taylor, Joual
Westfall, Ithamer
Wilkinson, Alexander S.
Wingfield, Lewis G.
Woods, Henry G.
Woods, Martin Z.
Zedler, Ferdinand *

Miscellaneous, Twenty-fourth Texas Cavalry Regiment

Arnold, J. R. G.
Bagott, J. R.

Boyett, J. R.
Barnett, Thomas G.

Collier, E. C.
Dickerson, J. M.

Gable, G. F.
Graham, C. M.
Grear, S. D.
Huyly, S. W.
Johnson, W.
Julia (Slave Matron)
King, J. W.

Leal, Rafael
Lucy (Slave Matron)
Mayes, Gondaw
McIntosh, G. F.
Neil, A. D.
Rilla (Slave Matron)
Shaw, Houston P.

Commissioned Staff, Twenty-fifth Texas Cavalry Regiment

Colonel:
   Clayton C. Gillespie
Lieutenant Colonel:
   William N. Neyland
   Edward B. Pickett
Major:
   Joseph N. Dark
   J. P. Montgomery
   Edward B. Pickett
Adjutant:
   R. H. Davis
   Moses L. Moulton
Surgeon:
   Jonathan T. Eldridge
   E. S. Whelan
Assistant Surgeon:
   ———— Fahrenholt
   E. S. Whelan
Assistant Commissary of Subsistence:
   J. E. Ferguson
Assistant Quartermaster:
   B. F. Davis
   B. R. Davis
   J. W. Compton
Chaplain:
   S. J. Hawkins
   James L. Neese

Company A, Twenty-fifth Texas Cavalry Regiment

Addisson, R.
Albritton, David
Allison, James M.
Allison, John V.
Barclay, Robert
Barclay, Walter
Barcly, Henry A.
Barefield, J. W.
Bendy, James H.
Blake, A.
Bradley, J. D.
Brown, A. W.
Brown, James V.
Burton, W.
Cherry, J.
Cherry, James W.
Chorn, W. W.
Craft, David
Cupp, John J.
Deason, Minor J.
Dollarhide, Cornelius
Farley, James T.
Farley, William H.

Felton, O. C.
Ferrell, M. H.
Fortenberry, Evan W.
Fortenberry, Gilbert C.
Fortenberry, J. C.
Frazier, James M.
Frisby, A. J.
Gibbs, J. G.
Goodman, John M.
Graham, J. N.
Graham, L.
Graham, W. H.
Gray, N. R.
Greenhaw, W. W.
Griffen, Z.
Grimm, Christian
Haddox, Alex
Harper, W.
Harris, H. C.
Hensly, Thomas
Hewlett, J. E.
Holt, Isaac
Holt, William M.

Hughes, Patrick A.
Huling, Thomas B.
Ipsinger, J. G.
Jackson, Ambrose
Jackson, William
Jenkins, O.
Johnson, J.
Jones, J. H.
Jones, R. D.
Jones, R. J.
Jutson, J.
Kincaid, J. B. F.
Kincaid, William J. A.
Kirby, Henry S.
Kirby, J. L.
Laky, R.
Mahaffey, William A.
Mann, D. J.
Mann, J. M.
Manson, J. C.
Markley, James
Martin, John
Miller, W. M.

Minter, James G.
Mixon, J.
Monser, D.
Moore, W. D.
McAlister, W. J.
McCartney, R. L. K.
McMillan, D. C.
McShan, J.
Nolin, Henry
Nowlin, Benjamin F.
Odam, Richard
Overstreet, Johnson
Phelps, D. J.
Prescott, James
Prescott, Thomas J.
Reynolds, P.
Rich, G. L.
Riley, A. J.
Riley, G. W.
Riley, J.
Risinger, J. G.
Risinger, Jordan J.
Risinger, N. T.

Rodgers, Joseph H.
Rodgers, W. H.
Ross, B. F.
Rowe, W.
Rundal, John
Sanford, R. H.
Scarls, W.
Seale, E. P.
Sharp, Rufus
Sims, J. A.
Sims, Thomas R.
Slater, F. A. M.
Smelley, J. E.
Smith, T. G.
Smith, T. J.
Smith, William H.
Speer, George W.
Squirs, A.
Squirs, S. H.
Squirs, W. H.
Stallbaum, Jacob
Sumrall, J. A.
Suttle, J. A.

Suttle, W.
Terry, F. M.
Theis, Phillip
Thompson, C. T.
Thompson, Samuel J.
Tolar, James
Turner, W. F.
Vastal, J. R.
Ward, J. T.
Ward, J. G.
Watson, J. R.
Weeks, Alexander
Weeks, Edward
Weeks, John W.
White, J. H.
Whitmore, H.
Wiggins, R.
Williams, E. H.
Williford, Benjamin A.
Williford, G. W.
Winter, J. M.
Winters, J. T.
Wooly, D. L.
Wooly, V. W.

Company B, Twenty-fifth Texas Cavalry Regiment

Allison, John V.
Alston, W. J.
Arnett, F. F.
Batson, James
Bell, E.
Bilow, J.
Bishop, B. F.
Blackman, A.
Boone, R.
Bracken, G. B.
Bracken, W. G.
Brantly, William T.
Bridges, L. M.
Bryant, John M.
Burt, W. L.
Callier, R. P.
Calloway, John
Chapel, C.
Cherry, James W.
Chesson, Joshua
Combs, James R.
Cook, J. D.
Cooper, James A.
Cotton, M. F.
Cotton, W. H.
Crawford, W.
Dark, J. N.
David, S. J.
Davis, John
Davis, Larkin
Davis, Ludwell R.
Davis, S. W.
Dean, Robert
Deets, Fred W.
Dollard, John J.

Dozier, J. L.
Dudley, Aaron H.
Duset, Joseph
Ellis, Jackson J.
Evans, James J.
Farling, M.
Forlond, M.
Fountain, J. B.
Franklin, J.
Franklin, T. P.
Franklin, Willie R.
Frazier, James M.
Frazier, J. J.
Gilbert, L. F.
Gilbert, Samuel
Gillard, J. W.
Gillard, S.
Gilley, A.
Gilley, I.
Goff, P. V.
Goff, Thomas R.
Goodman, John M.
Graham, A. J.
Graham, R. G.
Green, Ezra
Green, J. L.
Green, Philip
Gudny, N.
Guines, Z. M. *
Hall, W. H.
Hall, W. H.
Hamptin, G.
Haralson, J. H.
Hardin, C. O.
Harlson, W. P.

Harper, J.
Harrell, W. L.
Hart, Richard J.
Harvill, J. C.
Havered, S. J.
Havord, W. F.
Hebert, J. D.
Hempling, J.
Hillyer, F. R.
Holland, E. B.
Hooks, J. D. *
Hughes, James F.
Huling, Thomas B.
Jackson, Ambrose
Jackson, James
Jackson, William
Jarrell, John
Jones, J.
Jones, J. H.
Jones, J. K.
Jones, John R.
Jones, R. D.
Jones, R. J.
Jourdan, M. W.
Jourdan, W. H.
Kaim, V.
Kea, J. W.
Kennedy, J. D.
Kerr, C. D.
Kerr, J. M.
Kingcade, J. B. L.
Kincaid, J. B. F.
Langthrop, W.
Lee, B. J.
Levy, H.

Lewis, Simeon
Lewis, Willis N. B.
Long, James M.
Lum, Jesse D.
Marble, Jacob A.
Marks, Barney
Matthews, W. J.
Merchant, James A.
Meyer, Peter
Middleton, W.
Mixon, Henry
Montgomery, H.
Montgomery, John
Mott, Daniel
Mott, Hiram P.
Mott, Isaac
Mott, J. L.
Mott, Loveless
Mott, Thomas
McAllister, John H.
McCartney, R. L. K.
McMasters, Thomas R.
McNealy, D. S. D.
McNealy, Hugh *
McShan, G. W.
McWilliams, James *
Nichols, A.
Odam, J. W.
O'Neal, Paul
Overstreet, Coleman
Parker, Isaac

Parker, James
Parker, John
Parr, W. H.
Perryman, W. A.
Petty, J. T.
Philips, C. T.
Pool, J. J.
Porter, M. P.
Pugh, W. H.
Randolph, J. G.
Richey, Stephen
Riley, A.
Ripka, D.
Ross, B. F.
Ross, R. L.
Runnels, A. J.
Runnels, Alexander
Runnels, F. M.
Runnels, G. B.
Runnels, Jesse
Sellman, George W.
Shaw, Quincy
Shell, R. H.
Shepherd, J. M.
Simans, B. J.
Simmons, J.
Simms, James F.
Sims, John T.
Sims, E. G.
Sims, J. T.
Sims, Thomas R.

Smith, Robert
Smith, William H.
Snellgroves, J. A. C.
Snider, William S.
Spell, R. H.
Spier, A. J.
Speir, J. P.
Stanley, F. P.
Stanly, P. S.
Street, C. O.
Sutton, S. H.
Swiney, Milton
Tanner, J. R.
Tarling, M. C.
Taylor, J. G. L.
Taylor, Joseph
Teel, Richard
Terry, William
Thibodeaux, Charles
Thibodeaux, Joseph
Thompson, James
Thompson, J. E.
Thompson, Joseph
Thompson, S. K.
Thompson, Stacy W.
Thomson, J. W.
Underwood, A. J.
Van Deventer, J.
Whittington, W. H.
Williams, E. H.
Williams, J. R.
Williford, G. W.

Company C, Twenty-fifth Texas Cavalry Regiment

Adams, Everett N.
Adams, Jeradore
Autrey, A. S.
Biskamp, William F. *
Black, A. J.
Borgfeldt, Fred *
Burkholter, R. D.
Byerley, A. J.
Byerley, Frederick *
Byerley, Henry S.
Byerley, William F.
Calhoun, C. J.
Carraway, Thomas J.
Collins, Alexander B.
Collins, E. E.
Cowart, Holmes S.
Delaney, Thomas C.
Dias, Clement
Erwin, John T.
Evans, D. W.
George, Cary
George, J. G.
Gilbreath, T. N.
Gilmore, Josiah
Glenn, David
Glenn, Joseph
Goode, G. C.

Goode, H. F.
Goode, M. M.
Gover, Samuel
Gray, S. L.
Hamilton, B. W.
Hamilton, Dewit B.
Hancock, David L. *
Hancock, James B. *
Hancock, Jonathan A.
Harrison, William A.
Hempling, J.
Hill, John J.
Hollaman, William F.
Holton, J. J.
Huffman, L. A.
Isbell, G. W.
Jeter, Lovick M.
Jones, Aaron
Jones, Robert
Jones, Zero
Lackey, Green B.
Landman, John
Langley, John B.
Lapham, William S.
Mahany, M. M.
Moulton, Moses C.
Murff, W. L.

McCree, William S. *
McDonald, W. C.
McFarlane, William M.
Neyland, W. M.
Nichols, Aurelius C.
Nolan, J. H.
Owens, A. B.
Palmer, B. H.
Pattillo, Samuel A.
Perry, O. H.
Powell, Robert L.
Prescott, Freeman
Pry, Peter B.
Randal, Joseph
Rawles, Irvin H.
Reeder, William F.
Rhymes, John H.
Robinson, B. W.
Rogers, E. A.
Sanders, James W.
Sanders, Madison
Scarborough, J. W.
Scott, George W.
Scott, James T.
Scott, William R.
Sells, Henry D. *
Shelby, Robert P.

Sheppard, John
Shoffit, H. A.
Short, John J.
Simpson, William
Smith, Henry V.
Steel, George W.
Stewart, W. G.
Stovall, David M.

Stovall, William G.
Taylor, J. E.
Taylor, John R.
Taylor, William A.
Taylor, William M.
Traylor, William L.
Waller, Ichabod
Waller, Joseph

Waller, S.
Watson, M. R.
Watts, William
Weiland, Charles
Wigley, C. F.
Wigley, Rufus A.
Williams, S. J.
Wrigley, Paschal A.

Company D, Twenty-fifth Texas Cavalry Regiment

Bailey, James E.
Bayes, Henry L.
Boney, W.
Bowman, W. R.
Brown, John H.
Casey, John M.
Cash, John C.
Cissell, J. D.
Cole, William H.
Collins, C. G.
Cook, Daniel S.
Davis, Aaron R.
Delgado, Severo
Dwyer, Dennis
Eakin, S.
Fields, William R.
Fleming, T. F.
Flemming, Thomas N.
Fowler, Benjamin *
Gayle, R. D.
Gonzales, Emanuel
Gorden, Robert S.
Grantling, Robert E.
Grantling, Thomas B.
Hall, John
Hamm, Lewis
Hart, John F.
Holton, Lemon
Huey, Barrom B.
Huff, John O.
Huff, William K.
Huff, William P.
Hughes, James

Hughes, Nathan
Hughes, W. W.
Hughey, William K.
James, J. J.
Johnson, T. G.
Kennedy, John
Lasso, Alvino
Law, A.
Lee, Charles
Lewis, Simeon
Linney, Mike
Lott, Arthur
Lott, J. W.
Lott, William
Luna, James
Lunsford, James W. *
Lunsford, W.
Martin, Benjamin F.
Martin, Josiah O.
Montgomery, J. P.
Morris, Sedro
Myres, John C.
McCloud, Malcolm *
McNamer, James
O'Boyle, Michael
Owens, Benjamin
Parker, T. S.
Patterson, James
Patterson, John
Patterson, William
Payton, A. R.
Phelps, James P.
Phelps, William C.

Phillips, L.
Reed, James D.
Reeves, Robert
Rhodes, J. B.
Rhodes, Thomas *
Rigby, John O.
Rock, Edward D.
Rupe, James T.
Ryan, A. S.
Sanders, Madison
Scott, Henry
Sellars, J. J.
Sessell, William A.
Sessions, Jethro H.
Sessions, J. M. *
Sessions, J. W. B.
Sessions, W. B.
Sexton, M. V.
Shultz, August A.
Sichett, S. B.
Smith, Antony
Spires, Daniel J.
Taylor, Randolph B.
Thompson, James J.
Totty, James F.
Treadwell, John J.
Trivina, John
Tupe, Joseph T.
Turner, W. J.
Vivion, H. C.
Webb, Thomas
Williams, C. L.
Williams, Jeptha
Word, Bruce L.
Wright, James E.

Company E, Twenty-fifth Texas Cavalry Regiment

Allphin, D. M.
Asbury, D.
Ashbury, T. V.
Auley, J. B.
Bagley, J.
Bailey, James
Bailey, William
Bales, J. A.
Barrow, Zephaniah
Barter, James
Bass, L.
Baxter, J. J.
Bayles, W.
Beckham, James L.
Birmingham, W. R.

Bishop, J.
Bobbit, G. R.
Braley, Levi
Brooks, R. P.
Brown, James
Burns, D. D.
Burns, R. D.
Cabiness, F. L.
Caldwell, O. B.
Collard, J. S.
Cowan, Thomas
Crabill, James M.
Cunningham, Joseph
Cunningham, William H.
Daniel, William G.

Dawson, Richard B.
Deamond, A.
Delay, James
Easley, E. C.
Ellington, D. C.
Ellis, J.
Ellison, ———
Fairmond, ———
Farrier, ———
Field, J. M. B.
Foster, M. B. A.
Fulkerson, A. H.
Fuller, J. D.
Gains, William
Gayle, T. C.

Gann, William M. *
Green, J. C.
Grice, J. L.
Guin, William
Gwinn, ——
Hagan, ——
Hall, William S.
Halsey, ——
Harbuck, Ch.
Harden, John C.
Hardy, Henderson
Harper, J.
Harper, W. F.
Harris, John
Havens, Rice
Hays, Thomas
Hempfling, George
Hill, Charles
Hilton, Thomas
Hodge, F. Y.
Holliday, Titus
Hughes, William
Humphrey, ——
Hunt, O.
Hunter, Willis L.
Hunts, J. V. M.
Johns, ——
Johnson, J.
Johnston, James A.
Jones, Frank
Jones, J.
Jones, M. D.
Jones, S.
King, ——
Kizer, E. B.
Kizer, John C. *
Kizer, John P.
Kruger, Fritz
Landreth, John
Laurence, J.
Lawson, D. B.

Lloyd, Jesse P.
Lloyd, John L.
Lock, M. D.
Loring, L.
Lyons, Joseph
Man, ——
Man, G.
Man, H.
Man, J.
May, H. L.
Millican, Jasper
Millican, Wesley J.
Moloney, David
Moon, ——
Muldrew, R.
McCann, D. G.
McDaniel, J. A.
McIntyre, J. C.
McIntyre, J. R.
Obanon, D. B.
Onstott, Henderson
Onstott, Thomas
Onstott, West
Onstott, E.
Orr, Andrew J.
Patterson, E.
Patterson, Thomas E. E.
Peverly, Benjamin H.
Price, John M.
Price, Josiah W.
Ranay, Isaac
Raney, David
Raney, John
Rankin, John Y.
Richards, ——
Richardson, T. J. M.
Robertson, George *
Ross, C. C.
Ross, H.
Ryan, D. D.
Sammons, Theodore C.

Shanks, John P.
Shanks, Leroy
Shaw, J.
Simmons, J.
Simmons, Joel
Simmons, John B.
Simms, James F.
Simpson, J.
Simson, J. B.
Springsteen, W. G.
Stanley, Stephen
Stewart, T. B.
Stunley, B.
Sullivan, Milton
Symms, George
Taylor, ——
Taylor, W.
Terrell, C. R.
Terrell, John E.
Thompson, W. C.
Tidwell, William C.
Treadwell, W.
Tubb, H. J.
Vicker, ——
Walker, Andrew J.
Walker, George W.
Warnick, W. B.
Warren, W. L.
Wells, J. B.
West, William C.
Wicker, W. F.
Williams, G. W.
Williams, Joseph
Williams, Stephen
Wilson, J. B.
Wilson, Marvey D. D.
Winston, J. A.
Wiseman, W. J.
Womack, D. H.
Woods, J. A.
Wyman, ——
Young, James A.

Company F, Twenty-fifth Texas Cavalry Regiment

Ballard, A. W.
Ballard, L. W.
Barclay, Walter
Barclay, W. W. W. *
Barnes, E. J. W.
Barnes, William E.
Beynter, J.
Boyett, John H.
Bradley, N.
Callier, R. P.
Clough, William S.
Deason, A. J.
Deason, William M.
Dowe, W. M.
DuBose, John B.
DuBose, R. N.
Durden John J.

Everett, James E.
Felder, Daniel
Felder, David
Felder, James
Felder, John
Fielder, Daniel
Fitzgerald, J. H.
Fortenberry, Evan W.
Freeman, H. W.
Fulgham, J. H.
Fulgham, Robert F.
Fulgham, Samuel J.
Fulgham, William M.
Garaway, Robert W.
George, John B.
Gibson, L. D.
Gibson, W. W.

Goff, Thomas B.
Goode, William T.
Hand, W. P.
Hardie, J.
Hardie, W.
Hardy, John H.
Hardy, W. W.
Heard, W. F.
Helton, M. P.
James, S.
Johnson, Francis M.
Johnson, M.
Johnson, Tom S.
Lea, James M.
Leard, William A.
Lowe, William M.
Madden, James M. K.

Maddox, W. D.
Mahaffey, William
Meadows, E. J.
Murrell, William M.
McAllister, John H.
McBride, Daniel S.
McMasters, Thomas R.
McQueen, John
Nowlin, James S.
Pace, Hiram
Patterson, Thomas C. C.
Peters, Elijah
Peters, John
Peters, J. W.
Pew, H. M.
Pharr, Denley
Pitts, E. S.
Powell, Cader

Powell, Hiram
Powell, John R.
Powell, Ransom
Preast, James T.
Priest, William
Priest, W. C.
Register, Joel R.
Reid, F. H.
Reid, John
Richardson, John
Rotan, James M. *
Russell, Samuel A.
Russell, William D.
Simons, James J.
Simpson, J.
Smith, Henry V.
Stephens, E. M.
Sterling, John

Sterling, William H.
Stewart, C. H.
Stewart, E.
Stewart, George W.
Stewart, William M.
Sumeral, Moses
Tarver, C. C.
Tarver, George W.
Tarver, J. A. S.
Tarver, John H.
Tarver, Sterling
Tarver, William W.
Twichell, A. F.
Twichell, B. F.
Ulrich, Louis
Wallace, James E.
Whatley, E. W.
Windham, H. H.
Young, William A.

Company G, Twenty-fifth Texas Cavalry Regiment

Allen, Abner
Allen, Taylor
Arrant, D. G.
Arrant, E. G.
Arrant, H. B.
Baker, Mosely
Baker, W. S.
Barefield, Jesse
Bennett, Robert
Black, G. B.
Boothe, F. W.
Boothe, W. S.
Brandon, A. E.
Bright, Jesse E.
Brown, W. H.
Bryan, F. E.
Burnes, C. E.
Burns, P.
Byrd, G. W.
Byrd, J. C.
Carnegie, Alex E.
Cherry, A. J.
Cherry, Hiram
Cherry, John J.
Cherry, William C.
Coffelt, J.
Coker, A. J.
Cox, M. J.
Darr, A.
Davis, G. P.
Davis, W. D.
Dearman, S. M.
Donahoe, C. C.
Eaves, Tayler
Ellis, W. F.
Ellis, W. L.
Emanuel, Asa C.
Emanuel, F. M.
Emanuel, Henry

Emanuel, Jasper
Etheridge, W. G.
Evans, W. H.
Evans, Jonathan D.
Furr, Christian
Gambada, ——
Gibson, J. J.
Graham, W. W.
Granus, J. A.
Gray, D. L.
Grayman, W. M.
Gregory, David
Grimes, J. A.
Hanson, H. A.
Hardison, J. L.
Hardison, J. R.
Hardison, William L.
Hardison, W. M.
Holtsclaw, Eli
Howard, J. W.
Howel, H. B.
Hughs, J. L.
Jackson, D. M.
Jones, J. A.
Jones, J. H.
Jones, R.
Leggett, Reuben
Lewis, William
Masters, A. J.
May, F. E.
May, J. G.
May, William J.
Montgomery, W. A.
Morris, J. O.
Morriss, William G.
McCracken, Ansel
McCracken, Daniel
McCracken, G. S.
McCracken, J. J.

McCracken, W. B.
McCracken, W. E.
Neal, G. E.
Nix, W. M.
Pool, E.
Pratt, R.
Quada, John
Richards, R. A.
Ricks, William L.
Roberson, James
Roy, W. M.
Servat, Paul
Simms, James F.
Simpson, G. W. *
Simpson, H. J.
Simpson, Jesse
Simson, J. B.
Singler, William
Smith, Henry V.
Snow, Harrison S.
Sprecher, Andrew
Stanmots, Ph.
Tanner, J. R.
Thomas, A. J.
Thomas, H. A.
Tomlinson, A.
Turner, Richard
Walker, A.
Walton, W. G.
Weldon, V.
Wilbourne, John
Wilbourne, W. J.
Williams, Richard
Williams, H. J. E.
Woodlaw, H.
Woodsworth, S. S.
Wright, Henry
Wright, James
Wright, W. P.

Company H, Twenty-fifth Texas Cavalry Regiment

Alleans, John G.
Anderson, Thomas
Anderson, Thomas S.
Antonio, Christoff
Arnaud, Adolph
Arnett, John T.
Arnnett, Z.
Ayer, G. W.
Bachen, H.
Bailey, James E.
Baillio, Selvair P.
Baily, J.
Barrett, John F.
Bandreaux, J.
Beachan, H.
Bellard, Mecina
Beothyen, W.
Bitteman, Lucien A.
Block, H.
Bondreau, Joseph
Brown, Albert L.
Carter, B. F.
Carter, W.
Cashett, J.
Childs, James B.
Davison, George W.
Davidson, J.
Dawson, John
DeBlanc, Alcide
DeBlanc, Cesaire
DeBlanc, Jerome E.
Deblanc, Joe
Deblanc, Oscar *
Dugat, Arvellian
Dugat, John
Dugat, Lefrois
Duset, Joseph
Elliott, William B.
Fortier, C. Sulimbe
Francen, Hugo
Francis, W.
Freeman, W.
Fruge, L.
Fruger, Antonio Jr.
Fruger, Antonio Sr.
Fruger, David
Frugier, F.
Frugier, John P. Jr.
Frugier, John P. Sr.
Frugier, Joseph
Frugier, Julian

Frugier, Lazime
Frugier, R.
Fruzier, Valcine
Fulkerson, A. H.
Garvin, James T.
Gilchrist, Ursen
Gillard, Appolinair
Gillard, Ludolph
Gillard, N.
Goshen, ———
Graves, Joseph N.
Grice, Robert L.
Hardin, Swan
Harges, James M.
Hartman, Levi
Hatton, A. E.
Hicks, John H.
Hoards, John R.
Holland, Jeremiah
Houghstutter, C.
Honse, M
Howard, Pryor
Hughes, Jefferson C.
Hughes, W. M.
Hyde, R. E.
Ivey, Andrew J.
Jackson, A.
Jackson, William
Johnson, Earl B.
Johnson, Joseph B.
Johnson, William B.
Jones, J. Churchill
Joy, A. J.
Kinsey, Allen T.
Lacour, Siprien
Lacour, Edward N.
Lacour, Gilbert Jr.
Lacour, Gus
Lacour, J. M. C.
Lacour, John W.
Lacour, Jul. J.
Lacour, L. Ernest
Lacour, Zenon
Lacy, Francis M.
Lacy, John D.
Lawrence, William F.
Lofton, William H.
Longtoft, Louis R.
Morris, Osceola
Myers, T. H.
McAllister, John W.

McCorkle, Robert
McLaughlin, Charles
McNamer, James
Nead, Eugene
Noe, James W.
O'Brien, John
Owens, Alfred
Owens, John H.
Pentecost, J.
Peveto, John
Peveto, Joseph
Pice, John Henry
Pile, Henry R.
Proudfoot, John R.
Rachal, Frank S.
Reese, John H.
Richard, Alfred
Ripka, D.
Roberts, Benjamin
Rodgers, H.
Rodgers, M.
Rodgers, William G. B.
Sargent, J. Henry
Schwarner, James
Sells, Thomas W.
Simpson, Andrew J.
Simpson, Henry
Simpson, W. H.
Sisk, Jacob J.
Smith, E. J.
Smith, James T.
Smith, J. C.
Smith, W. C.
Stanley, William G.
Swaner, James W.
Tanney, H.
Tanney, W.
Tapin, J.
Tenney, L. M.
Thibodeaux, Charles
Thibodeaux, Joseph
Tompkins, Augustus
Vanhuten, R.
Vinier, John
Wallen, Charles
Watts, John W.
Weaver, John
Wilson, Theodore O.
Wilson, William H.
Wright, David C.
Wright, William M.
Zaran, F. M.

Company I, Twenty-fifth Texas Cavalry Regiment

Abbott, W. H.
Andler, Charles
Arnaud, Adolph
Ayer, G. W.
Bagerly, W. H.
Baily, B. W.
Berthier, J. B.

Bilow, J.
Blum, ———
Borth, Joseph
Bristley, M.
Britton, Thomas J.
Britton, W. H.
Brown, J. Douglas

Brown, William C.
Burrell, David
Cade, W. J.
Campbell, G. H.
Cannon, G. H.
Cantrell, Rice
Carey, D. J.

Carlin, James F.
Casey, James
Chambers, Thomas J. Jr.
Chambers, William
Charpiot, Vincent
Clayton, Josephus C.
Clingman, A. A.
Crosby, Gilbert
Curbello, Antoine
Deets, W. S.
Deval, Lewis
Devore, C. C.
Dickinson, J. J. E.
Dodge, William H.
Dugat, W. M.
Ducet, James
Fisher, S.
Freeman, Thomas J.
Fuller, John
Gains, P. S.
Garcia, Robert
Garner, W.
Gill, A. J.
Gray, J. A.
Green, Ezra
Green, J. J.
Green, Reoson
Greene, F. D.
Gregg, James A.
Griffin, J. H.
Guise, P. S.
Gunter, C.
Hardin, C. O.
Hardin, Swan
Hartman, Douglas
Hartman, S. C.
Hayden, Joseph
Hillboldt, S.
Holley, Nat
Horton, Calvin B. M.
James, G. W.
Jarrell, Stephen

Johnson, Moses
Johnston, D. E.
Johnston, Samuel H.
Jones, Stephen
Jourdan, E. F.
Jourdan, James J.
Kilgore, Robert
Leary, James C.
Levy, H.
Linney, Henry
Loggins, R. T.
Loggins, W. H.
Lucas, William
Lyons, James
Manly, John
Martin, G. W.
Martin, O. H.
Massa, Eugene T.
Massa, Lewis
Maynard, C. D.
Meadors, T. J.
Merrill, W. R.
Montgomery, John
Moon, Joseph
Myer, Henry
McCallister, M. D.
McCarty, James P.
McDowell, James B.
McIntyre, William H.
McKinley, J. L.
McLaughlin, C. T.
McManus, William
McMurtry, Abner
McMurtry, A. L.
McMurtry, James Jr.
McMurtry, Levi
Neal, David
Nichols, S. S.
Paul, L. D.
Payne, Moses P.
Pevotot, J.
Pickett, E. B.

Pickett, J. J.
Pickett, Joseph T.
Porter, William M.
Pounds, William D.
Preacher, George A.
Prewitt, James
Quinn, John F.
Rainier, A.
Ricca, F. G.
Ricks, George
Ricks, William L.
Roach, B. F.
Roberson, James
Rock, Thomas
Servat, Paul
Shannon, William
Shelby, John O.
Simans, B. J.
Simmons, Bernard
Simmons, B. H.
Simpson, Andrew J.
Simpson, H. J.
Simpson, Jesse
Singler, William *
Smith, P. K.
Smith, Sam Y.
Snow, Harrison S.
Sprecher, Andrew
Swearingen, S.
Tarkington, J.
Thiel, C.
Touchstone, H.
Turner, Richard
Vannier, J.
Vorbeck, John
Wells, J. M.
Wells, M.
Wiggins, J. H.
Wilbourne, John
Wilbourne, W. J.
Wilburn, J. W.
Williams, H. J. E.
Woodsworth, S. S.
Wright, Henry *

Company K, Twenty-fifth Texas Cavalry Regiment

Allphin, B. S.
Allphin, Thomas S.
Armitage, Wilber F.
Atkins, H. S.
Bell, F. M.
Bingham, F. E.
Bostwick, J. T.
Brooks, R. P.
Burnett, John
Bushen, Bennett
Cary, John W.
Chatham, John C.
Childress, John P.
Childress, Thomas Y.
Clark, J. F.
Cockrell, Samuel P.

Cook, C. Monroe
Cook, John W.
Cross, John B.
Cureton, John W. *
Davis, Henry P.
Dean, William J.
Dobbins, John
Douglas, W. L. *
DuBose, J. C.
Dunn, John C. *
Durham, George G.
Edwards, J. M. *
Edwards, Jonathan
Elliott, Martin
Everett, J. R.
Gibson, R. M.

Grady, B. F.
Grant, R. D.
Gunter, W. S.
High, Edward
Hopkins, James J.
Hyde, Robert H.
James, Edward
Kelly, W. R.
Marler, W. W.
Mathews, S. H.
Merryman, P.
Milliken, Robert
Mills, Edward
Monro, H.
McAdams, Thomas L.
McClintock, William B.

McGary, John A.
Nash, Lafayette
Pepera, Oraste
Patterson, Thomas C. C.
Pilgrim, James
Plaster, H. F.
Potter, Edward
Prescott, C. S. *
Pursley, W. G.
Ragsdale, John N.
Raley, F. M. *

Rawls, J. C.
Roberts, George G.
Shaffer, John
Shaffer, J. Thomas
Shannon, Isaac
Singletary, L. L.
Singletary, M. M.
Smith, Lemuel
Smith, Samuel
Smith, Thomas
Smyrl, Jonathan K. *

Taylor, W. P.
Thomas, John
Thompson, Alvis
Tyler, W. J.
Waller, A. C.
Webb, James H.
Webb, Thomas B.
West, Henry
White, George A.
Wood, George W.
Wyche, D. W. *

Miscellaneous, Twenty-fifth Texas Cavalry Regiment

Allstaden, E.
Bailey, J. C.
Baldinger, H. A.
Barney, R. A.
Bavoux, J. B.
Bedmore, R. H.
Bentict, J.
Bermondy, A. W.
Berry, J.
Besing, C. H.
Bodiker, W.
Bowles, J. H.
Brenner, T. W.
Brick, T.
Brintnall, J. J.
Brownlee, J. H.
Burthall, J. C.
Bussie, F.
Byrnes, F. E.
Colton, T. J.
Conor, P.
Coulton, F. R.
Crane, E.
Dabide, J.
Dedrick, C.
Derick, J.
Doe, E. S.
Doiris, J.
Estes, J. F.

Ferill, T. R.
Fisher, J. B.
Fleming, J. J.
Foster, A. H.
Gaither, James C.
Gee, John
Gee, L.
Gentry, C. R.
Gill, E. P.
Gillet, F.
Gillett, J.
Green, D. C.
Groce, G. W.
Guinn, J. W.
Hamitt, T. L.
Hanson, J. L.
Haskill, P. A.
Hayes, C. A.
Hubbard, T. P.
Johnson, G.
Johnson, W.
Jones, J.
Jones, W. D.
King, J. E.
King, S. H.
Kuntz, F.
Lemon, G. W.
Liley, W.
Lungill, T.

Menard, A. B.
Milby, W. H.
Moss, M.
McGillbery, C.
McKeetton, D. R.
Nemier, W.
Osh, R. F.
Percey, H. R.
Rea, J. W.
Richard, F. A.
Rigley, A. H.
Roberts, R. J.
Rodgers, W.
Scatchell, J.
Scoble, A. W.
Sealy, G.
Sessions, E. R.
Shaw, P. N.
Shearer, T. C.
Simmons, J. F.
Stacey, D. C.
Stafford, J. S.
Swares, E.
Talman, J. L.
Thacken, T.
Thompson, Van Buren
Wertman, B. F.
Wilbourn, D. C.
Wooly, M.

Richardson's Company of Independent Texas Cavalry

Adams, David H.
Adams, William J.
Agurs, William C.
Allen, Robert S.
Alley, James W.
Anderson, Alvin H.
Anderson, Martin V.
Attaway, Lewis L.
Bann, Alexander
Barker, John N.
Barrett, William G.
Bayless, A. Benjamin
Bayliss, Laban R.
Beard, John
Beavers, William M.
Bedell, Edmund Thomas
Benge, Richard Provine

Black, Benjamin P.
Black, Silas E.
Board, John S.
Board, Sterrett B.
Bonner, Reuben P.
Boswell, Charles P.
Bradfield, John Anderson
Briggs, Robert W.
Brown, Bolar A.
Bullock, Henry Clay
Bullock, Zach T.
Burnett, William H.
Burns, Christopher C.
Burns, Sim M.
Burton, Samuel J.
Carlow, Sam J.
Carlow, William H.

Chambers, James Robert
Chatham, William H.
Chilcoat, William P.
Choat, Austin
Choat, P. Henderson
Clark, Adolphus Newton
Clark, George B.
Clark, Isaac Wesley
Clark, James M.
Cocke, Henry B.
Cocke, Jonathan H.
Coffey, Thomas J.
Cole, Daniel H.
Cole, William Bright
Coleman, James M.
Collier, Calvin Wiggins
Collier, William Irvine

Conway, George B.
Cosgrove, James H.
Cotten, Joseph
Cowan, Thomas J.
Cox, Hardy P.
Crisenberry, Hiram Mason
Cunningham, R. H.
Curtis, James C.
Davis, Newton B.
Dawson, Richard P.
Dean, Charles A.
Dobbins, Sylvester
Duke, John Martindale
Elgin, Thomas Ashford
Fair, James Matt
Felton, Hilliard F.
Fitzpatrick, Schuyler G.
Furst, Samuel
Gaither, George W.
Garrett, Robert C.
Geer, George L.
Gibson, Drayton
Goode, Tim G.
Gravitt, Jonathan M.
Greer, Ed B.
Gully, James M.
Hamlett, Francis Marion
Harris, Henry S.
Harris, Micajah Jessee
Harris, William A.
Harris, William F.
Hart, Andrew Jackson
Harwell, Alfred Washington
Hawlee, Lee C.
Heartsill, William Williston
Hemby, Thomas M.
Henderson, Luther Andrews
Higgins, Thomas V.
Hill, Dennis C.
Hilliard, Walter
Hinds, Joseph D.
Holcombe, John Theodore
Holcombe, Phil
Hudson, Thomas Jefferson
Hughes, James W.
Hummel, George H.
Hyde, James Robert
Irvine, S. Doak M.
Ish, Jonathan H.
Jarrott, Erasmus L.
Jarrott, George Witherspoon
Jarrott, James R.
Jarrott, John M.
Jarrott, Jonathan R.
Johnson, Joseph J.
Johnson, Marcellus W.
Johnson, Robert Sidney
Johnson, William Oscar
Johnston, Wesley B.
Jones, Felix A.
Jones, Henry H.

Jones, Martin E.
Jones, Russell D.
Jones, William M.
Keener, Lawson J.
Keith, William D.
Kennedy, Samuel J.
Kneeland, Walter E.
Lane, Walter P. Jr.
Lawrence, Jessee M.
Lott, Stephen S.
Loughery, Robert W. Jr.
Magrill, James M.
Magrill, Jonathan B.
Marshall, Andrew S.
Marshall, Frank M.
Mathis, George
Matthews, Benjamin E.
Miller, D. C.
Moodie, Samuel O.
Mooney, Seabourn J.
Morris, Anderson
Morris, Jonathan
Morris, Jonathan G.
Moshier, Henry H.
Murphy, William J.
McCain, Rufus A.
McCain, William J.
McCarey, D. L.
McDonald, John W.
McKinney, Claudius A.
McKinney, William M.
Nance, Benjamin A.
Norris, Joel H.
Oliver, J. L.
Palmer, William H.
Pattillo, A. Dixon
Pattillo, J. Zach
Pattison, Jonathan T.
Pattison, William R.
Peete, George A.
Perry, Walter C.
Perry, Zach T.
Pounds, Thomas J.
Preston, William B.
Rabb, William Penn
Ragland, Areloise
Ragsdale, Thomas B.
Ramsey, Jonathan W.
Ramsey, Robert E.
Rees, John B.
Reilly, Francis
Reynolds, Samuel H.
Richardson, Samuel J.
Rives, George M.
Rogers, Jonathan M.
Sample, Alex W.
Sanford, William Daniel
Saufley, Jonathan C.
Scott, Jonathan W.
Sedberry, Mike K.
Shepherd, John W.

Sims, James M.
Smisson, John A.
Smith, Nathan Alexander
Snediker, William
Spencer, John
Starkey, William C.
Steally, Henry A.
Thompson, William S.
Tillery, Milton Jarrod
Trosper, James M.
Twitty, Thomas
Underwood, Sam A.
Vance, William L.
Vanderhuff, William
Vanvickle, ———
Vaughan, James Marshall
Vines, John M.
Walker, Johnson
Wallace, Benjamin A.
Warwick, Robert M.
Watson, George W.
Watt, William
Wattson, Samuel
Weaver, Thomas O.
Wheeler, George W.
Willeford, J. Wallace
Williams, Robert W.
Williams, William P.
Williamson, William Wesley
Witt, Luther Rice
Young, Charles F.
Young, James W.
Young, William H.

Notes

One: Texans Go To War

1 Franz Coller, "Coller of the Sixth Texas," edited by Gilbert Cuthbertson, *Military History of Texas and the Southwest*, Vol. IX, 1972, Number 2, p. 131.

2 Jim Turner, "Jim Turner Co. G, 6th Texas Infantry, C.S.A. from 1861 to 1865," *Texana*, Vol. XII, Number 2, 1974, p. 152.

3 Robert R. Gilbert, *High Private's Confederate Letters*, p. 6.

4 Dallas *Herald*, January 28, 1863.

5 Recruiting poster dated Chappell Hill, Nov. '61

6 J. P. Blessington, *The Campaigns of Walker's Texas Division*, p. 22–23.

7 Government Printing Office, *The War of the Rebellion: A Compilation of the Official Records of the Union and Confederate Armies*, XV, p. 823 (hereafter referred to as *OR*).

8 Robert Hodges, "Robert Hodges, Jr.,: Confederate Soldier," edited by Maury Darst, *East Texas Historical Association*, Vol. IX, Number 1, March, 1971, p. 31.

9 Isaiah Harlan to his brother, Alpheus, dated November 24, 1862, typescript in collection of Confederate Research Center at Hillsboro, Texas.

10 Benjamin M. Seaton, *The Bugle Softly Blows*, edited by Harold B. Simpson, p. 18–19.

11 George L. Griscom, *Fighting with Ross' Texas Cavalry Brigade C.S.A.*, edited by Homer L. Kerr, p. 21.

12 Robert M. Collins, *Chapters from the Unwritten History of the War Between the States*, p. 25.

13 Collins, p. 19.

14 Collins, p. 20–21.

15 Flavius W. Perry, "The Letters of Lt. Flavius W. Perry 17th Texas Cavalry, 1862–1863," edited by Joe R. Wise, *Military History of Texas and the Southwest*, Vol. XIII, Number 3, p. 12.

16 Dallas *Herald*, November 6, 1861.

17 Dallas *Herald*, November 13, 1861.

18 *OR*, XIII, p. 956.

19 Marshall Pierson, "The Diary and Memoirs of Marshall Samuel Pierson, Company C, 17th Reg., Texas Cavalry 1862–1865," edited by Norman C. Delaney, *Military History of Texas and the Southwest*, Vol. XIII, No. 2, p. 26.

20 Collins, p. 62.

21 Seaton, p. 22.

22 Perry, p. 21.

23 Isaiah Harlan to his brother, Eliphalet, dated August 15, 1862.

24 John Q. Anderson, editor, *Campaigning with Parsons' Texas Cavalry Brigade*, p. 69.

25 Anderson, p. 71.

Two: The Battle of Arkansas Post

1 L. V. Caraway, "The Battle of Arkansas Post," *Confederate Veteran*, XIV, 1906, p. 127–128; S. W. Bishop, "The Battle of Arkansas Post," *Confederate Veteran*, V, 1897, p. 151–152; Collins, p. 68.

2 Samuel T. Foster, *One of Cleburne's Command*, edited by Norman D. Brown, p. 5.

3 Anderson, p. 88.

4 *OR*, XVII, Part 1, p. 781.

5 Government Printing Office, *The War of the Rebellion: A Compilation of the Official Records of the Union and Confederate Navies*, XXIV, p. 104 (hereafter referred to as *ORN*).

6 Bishop, p. 151–152.

7 Caraway, p. 127–128.

8 *OR*, XVII, Part 1, p. 768.

9 W. H. Bentley, *History of the 77th Illinois Volunteer Infantry Sept. 2, 1862-July 10, 1865*, p. 116.

10 William J. Oliphant memoirs.

11 *OR*, XVII, Part 1, p. 794.

12 Caraway, p. 127–128.

13 *OR*, XVII, Part 2, p. 553.

14 *OR*, XVII, Part 1, p. 781.

Three: Prison

1 Collins, p. 72–73.

2 Dallas *Herald*, February 18, 1863.

3 *OR*, Series 2, IV, p. 157.

4 Joseph A. Hinkle, "The Odyssey of Private Hinkle," *Civil War Times Illustrated*, Dec. 1969, p.27.

5 William J. Oliphant memoirs.

6 *OR*, Series 2, V, p. 400, 409.

7 T. M. Page, "The Prisoner of War," *Confederate Veteran*, VIII, 1904, p. 64.

8 Unknown, *Southern Bivouac*, New Series, I, No. 4, Sept., 1885, p. 256.

9 Collins, p. 86–87.

10 *OR*, Series 2, V, p. 305.

11 *OR*, Series 2, V, p. 317.

12 Collins, p. 94.

13 Collins, p. 99.

14 Collins, p. 108.

15 *OR*, Series 2, V, p. 477

16 *OR*, Series 2, V, p. 477–478.

17 *OR*, Series 2, V, p. 487.

Four: Assigned to the Army of Tennessee

1 Foster, p. 43.

2 Collins, p. 135.

3 *OR*, XVII, Part 1, p. 787.

4 Foster, p. 49.
5 Daniel H. Hill, "Chickamauga — The Great Battle of the West," *Battles and Leaders*, III, p. 641.
6 *OR*, XXX, Part 3, p. 481.
7 *OR*, XXX, Part 2, p. 294–295.
8 *OR*, XXX, Part 2, p. 296.

Five: The Battle of Chickamauga

1 *OR*, XXX, Part 2, p. 49.
2 *OR*, XXX, Part 2, p. 52.
3 William W. Heartsill, *Fourteen Hundred and 91 Days in the Confederate Army*, p. 159

Six: Missionary Ridge

1 John Allen Wyeth, *That Devil Forrest*, p. 236.
2 Stanley F. Horn, *The Army of Tennessee*, p. 285; *OR*, XXX, Part 4, p. 705.
3 Horn, p. 285–286; *OR*, XXX, Part 2, p. 65–66.
4 Horn, p. 291.
5 Collins, p. 168.

Seven: Winter Quarters

1 *OR*, XXXI, Part 2, p. 753.
2 Collins, p. 186.
3 *OR*, XXXI, Part 2, p. 608.
4 *OR*, XXXI, Part 2, p. 758.
5 Bryan Marsh, "The Confederate Letters of Bryan Marsh," *Chronicles of Smith County, Texas*, XIV, No. 2, Winter, 1975, p. 45.
6 Unknown, "Severe Discipline," *Confederate Veteran*, I, 1893, p. 374.

Eight. Dalton to Atlanta

1 Foster, p. 78.
2 Horn, p. 328.
3 *OR*, XXXVIII, Part 3, p. 725.
4 *OR*, XXXVIII, Part 3, p. 725.
5 G. W. Lewis, *The Campaigns of the 124th Ohio Volunteer Infantry*, p. 153.
6 *OR*, XXXVIII, Part 3, p. 726.
7 Mamie Yeary, *Reminiscences of the Boys in Grey, 1861–1865*, p. 656.

Nine: Atlanta

1 D. R. Lucas, *New History of the 99th Indiana Infantry*, p. 107.
2 Unknown, "Return of a Confederate Flag," *Confederate Veteran*, XXII, 1914, p. 302.
3 Foster, p. 125, 126.
4 *OR*, XXXVIII, Part 3, p. 744.

5 Peggy Robbins, "Hood vs. Sherman: A Duel of Words," *Civil War Times Illustrated,* XVII, No. 4, July, 1978.
6 Foster, p. 135.
7 Foster, p. 133.

Ten: The Tennessee Campaign

1 Stanley F. Horn, "The Spring Hill Legend," *Civil War Times Illustrated,* VII, Number 1, p. 24.
2 John K. Shellenberger, *The Battle of Spring Hill, Tennessee,* p. 28–29.
3 John B. Hood, "The Invasion of Tennessee," *Battles and Leaders,* IV, p. 432.
4 Foster, p. 151.
5 Hood, p. 436.
6 *OR,* XLV, Part 1, p. 527.
7 Stanley F. Horn, *The Decisive Battle of Nashville,* p. 153.

Eleven: The End of the War

1 Horn, *The Army of Tennessee,* p. 424.
2 Collins, p. 275–276.
3 H. W. Slocum, "Final Operations of Sherman's Army," *Battles and Leaders,* IV, p. 757.
4 *OR,* XLVII, Part 3, p. 848–849.
5 Foster, p. 178.
6 Joseph McClure, "Wounded Texan's Trip Home on Crutches," *Confederate Veteran,* XVII, 1909, p. 162–163.

Twelve: Aftermath

1 Dixon Wecter, *When Johnny Comes Marching Home,* p. 177.
2 *Fort Worth Gazette,* August 12, 1891.
3 *Minutes of the Proceedings of the Association of Survivors of Ross', Ector's and Granberry's [sic] Brigades, U.C.V. Held at Garland, Texas August 8 and 9, 1899,* p. 7.
4 Weatherford *Enquirer,* August 11, 1892.

Appendix A: The Flags of Granbury's Brigade

1 Letter from William J. Oliphant to H. P. Bee, Commissioner of Insurance, Statistics and History (and former Confederate General) dated November 25, 1885.
2 *OR,* XVII, Part 1, p. 794.
3 Heartsill, p. 4.
4 Turner, p. 150.

Bibliography

Books

Banks, R. W. *The Battle of Franklin November 30, 1864.* New York and Washington: The Neale Publishing Company, 1908. (Banks was the captain of Company D, 37th Mississippi Consolidated Infantry Regiment.)

Bear, Henry C. *The Civil War Letters of Henry C. Bear: A Soldier in the 116th Illinois Volunteer Infantry.* Edited by Wayne C. Temple. Harrogate, Tennessee: Lincoln Memorial University Press, 1961.

Bentley, Lieutenant W. H. *History of the 77th Illinois Volunteer Infantry Sept. 2, 1862–July 10, 1865.* Peoria, Illinois: Edward Hine, 1883. (Bentley served as an enlisted man in Company I, 77th Illinois Infantry and later as a lieutenant in Company D, 77th U.S. Colored Infantry and Company H, 10th U.S. Colored Artillery.)

Bering, John A. and Thomas Montgomery. *History of the Forty-Eighth Ohio Veteran Volunteer Infantry.* Hillsboro, Ohio: Highland News Office, 1880. (Bering was the major of the 48th Ohio and Montgomery was a captain in the same regiment.)

Blessington, J. P. *The Campaigns of Walker's Texas Division.* New York: Lange, Little and Company, 1875. (Blessington was a member of Company H, 16th Texas Infantry Regiment.)

Boynton, Henry V. *Was General Thomas Slow at Nashville?.* New York: Francis P. Harper, 1896. (Boynton was the lieutenant colonel of the 35th Ohio Infantry Regiment.)

• Bryant, C. C. *History of the Sixth Regiment Indiana Volunteer Infantry.* Indianapolis: William B. Burford, 1891. (Bryant was the captain of Company K, 6th Indiana Infantry Regiment.)

Buck, Irving A. *Cleburne and His Command.* New York: The Neale Publishing Company, 1908. (Buck served on General Cleburne's staff.)

Buck, Paul H. *The Road to Reunion — 1865–1900.* Boston: Little, Brown, 1937.

Catton, Bruce. *The Coming Fury.* Garden City, New York: Doubleday and Company, Inc., 1961.

——— *Never Call Retreat.* Garden City, New York: Doubleday and Company, Inc., 1965.

———. *Terrible Swift Sword.* Garden City, New York: Doubleday and Company, Inc., 1963.

Chamberlin, William H. *History of the Eighty-First Regiment Ohio Infantry Volunteers During the War of the Rebellion.* Cincinnati: Gazette Steam Printing House, 1865. (Chamberlin was the major of the 81st Ohio Infantry Regiment.)

Clark, Charles T. *Opdyke Tigers: 125th Ohio Volunteer Infantry.* Columbus, Ohio: Spahr and Glenn, 1895. (Clark was the captain of Company F, 125th Ohio Infantry Regiment.)

Collier, Calvin L. *First In-Last Out: The Capitol Guards, Arkansas Brigade.* Little Rock: Pioneer Press, 1961.

Collins, Robert M. *Chapters From the Unwritten History of the War Between the*

States. St. Louis: Nixon–Jones Printing Company, 1893. (Collins was a lieutenant in Company B, 15th Texas Cavalry Regiment.)

A Committee. *Military History and Reminiscences of the Thirteenth Regiment of Illinois Volunteer Infantry in the Civil War in the United States 1861–1865*. Chicago: Woman's Temperance Publishing Association, 1892.

A Committee. *The Story of the Fifty-fifth Regiment Illinois Volunteer Infantry in the Civil War 1861–1865*. Clinton, Massachusetts: W. J. Coulter, 1887.

Dinkins, James. *1861 to 1865 — By An Old Johnnie*. Cincinnati, 1897. (Dinkins was a captain in the Confederate Army.)

Downey, Fairfax. *Storming of the Gateway: Chattanooga, 1863*. New York: David McKay Company, Inc., 1960.

Eisenschiml, Otto and Ralph Newman. *The Civil War: The American Iliad*. New York: Bobbs-Merril Company, 1956.

Evans, Clement A., editor. *Confederate Military History*. Reprinted by the Blue and Grey Press. (Evans was a brigadier general in the Army of Northern Virginia.)

Foster, Samuel T. *One of Cleburne's Command: The Civil War Reminiscences and Diary of Captain Samuel T. Foster, Granbury's Texas Brigade, C.S.A.* Edited by Norman D. Brown. Austin, Texas: University of Texas Press, 1980. (Foster was a captain of Company H, 24th Texas Cavalry Regiment.)

Gay, Mary A. H. *Life in Dixie During the War*. Fourth Edition. Atlanta: Foote and Davies Company, 1901. (Miss Gay was the half sister of Lieutenant Thomas J. Stokes of the 10th Texas Infantry Regiment.)

Gilbert, Robert R. *High Private's Confederate Letters*. Second Edition. Austin, Texas: Eugene Von Boeckmann, 1894. (Gilbert was a member of Company B, 6th Texas Infantry Regiment.)

Gracie, Archibald. *The Truth About Chickamauga*. Boston and New York: Houghton Mifflin Company, 1911.

Grainger, Gervis D. *Four Years With the Boys in Gray*. Franklin, Kentucky: The Favorite Office, 1902. (Grainger was a member of Company I, 6th Kentucky Infantry, C.S.A.)

Gray, Edgar. *Confederate Soldiers, Sailors and Civilians Who Died as Prisoners of War At Camp Douglas, Chicago, Illinois 1862–1865*. Kalamazoo, Michigan: Edgar Gray Publications, ca. 1976.

Grimes, Roy, editor. *300 Years in Victoria County*. Victoria, Texas: The Victoria Advocate Publishing Company, 1968.

Hay, Thomas Robson. *Hood's Tennessee Campaign*. New York: Walter Neale, 1929.

Hays, Ebenezer Z., editor. *History of the 32nd Regiment Ohio Veteran Volunteer Infantry*. Columbus, Ohio: Cott and Evans, 1896. (Hays was a lieutenant in Company K, 32nd Ohio Infantry.)

Handy, Isaac W. K., D. D. *United States Bonds or Duress by Federal Authority: A Journal of Current Events During an Imprisonment of Fifteen Months, At Fort Delaware*. Baltimore: Turnbull Brothers, 1874.

Heartsill, William W. *Fourteen Hundred and 91 Days in the Confederate Army*. (Reprint) Jackson, Tennessee: McCowat-Mercer Press, 1954. (Heartsill was a sergeant in Richardson's Texas Cavalry Company and later of Company L, 6th, 10th and 15th Texas Regiment.)

Hegarty, Lela Whitton, editor. *Father Wore Gray.* San Antonio, Texas: The Naylor Company, 1963.

Hesseltine, William B. *Civil War Prisons: A Study in War Psychology.* Columbus, Ohio: Ohio State University Press, 1930.

Hood, John B. *Advance and Retreat.* New Orleans, 1880. (General Hood's memoirs.)

Horn, Stanley F. *The Army of Tennessee.* New York: Bobbs-Merril Company, 1941.

———. *The Decisive Battle of Nashville.* Baton Rouge: Louisiana State University Press, 1956.

Jewell, Carey C. *Harvest of Death: A Detailed Account of the Army of Tennessee at the Battle of Franklin.* Hicksville, New York: Exposition Press, 1976.

Johnson, Robert Underwood and Clarence Clough Buel, editors. *Battles and Leaders of the Civil War.* New York: A. S. Barnes and Company, Inc., 1887 (Volumes I and II), 1884 (Volume III), 1888 (Volume IV).

Johnston, Joseph E. *Narrative of Military Operations.* New York: D. Appleton and Company, 1874. (General Johnston's memoirs.)

Key, Thomas J. and Robert J. Campbell. *Two Soldiers: The Campaign Diaries of Thomas J. Key, C.S.A. and Robert J. Campbell, U.S.A.* Edited by Wirt Armistead Cate. Chapel Hill, North Carolina: The University of North Carolina Press, 1938. (Key's artillery battery sometimes fought alongside Granbury's Brigade.)

Kimberley, Robert L. and Ephraim S. Holloway. *The Forty-first Ohio Veteran Volunteer Infantry in the War of the Rebellion 1861–1865.* Cleveland, Ohio: W. R. Smellie, 1897. (Kimberley was the lieutenant colonel of the 41st Ohio before becoming colonel of the 191st Ohio. Holloway was the lieutenant colonel of the 41st Ohio at the end of the war.)

King, John H. *Three Hundred Days in a Yankee Prison: Reminiscences of War Life Captivity Imprisonment at Camp Chase Ohio.* Atlanta: James P. Davies, 1904. (King was a member of Company H, 40th Georgia Infantry Regiment.)

Knauss, William H. *Story of Camp Chase.* Nashville and Dallas: Publishing House of the Methodist Episcopal Church, South, 1906. (Knauss was an ex-Union soldier.)

Lewis, G. W. *The Campaigns of the 124th Regiment Ohio Volunteer Infantry.* Akron, Ohio: The Werner Company, no date. (Lewis was captain of Company B, 124th Ohio Infantry Regiment.)

Lucas, D. R. *History of the 99th Indiana Infantry.* Lafayette, Indiana: Rosser and Spring, 1865. (Lucas was the chaplain of the 99th Indiana Infantry Regiment.)

———. *New History of the 99th Indiana Infantry.* Rockford, Illinois: Horner Printing Company, 1900.

Madaus, Howard Michael and Robert D. Needham. *The Battle Flags of the Confederate Army of Tennessee.* Milwaukee, Wisconsin: Milwaukee Public Museum, 1976.

McMurray, W. J. *History of the Twentieth Tennessee Regiment Volunteer Infantry* C.S.A. Nashville, 1904.

McMurry, Richard M. *The Road Past Kennesaw: The Atlanta Campaign of 1864.* Washington, D.C.: U.S. Department of the Interior, 1972.

Miller, Francis Trevelyan, editor-in-chief. *The Photographic History of the Civil War.* New York: A. S. Barnes and Company, Inc., 1911.

Minutes of the Proceedings of the Association of the Survivors of Ross', Ector's and Granberry's [sic] Brigades, U.C.V. Held at Garland, Texas August 8 and 9, 1899.

Minutes of the Proceedings of the Association of Survivors of Ross', Ector's and Granberry's [sic] Brigades, U.C.V. Held at Lancaster, Texas, August 14 and 15, 1900.

Minutes of the Proceedings of the Ross, Ector and Granbury Brigades, with the Douglass Texas Battery, Constituting the First Division of Texas, U.C.V. in Reunion Assembled at Tyler, Texas, August 16, 17, 1905. (Reprinted in *Chronicles of Smith County, Texas,* Volume VIII, No. 1, p. 43–54.)

One of the Boys. *The Story of the Service of Company E, and of the Twelfth Wisconsin Regiment of the Veteran Volunteer Infantry in the War of the Rebellion.* ca. 1893.

Orr Brothers. *Campaigning With Parsons' Texas Cavalry Brigade C.S.A.: The War Journal and Letters of the Four Orr Brothers, 12th Texas Cavalry Regiment.* Edited by John Q. Anderson. Hillsboro, Texas: Hill Junior College Press, 1967. (Two of the four Orr brothers transferred to the 18th Texas Cavalry Regiment in late 1862.)

Praus, Alexis A. *Confederate Soldiers and Sailors Who Died as Prisoners of War at Camp Butler, Illinois 1862–1865.* Kalamazoo, Michigan: Edgar Gray Publications, ca. 1976.

Purdue, Howell and Elizabeth. *Pat Cleburne: Confederate General.* Hillsboro, Texas: Hill Junior College Press, 1973.

Ramsdell, Charles William. *Reconstruction in Texas.* New York: Columbia University Press, 1910. (Reprinted by University of Texas Press in 1970.)

Report of the Proceedings of Granbury's Brigade Association, at Dallas, August 6th to 9th Inclusive, 1884.

Ridley, Bromfield L. *Battles and Sketches of the Army of Tennessee.* Mexico, Missouri: Missouri Printing and Publishing Company, 1906. (Ridley was on the staff of Lieutenant General Alexander P. Stewart.)

Scofield, Levi T. *The Retreat from Pulaski to Nashville.* Cincinnati: H. C. Sherick and Company, 1886. (Scofield was a captain in the Union Army.)

Seaton, Benjamin M. *The Bugle Softly Blows: The Confederate Diary of Benjamin M. Seaton.* Edited by Harold B. Simpson. Waco, Texas: Texian Press, 1965. (Seaton was a member of Company G, 10th Texas Infantry Regiment.)

Shellenberger, John K. *The Battle of Franklin, Tennessee November 30, 1864.* Cleveland, Ohio: Arthur H. Clark, 1916. (Shellenberger was captain of Company B, 64th Ohio Infantry Regiment.)

————. *The Battle of Spring Hill, Tennessee November 29, 1864*. Cleveland, Ohio: Arthur H. Clark, 1913.

Sherman, William T. *Memoirs of General William T. Sherman*. New York: D. Appleton and Company, 1875.

Smith, Charles H. *The History of Fuller's Ohio Brigade 1861–1865*. Cleveland, Ohio: 1909. (Smith was the major of the 27th Ohio Infantry Regiment.)

Stevenson, Benjamin Franklin. *Letters from the Army*. Cincinnati: W. E. Dibble and Company, 1884. (Stevenson was the surgeon of the 22nd Kentucky Infantry, U.S.)

Stevenson, Thomas M. *History of the 78th Regiment Ohio Veteran Volunteer Infantry*. Zanesville, Ohio: Hugh Dunne, 1865. (Stevenson was the chaplain of the 78th Ohio Infantry Regiment.)

Sullivan, James R. *Chickamauga and Chattanooga Battlefields*. Washington, D.C.: U.S. Department of the Interior, 1956.

Sunderland, Glenn W. *Lightning at Hoover's Gap: Wilder's Brigade in the Civil War*. New York, South Brunswick, London: Thomas Yoseloff, 1969.

Thompson, Edwin Porter. *History of the First Kentucky Brigade*. Cincinnati: Caxton Publishing House, 1868. (Thompson was the first lieutenant of Company E, 6th Kentucky Infantry Regiment, C.S.)

Tucker, Glenn. *Chickamauga: Bloody Battle in the West*. New York: Bobbs-Merril Company, Inc., 1961.

Turchin, John B. *Chickamauga*. Chicago: Fergus Printing Company, 1888. (General Turchin led the Third Brigade, 4th Division, XIV Army Corps at Chickamauga.)

U.S. Government Printing Office. *The War of the Rebellion: A Compilation of the Official Records of the Union and Confederate Armies*. Washington, D.C.: 1881–1900.

U.S. Government Printing Office. *The War of the Rebellion: A Compilation of the Official Records of the Union and Confederate Navies*. Washington, D.C.: 1881–1900.

Walton, Buck. *An Epitome of My Life: Civil War Reminiscences*. Austin, Texas: The Waterloo Press, 1965. (Walton was a member of Company B, 21st Texas Cavalry Regiment.)

Warner, Ezra J. *Generals in Gray*. Baton Rouge, Louisiana: Louisiana State University Press, 1964.

Watkins, Sam R. *"Co. Aytch": A Side Show of the Big Show*. (Reprint) New York: Collier Books, 1962. (Watkins was a member of Company H, 1st Tennessee Infantry Regiment, C.S.)

Wecter, Dixon. *When Johnny Comes Marching Home*. Boston: Houghton Mifflin, 1944.

Wiley, Bell Irvin. *The Common Soldier in the Civil War*. New York: Grosset and Dunlap, ca. 1960.

Woods, J. T. *Services of the Ninety-Sixth Ohio Volunteers*. Toledo, Ohio: Blade Printing and Paper Company, 1874. (Woods was the surgeon of the 96th Ohio Infantry Regiment.)

————. *Steedman and His Men at Chickamauga*. Toledo, Ohio: Blade Printing and Paper Company, 1876.

Wright, Marcus J. *Texas in the War 1861–1865*. Edited and notes by Harold B. Simpson. Hillsboro, Texas: Hill Junior College Press, 1965. (Wright was a Confederate brigadier general.)

Wyeth, John Allan. *That Devil Forrest*. (Reprint) New York: Harper and Brothers, 1959. (Wyeth was a member of the 4th Alabama Cavalry Regiment.)

Yeary, Mamie, editor. *Reminiscences of the Boys in Gray, 1861–1865*. Dallas: Smith and Lamar, ca. 1912.

Zuber, William Physick. *My Eighty Years in Texas*. Austin, Texas: University of Texas Press, 1971. (Zuber was a member of Company H, 21st Texas Cavalry Regiment.)

Articles

Allen, George W. "Civil War Letters of George W. Allen," Edited by Charleen Plumly Pollard. *Southwestern Historical Quarterly*. Vol. LXXXIII, No. 1. (July, 1979), p. 47–52. (Allen was a member of Company A, 10th Texas Infantry Regiment.)

Anonymous. "The Gray and the Blue," *Confederate Veteran*, Vol. I (1893), p. 75–76.

Anonymous. "Severe Discipline," *Confederate Veteran*, Vol. I (1893), p. 374.

Anonymous. "Texas Confederate Veterans Gather," *Confederate Veteran*, Vol. XVI (1908), p. 501–504.

Barr, Alwyn. "Confederate Artillery in Arkansas," *The Arkansas Historical Quarterly*, Vol. XXII, No. 3 (Fall, 1963), p. 238–273.

Bearrs, Edwin C. "The Battle of the Post of Arkansas," *The Arkansas Historical Quarterly*, Vol. XVIII, No. 3 (Autumn, 1959), p. 237–279.

————. "The White River Expedition June 10-July 15, 1862," *The Arkansas Historical Quarterly*, Vol. XXI, No. 4 (Winter, 1962), p. 305–362.

Bowser, Oliver P. "Notes on Granbury's Brigade," *Comprehensive History of Texas, 1685–1897*, edited by Dudley G. Wooten. Dallas: W. G. Scarff, 1898. (Bowser was a member of Company E, 18th Texas Cavalry Regiment.)

Burge, F. Weldon. "Fort Delaware: Andersonville of the North," *North South Trader*, Vol. VII, No. 3 (March–April, 1980), p. 20–25.

Campbell, W. R. "Concerning the Fighting About New Hope Church," *Confederate Veteran*, Vol. IX (1901), p. 548. (Campbell was a member of Company K, 4th Louisiana Infantry Regiment.)

Cooke, Samuel Alonzo. "The Civil War Memoirs of Samuel Alonzo Cooke," edited by Bill O'Neal. *Southwestern Historical Quarterly*, Vol. LXXIV, No. 4, (April, 1971), p. 535–548. (Cooke was a lieutenant in Company E, 17th Texas Cavalry Regiment.)

Crow, Zachariah H. "A Smith County Confederate Writes Home: Letters of Z. H. Crow," edited by F. Lee Lawrence and Robert W. Glover. *Chronicles of Smith County, Texas*, Vol. IV, No. 2 (Fall, 1965), p. 11–14. (Crow was a member of Company C, 17th Texas Cavalry Regiment.)

Cuthbertson, Gilbert. "Coller of the Sixth Texas: Correspondence of a Texas Infantry Man, 1861–64," *Military History of Texas and the Southwest*, Vol. IX, No. 2 (1972), p. 129–136. (Coller was a member of Company B, 6th Texas Infantry Regiment.)

Darst, Maury. "Robert Hodges, Jr.: Confederate Soldier," *East Texas Historical Journal*, Vol. IX, No. 1 (March, 1971), p. 20–49. (Hodges was a member of Company F, 24th Texas Cavalry Regiment.)

Eisendrath, Joseph L., Jr. "Chicago's Camp Douglas, 1861–1865," *Journal of the Illinois State Historical Society*, Vol. LIII, No. 1 (Spring, 1960), p. 37–63.

Hinkle, Joseph A. "The Odyssey of Private Hinkle," *Civil War Times Illustrated*, Vol. VIII, No. 8 (December, 1969), p. 24–31. (Hinkle was a member of the 30th Tennessee Infantry Regiment, C.S.)

Jacobs, E. Lowell. "Restoration: Visitors Return to Pea Patch Island," *Consulting Engineer*, Vol. 53, No. 4 (October, 1979), p. 92–97.

Lee, Stephen Dill. "From Palmetto, Ga., To Defeat at Nashville," *Confederate Veteran*, Vol. XVI (1908), p. 257–259. (General Lee wrote this article about 1876.)

Marsh, Bryan. "The Confederate Letters of Bryan Marsh," *Chronicles of Smith County, Texas*, Vol. XIV, No. 2 (Winter, 1975), p. 9–39 and 43–55. (Marsh was captain of Company C, 17th Texas Cavalry Regiment.)

Oliphant, William J. "Arkansas Post," *Southern Bivouac*, New Series, Vol. I, No. 12 (May, 1886), p. 736–739. (Oliphant was a member of Company G, 6th Texas Infantry Regiment.)

Page, T. M. "The Prisoner of War," *Confederate Veteran*, Vol. VIII (1900), p. 62–64. (Page was captured at Chickamauga and sent to Camp Douglas.)

Perry, Flavius W. "The Letters of Lt. Flavius W. Perry 17th Texas Cavalry, 1862–1863," edited by Joe R. Wise. *Military History of Texas and the Southwest*, Vol. XIII, No. 2, p. 11–37.

Perry, Henry W. "The Negotiations Between General Johnston and General Sherman, April, 1865." *Military Analysis of the Civil War: An Anthology by the Editors of "Military Affairs,"* p. 405–414.

Pierson, Marshall Samuel. "The Diary and Memoirs of Marshall Samuel Pierson Company C, 17th Regiment Texas Cavalry 1862–1865," edited by Norman C. Delaney: *Military History of Texas and the Southwest*, Vol. XIII, No. 3, p. 23–29.

Sheppley, Helen Edith. "Camp Butler in the Civil War Days," *Journal of the Illinois State Historical Society*, Vol. XXV (January, 1933), p. 285–317.

Stewart, Alexander p., Gen. " 'A Critical Narrative', ", *Confederate Veteran*, Vol. XVI (1908), p. 462–463.

Thomas, J. Knox. "Escape From Camp Douglas," *Confederate Veteran*, Vol. IX (1901), p. 30. (Thomas was a member of Company H, 55th Georgia Infantry Regiment.)

Turner, Jim. "Jim Turner Co. G, 6th Texas Infantry, C.S.A. From 1861 to 1865," *Texana*, Vol. XII, No. 2 (1974), p. 149–178.

Watkins, S. R. "Snow Battle at Dalton — Little Jimmie White," *Confederate Veteran*, Vol. I (1893), p. 261–262. (Watkins was a member of Company H, 1st Tennessee Infantry Regiment, C.S.)
———. "Snowball Battle at Dalton," *Confederate Veteran*, Vol. II (1894), p. 204–205.
Young, J. P. "Hood's Failure at Spring Hill," *Confederate Veteran*, Vol. XVI (1908), p. 24–41.

Periodicals

Civil War Times Illustrated
Dallas *Herald*, 1861–1864
Fort Worth Gazette, August 12, 1891
Tyler *Daily Courier*, August 16, 17, 1905
Waco *Daily Examiner*, June 29, 1871
Weatherford *Enquirer*, August 11, 1892

Unpublished Works

Harlan, Isaiah. Letters to various members of his family from November 1, 1861 through April 25, 1864. Harlan was a member of Company G, 10th Texas Infantry Regiment.
Hurst, James H. Diary from April 18, 1862, through June 29, 1862. Hurst was a member of Company A, 10th Texas Infantry Regiment.
Oliphant, William J. Memoirs. Oliphant was a member of Company G, 6th Texas Infantry Regiment.

By the time the war was half over John Scott Pickle (shown here with his wife) wore a much plainer uniform than he had worn when he first joined the army.
— Courtesy Austin History Center, Austin Public Library.

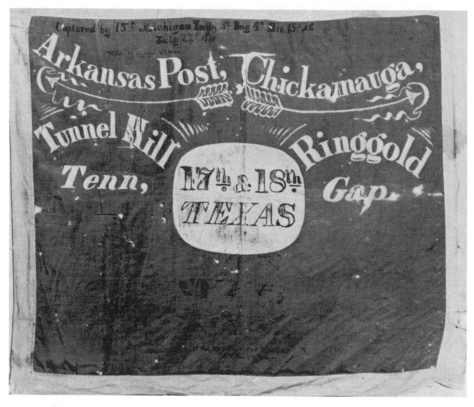

This blue Hardee-pattern battle flag was captured at the Battle of Atlanta on July 22, 1864, and returned to the state of Texas fifty years later.

— Courtesy Texas State Archives.

This early war photograph shows John Scott Pickle of Company B, Eighteenth Texas Cavalry Regiment wearing a gray double-breasted frock coat and gray trousers with yellow stripes. He is holding what appears to be a Whitney pistol while another revolver can be seen tucked into his belt.

— Courtesy Austin History Center, Austin Public Library.

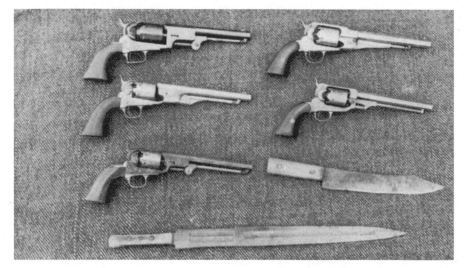

Some of Granbury's Texans carried sidearms — at least early in the war. Left, top to bottom; Confederate made copy of a .44 caliber Colt Dragoon, a .44 calibre Model 1860 Colt Army, .36 caliber Model 1851 Colt Navy. Right, top to bottom; .44 caliber Remington New Model Army, .36 caliber Remington New Model Navy, side knife made from an old blacksmith's file. Bottom; Model 1832 Foot Artillery short sword blade fitted with a homemade wooden handle.

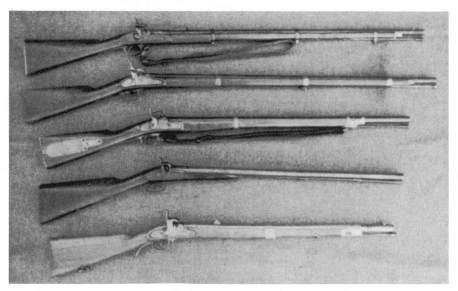

This photograph shows some of the types of long arms carried by members of Granbury's brigade. Top to bottom; English made Enfield rifle, U.S. Model 1864 Springfield rifle, U.S. Model 1841 (Mississippi) rifle, double-barreled shotgun, Austrian made rifle.

Malcomb M. Hornsby of Company B, Eighteenth Texas Cavalry Regiment is said to be an ancestor of baseball great Rogers Hornsby.

— Courtesy Texas State Archives.

Sixteen-year-old William James Oliphant of Company G, Sixth Texas Infantry Regiment was not much taller than his flintlock musket. His warlike image is further enhanced (at least for the photographer) with a large knife and a huge six-shooter. His gray uniform is trimmed in green.

— Courtesy Austin History Center, Austin Public Library.

INDEX